Judges, politics and the Irish Constitution

Manchester University Press

Judges, politics and the Irish Constitution

Edited by Laura Cahillane, James Gallen and Tom Hickey

Manchester University Press

Copyright © Manchester University Press 2017

While copyright in the volume as a whole is vested in Manchester University Press, copyright in individual chapters belongs to their respective authors, and no chapter may be reproduced wholly or in part without the express permission in writing of both author and publisher.

Published by Manchester University Press
Altrincham Street, Manchester M1 7JA

www.manchesteruniversitypress.co.uk

British Library Cataloguing-in-Publication Data
A catalogue record for this book is available from the British Library

Library of Congress Cataloging-in-Publication Data applied for

ISBN 978 1 5261 1455 6 hardback
ISBN 978 1 5261 0731 2 paperback

First published 2017

The publisher has no responsibility for the persistence or accuracy of URLs for any external or third-party internet websites referred to in this book, and does not guarantee that any content on such websites is, or will remain, accurate or appropriate.

Typeset in Sabon and Gill Sans by
Servis Filmsetting Ltd, Stockport, Cheshire

Dedicated to the memory of Justice Adrian Hardiman

Contents

List of contributors	p. x
Tribute to Justice Adrian Hardiman	xiv
Acknowledgements	xvii

Introduction   1
Laura Cahillane, James Gallen and Tom Hickey

Part I Judicial power in a constitutional democracy: theoretical foundations

1. In defence of judicial innovation and constitutional evolution   9
   Fiona de Londras
2. Reappraising judicial supremacy in the Irish constitutional tradition   29
   Eoin Daly
3. Unenumerated personal rights: the legacy of *Ryan v. Attorney General*   49
   The Hon. Mr Justice Gerard Hogan
4. Judges and the idea of 'principle' in constitutional adjudication   64
   Tom Hickey

Part II Judging in the case of *O'Keeffe v. Hickey*: analysis and debate

5. *O'Keeffe v. Ireland*: overview and analysis   85
   James Gallen

6 The jurisdiction of the European Court of Human Rights
   and the case of *O'Keeffe v. Hickey* 94
   The Hon. Mr Justice Adrian Hardiman
7 Subsidiarity of ECHR and *O'Keeffe v. Ireland*: a response to
   Mr Justice Hardiman 108
   Conor O'Mahony

Part III Judges and the political sphere: appointments and dialogue

8 Judicial appointments in Ireland: the potential for reform 123
   Laura Cahillane
9 Merit, diversity and interpretative communities: the (non-
   party) politics of judicial
   appointments and constitutional adjudication 136
   David Kenny
10 Speaking to power: mechanisms for judicial–executive
   dialogue 153
   John O'Dowd

Part IV Judges and the Constitution in historical perspective

11 The Irish Constitution 'from below': squatting families
   versus property rights in Dublin, 1967–71 169
   Thomas Murray
12 'The union makes us strong': *National Union of
   Railwaymen v. Sullivan* and the demise of vocationalism in
   Ireland 182
   Donal Coffey
13 Ulster unionism and the Irish Constitution, 1970–85 199
   Rory Milhench
14 'Towards a better Ireland': Donal Barrington and the Irish
   Constitution 217
   Tomás Finn

Part V Perspectives on the Constitution and judicial power

15 Administrative action, the rule of law and unconstitutional
   vagueness 237
   Oran Doyle

16	Article 16 of the Irish Constitution and judicial review of electoral processes *David Prendergast*	252
17	Social and economic rights in the Irish courts and the potential for constitutionalisation *Claire-Michelle Smyth*	269

Index   289

Contributors

Laura Cahillane is a lecturer in the School of Law at the University of Limerick. Her research interests lie in the areas of constitutional law, legal history, judicial politics and comparative law. Her book, *Drafting the Irish Free State Constitution* is due for publication in 2016 (Manchester UP).

Donal Coffey is a postdoctoral research associate in the Max Planck Institute for European Legal History. His work focuses on constitutional law and constitutional history. He is currently working on a legal history of the British Commonwealth in the interwar years.

Eoin Daly is a lecturer in the School of Law, NUI Galway, specialising in political and constitutional theory. He is co-author (with Tom Hickey) of *The Political Theory of the Irish Constitution* (Manchester UP, 2015).

Fiona de Londras is the Chair in Global Legal Studies at the University of Birmingham. She holds visiting positions at the law schools of UCD and UNSW. Her work addresses questions of constitutionalism and the limitation of power, with particular interests in crisis, comparativism and the judicial role. She is (co) author or (co) editor of more than sixty books, articles and chapters, joint editor in chief of the *Irish Yearbook of International Law*, co-editor of *Legal Studies*, and founder of HumanRights.ie

Oran Doyle is Head of School and Associate Professor at the School of Law, Trinity College Dublin. His areas of interest include constitutional law, jurisprudence and environmental law. He is author of several books and articles in those areas including *Constitutional Equality Law*

(Thomson Round Hall, 2005) and *Constitutional Law: Texts, Cases and Materials* (Clarus, 2007).

Tomás Finn lectures in history at NUI, Galway. His research interests include the role of intellectuals, church–state relations and Northern Ireland. Tomás's recent publications include *Tuairim, intellectual debate and policy formulation: Rethinking Ireland, 1954–7* (Manchester UP).

James Gallen is a lecturer in the School of Law and Government at DCU. His research interests include human rights, international law and legal and political philosophy. His present research agenda concerns the development of jus post bellum in international and policy for post-conflict states and a transitional justice approach to child sex abuse in the Roman Catholic Church. His recent publications include Sue Farran, James Gallen, Jen Hendry and Christa Rautenbach (eds), *Diffusion, The Movement of Law and Norms* (Ashgate, 2015) and 'Odious Debt and Jus Post Bellum' (*Journal of World Investment and Trade* 2015)

Adrian Hardiman (RIP) was a judge of the Irish Supreme Court. He was also Judge-in-Residence at the School of Law and Government, DCU. He contributed widely to academic discourse, having published across a vast range of areas in constitutional law as well as in other fields. The volume is dedicated to his memory.

Tom Hickey is a lecturer at the School of Law and Government, Dublin City University. His work addresses constitutional and public law, often drawing on republican theory. Recent publications include 'The Republican Virtues of the New Commonwealth Model of Constitutionalism' (2016) 14(4) *International Journal of Constitutional Law* 794 and *The Political Theory of the Irish Constitution* (Manchester UP, 2015), co-authored with Eoin Daly.

Gerard Hogan is a judge of the Court of Appeal. He was previously a lecturer at the School of Law, Trinity College Dublin. He has published widely in fields including constitutional law, history and theory and administrative law. His latest book is *Origins of the Irish Constitution* (RIA, 2012).

David Kenny is Assistant Professor at the School of Law, Trinity College Dublin. His main teaching and research interests are in the fields of constitutional and administrative law. He has published several articles in these fields, many addressing themes in the separation of powers and proportionality doctrines.

Rory Milhench recently completed his Ph.D. in history at Trinity College Dublin. Its full title was 'Ulster Loyalism, Ulster Unionism and the Irish State, 1970–85' and was completed under the guidance of Professor Eunan O'Halpin. Rory is currently working outside of academia but intends to return and undertake post-doctoral research into Ulster Unionism and Irish Nationalism soon.

Thomas Murray is a lecturer at the UCD School of Social Policy, Social Work and Social Justice. His work addresses the comparative politics of constitutions and socio-economic rights. His recent publications include 'Socio-economic Rights versus Social Revolution? Constitution-Making in Germany, Mexico, and Ireland, 1917–23' in *Social & Legal Studies* (2015) and 'Socio-Economic Rights and the Making of the 1937 Irish Constitution' in *Irish Political Studies* (forthcoming).

John O'Dowd is a lecturer at the Sutherland School of Law, University College Dublin. His main research and teaching interests are in the fields of administrative law, constitutional law and European human rights law. He has published several articles and book chapters in these fields.

Conor O'Mahony is a senior lecturer at the School of Law at University College Cork. He works in the areas of constitutional law and child law, focusing on constitutional interpretation, enforcement of rights and children's rights in particular. Recent publications include 'If a Constitution is Easy to Amend, Can Judges be Less Restrained? Rights, Social Change, and Proposition 8' (2014) 27 *Harvard Human Rights Journal* 191–242; 'Evolutive Interpretation of Rights Provisions: A Comparison of the European Court of Human Rights and the US Supreme Court' (2013) 44(1) *Columbia Human Rights Law Review* 1–58, and 'There is No Such Thing as a Right to Dignity' (2012) 10(2) *International Journal of Constitutional Law* 551–574.

David Prendergast is Assistant Professor at the School of Law, Trinity College Dublin. His main teaching and research interests are in the fields of criminal and constitutional law: he has published several articles in these fields. He is co-editor of the Dublin University Law Journal and the Criminal Law and Practice Review.

Claire-Michelle Smyth is a senior lecturer in Law at the University of Brighton where her research focuses on international and comparative human rights law, with a particular emphasis on the constitutionalisation of social and economic rights.

Tribute to Justice Adrian Hardiman, 1951–2016

Justice Adrian Hardiman delivered the opening keynote paper on 4 September 2014 at the conference that culminated in the publication of this volume. His chapter here is an almost verbatim account. He was himself on the day: pugnacious; yet genial; serious, yet theatrical. His paper prompted deep scholarly argument – opposition, even (as Conor O'Mahony's chapter in this volume attests). To that extent, it set us off on the right note for the day.

In recent years, Justice Hardiman was a regular visitor to the School of Law and Government at Dublin City University, where we were so glad to have him as our Judge-in-Residence. He had several such commitments, of course. But he certainly took this one seriously, and seemed to enjoy it a great deal. Those of us who were at his lectures recall fondly the vigour with which he made his arguments, and the sometimes sharp exchanges that followed. He seemed to at once take it all so seriously and yet not seriously at all: once the intellectual argument had been had, he'd promptly revert to conviviality. As we say in the Acknowledgements section – written while he was still among us – we at the School of Law and Government very much enjoyed him and are very grateful to him for his contributions to the School and for our students.

His judgments in particular leave a vast legacy. Ruadhán Mac Cormaic wrote in an *Irish Times* column following his death that his would invariably be the judgment picked up by the media, even if the main judgment had been written by someone else.[1] Speaking as constitutional and human rights law lecturers, we can relate: we use his judgments more or less routinely in class to explore many of law's deep conundrums. On complex concepts such as the separation of powers (although he, of course, claimed it to be a simple or rigid concept!),[2] the role of judges, the control of public power, the rights of accused persons, even the idea of freedom, his were the judgments to assess. Yes – often because he articulated an idea that we felt might warrant particular scrutiny; but he would have articulated it so sharply, setting out the clashing principles with such clarity.

He leaves a legacy of several important judgments. Almost every tribute on his death pointed in particular to his strident dissent in a case reported almost exactly a year before his passing: *DPP v. JC*.[3] His opening paragraph there is worth another look. It points to a theme that reverberates through several of his judgments: that the freedom of individual citizens depends upon judges robustly enforcing their *civil* rights as against what he referred to as 'their own country's *force publique*'. He elaborated the ornate phrase to signify:

> not only the police force but the army, the tax collectors, the customs and revenue officials and the whole body of public officials who are vested with coercive and compulsory powers over ordinary citizens, their property, including their homes, their records and papers, their money and monies worth and other aspects of their lives.[4]

It is heady stuff and it illuminates why he was so perturbed by the majority judgments in the case. But it also points, arguably at least, to the scepticism he had of state power more generally. Perhaps he saw it as something of a necessary evil: that without it no one could have any viable kind of freedom but that equally, as the state's powers of interference in the lives of individual citizens grew, the freedom of those citizens necessarily shrunk. That understanding might also go some way to explaining his forceful stance in the infamous *Portmarnock Golf Club* case,[5] as well, perhaps, as those in the socio-economic rights cases, *TD v. Minister for Education*[6] and *Sinnott v. Minister for Education*.[7]

He would have much to say about any such claim, of course. That he is not around to contribute to such debates is very sad, and a great loss. The loss to his family is far greater, of course. We at the School of Law and Government at DCU – and all of the contributors to this volume – extend our deepest sympathy to his wife, former Circuit Court Judge Yvonne Murphy, to their sons, Daniel, Eoin and Hugh, to his grandchildren (who were so touchingly referenced in his funeral oration) and to his extended family and friends.

May he rest in peace
Laura Cahillane, James Gallen, Tom Hickey
April 2016

Notes

1. R. Mac Cormaic, 'Adrian Hardiman: A unique courtroom voice falls silent', *Irish Times* (7 March 2016).
2. See his judgment in *TD v. Minister for Education* [2001] 4 IR 259, 367–371.
3. *DPP v. JC* [2015] IESC 31.
4. *Ibid.*
5. *Equality Authority v. Portmarnock Golf Club* [2010] 1 ILRM 237.
6. [2001] 4 IR 259.
7. [2001] 2 IR 545.

Acknowledgements

The editors thank all at the Socio-Legal Research Centre at Dublin City University for their work on and support of this project. We particularly note the contributions made by students at the School of Law and Government in advance of and at the 'Judges, Politics and the Irish Constitution' conference, from which this volume emerged, and subsequently, through their work in bringing together the edition of DCU *Socio-Legal Studies Review*, in which some of the conference papers were published. Those students are: Stephen Brereton, Jordan Byrne, Shaunagh Byrne, Adam Casey, Ciara Dowd, Katherine Hall, Kimberly Hayden, Kaleb Honer, Davy Lalor and Rebecca McGrath.

We thank Professor Gary Murphy, Head of the School of Law and Government at DCU for his support of this and other projects at the Socio-Legal Research Centre. We acknowledge the contributions of our Judges-in-Residence at the School, Justice Adrian Hardiman and Justice John Hedigan, both at and around the conference and indeed subsequently in various contexts. We thank the Attorney General, Máire Whelan for her keynote paper at the conference. Thank you also to Justice Gerard Hogan who brought his insight and his warmth to the project.

We extend a particular note of appreciation to Dr Claire-Michelle Smyth who very much drove the project while working at DCU, but who withdrew as co-editor of this volume due to various commitments. She has since joined the University of Brighton: her loss is keenly felt at DCU.

We thank all at Manchester University Press for their work in helping us bring this volume together.

Most of all, thank you to all who participated at the conference. Many did not contribute chapters here but have done so in the *DCU*

Socio-Legal Studies Review and elsewhere. Those who did contribute chapters to this volume have been patient and highly efficient in reading other chapters to which their own related, integrating insights in redrafting their own chapters, submitting them on time, and all besides.

Finally, we thank the Faculty of Humanities and Social Sciences at Dublin City University: this book received financial support from the Faculty Book Publication Scheme.

Laura Cahillane, James Gallen, Tom Hickey
November 2015

Introduction

Laura Cahillane, James Gallen and Tom Hickey

This volume follows from a conference hosted by the School of Law and Government at Dublin City University in September of 2014, which brought academic scholars and judges together to consider themes flowing from the often complex relationships between 'law' and 'politics', 'adjudication' and 'policy-making', the 'judicial' and the more obviously (some might say more overtly) 'political' branches. The whole atmosphere of the conference was open and authentically scholarly: papers were delivered in an accessible and deliberative way, making for sessions that developed into meaningful intellectual exchanges (sometimes on high-minded theoretical themes or discrete historical questions, other times on practical or policy matters). The consensus was that it was the kind of conference that really warranted a follow-up edited collection. That aspiration has been realised in the form of this volume: it is thanks to the participants for following up their immediate post-conference commitments by developing their ideas on foot of the exchanges and delivering them in book chapter form.

In the Introduction to the fourth edition of the by now famous *Hogan and Morgan's Administrative Law*, David Gwynn Morgan bemoans the dearth of deep thinking about 'the character of the Irish State' and 'consequently [about] the values underlying its administrative law'.[1] The same might have been said until recently of Irish public law more generally; of constitutional law and indeed the constitutional order in the broader sense. It is hard to think of subdisciplines in which broader work of this kind is more urgent: public law and the constitutional order are concerned in the most fundamental way with the relationship between the citizen and the state (or rather between various communities of individuals, an overall community of citizens and the state). It engages the deepest of questions around liberty, equality and justice. We certainly do not present this volume as a definitive or comprehensive work that fills that gap. Far from it: most of the chapters address quite discrete questions. But we would hope that the book contributes in a small way to what seems to be a kind of emerging movement among contemporary Irish public lawyers – exemplified by the work of the Northern/Irish Feminist Judgments Project or Gerry Whyte's updated edition of *Social Inclusion and the Legal System* among so much besides – to bring broader insight to bear and to go beyond what is arguably a stifling and insular 'black letter' tradition.[2]

We have arranged the volume in five parts. Part I addresses questions concerning the nature and extent of judicial power from a largely theoretical perspective. The chapters engage with abstract work on democracy and legitimacy in the context of the wielding and exercise of public (particularly judicial) power. The volume opens with a general defence of judicial supremacy by Fiona de Londras. Her thesis can certainly be read as a general one, although it is applied here in the context of the Irish constitutional system. It may be understood as a rallying cry for legal constitutionalism: de Londras defends judicial power generally based on her claims that it leads to better outcomes and that it should be understood as just one part of a broader and ongoing constitutional 'ecosystem'. Her chapter is followed by a starkly contrasting contribution from Eoin Daly, which casts a sceptical eye on judicial supremacy. Daly argues that the doctrine goes almost unquestioned in Irish constitutional scholarship (and practice) and that its value and potential is vastly overstated, while its costs – particularly its tendency to stultify rights discourse in the sphere of ordinary politics – go largely underappreciated.

Gerard Hogan's chapter turns to a more specific theme, revisiting the famous case of *Ryan v. Attorney General*. He considers the consequences of the reliance by judges in the case on extra-textual norms (e.g. on the 'Christian and democratic nature of the state'), arguing that they could instead have relied on norms that had a clearer textual basis. Their failure to do so, he argues, distorted the rights elements of Irish constitutional jurisprudence in part through a related failure to develop a thorough analysis of the meaning of the rights that were expressly enumerated in the text itself.

Tom Hickey's chapter turns back to general theory, responding to a great extent to the chapters that precede it. So far as a model of constitutionalism is concerned, it may seem to prescribe something of an intermediate position between those defended by de Londras and by Daly, respectively. It argues for a model that formally combines judicial and legislative power over rights on the basis that each brings particular strengths to bear, but that at the same time appropriately accounts for what he sees as the costs of vesting exclusive authority (and, by extension, responsibility) for rights in either branch. He defends a constrained form of judicial review on the basis of its capacity to identify and develop deliberative understandings of rights that might seem to correspond with the common good, but challenges the tendency to invest excessive faith in judges both on this front and more generally, using the de Londras and Hogan chapters as different exemplars of that tendency.

Part II takes the form of a debate: it addresses the particular case of *O'Keeffe v. Hickey*.[3] It opens with an overall account of the case, in James Gallen's chapter, which discusses the challenges facing Louise O'Keeffe in holding the state responsible for its failure to prevent the child sexual abuse she endured. Gallen discusses the evolution of the case from Irish courts to an appeal to the European Court of Human Rights, previews the arguments of the other contributors in Part II, and notes the potential impact of the decision for the European Convention of Human Rights and for victims of child sexual abuse in Ireland. Mr Justice Adrian Hardiman delivered the keynote address to the 2014 conference. His chapter critiques the decision of the Strasbourg Court, in particular claiming the reasoning employed marks a notable departure from prior jurisprudence and fails to respect the subsidiary role of the Convention in national legal systems. In reply, Conor O'Mahony argues that the reasons offered by the Court were sufficient in themselves to declare the case admissible, and that the decision was entirely in line with the jurisprudence of the ECtHR on admissibility. The discussion between these authors reveals the tension between the principle of subsidiarity and the right to effective protection and an effective remedy in the Convention.

Part III comprises chapters that address questions around the process of appointing judges and judicial representation or dialogue between the judicial and executive branches. Laura Cahillane's chapter begins with an appraisal of the current system of appointing judges in Ireland and proceeds to suggest some potential reforms in this area with the aim of opening the debate on this topic. David Kenny's chapter also considers the judicial appointment process but his focus is specifically on the 'politics' of the appointment process: he argues that we can never eliminate politics from this process (and that this should not be seen as a necessarily bad thing) and so that the way forward lies in appropriately engaging with, rather than concealing, the politics at play in judicial appointments. O'Dowd concentrates on the relationship between the executive and judiciary, specifically the communication, or lack thereof, between these institutions. He refers to some recent controversial episodes where this lack of communication has been problematic and suggests looking to Canada for potential solutions.

Part IV is devoted to certain historical questions pertaining to judges and adjudication. Thomas Murray's chapter begins this part by proposing an alternative interpretation of the Constitution which views the document from the perspective of those constitutionalised. He examines the squatting campaigns of the Dublin Housing Action Committee in the late 1960s and early 1970s to demonstrate the tension and differing interpretations of property rights as commodity versus social need. Donal Coffey's chapter[4] takes another look at the case of *National Union of Railwaymen v. Sullivan*, a case which, he argues, has been undervalued in terms of its historical importance.[5] Coffey makes the argument that the case undermined the vocational project in Ireland, which was an ongoing concern in 1945 when the decision was handed down and that it also marks a decisive turn in the development of judicial review in Ireland. Rory Milhench considers the Irish Constitution from the perspective of Ulster Unionists. He examines the relationship between Ulster Unionists and successive Irish governments, with particular emphasis on how certain Articles of the Irish Constitution helped form the Unionist image of the Irish Republic and how this conditioned the relationship between the two parties. Finally, Tomás Finn considers one particular judge as a historical figure and examines the impact he had on the Irish constitutional landscape.

Finally, Part V comprises three chapters, each of which has a quite specific focus but all engaging questions pertaining to judicial power and political processes. Oran Doyle's chapter addresses a discrete rule-of-law question around control of discretionary power granted under legislation to public actors. He traces and critiques the uncertain emergence of a new judge-made constitutional doctrine responding to the concern that individuals subject to such discretionary power may be diminished by their vulnerability to power that – at least in the absence of this judicial intervention – would be insufficiently checked. Although conscious of the lack of a clear textual basis for this development (and thus perhaps in some ways in tension with Gerard Hogan's argument), Doyle claims the judicial development of the doctrine is justified through rule-of-law values around certainty and predictability.

David Prendergast examines the judicial development of Article 16 and the role of the judiciary in safeguarding the Irish electoral process. He rejects the idea that Article 16 forms a 'total code' for Dáil elections, but argues that the courts' work can be characterised overall as seeking to protect the electoral process, but not perfect it. Claire-Michelle Smyth's chapter examines the question of socio-economic rights in the Irish Constitution. She argues that it is possible to identify the avenues for constitutionalisation of socio-economic rights without the need for express incorporation by way of referendum.

Notes

1 See D. Gwynn Morgan, *Hogan and Morgan's Administrative Law* (4th edn, Round Hall, 2012) p. 8.
2 See www.feministjudging.ie (accessed 20 October 2015); G. Whyte, *Social Inclusion and the Legal System: Public Interest Law in Ireland* (2nd edn, Institute of Public Administration, 2015).
3 [2009] 2 IR 302.
4 Donal's chapter won the Irish Legal History Society prize for best paper with a historical dimension at the conference.
5 [1947] IR 77.

Part I
Judicial power in a constitutional democracy: theoretical foundations

1

In defence of judicial innovation and constitutional evolution

Fiona de Londras

The meaning of broadly drawn constitutional provisions is rarely static or self-evident. Thus, certain branches – including the judiciary – usually have a role in interpreting them. Although this task is often shared between different branches of government (and, thus, essentially collaborative), the role of superior courts is particularly significant, especially (although not only) in so-called 'legal constitutions' (i.e. written constitutions in which constitutional, rather than parliamentary, supremacy is the norm). In carrying out their interpretative role, judges are at least sometimes innovative (or what some might call 'activist'),[1] and that innovation is a key element of constitutional evolution. This is not uncontroversial; many argue that judges 'overreach' when they engage in such innovation and, as a result, prefer a more restrained judicial role.[2] However, exploring this in the Irish context, I argue in this chapter that judicial innovation is an important and legitimate part of constitutional evolution, taking into account the broader constitutional tradition and structure within which Irish superior courts operate.

At this stage, it is useful to outline what I mean by judicial innovation here. Judicial innovation includes, but goes beyond, judicial activism. In his excellent short study of judicial activism in Ireland, David Gwynn Morgan defined judicial activism thus:

> [when] in order to resolve the case one way or another ... a judge has to call on some element of policy choice or preference ... the judge selects the option of not accepting the status quo as it is given in the form of law or government action, but instead strikes down the law or action as unconstitutional.[3]

Innovation can form part of judicial activism but is not limited to cases where courts strike down law or government action. Rather, wherever the court develops an understanding of the text or unenumerated content of the Constitution that is at odds with and moves the constitutional *acquis* on from the prevailing understanding we can say judicial innovation has taken place. While this may then be deployed in striking down a law, it can also be used to 'discover' a new constitutional right, to save a provision from strike down, or to rethink the relationships between different bodies of law. I consider this here in the context of an evolving constitution: the development of an understanding of the content of the Constitution, the nature of its limits, and the form of the constitutional settlement it frames and represents.

Constitutions require interpretation. This is so not only because of the relatively open-textured nature of constitutional texts (or what might be called their 'indeterminacy'), but also because of the reality of constitutionalist governance. Governance is an activity, a practice, and a mode of being that does not take on a static form; it is an activity that must constantly address new and emerging issues. In so doing, any system of governance that has a constitutionalist orientation (i.e. that is committed to ensuring the state remains within its constitutional bounds) is constantly faced with the task of establishing and assessing the constitutionality of new responses to old and emergent challenges. This is not least because no politico-legal system could possibly have predicted all of the challenges that it would face in the future at the time of drafting its constitution. Nor could it have foreseen the development of social mores to consider as illegitimate forms of behavioural proscription that were previously considered to be entirely legitimate and vice-versa.[4] Innovative constitutional interpretation is necessary so that the boundaries and limits of constitutionally permissible action can be identified in the face of new and different forms of government activity and governance. If constitutions and constitutionalism are about setting the limits of permissible government action, then there simply cannot be government activities that fall outside of constitutional governance.[5] In order to ensure that this is the case, evolution of the constitution is required. Through their engagement in constitutional interpretation, courts play a vital role in that enterprise.

It is important that we identify what is meant by constitutional interpretation in this context. Although useful distinctions can be drawn between interpretation and construction per se, adherence to such a distinction is not required here because judicial innovation can occur in both of these senses. Solum offers the clearest articulation of these two activities in his 'interpretation–construction distinction'.[6] For Solum, applying or explicating a constitution (or other authoritative legal text) involves two stages or processes. The first is interpretation, which he says 'is the process (or activity) that recognizes or discovers the linguistic meaning or semantic content of the legal text'.[7] The second is construction: 'the process that gives a text legal effect (either my [sic] translating the linguistic meaning into legal doctrine or by applying or implementing the text)'.[8] If the need for constitutional interpretation arises from *both* linguistic indeterminacy or open texturedness *and* the need to ensure constitutional coverage of new modes and subjects of governance, there is scope for judicial innovation in respect of both linguistic/semantic aspects of the constitution *and* giving legal effect to the constitution. In neither case is such innovation necessarily an illegitimate exercise of judicial power.

Making out this argument requires both a positive and a negative case. The positive case posited here is that innovation in constitutional interpretation is a necessary part of the judicial role; the negative case I forward is that such innovation is not an illegitimate judicial activity. This chapter starts by sketching what I term an 'ecosystem' of constitutional interpretation, placing the judicial role in constitutional interpretation into a broader context. I then proceed to outline the positive and negative cases. While the chapter is primarily oriented towards defending judicial innovation in Ireland, the arguments contained here are more broadly applicable allowing for technical adjustments based on the particularities of different politico-legal systems. Thus, the chapter draws on examples from within and beyond Irish jurisprudence throughout.

The ecosystem of constitutional interpretation

Constitutional interpretation does not take place only in courtrooms and by means of litigation and judicial adjudication. Rather, constitutional interpretation is a constant and a collaborative process between all branches of government and the bureaucracy of the state.[9] Thus, courts are not the only organ of state with a right or a need to interpret the constitution. However, critiques of judicial activism, or what I term judicial innovation, routinely proceed as if that were the case, largely looking at judicial interventions in constitutional evolution in isolation. Such an approach artificially inflates claims of the superiority of the judicial role in constitutional interpretation. It is more appropriate, and more reflective of the reality of constitutionalist practice, to conceive of constitutional interpretation as a knowledge ecosystem in which dynamism and evolution are fostered by inter-entity interaction, which in turn improves decision-making and enhances collaboration.

The precise contours of the interpretative roles of different branches of the state will be different from system to system, but we can say that, in general, at least three entities *apart from courts* have a role in interpreting the constitution on a fairly constant basis.

The executive

In going about its daily business, the executive must make decisions as to the constitutional permissibility of its actions. This is often done with the advice and assistance of law officers such as Attorneys General, but these law officers merely advise; at the end of the day it is the executive that makes the actionable decision about the permissible limits of the state's constitutionally endowed power, and the executive that must carry the political and legal consequences flowing from that.

Beyond the obvious political significance of these decisions, the executive's position on the constitutional permissibility of any desired action has interpretative weight, notwithstanding its non-determinative nature. First of all, these decisions can set a practical precedent, especially while they go unchallenged in litigation, so that they develop into constitutional understandings and maybe even conventions over time. By means of example, from the mid 2000s the Irish government claimed, on the advice of law officers, that same-sex marriage was unconstitutional. However, whether or not marriage between people of the same birth gender was constitutionally impermissible was by no means a matter of settled law at that time. Indeed, there was reasonable disagreement on the question among scholars and the only precedent directly addressing the question emanated from the High Court and was somewhat unconvincingly reasoned.[10] Notwithstanding that, it became accepted wisdom that marriage equality could be achieved only by referendum and constitutional change, and not by political decision-making, leading eventually to the 2015 referendum on the 34th amendment to the Constitution which introduced a constitutional right to marry the person of one's choosing, as regulated by law, regardless of sex.

Furthermore, executive interpretations of the constitution can be heavily influential on other branches of government including on the legislature (especially but not exclusively in fused systems) and the judiciary (given principles of deference and self-restraint further considered below). The legislature will often be guided in its consideration of the constitutionality of proposed legislative or policy action by the judgement of the executive (which in turn is influenced by advice from relevant law officers). Indeed, where parliamentary votes are subject to party whips there can be limited opportunities for public contestation so that executive decision-making as to constitutionality and constitutionalism may be effectively determinative of legislative opinion in this respect.[11] This is not to suggest that executive determinations completely overwhelm legislative judgement as to constitutionality, or that opportunities for backbench or internal-party contestation do not exist outside of the relatively reified air of the legislative debating chamber (for example, in meetings of the parliamentary party).[12] Rather, it is to point out the broad interpretative weight that can attach to executive interpretations of constitutional limits.

The executive can also have a role in constructing judicial interpretations of the constitution. It is sometimes thought that a judicial interpretation is the final word, to borrow from Gardbaum,[13] particularly in a legal constitution, but that is to oversimplify matters. Even when a superior court has handed down an interpretation of a part of the constitutional text, questions often remain about the broader implications of that, its meaning in the context of the constitutional text as a whole, and its practical application. These are all matters that require executive interpretation of the constitution, and especially of the constitution in action.

The legislature
Although it may not seem to be a task that is often seriously or explicitly discussed by parliamentarians, the legislature also has a role in constitutional interpretation. This is so in both legal and political constitutions (if such a rigid bifurcation can possibly be sustained), although the weight of legislative interpretation may differ from system to system. In a system of separate but equal power – such as that found in the United States – legislative constitutional interpretation arguably takes on a particularly significant role. Under the oath of office, Members of Congress have a duty to abide by the Constitution and rely to a lesser extent on executive guidance in doing so than is the case in fused systems such as the UK and Ireland.[14] Notwithstanding that, there is a clear pattern of what Limbach and Tushnet call 'anticipatory obedience' where the legislature anticipates what a constitutional court might decide as to constitutionality and attempts to align with that anticipated outcome.[15] It is, after all, the fundamental basis of principles such as the presumption of constitutionality that we assume the legislature intends to act constitutionally in all of its enactments,[16] and thus some anticipatory obedience is to be expected. Leaving this to one side, and disregarding issues about which reasonable people can reasonably disagree in which a large amount of political capital might be invested, Tushnet finds that in the United States Congress frequently acts as a responsible constitutional interpreter.[17] Indeed, this is important to his conception of constitutionalism as a collaborative (and quasi-competitive) activity between branches of government.

In systems of legal constitutionalism where there is a fused executive and legislature, such as in Ireland, explicit exercises in constitutional interpretation by legislators seem to arise relatively infrequently, perhaps especially in respect of rights. In Ireland, for example, rights are politically conceptualised as legal instruments; the domain of law and of lawyers and not easily amenable to political contestation on their own terms.[18] Added to this is the influence of the party whip in closely disciplined party political systems. In some such systems, such as the UK, there is a (limited) tradition of backbench revolt where parliamentarians advance their own interpretation of that which is constitutionally permissible in contravention of that articulated by their party.[19] Although such revolt is relatively rare, and cannot be relied upon as a mechanism of ensuring effective legislative oversight per se, it is an important example of constitutionalism and constitutional interpretation by individual members of parliament. In other systems, revolt of this kind is uncommon, but even then there are important opportunities and systems of constitutionalist contestation among legislators.[20] Even in Ireland, hints of a kind of dissent as to constitutional interpretation can sometimes be identified in parliament. Take, for example, recent attempts by Clare Daly TD and Michael McNamara TD to introduce legislation allowing for abortion in cases of 'fatal foetal abnormalities'.[21] Both of these TDs contested the assertion that no such legislation was possible under the 8th Amendment; advice said by the executive to have been communicated by the Attorney General.[22] By proposing these Bills Daly and McNamara (himself a backbench member of a government party) publicly registered their counter-interpretations of what the Constitution permits in relation to a matter that, in truth, is not clearly resolved by the wording of the Constitution as it is currently understood.[23]

Public authorities

Constitutional interpretation is a quotidian activity for public authorities (or 'organs of the state').[24] Engaged on a continuous basis in delivering state services to the public, these authorities – whether local authorities, government departments, police authorities, hospitals or others – are the daily link between the state and the individual. They are also required, as a matter of practicality, to operationalise legal provisions; an activity that necessarily requires interpretation of those provisions by reference to the constitutional context in which they were introduced.

When applying or fulfilling statutory duties, public authorities must act with an eye to the constitutional parameters of state authority, constitutional principles such as natural justice, and the constitutional rights of those with whom they interact. Legislative provisions are less open-textured than are constitutional texts, but they can, nevertheless, require some processes of translation from statutory wording to practical reality. While these processes are, on occasion, assisted by the promulgation of regulations and other forms of delegated legislation, this is not always the case. Furthermore, there are occasionally 'gaps' between the time of promulgation and commencement of a measure and the publication of relevant guidelines.[25] In this time, the public authorities responsible for delivering the statutory scheme in question must put it into action in a manner that, to the best of their ability, aligns with constitutional limitations on public power.

Furthermore, public authorities can engage in constitutional interpretation quite outside of giving effect to statutory provisions, i.e. when they act in a way that bears directly on the delivery of constitutional rights. In such circumstances, public authorities are engaged in close constitutional interpretation, assessing the extent to which their decisions and actions are constrained by the constitution and any relevant jurisprudence. Such direct engagement with the constitution, i.e. without legislative refraction, would arise in situations where there is an absence of legislation to give effect to the constitutional right or provision. This is well demonstrated by the position in which public hospitals found themselves in Ireland between 1983 and 2013 in respect of the provision of abortions. In that time (and now), providing an abortion was a serious criminal offence carrying severe penalties,[26] and abortion was effectively prohibited by the Irish Constitution, which recognises the 'equal right to life' of pregnant women and unborn children in Article 40.3.

That provision was inserted in the Constitution following a referendum of the people in 1983, but its terms clearly allowed for termination of a pregnancy by abortion (or other means) where this was required in order to respect the constitutionally protected right to life of a pregnant woman. What the Constitution did not make clear, however, was whether the risk to life had to be imminent, or how severe the risk threshold was, or whether there was something equivalent to a time limit beyond which an early inducement would be the only constitutionally permissible course of action (rather than an abortion *per se*). In spite of this, no legislation was introduced to give procedural substance to this right or guidance to public authorities. The confusion and lack of certainty as to what a doctor could or could not do, and when, was exacerbated by the decision in of *Attorney General v. X*,[27] in which the Supreme Court found that abortion was permissible where there 'is a real and substantial risk to the life, as distinct from the health, of the mother, which can only be avoided by the termination of her pregnancy'.

That risk to life, the Court confirmed, included a risk of suicide. In spite of repeated calls to 'legislate for the *X Case*' in order to provide clarity to women and medics about how the (limited) right to access abortion could be exercised,[28] no legislation was forthcoming. Instead, hospitals were required to develop their own interpretations and internal practices around termination of pregnancies by means of abortion and to apply those in an attempt to protect their medics from criminal liability and avoid unconstitutional activity.

It was not until 2013, nudged by a series of exogenous events, that a legislative scheme to allow for access to abortion in Ireland was finally introduced in the form of the Protection of Life during Pregnancy Act 2013. Even then, however, providers of medical care were left without guidance as to the means of operationalising this highly procedural Act until the autumn of 2014. In the intervening time, they (and the lawyers who advise them) were necessarily engaged in processes of constitutional interpretation for the purposes of practicability.

Judicial innovation is necessary

The fact that constitutional interpretation and evolution is a collaborative process, involving multiple parts of the state, does not, of course, mean that courts do not have a particular role in this relation. When making decisions that require constitutional interpretation, courts are engaged in more than 'mere' adjudication of the dispute before them; they are also engaged in constitutionalism. In such contexts, courts' constitutional interpretations carry out particular functions.

First, *judicial interpretation of the constitution settles particular disputes*. Thus, courts decide on the constitutionality of impugned measures or activities in a particular set of factual circumstances and in this respect – and this respect alone (considered further below) – courts have the final say as to the future of that measure or activity. In other words, in the context of a particular case the courts have the final say as to constitutionality at that moment in time and in respect of the particular measures or activities in question. In deciding on this, constitutional principles may be elucidated, which in turn may have a broader and longer significance to constitutional adjudication and interpretation than the case at the Bar.[29] However, in the context of a particular dispute, it is courts that have the capacity to bring resolution and, where appropriate, provide for a remedy.

Second, judicial interpretation of the constitution can engage broader questions of constitutionalism that are rarely addressed in quotidian constitutional politics. The political system tends only to address questions of constitutional evolution directly when a systemic imperative requiring such attention arises, such as a political crisis, a populist demand, or an exogenous force. When resolving issues in such a context, politics must endure certain popular and political impulses, demands, panics or fears. Thus, political debate as to constitutional evolution faces challenges of deliberative quality. Although, as outlined above, actors within the political system may have to (implicitly or expressly) consider constitutional meaning and limits on a regular basis, they do so as political animals cognisant of political realities and constituents' demands, and seldom with a level-headed view to the long term. In such circumstances, questions of constitutional meaning may not receive a consideration that benefits from 'distancing devices' available to courts,[30] which tend to be able to address matters in a different atmosphere. Certainly, the decisions that courts make in relation to constitutional matters have weighty political implications. It would be trite to suggest that a court considering whether to strike down the criminalisation of certain narcotics or a statutory rape offence, or a court considering whether children born to asylum seekers in Ireland had a constitutional right to remain in the country and, as a result, to have their parents remain with them would not be cognisant of the potential political fallout of however they decide. However, this does not mean that their deliberations are subjected to the same demands and anxieties of populism as are those of politicians.

Judges enjoy an independence that brings with it a certain insulation from direct criticism and, of course, a protection from removal, that give them sufficient security to make unpopular decisions where they consider them to be mandated by the text and meaning of the constitution. These will not be inevitably progressive; neither will they be inevitably popular. But they are decisions that courts are well positioned to make in respect of matters that have, after all, been the subject of some political, executive or practical consideration by the state leading to the impugned law or action. This is simply because the infrastructure of the judicial administration of justice – the independence of the judiciary, the separation of powers, the security of tenure – allows space for a form of principled courage that is not facilitated by the structure of the political system. Thus, although of course we know that courts are not wholly neutral and that judges are human just as the rest of us are, the infrastructure of the state is such that political and populist forces are hindered from imposing their will on the judiciary.

Bearing in mind the role of courts in constitutional interpretation, judicial innovation in the form of evolutionary interpretation is a necessary part of the judicial function. This does not, on its own, establish its legitimacy – an issue to which I turn below – but the question of necessity is not insignificant. This claim of necessity rests on one's conception of the constitution and its function. If constitutions are about constitutionalism and not merely about text, i.e. fundamentally about *telos*, they simply cannot remain static and, at the same time, carry out the functions that we expect of them. Indeed, as Conor O'Mahony has noted, Irish constitutional jurisprudence has tended to be developed upon an underlying understanding that it would be 'capable of evolution, and that judges should be free to mould it to changing conditions and ideas without the need for repeated referenda'.[31]

The particular nature of courts' role in constitutional interpretation calls for innovation in the form of evolution if the constitution is not to remain static or to fail in its prescriptive *telos*. Think of the core constitutional principles developed through judicial innovation and now considered fundamental in many legal systems; what would the constitutionalist identity of those systems be had courts not engaged in such innovation? Were a constitution to remain static, for example, the United States Constitution would not protect a right to access abortion,[32] a right to marry someone of another race,[33] a right to equal access to education regardless of race or,[34] indeed, the right of the Supreme Court to adjudicate upon and strike down unconstitutional laws.[35] The Irish Constitution would not protect the right to use contraception as a part of one's fundamental right to privacy,[36] the right to bodily integrity,[37] or any of the unenumerated rights that form such an important part of our constitutional system. The European Convention on Human Rights would not have developed to protect individuals from criminalisation on the basis of sexual orientation,[38] or to protect the rights of unmarried parents and their children.[39] The German Constitutional Court would not have engaged in the *Solange* line of decisions that so enriched the development of fundamental rights at European Union level.[40] Ultimately, a static constitution cannot serve the needs of the polity and the avoidance of stasis requires judicial innovation. This, of course, is not to valorise the judicial role over all others or to ignore courts' capacity to savagely undermine liberty,[41] scathingly excoriate those who do not conform to the perceived 'norm',[42] or draw on perceived societal values or realities to undermine rights.[43] The argument here is *not* that judges always get it 'right' from a progressive perspective when they innovate, or that innovation always enhances liberty or positively develops the constitutional settlement. One can criticise the outcome and mechanism of reasoning deployed without deeming the judicial activity of innovation *per se* illegitimate, just as one can criticise dangerous driving without calling for roads to be shut down and private car ownership abolished.

It was not inevitable that questions such as reproductive autonomy, fundamental rights within the EU, or LGBT rights (for example) would require rights-based resolution through judicial innovation. Such innovation is not necessarily judicial: there is no reason why the other interpretative actors within the constitutional ecosystem could not have engaged in such innovation themselves before or instead of the courts. However, where a political system allows for stagnation, or imposes laws and restrictions that appear at odds with contemporary practice and mores, it falls to the courts to decide on the continuing compatibility of those laws and practices with the constitution in its current form. Certainly, there may be disagreement about where that point in time lies, but as Justice Kennedy observed in *Obergefell*:

> The nature of injustice is that we may not always see it in our own times. The generations that wrote and ratified the Bill of Rights and the Fourteenth Amendment did not presume to know the extent of freedom in all of its dimensions, and so they entrusted to future generations a charter protecting the right of all persons to enjoy liberty as we learn its meaning. When new insight reveals discord between the Constitution's central protections and a received legal stricture, a claim to liberty must be addressed.[44]

In such cases, judicial innovation – i.e. activism or evolutionary interpretation – is necessary. Indeed, judicial innovation of this kind is arguably compensatory. By this I mean that it may involve the courts in innovation in order to compensate for the failure of other organs of the state to advance constitutional evolution in line with the *telos* of the constitution.[45] In this way, judicial innovation is quite simply necessary for a constitutional system to remain fit for purpose, i.e. capable of addressing contemporary issues in a way that delimits government power, enhances individual liberty and organises governance accordingly.

Judicial innovation is not illegitimate

As already conceded, necessity does not equate to legitimacy. There is continuing and long-standing anxiety about judicial activism/innovation/evolution across multiple jurisdictions. These anxieties relate primarily to what is considered to be the legitimate role of the judiciary as a body that applies rather than makes law, i.e. a concern that through innovation, judges engage in lawmaking, thus infringing illegitimately on the roles of the other branches of the state. Furthermore, the particular purchase of these anxieties may depend on the nature of the politico-legal system within which they are expressed: one can imagine that in a system where constitutional texts can be amended by legislation, that anxiety is less sharp than in systems where the constitutional text is extremely difficult to amend. However, in a legal constitution such as Ireland's, a broader conception of the role of the judiciary would, and as argued above should, recognise courts' role as part of the ecosystemic and collaborative process of constitutionalism. Thus, while the courts ought not to 'make law' per se, they also ought to not *shy away from developing legal standards through interpretation*, albeit within some limits.

Courts being limited in this relation is no different from a qualitative perspective than is the limitation of executive and legislative power: no one branch of the state can act unlimited, rather all place limits on themselves and on one another. In the case of courts, judicial self-restraint is an especially important limitation as the principle of independence of the judiciary would be potentially endangered by the express limitation of judicial power by the other branches of government even, it is increasingly suggested, in a traditionally political constitution.[46] And so, if legitimacy here is to be measured against *both* the role of the courts *qua* courts and the role of the courts as part of the broader system of constitutional governance, I suggest that there are a number of arguments underpinning the claim that judicial innovation is not illegitimate.

As considered above, judges do not exist merely to adjudicate. The judicial function is in fact more complex that than. When we ask judges to apply the law we accept that in so doing they must interpret it. This includes the law that forms part of the constitution. We also entrust judges with a role in the overall governance of the state and with an important function of delimiting democratic possibilities through the identification of constitutionalist boundaries on political choice. As noted above, the constitutional text, jurisprudence and conventions that have developed over time cannot foresee every possible issue that will arise in a developing polity. Rather, constitutions generally lay down broad approaches to fundamental rights, organisation of the state, and state identity that then require (re)shaping, evolution and innovation over time. In adjudicating upon disputes that come before them, courts have a role in that process of ensuring constitutional(ist) growth to accompany the complexity of contemporary governance. Thus, judicial innovation – and perhaps particularly compensatory judicial innovation – is part and parcel of the judicial role, for it constitutes an important element of shepherding the constitutionalist maturation of the polity. This is not to suggest that courts make the ultimate decision as to the constitutionalist identity of the polity; while judicial innovation is part and parcel of the judicial role, the results of such innovation are also subject to rejection by the polity. In other words, and bringing us to the second prong of this part of the argument, courts do not have the 'final word' on the constitution.

One of the primary objections people make to judicial innovation across contexts is that the courts are somehow stealing the thunder of the legislature and claiming the 'final word' for themselves. In my view this is also true in the context of review of legislation. Even if a court strikes a measure down, the message to government is usually not 'you may not do that' but rather 'you may not do that in this way'. The fact that government or the legislature may neglect to innovate in response or to hold a corrective referendum (considered further below) does not mean that courts have had the final word on policy or even on the constitution. Rather, as considered above, the court has had the last word on the specific measure impugned, and only that. However, the reality of constitutional governance is that there is *never* a last word: constitutional development is ongoing, incremental, collaborative and constant, particularly in its practical application. Thus, courts do not act illegitimately by developing and applying an understanding of constitutional texts, principles or conventions on the basis of usurping the other branches of government: those branches always have the option of revising the constitutional text or opposing the interpretation outlined by the courts, although the form of such resistance will vary across contexts.

In the Irish system, this takes places primarily by means of what David Gwynn Morgan and I have termed corrective referenda,[47] i.e. referendums in which the people (or 'the People') are asked to reverse or amend an understanding of the Constitution as laid down by the courts. This is, in fact, not at all an uncommon phenomenon in Ireland. The Irish Constitution can only be amended by referendum of the people,[48] and there is no initiative process. In other words, referenda must be proposed by the government, and then put to the people. If successful, a special piece of legislation then implements the change by means of amendment of the constitutional text. The rate of referendum frequency has increased significantly since the 1970s; there were only three referenda between the introduction of the Constitution in 1937 and 1972. Now, however, referenda are almost commonplace and, as mentioned above, encapsulate the capacity of the political system and, ultimately, the people to challenge a judicial interpretation of the Constitution by means of referendum.

An example of this is the incendiary topic of abortion. Following *Attorney General v. X*,[49] considered above, it was claimed that those who voted for the 8th Amendment in 1983 never contemplated the possibility of acquiring an abortion on the basis of risk of suicide;[50] that the Supreme Court had, in other words, frustrated the will of the people. Compelled by this argumentation, two referenda were held (one in 1992 and another in 2002) to (*inter alia*) give the Irish electorate the opportunity to explicitly exclude abortion on the basis of a risk of death from suicide from the limited constitutional right. In this case, although it was the Supreme Court that had applied an innovative approach to constitutional interpretation in terms of understanding the constitutional text, it was ultimately the people who had the last word through their rejection on both occasions of a proposed reversal of this interpretation.[51] A referendum to empower parliamentary committees held in 2012 brought about a similar outcome, while the people did reverse the effect of Supreme Court decisions in referenda pertaining to bail[52] and the electoral system,[53] for example.

By deciding to hold a corrective referendum – or, beyond Ireland, to amend the constitution by the jurisdictionally appropriate means – in response to judicial innovation other branches of the state expressly exercise their right to the last word; or, at least, to the *next* word in constitutional interpretation. However, a decision not to challenge or attempt to reverse judicial interpretation is also an exercise in the next word; it suggests that the other branches of government accept the court's constitutional interpretation (or at least do not sufficiently oppose it to attempt 'correction').

In a political constitution, such as that in the United Kingdom, parliament is supreme and sovereign and so has the capacity to reverse judicial pronouncements not only through statutory amendment but also by voicing clearly articulated opposing constitutional interpretations, although a statutory amendment is more effective. The fact that, over the past fifteen years, a culture of compliance in relation to a particular kind of *quasi*-constitutional interpretation (i.e. the interpretation and application of the Human Rights Act 1998) has developed does not undo this constitutional right of parliament within the United Kingdom,[54] although there are some suggestions that at least some members of the judiciary may consider that some elements of the developing constitution (such as judicial review) are now beyond the reach of the legislature.[55] Rather, the decision to comply is a decision to accept the interpretation of the court; it is in itself the next word in a dispute as to constitutional interpretation and the appropriate role of the courts. In such systems, particular innovations (such as the declaration of incompatibility) have been developed to structure and nudge dialogue between the judiciary and other branches of government and to clearly communicate the courts' subordinate position;[56] their constitutional inability to have 'the final word'.

In a system of separate and equal powers, such as that found in the United States, this principle – that courts do not have the final word – is very much writ large. Congress and the executive are both at liberty to present contrary views of the Constitution and, although the Supreme Court has the ultimate interpretative authority under *Marbury v. Madison*[57] (itself an example of judicial innovation), there are numerous 'workarounds' that might be used such as constitutional amendment (albeit a particularly difficult thing to achieve in the US),[58] jurisdiction-stripping clauses[59] (which are not subjected to the same level of scrutiny as ouster clauses in UK administrative law,[60] for example) and, in the field of international law, the last-in-time principle under the Supremacy Clause of the Constitution.[61] In addition, the federal system gives rise to particular cleavages of constitutionalism and constitutionalist resistance and collaboration by means of state law that inevitably influence the stability, nature and content of federal constitutional interpretation and evolution. The aftermath of *Roe v. Wade*[62] serves as an instructive example of this. In that case the US Supreme Court famously found that the Constitution protects the right to access abortion within certain parameters. However, in the aftermath of that decision, a large number of states have introduced laws ostensibly to regulate medical practice, but which effectively constitute rejections of the Court's constitutional interpretation by introducing procedural requirements such as pre-abortion foetal scans, paternal consent laws and licensing requirements for medical professionals that make it extremely difficult to access an abortion as a matter of fact.

Furthermore, when engaging in judicial innovation in the field of constitutional interpretation, courts are fully cognisant of and take into appropriate account the views of other branches of government, recognising their role as collaborators in the process of constitutional interpretation and development. In this sense, courts demonstrate judicial self-restraint, even when engaging in compensatory innovation. This is manifested in a number of different elements of constitutional interpretation that are common across systems: deference, the presumption of constitutionality, and the taking into account of 'original' intent in constitutional interpretation.

Thus, claims that judicial innovation by means of activism is illegitimate because it robs the political branches of government of their right and capacity to make law simply fail to take into account the fact that – apart from in relation to the particular dispute before them – courts do not have the final say on the content of constitutions or the interpretation of their provisions. The fact that the political branches may opt not to engage in processes to reverse, adjust or otherwise amend judicial interpretation of the constitution does not mean that they do not have that power or capacity or that their failure to exercise this power makes judicial innovation *a fortiori* illegitimate. Rather this reinforces the iterative and collaborative nature of constitutional interpretation; its ecosystemic form.

Conclusion

Many scholars, politicians and activists are deeply uncomfortable with judicial innovation. This chapter mounts a defence of such innovation, arguing that persistent discomfort is founded on: (a) an overweighting of the role of the courts and failure to recognise the ecosystemic nature of constitutional interpretation; (b) a restricted conception of the constitution that underplays its teleological nature; and (c) a misrecognition of judicial pronouncements as 'the final word'. While framed in the context of the Irish Constitution, this argument is not jurisdictionally limited; rather, with appropriate adjustment for the particularity of constitutional amendment in different jurisdictions for example, it can translate across national boundaries and into other constitutional polities.

Notes

1 Judicial activism is often, but not inevitably, progressive, although some conservatives argue that an activist court cannot be truly conservative as conservatism favours judicial restraint (see, e.g., R. Bork, *The Tempting of America: The Political Seduction of the Law* (Free Press, 1990) pp. 223–240). For a rich discussion of the meaning and history of judicial activism, including its conservative manifestations, see B. Canon, 'Defining the Dimensions of Judicial Activism' (1982–83) 66 *Judicature* 236.
2 There are almost too many examples of such arguments to cite, but a good account of the arguments is provided in J. Waldron, 'The Core of the Case against Judicial Review' (2006) 115(6) *Yale Law Journal* 1346.
3 D. Gwynn Morgan, *A Judgment Too Far? Judicial Activism and the Constitution* (Cork UP, 2001) p. 7.
4 Take for example the general acceptability of anti-miscegenation laws in the United States at the time of the drafting of the US Constitution, on which see, e.g., A. Avins, 'Anti-Miscegenation Laws and the Fourteenth Amendment: The Original Intent' (1966) 52(7) *Virginia Law Review* 1224, compared to the Supreme Court's decision striking down laws prohibiting interracial marriage in *Loving v. Virginia* 388 US 1 (1967) and the subsequent development of a dignitarian conception of a right to marry the person of one's choosing, including a person of the same sex, in the 2015 decision in *Obergefell v. Hodges* 576 US ___ (2015).
5 Some scholars advocate the identification of 'extra-constitutional' issues, i.e.

issues that are to be governed by political processes alone as they are not contemplated by the Constitution and are, thus, considered to be outside of the appropriate judicial sphere. Such issues are, first of all, not strictly outside of constitutionalist contestation as political contestation is part of constitutionalism. Second, the claim that they ought to remain outside of the courts' contemplation (i.e. that courts ought to declare them extra-constitutional and thus not adjudicate on them) is hotly contested. For an overview and a defence, see the views propounded by Davis in F. de Londras and F. F. Davis, 'Controlling the Executive in Times of Terrorism: Competing Perspectives on Effective Oversight' (2010) 30(1) *Oxford Journal of Legal Studies* 19.
6 L. Solum, 'The Interpretation–Construction Distinction' (2010) 27 *Constitutional Commentary* 95.
7 *Ibid.*, 96.
8 *Ibid.*
9 E. Carolan, 'Between Supremacy and Submission: A Model of Collaborative Constitutionalism?' (2013), available at http://ssrn.com/abstract=2309875 (accessed 18 June 2015).
10 *Zappone & Gilligan v. Revenue Commissioners* [2008] 2 IR 417. On scholars' and campaigners' reaction to the crystallisation of this claim in the popular imagination, see, e.g., U. Mullally, *In the Name of Law: The Movement for Marriage Equality in Ireland. An Oral History* (History Press, 2014) ch. 5.
11 While the extent to which the executive really dominates the legislature may be somewhat lesser than is often thought to be the case (on a study of executive dominance in the UK, see M. Russell, D. Gover and K. Wollter, 'Does the Executive Dominate the Westminster Legislative Process? Six Reasons for Doubt' (2015) 69(2) *Parliamentary Affairs* 286, the claim that executive judgement as to constitutional meaning and limitations is heavily persuasive is uncontested in the broader sense.
12 Indeed, in some political systems the 'party room' is the key site of constitutionalist contestation, rather than the debating chamber. On the workings of contestation in the Australian system, for example, see F. F. Davis, 'The Politics of Counterterrorism Judicial Review: Creating Effective Parliamentary Scrutiny' in F. F. Davis and F. de Londras (eds), *Critical Debates on Counter-Terrorism Judicial Review* (CUP, 2014).
13 S. Gardbaum, *The New Commonwealth Model of Constitutionalism: Theory and Practice* (CUP, 2014).
14 On the role of the Oath in duties and capacities for constitutional interpretation, see R. Re, 'Promising the Constitution' (2016) 110(2) *Northwestern University Law Review* 299.
15 J. Limbach, 'The Role of the Federal Constitutional Court' (2000) 53 *Southern Methodism University Law Review* 429, 433; M. Tushnet, *Taking the Constitution Away from the Courts* (Princeton UP, 1999). Eoin Daly assesses this idea of anticipatory obedience in his chapter in the current volume, arguing that it is a cost of judicial supremacy (see Chapter 2, pp. 29–48).
16 The classical statement is that of Justice Hanna in *Pigs Marketing Board v.*

Donnelly [1939] IR 413, 424: 'When the court has to consider the constitutionality of a law it must, in the first place, be accepted as an axiom that a law passed by the Oireachtas, the elected representatives of the people, is presumed to be constitutional unless and until the contrary is clearly established.'

17 M. Tushnet, 'Evaluating Congressional Constitutional Interpretation: Some Criteria and Two Informal Case Studies' (2001) 50 *Duke Law Journal* 1395.

18 I make this argument out more completely in F. de Londras, 'Declarations of Incompatibility under the ECHR Act 2003: A Workable Transplant?' (2014) 35(1) *Statute Law Review* 50 and 'Neither Herald Nor Fanfare: The Limited Impact of the ECHR Act 2003 on Rights Infrastructure in Ireland' in S. Egan, L. Thornton and J. Walsh (eds), *Ireland and the European Convention on Human Rights: 60 Years and Beyond* (Bloomsbury, 2014) p. 37.

19 For an excellent and constantly evolving resource on the 'revolt' in UK parliamentary politics, see the website www.revolts.co.uk, reporting the research of professors Philip Cowley and Mark Stuart.

20 Here again the Australian example is germane; see Davis (n. 12).

21 This refers to private member's bills introduced by Clare Daly TD (Protection of Life During Pregnancy (Amendment) (Fatal Foetal Abnormalities) Bill 2013, s. 1(2)) and Michael McNamara TD (Protection of Life during Pregnancy (Amendment) (Fatal Foetal Abnormalities) Bill 2015, s. 2(1)); neither was successful.

22 See the comments reported in M. O'Halloran, 'Unconstitutional to include fatal foetal abnormalities in legislation, Taoiseach says', *Irish Times* (26 June 2013).

23 For an argument that it would not be unconstitutional to permit abortion in cases of fatal foetal abnormalities, see R. Fletcher, Opening Statement to Oireachtas Health Committee (21 May 2013), available at www.oireachtas.ie/parliament/media/committees/healthandchildren/Dr-Ruth-Fletcher,-Keele-University.pdf (accessed 28 May 2015).

24 This is the term used in the European Convention on Human Rights Act 2003 to identify those entities with obligations under the Act. The term, as defined in that Act, captures nicely the range of entities involved in administering the state. Section 1 of the 2003 Act defines an organ of the state as 'a tribunal or any other body (other than the President or the Oireachtas or either House of the Oireachtas or a Committee of either such House or a Joint Committee of both such Houses or a court) which is established by law or through which any of the legislative, executive or judicial powers of the State are exercised'.

25 An excellent example is the gap in time (a matter of some months) between promulgation and commencement of the Protection of Life During Pregnancy Act 2013 and the issuance of Department of Health, *Implementation of the Protection of Life During Pregnancy Act 2013: Guidance Document for Health Professionals* (19 September 2014).

26 Until 2013 abortion was criminalised under s. 58, Offences against the Person Act 1851. It is now criminalised under s. 22, Protection of Life during Pregnancy Act 2013.

27 *Attorney General v. X* [1992] 1 IR 1.

28 This included recriminations from the judiciary. See [1992] 1 IR 1, *per* Justice McCarthy, p. 147, See comments of Justice McCarthy in *Society for the Protection of the Unborn Child v. Grogan* [1989] IR 753, p. 770 *per* Justice McCarthy and Justice McKechnie in *D (A Minor) v. Judge Brennan, the HSE, Ireland, and the Attorney General* unreported (HC, 9 May 2007).

29 As Tom Hickey suggests in his chapter in this volume, there are certain similarities between his and my arguments for judicial power, notwithstanding considerable differences overall. This idea of judicial elucidation of principles that may have broader significance is evocative of his ideas around the capacity of courts to develop norms that might apply and develop elsewhere (see Chapter 4, pp. 64–82).

30 See J. Raz, *Between Authority and Interpretation: On the Theory of Law and Practical Reason* (OUP, 1999).

31 'Societal Change and Constitutional Interpretation' (2010) 1(2) *Irish Journal of Legal Studies* 71, 72.

32 *Roe v. Wade* 410 US 113 (1973).

33 *Loving v. Virginia* 388 US 1 (1967)

34 *Brown v. Board of Education of Topeka, Kansas* 347 US 483 (1954).

35 *Marbury v. Madison* 5 US 137 (1803).

36 *McGee v. Attorney General* [1974] IR 284.

37 *Ryan v. Attorney General* [1965] IR 294

38 *Dudgeon v. United Kingdom* (1981) 4 EHRR 149

39 *Johnston v. Ireland* (1987) 9 EHRR 203.

40 BVerfGE 37, 271 2 BvL 52/71 Solange I-Beschluß; BVerfGE 73, 339 2 BvR 197/83 Solange II-decision.

41 Famous examples include the US Supreme Court's decision in *Dred Scott v. Sandford* 60 US 393 (1857), finding that neither free nor enslaved blacks could be US citizens.

42 For this one need look no further than the judgment of O'Higgins CJ in *Norris v. Attorney General* [1984] IR 36

43 The recent case of *Shelby County v. Holder* 570 US ___ (2013), in which the US Supreme Court overturned a key element of the Voting Rights Act 1965 on the basis that there was no longer a need to require federal clearance before local government implements changes to voting law and practice. This is notwithstanding the overwhelming evidence that structural racism in the United States, including in respect of ability to vote, persists.

44 *Obergefell v. Hodges* 576 US ___ (2015) p. 11 Slip Opinion.

45 David Gwynn Morgan makes an aligned analysis to this effect in Morgan (n. 3) ch. 10.

46 See for example Bingham LJ in *R (Jackson) v. Attorney General* [2005] 4 All ER 1253 [102].

47 F. de Londras and D. Gwynn Morgan, 'Constitutional Amendment in Ireland' in X. Contiades (ed.), *Engineering Constitutional Change: A Comparative Perspective on Europe, Canada and the USA* (Routledge, 2012).

48 Article 46.

49 [1992] 1 IR 1.
50 W. Binchy, 'New abortion regime has no effective limits', *Irish Times* (6 March 1992).
51 See generally F. de Londras, 'Constitutionalizing Fetal Rights: A Salutary Tale from Ireland' (2015) 22(2) *Michigan Journal of Gender and Law* 243.
52 Reversing *The People (Attorney General) v. O'Callaghan* [1966] IR 501 and *Ryan v. Director of Public Prosecutions* [1989] IR 399.
53 Reversing *Re Article 26 and the Electoral (Amendment) Bill 1983* [1984] IR 268.
54 On possible changes wrought by the Human Rights Act 1998 in this relation, see, e.g., R. Masterman, 'Labour's "Juridification" of the Constitution' (2009) 62(3) *Parliamentary Affairs* 476.
55 Bingham LJ in *R (Jackson) v. Attorney General* [2005] 4 All ER 1253 [102].
56 R. Masterman and J. Mürkens, 'Skirting Supremacy and Subordination: The Constitutional Authority of the United Kingdom Supreme Court' (2013) *Public Law* 800.
57 *Marbury v. Madison* 5 US 137 (1803).
58 Article V, US Constitution.
59 Congress has jurisdiction-stripping powers under congressional powers clause (Article 1(8)(9), US Constitution), the vesting clause (Article 3(1), US Constitution) and the exceptions clause (Article 3(2), US Constitution).
60 Classically, see *Anisminic Ltd v. Foreign Compensation Commission* [1969] 1 All ER 208.
61 See, e.g., J. Ku, 'Treaties as Laws: A Defense of the Last-in-Time Rules for Treaties and Federal Statutes' (2005) 80(2) *Indiana Law Journal* 319.
62 *Roe v. Wade* 410 US 113 (1973).

2

Reappraising judicial supremacy in the Irish constitutional tradition

Eoin Daly

Ireland is unusual among anglophone jurisdictions in the degree of consensus that exists in its constitutional and political culture concerning the merits of 'strong-form' judicial review – that is, the exclusive power vested in the superior courts to invalidate primary legislation on constitutional grounds. While there is a relatively elaborate judicial and academic discourse concerning how this power should be exercised – the standards and methodology of judicial review; the doctrines of proportionality and deference and so forth – there has been remarkably discussion of its desirability as such. This can be contrasted with both the United States and the United Kingdom, where the alternative model – 'political constitutionalism' or legislative supremacy – attracts strong intellectual support.[1] Here, I aim first, to consider why judicial supremacy has gone almost unquestioned in political and intellectual circles, and second to consider whether or not, and to what extent, some of the better-known theoretical arguments against strong-form judicial review are borne out in certain aspects of the Irish experience.

Roughly speaking, the doctrine of *judicial supremacy* means that while various organs might legitimately interpret the Constitution, the judiciary enjoys ultimate authority or the 'final say' concerning its meaning, at least with respect to the constitutionality of laws. On the one hand, this simply describes the institutional status quo in Ireland since the enactment of the 1937 Constitution, which explicitly grants the superior courts the power to invalidate unconstitutional legislation. However, judicial supremacy also refers to a political doctrine concerning the best form of constitutional structure. It tends to encompass the view, first, that judges are better positioned than 'political' organs to render authoritative and *correct* interpretations of constitutional rights; indeed, strong-form judicial review is often considered synonymous with written constitutionalism itself. Second, and more broadly, it embraces the view that judicial fetters on legislative power are needed to protect individual liberties against the state – that judicial powers of legislative invalidation are 'good for rights' in more general terms, based on a more open-ended moral concern for individual human rights.

This chapter offer a sceptical appraisal of judicial supremacy in Irish constitutional culture. In particular, I will argue that the benefits and potential of rights-based constitutional adjudication have been broadly overstated, and its costs under-acknowledged. I will consider how various familiar, principled objections to strong-form judicial review, of the sort typically aired in other anglophone jurisdictions, may be borne out in the Irish context. Two arguments in particular are salient in the Irish experience. First, the understanding of strong-form judicial review as being 'good for rights' conceives of rights narrowly, ignoring the connection between individual freedom and citizenship, and overlooking problems of domination in social and political life. Second, rights-based review of legislation undermines democratic citizenship in the Irish context, not because it undermines majority decision-making as such, but rather, because it has meant that ever-increasing areas of political argument are framed in esoteric constitutional terms. Many areas of legitimate disagreement about rights are divested from the political to the legal spheres, thus stifling democratic discourse.

Judicial supremacy in the Irish constitutional tradition

First it is worth qualifying the scope of the argument. I use 'judicial supremacy' both descriptively and normatively. On the one hand, it refers to a constitutional system where the judiciary enjoys the 'final say' as to the constitutionality of parliamentary legislation. Thus it is limited, for the purposes of this discussion at least, to judicial review of legislation as distinct from executive action, as this raises quite separate normative and institutional issues.[2] Neither does the argument extend to weaker systems of rights-based review that deny courts an outright power of legislative invalidation – for example, the UK or New Zealand models – and that create a weaker declaratory remedy.[3] On the other hand, I refer to a normative proposition that a system of the kind described is necessary and legitimate in protecting individual rights against legislative encroachment.

In Ireland, the normative idea is rarely articulated partly because it is taken as self-evident. In fact it is difficult to find sources to support that claim because a belief in judicial supremacy is so pervasive in our legal culture that it is rarely discussed or mentioned. Judges will tend to justify their exercise of this power on the straightforward grounds that, unlike the United States, it is explicitly mandated by the Constitution.[4] They do not need to provide a principled defence of judicial supremacy and are naturally disinclined to proffer one, even if they initially dithered as to the justiciability of constitutional rights.[5] In academia, there is a growing body of analytical literature concerning how the courts' power of constitutional review should be exercised, particularly in the area of proportionality doctrine.[6] But, curiously, in Ireland there is little discussion of whether or not the existence of this power is a good thing in the first instance. Perhaps this is partly because there seems to be little point in discussing what is, in reality, an institutional fait accompli: once constitutional courts acquire such powers, they are rarely reversed.[7] But this is an incomplete explanation, especially bearing in mind the comparatively lively discourse that exists in equivalent jurisdictions, such as the United States, where judicial supremacy is at least as intractably established.

Why has judicial supremacy become an article of faith in Ireland? This could be attributed, in part, to a relative lack of public regard for the quality of legislative process and legislative deliberation – although this is inevitably a rough-and-ready assessment in comparative terms. But, in general terms, perhaps, the lesser esteem a public (or elite public) will have for legislative politics, the more it will likely tolerate judicial activism.[8] On the one hand, the culture of the legal academy itself is somewhat judicial-centric. In Ireland, legal academics remain closer to the culture of the legal professions than is the case in England and Wales (and certainly more so than in continental European jurisdictions). They will tend to be more appreciative of the reasoned deliberation of precedential and principled decision-making in courts than the seemingly baser dynamics of legislative politics. Of course, they will not usually be inclined to understate the social value of a discipline or profession to which they belong or with which they have an affinity: beliefs concerning the merits of judicial review do not form in the abstract, but are surely a product, in part, of professional *habitus*.[9] And so with few exceptions, law generally, and judicial review, specifically, are understood as bulwarks for justice and liberty.[10]

Anecdotally at least, the prevailing assumption among most legal academics is that the more extensive the power of judicial review, the better it must be for 'rights'. Indeed there can hardly be a jurisdiction in the English-speaking world that more enthusiastically embraces Dworkin's idea that whereas 'policy' is the domain of parliaments and politics, 'rights' are the domain of judges and courts.[11] And while British legal tradition has been so obviously influential in so many ways, its model of parliamentary sovereignty is usually seen, in Ireland, as a historical quirk rather than as a live institutional option for a mature democracy, especially given that strong-form judicial review has become the European norm since the Second World War, and subsequently the fall of the Iron Curtain.[12] In our legal culture, it would be seen as quite outlandish to suggest, for example, that we would be better off if the Oireachtas enjoyed a constitutionally unfettered legislative power. By and large, students probably absorb this view as well. In its most clichéd form, this manifests itself as a lawyerly conceit that suggests that only the courts stand between 'politics' and 'rights'.

Since I am not an anthropologist of the legal academy or the legal professions, I offer no original explanations for this specificity of Irish legal culture. However, some clues lie, perhaps, in the historical context in which the current Constitution emerged. The 1922 Irish Free State Constitution is often considered a dead letter simply because its fundamental-rights provisions were rendered meaningless by the flexible amendment procedure that was more or less abused routinely throughout the 1920s and 1930s, at a time of relative political instability.[13] Although the Supreme Court enjoyed a power to invalidate primary legislation, the Oireachtas could simply circumvent this through ordinary legislation. And given the political turbulence of the 1920s and 1930s, the Constitution proved quite ineffective in safeguarding civil liberties. By way of contrast, the 1937 Constitution properly entrenched rights-based review of legislation by precluding the possibility of any extended flexible-amendment procedure. And according to the dominant narrative, this paved the way for a period of rights-based judicial activism in the 1960s and 1970s, once the Supreme Court discarded its initial reticence. Therefore, judicial supremacy became synonymous with a transition to constitutional stability and greater respect for rights, particularly in the criminal justice and procedural domains.

Thus the provision for strong-form judicial review came to be seen as a definitive characteristic of Irish constitutionalism and indeed the main point of contrast with the parliamentary-focused British tradition. Indeed the 1937 Constitution can be seen as anticipating the postwar global trend towards entrenched constitutionalism, away from the legislative supremacy that had dominated previously.[14] In one respect, however, Ireland remains distinctive, because judicial supremacy has not, in general terms, been understood as a 'counter-majoritarian' fetter or as a check on popular sovereignty: in fact it has often been understood as quite consistent with a majoritarian and populist account of democracy. Since the Constitution was enacted by an extraordinary plebiscite and could only be amended by referendum, this meant that judicial review could be understood as a manifestation of popular sovereignty rather than as a fetter on it.[15] It is understood not in terms of a transition from majoritarian to counter-majoritarian constitutionalism, but rather as a shift from parliamentary to popular sovereignty.[16]

Objections to judicial supremacy

While there is a rich and extensive political literature offering a sceptical perspective on rights-based constitutional review, here I will only sketch the main themes and highlight those points that are particularly salient in the Irish context. What I outline here is a very specific proposition that does not call into question rights-based judicial review as such. Rather it challenges an idea of judicial supremacy in rights-based constitutional adjudication – that is, the idea that judges should enjoy the 'final say' in determining the constitutionality of parliamentary legislation.

The debate on rights-based constitutional review is often framed as a conflict between majoritarian democracy and individual rights, where parliamentary legislation is understood as reflecting the will of a political majority, and judicial power as representing a bulwark for minority and individual rights. Judicial review is often defended as a so-called 'counter-majoritarian' mechanism, a means of protecting minorities and individuals from political majorities.[17] But this is an oversimplification which relies on a caricatured version of the argument against judicial supremacy. On the one hand, judicial review can be defended in some contexts as an exercise or expression of popular sovereignty rather than as a check upon it.[18] Conversely, on the other hand, the counter-majoritarian view only makes sense if one understands the function of representative democracy as being to effectuate majority will or majority opinion on discrete issues, which is a crude and unrealistic account of legislative process.[19] Waldron argues it is unclear why a policy or law is intrinsically problematic or oppressive merely because it emanates from a majority rather than a minority. There is no reason to assume that a tyranny of the majority is worse than a tyranny of the minority; in either instance we have to consider the content or the source of the law in question to decide whether and why is it 'tyrannical' at all.[20] And while judges can be portrayed as agents of majoritarian power as well as individual rights, conversely legislative supremacy might be defended as a better mechanism for protecting rights, or for reconciling competing rights claims, rather than on narrowly 'majoritarian' grounds. Thus the 'counter-majoritarian' dilemma makes little sense insofar as judicial power can be understood (partly) in majoritarian terms and legislative power (partly) in rights-based terms.

The philosophical arguments against judicial supremacy can be classified as proceduralist versus consequentialist, or as process-based versus outcomes-based. Roughly speaking, the consequentialist or outcomes-based argument holds that strong-form judicial review fails to enhance some concept of rights, or that in practice it does more harm than good with a particular political or moral philosophy in mind. In contrast, the proceduralist or process-based argument holds that regardless of outcomes, there is an intrinsic value in respecting the legislative products of a democratic electoral process that enshrines and reflects a principle of political equality.

On the consequentialist side, there is a strong history of left-wing and progressive ambivalence towards judicial power.[21] Traditionally, for example, much of the British left opposed strong-form judicial review based on a concern that it would be used to check progressive state intervention and the welfare state. Similarly, French republicans were generally hostile to judicial power in the political domain as they associated it with the privileges and the abuses of the *ancien régime*.[22]

Many of these left-wing consequentialist objections centre on the intractably ideological character of rights-based adjudication. In particular, they contest the central premise of liberal constitutionalism – the idea that a codified set of constitutional rights can place determinate boundaries on the power of the state in a manner that transcends political conflict. Similarly, critical scholars will deny that constitutional rights have any discernible objective content that stands apart from open-ended political and ideological controversies, or that social conflicts about the meaning of rights can be adjudicated based on any specifically legal mode of reasoning. They will argue that rights-based reasoning simply reproduces the full spectrum of (acceptable) political opinion using legal terminologies.[23] They reject the idea that constitutional jurisprudence can ever provide a self-sufficient, non-political mechanism for resolving social conflicts about rights. Since constitutions are drafted in abstract and open-textured terms, they are essentially indeterminate. More or less any pre-existing prejudice or moral intuition concerning the purposes and limits of state power can be framed in rights-based terminologies, and more or less any social and political problem can be presented in 'rights' terms. In short, any attempt to depoliticise 'rights' ignores the ideological character of rights-based reasoning.

Of course, for a consequentialist, judicial activism might work in both directions, serving progressive as much as conservative ends. Then, the merits of strong-form review might simply depend on local contingencies and the vagaries of institutional culture. However, since constitutional law generally works in a negative way by striking down legislative encroachments, arguably it is conceptually geared towards a conservative view of individual liberty focused on protecting the individual from public encroachment, but which lacks the remedies and the conceptual toolkit that are necessary to address the structural inequalities – and thus the various forms of domination – that persist in the social and economic domains. Unfreedom understood as *domination* – that is, the power hierarchies encoded in unequal social relationships – is hardly amenable to being resolved through the usual judicial remedies.[24] At best, constitutional justice is ineffective against, and at worst reinforces, those problems of social and economic domination that are perhaps incapable of being captured or expressed by 'rights' language at all. And irrespective of whether judges 'get it right' in particular cases, there is an independent cost to participative citizenship as citizens are precluded, collectively, from (definitively) making such decisions themselves.

These structural limitations of constitutional justice offer progressive and left-wing consequentialists cause for opposing strong-form judicial review independently of contextual considerations. In the wake of decisions like *Citizens United*, progressive and left-wing lawyers in the US might be inclined to regard the judgments of the post-war Warren Court as something of a historical aberration.[25] Why hold out for the hope of isolated victories, they might ask, within a system that is structurally allied to a conservative form of liberalism; that is consistently amenable to elite interests; and that ultimately shores up social and economic domination?

These arguments suffer from the same problems that plague all consequentialist political theories (how competing harms and goods are weighted and measured, etc.). By contrast, proceduralist theories provide arguments against strong-form judicial review that avoid the need to rely on conjectural claims concerning the political effects of judicial review under particular conditions. In short, the process-based argument eschews debates about the net efficaciousness or otherwise of constitutional judgments in promoting any particular concept of rights or of justice. Rather, it suggests that the central problem of institutional design is not the concept of rights that ought to be enshrined and protected, but rather, the institutional procedure through which competing rights claims are settled. In turn, it claims that, all things considered, systems centred on legislative supremacy do better in this light, given the contestatory nature of legislative process and its direct structural connection to a principle of political equality.

Waldron, for example, argues that legislative process offers the fairest mechanism for resolving competing rights claims: it 'treats participants equally'.[26] 'Rights' are not the preserve of the courts: legislative debate routinely weights and orders 'rights claims'. Thus he denies that judicial review offers a better means of 'getting to the truth about rights'. Far from representing a purer deliberative forum, judicial reasoning tends to avoid full-throated moral debate concerning rights, obscuring the essential moral issues 'with side-issues about precedent, texts, and interpretation'.[27] In contrast, legislative debate 'gets to the heart of the matter ... there are things about legislatures that sometimes make them vulnerable to the sorts of pressures that rights are supposed to guard against; but there are also things about courts that make it difficult for them to grapple directly with the moral issues that rights-disagreements present'.[28]

Bellamy, working from a republican perspective, offers a similar case against judicial supremacy.[29] Like other neo-Roman republican thinkers, Bellamy conceives of freedom not in the liberal sense of non-interference, but rather as non-domination, understood as resilient security against arbitrary power.[30] Effectively, Bellamy's argument is that reasonable citizens are deeply divided on issues of rights, the central task of constitutional design it not to enshrine a particular concept of rights but rather to establish some non-arbitrary mechanism through which competing rights claims can be settled. In turn, he argues that non-arbitrary rule can only be realised through a contestatory political process that accords each voting citizen equal weight and respect. This kind of majoritarian democracy – a procedural democracy unfettered by strong-form judicial review – encourages ongoing and open-ended contestation about the meaning of rights. By contrast, it is the very features that are thought to make constitutional courts uniquely suitable for protecting rights – that is, their non-political and non-electoral nature – that ultimately makes them inconsistent with political freedom in this sense. In fact, it is the very attempt to depoliticise rights that leads to political domination. In short, given that reasonable citizens disagree fundamentally about rights, strong-form judicial review constitutes a kind of arbitrary power: 'depoliticisation can fuel domination'.[31] Indeed for most republican thinkers, freedom is not established *despite* politics, as a residual sphere of non-interference against state power, but rather constituted by politics itself – a perspective that is rather marginalised in Irish judicial and legal culture.[32]

An Irish version of political constitutionalism?

How might the familiar theoretical arguments against judicial review be borne out in the Irish experience? First, it should be noted that a number of aspects of Irish constitutional culture, compared, say, to the United

States, might attenuate some concerns about the political legitimacy of judicial supremacy.

First, the Supreme Court jurisprudence of recent decades has recoiled from the high watermark of judicial supremacy that it (arguably) reached in the 1970s. Much of the judicial discourse has, in effect, tacitly accepted a theory of constitutional indeterminacy – that is, an understanding that the correct or *true* meaning of constitutional rights cannot be established according to any specifically legal or judicial mode of reasoning – a belief, in effect, that constitutional clauses are essentially indeterminate and open-textured. Alternatively, this can be understood as accepting that legislatures routinely protect and balance competing rights claims, and that they are better positioned in some respects to make such appraisals. Accordingly, the Court has indicated it will defer to interpretations of rights that are enacted by the Oireachtas via primary legislation. *Tuohy v. Courtney*, for example, established a rather deferential threshold concerning legislative limitations on rights.[33] Effectively it acknowledged that legislation not only limits constitutional rights for the sake of utilitarian and social-policy goals, but also to protect other rights; it 'balances' rights. Moreover, the Court affirmed that judges will not 'impose their view of the correct or desirable balance in substitution for the view of the legislature ... but rather ... determine from an objective stance whether the balance contained in the impugned legislation is so contrary to reason and fairness as to constitute an unjust attack on some individual's constitutional rights'.[34]

Thus, the limits of individual rights and public interests fall to be determined through the legislative process in the first instance, and the role of the courts is limited to determining whether restrictions on the exercise of constitutional rights are arbitrary, invidious or disproportionate. An example of this kind of reasoning about rights was found in *Fleming v. Ireland*, a case concerning the constitutionality of the ban on assisted suicide. Justice Kearns noted: 'the prohibition on assisted suicide is rationally connected to [the] fundamental objective of protecting life and is not remotely based on *arbitrary, unfair or irrational considerations*'.[35] Arguably, in turn, this minimalist understanding of the Court's role in interpreting rights is implicit in the proportionality doctrine that was endorsed in *Heaney v. Ireland*.[36] This was evident in an earlier version of the doctrine as articulated in *Ryan v. Attorney General*, where Justice Kenny affirmed:

> When dealing with controversial social, economic and medical matters on which it is notorious views change from generation to generation, the Oireachtas has to reconcile the exercise of personal rights with the claims

of the common good and its decision on the reconciliation should prevail unless it was oppressive to all or some of the citizens or unless there is no reasonable proportion between the benefit which the legislation will confer on the citizens or a substantial body of them and the interference with the personal rights of the citizen.[37]

A similarly modest judicial methodology was in evidence in *Roche v. Roche*, a case which considered whether the constitutional reference to the 'unborn' encompassed embryos *in vitro*. Most of the Supreme Court judges were at pains to emphasise that the responsibility for defining 'unborn' life fell initially to the Oireachtas, not the courts, and that as a 'court of law' they would eschew theological and philosophical 'imponderables' concerning the starting point of the right to life.[38]

Thus effectively – albeit tacitly for the most part – the Court has embraced an epistemological modesty (whether intentionally, consciously or otherwise), and has disavowed any role it might assume in 'getting to the truth about rights'. In *McGee v. Attorney General* in 1974, Justice Walsh boldly claimed that it fell to judges to ascertain the content of certain 'natural rights' which were to be placed above 'positive law' (meaning legislation), thus suggesting that judges could, and should attempt to discern an objective truth about rights.[39] However, the other cases suggest this case is an outlier in terms of judicial philosophy.

Certainly, compared to other jurisdictions the Irish Supreme Court has assumed a comparatively modest role in interpreting and enforcing the Constitution, and this might go some say towards attenuating any philosophical concerns about the legitimacy of judicial review.

Second, it is arguable that the Supreme Court's power of constitutional review is not as democratically problematic as that exercised by its American counterpart simply because the Constitution can be amended, and thus the Supreme Court overruled, through the referendum process; in fact there have been several instances in which the Constitution has been amended specifically to reverse unpopular Supreme Court judgments.[40] While judges might enjoy the 'final say' concerning the meaning of the constitutional text, the ultimate determination is reserved to the people.

From the proceduralist perspective, it is pointless to consider the specificities of Irish constitutional culture and of the Irish experience – the pluses and the minuses, the benefits and costs, etc. – because the objection is then rooted at a fundamental level of political legitimacy in institutional design.[41] The difficulty with a consequentialist argument is that it presupposes some means of weighting the advantages and disadvantages of strong-form judicial review, with a view to determining whether it advances a particular concept of rights – and so it may hinge, to an extent, on local contingencies such as judicial culture and the quality or rigour of parliamentary deliberation.

It is extremely difficult to establish an outcomes-based case against (or indeed for) strong-form judicial review based on an analysis of judicial decisions, and particularly to establish whether or not their net effect has been to advance some concept of rights. This would require some fairly dubious appraisal of moral trade-offs and weightings; indeed, I offer no original perspective on this familiar problem. How does one weigh up due process protections for criminal defendants against, say, restrictions on progressive labour legislation? One could try to make out an argument that in Ireland, the costs of judicial review – the bad decisions – simply outweigh the good decisions, thus undermining the moral claims of judicial supremacy as a mechanism for protecting rights. One could attempt to identify a conservative ideology in various patterns of rulings, for example, by highlighting the regressive effects of judicial rulings in the area of labour relations,[42] its ambivalence towards socio-economic rights, or indeed its reluctance to enforce resource-dependent educational rights, and so on.[43] Such analyses necessarily have a rough-and-ready sort of character, and are inevitably somewhat conjectural. My aim, therefore, is more modest – it is, simply, to identify some of the social and political costs of strong-form judicial review – costs that, I believe, have not been sufficiently acknowledged in domestic discourse concerning constitutional design.

In turn, the core of my argument is that the political costs of strong-form judicial review are not felt, primarily, in those constitutional judgments actually rendered, but rather that they are manifested as pre-emptive or anticipatory effects in the legislative and pre-legislative process – before constitutional controversies ever reach the courts. Regardless of the net effects of judgments themselves – the balance of pluses and minuses, so to speak – I will argue that in Ireland, judicial supremacy in constitutional matters carries an independent cost for democratic citizenship. This cost arises simply because as soon as legislative choices are subject to justiciable constitutional limitations, a vast swathe of legitimate political choice is framed in legalistic constitutional terms – and thus, political issues that would otherwise be regarded as open-ended political–moral considerations are divested from the political sphere to what is broadly perceived as the technocratic and expertised domain of constitutional law.

Since a vast range of policy and political issues can be framed in 'rights' terms – and since vast swathes of legislation limit the exercise of constitutional rights in some way – this means that vast areas of political debate may be constitutionalised.[44] Thus the stifling effects of constitutional discourse on 'ordinary politics' should not be underestimated. The constitutionalisation of political debate then leads to a kind of democratic deficit, as political and ideological questions are obscured in technical legal language. Constitutional argumentation, ostensibly the product of an expert technical knowledge rather than mere moral and political intuition, can be invoked to disarm 'lay' interlocutors in political debate. Just as any social issue can be framed in 'rights' terms, diverse moral and political intuitions can be presented as the product of expert or technical appraisal.

In short, then, the constitutionalisation of politics stifles our political discourse. In legislative and pre-legislative deliberations, constitutional considerations are typically invoked only as obstacles to political action, rather than as arguments for or against specific policies in a more general sense. Constitutional barriers to legislative reform are usually attributed to the (usually unpublished) advice of the Attorney General, disclosed at the discretion of the government. In other instances, constitutional discourse may be successfully instrumentalised by sectional-interest groups during the pre-legislative process to prevent a certain reform. Of course, it might work both ways, so to speak – constitutional objections might successfully be raised against repressive or reactionary measures – but again, bearing in mind that an over-constitutionalised politics will operate in a negative way, as a barrier to legislative change, on balance it will likely have an anti-reformist, conservative orientation.

Several examples illustrate this tendency. For example, in the 1970s, the chief recommendation of the Kenny Report on land prices – to permit local authorities to acquire land for housing at its agricultural value plus 25% thus potentially controlling property speculation in the public interest – was rejected on the pretext of constitutional property rights.[45] It is widely considered that any such legislation would likely have passed constitutional muster, in the event of a challenge, given that Article 43 permits proportionate restrictions on private-property rights.

A further example is provided by derogations from anti-discrimination law. In some analyses, the scope of equality legislation is limited by the constitutional rights to freedom of religion and freedom of association. While this reflects an indeterminate tension or 'balance' between competing constitutional principles (or indeed competing normative goals generally), this has generally been used as a pretext for extensive derogations from equality law both for religious-ethos institutions and private clubs. For example, constitutional religious freedom has been used to justify the commonplace practice of publicly funded schools requiring baptismal certificates as a criterion for enrolment.[46] In this light, recent deliberations on school admissions law provides an excellent example of how constitutional-rights arguments are often successfully marshalled by powerful vested interests to obstruct modestly progressive social reforms. In 2014, the Oireachtas Education Committee debated draft legislation aimed at prohibiting certain forms of 'cherry-picking' in school-admissions practices.[47] While it considered submissions concerning denominational schools' exemption from the religious-discrimination prohibition, the Committee declined to make any firm recommendation on this issue: it appeared to be dissuaded from doing so by submissions claiming that the derogation is constitutionally protected.[48]

This seems to contradict the deferential judicial stance towards legislative balancing of rights repeatedly affirmed since *Ryan*'s case. Moreover, it helps illustrate the mystifying effects of constitutional discourse in 'lay' political discourse: a precautionary approach may thwart legislative reforms even where the relevant arguments are more or less groundless as a matter of constitutional doctrine. Similarly, in 2014, it was reported that the Catholic Church intended to mount a constitutional challenge to proposed legislative reforms curbing the derogation provided to religious employers in employment equality legislation.[49] Such arguments may not always succeed, but their dissuasive effect is clear, and this represents the main political cost of strong-form judicial review. While these legislative issues involve competing rights claims, and although *Ryan*'s case affirmed pre-eminent role of the Oireachtas in balancing constitutional rights – the dominant understanding is, nonetheless, of legislation only as an invasion or limitation of constitutional rights, and the Constitution as its foil.

In light of the arguments already made, such constitutional argumentation simply masks, in one sense, what are effectively political–moral intuitions concerning the appropriate extent and use of state power – concerning, say, the appropriate extent of any private licence to discriminate. The 'rights' terminology used serves only to obscure this political and ideological content. On the other hand, the indeterminacy of the Constitution on this point introduces a genuine degree of unpredictability concerning the fate of any such legislative reform in the event of a constitutional challenge – even though, on balance, for example, it seems most likely, based on the established doctrines, that restrictions on religious discrimination in state-funded bodies would be ruled to be an invidious or arbitrary limitation on religious freedom. This factor of unpredictability seems to have a conservative effect irrespective of the mystifying effects of constitutional terminology. Again, it is impossible to definitively establish, in any particular case, whether the constitutional complaint is the cause, or simply a rationalisation, of legislative reticence. Equally it is unclear whether, collectively and individually, legislators are simply bamboozled by esoteric constitutional arguments – which they believe to be objective and true in a specifically legal sense – or whether instead they are dissuaded simply by the genuine uncertainty of constitutional litigation. While both these phenomena apply to varying extents, in situations where constitutional arguments are raised, the negative effects of judicial supremacy are evident in either case.

In principle, judicial supremacy does not preclude other organs and political agents from participating in constitutional discourse, or from deliberating on the meaning of constitutional norms in particular contexts.[50] And indeed, in theory, strong-form judicial review does not preclude inter-institutional dialogue on constitutional questions. Despite the Supreme Court's power of legislative invalidation, political actors might debate constitutional principles anticipatively (based on precedent, for example) or perhaps defiantly (based on an understanding of judicial determinations as ideological and/or contestable in the political realm). Legislators might seek to engage in 'anticipatory' disobedience, tactically testing ambiguous precedents, etc., or seeking to have the law clarified in a particular direction. Furthermore, in theory, this ought to be supported by the reticent and modest role the judiciary itself had adopted in respect of constitutional adjudication, and specifically the deference it has explicitly extended to the legislature in relation to the limitation and balancing of constitutional rights.

However, in Ireland such inter-institutional dialogue rarely, if ever occurs. In reality, constitutional barriers, raised at the pre-legislative stage, are understood as products of technical legal knowledge rather than as inputs in a broader principled discourse about public norms. Indeed, there is an unusual degree of public buy-in to the myth that constitutional interpretation is a technical, legal and apolitical matter, that it is the preserve of lawyers. Constitutional expertise succeeds in self-mystification to an extraordinary degree in Ireland. Constitutional claims are rarely contested in public discourse; they potentially serve as a trump card. There is a deep contradiction between how the Supreme Court conceives of its own role in relation to rights-based deliberation – that is, simply as a check on the Oireachtas' appraisal and interpretation of constitutional rights in its legislative outputs – and how the public (or at least the elite public) perceives constitutional considerations as a technical–legal and essentially non-political matter.[51]

Why, then, do legislators not typically exercise and assert their prerogative – one recognised by the Supreme Court itself – to proffer their own interpretation of constitutional rights, or their own sense of how constitutional rights should be balanced and reconciled in the context of specific legislative debates? It might be attributed to ignorance concerning the existence of *Ryan*'s doctrine or the proportionality concept, or alternatively, constitutional factors might simply offer an excuse for sidestepping difficult political choices. There may be some truth in both.

However, this seemingly bizarre culture of uncritical anticipatory obedience – that is, obedience to perceived or spurious judicial obstacles to legislative reform – cannot, I argue, be dissociated from the Constitution's institutional mechanism for judicial review of legislation. And, specifically, I argue that the stultifying effects of constitutional argumentation, in legislative discourse, are not attributable to the existence of a codified constitution as such, or even to its sometimes ambiguous, archaic and terse content, but rather, more specifically, to the exclusive and supreme jurisdiction given to the superior courts with respect to adjudicating the constitutionality of laws. It is the fact of an unfettered judicial supremacy, in this sense, that will dissuade even the most conscientious or thoughtful of legislators from proffering alternative interpretations of or deliberations on constitutional rights. They will not tend to see constitutional rights as their business or concern, notwithstanding judicial protestations to the contrary. Alternatively, under a hybrid, 'commonwealth'-style system that in some sense qualified judges' 'final say' and allowed a degree of political input on rights issues – both pre- and post-enactment[52] – there may be a greater chance that legislators will deliberate on and interpret constitutional rights, simply because the relevant institutional mechanisms will prompt them to do so, and send the message that it is indeed their business and their concern.[53]

There may be a deeper and more intractable barrier to the development of a vibrant democratic discourse about rights in a constitutional democracy. The idea that such a discourse can coexist with strong-form judicial review probably ignores the social perception of constitutional law, in complex liberal societies, as an expert practice. It probably underestimates the mystifying, and indeed the exclusionary effects of constitutional argumentation, which is broadly understood and perceived – by politicians as well as 'lay' people – as a form of expert technical knowledge. Indeed, while the Supreme Court itself has tacitly acknowledged the indeterminate and open-ended nature of rights-based argumentation, like any judicial authority it will be inclined to officially downplay the normative and political dimensions of its power, based on a concern for legitimacy. This simply reflects the fact that in complex late-modern societies, law is perceived and legitimated as a body of expert knowledge rather than as an exercise of political and normative power in the barer sense.[54] However, while this social understanding of law may disempower lay interlocutors, this applies as a matter of degree;

it can be attenuated or accentuated by institutional structures. In turn, strong-form judicial review, I have argued, intensifies the democratically harmful tendency for 'rights' to be treated as a matter of expert technical knowledge.

I have argued that the main political cost of strong-form judicial review lies in is its stifling effect on political discourse. The argument is essentially that the negative effects of constitutional justice are felt not so much in constitutional judgments as such, but rather in the use of constitutional arguments in the legislative process itself, as well as political discourse more generally. In turn, this undermines the two obvious defences of Irish-style judicial supremacy, considered above. While the Supreme Court has exercised great restraint in exercising its power of invalidation, this has little effect on the stifling and distorting effects that constitutional argumentation may wield in the legislative and pre-legislative process, partly because constitutional advice is usually received as a fait accompli. Furthermore, notwithstanding judicial reticence, there remains a good deal of unpredictability in how the court will exercise its powers, and this likely prompts a degree of precautionary inertia with respect to those legislative measures that are amenable to constitutional contestation. Such proposed legislation will sometimes be dropped as a result of constitutional objection, no matter how dubious, on a precautionary basis.

In this respect, the *form* of constitutional review is important: as in most anglophone jurisdictions, there is no mechanism in Ireland for settling constitutional questions before the enactment of legislation apart from the possibility of a reference by the president via Article 26 – a rarely utilised and problematic procedure.[55] Effectively, this allows constitutional concerns, often with an unclear footing, to be used as a pretext for legislative inaction. In continental jurisdictions such as France, at least there is provision for an extensive system of pre-enactment review, on the initiative of a number of different political actors.[56] In turn, this removes constitutional pretexts for legislative inaction, as contested bills can simply be referred by government, in particular, to dispel any constitutional doubts. It provides a mechanism for bluff-calling, so to speak. Of course, it can be argued that in the Irish system, governments could in principle wait for constitutionally contestable legislation to be challenged through the courts once enacted. But this is unsatisfactory in various ways, not least because of the practical difficulties that may be encountered in remediating the effects of legislation subsequently found to be unconstitutional.

Thus, while the over-constitutionalisation of our politics – the stifling and conservative effect of constitutional argumentation in the legislative and pre-legislative process – stems primarily from the dominant social perception of constitutional interpretation along with the exclusivity and uncontestability of the judicial invalidation power, this is accentuated by the absence of any institutional mechanism for settling constitutional controversies within the legislative process itself.

There remains the argument that any political risk in legislating on constitutionally contested issues is attenuated by the availability of corrective referendums that can reverse the effects of undesirable judgments. On the one hand, from a standpoint of political legitimacy Waldron asks why citizens espousing a particular view should accept having the 'decks stacked against them' in this way.[57] And, in practical terms, the significant cost and political risk that constitutional referendums entail will largely nullify any potential they might have to serve as correctives to judicial error or overreach. Thus the counterargument centred on the corrective potential of the constitutional referendum has little more than theoretical value, simply because as a matter of political reality it does virtually nothing to remediate the stifling effects of constitutional argumentation in legislative and pre-legislative deliberation. A government that perceives a constitutional barrier to some legislative reform will resort to a referendum only in exceptional circumstances.[58]

Conclusion

While the political legitimacy and effects of rights-based judicial review probably ranks as one of the central concerns of normative legal theory, there is remarkably little literature concerning the 'anticipatory' political costs of judicial supremacy in the legislative and pre-legislative process. Ireland provides a striking example of a system where judicial supremacy effects a great (and negative) influence on politics despite a marked historical trend towards reticence and epistemological modesty on the part of the Supreme Court itself. I have argued that the stultifying effects of constitutional law in legislative and pre-legislative discourse cannot be attributed simply to the ordinary vicissitudes of principled deliberation – to the uncertainties and disagreements that would be involved in any process for adjudicating competing interpretations of constitutional ideas and principles. Instead, it is attributable directly to the mechanism and *form* of constitutional review: the fact, specifically, that an unfettered judicial supremacy, unanswerable by any mechanism other than a cumbersome and ad hoc referendum, deprives legislators of any meaningful role in constitutional interpretation and relegates them to mere spectators and anticipators of judicial power. In turn, the political problem is not so much the ideology and orientation of this judicial power itself, but rather the way it is mediated, translated and refracted into the political process. Accordingly, any reappraisal of the form of strong-form judicial review enshrined in the 1937 Constitution must focus not primarily on the vicissitudes of judicial politics itself, in the victories and defeats that the Supreme Court's case law has produced, but rather to the potentially distorting effects of constitutional discourse felt in the political realm itself.

Notes

1 See, for example, M. Tushnet, *Taking the Constitution Away from the Courts* (Princeton UP, 1999); J. Waldron, *Law and Disagreement* (OUP, 1999); R. Bellamy, *Political Constitutionalism: A Republican Defence of the Constitutionality of Democracy* (CUP, 2007).
2 See M. Tushnet, 'New Forms of Judicial Review and the Persistence of Rights- and Democracy-based Worries' (2003) 38 *Wake Forest Law Review* 813.
3 In this and other ways the chapter can be read in tandem with Hickey's chapter in this volume (see Chapter 4).
4 This power was inferred in *Marbury v. Madison* 5 US 137 (1803).
5 See, for example, *Pigs Marketing Board v. Donnelly* [1939] IR 413.
6 See, for example, B. Foley, 'Diceyan Ghosts: Deference, Rights and Spatial Distinctions' (2006) 29 *Dublin University Law Journal* 141.
7 Thus, in work that does question the value of judicial supremacy in the Irish context, Hickey concedes that the alternative model which he argues for is, in practice, unlikely to come about. See T. Hickey, 'Revisiting *Ryan v. Lennon* to Make the Case against Judicial Supremacy (and for a New Model of Constitutionalism in Ireland)' (2015) 53 *Irish Jurist* 125, p. 150.
8 For a general discussion, see J. Ferejohn, 'Judicializing Politics, Politicizing Law' (2002) 65 *Law and Contemporary Problems* 41.
9 P. Bourdieu, 'The Force of Law: Towards a Sociology of the Juridical Field' (1987) 38 *Hastings Law Journal* 805.
10 A cautionary note against judicial activism in a more general sense was sounded in D. G. Morgan, *A Judgment Too Far? Judicial Activism and the Constitution* (Cork UP, 2001).
11 R. Dworkin, *A Matter of Principle* (Harvard UP, 1985).
12 See generally A. Stone Sweet, 'Constitutional Courts and Parliamentary Democracy' (2001) 25 *West European Politics* 77.
13 L. Cahillane, 'An Insight into the Irish Free State Constitution' (2014) 54 *American Journal of Legal History* 1.
14 S. Moyn, 'The Secret History of Human Dignity' (2012), available at http://papers.ssrn.com/sol3/papers.cfm?abstract_id=2159248 (accessed 18 July 2012).
15 E. Daly, 'A Republican Defence of the Constitutional Referendum' (2013) 35 *Legal Studies* 30
16 Thus the Supreme Court described the Constitution as 'representing … the

will of the People'. *Re Article 26 and the Regulation of Information (Services Outside the State for Termination of Pregnancies) Bill 1995* [1995] 1 IR 1.
17 J. Waldron, 'The Core of the Case against Judicial Review' (2006) 115 *Yale Law Journal* 1346.
18 For a fuller account of this argument, see Daly (n. 15).
19 S. Lemieux and D. Watkins, 'Beyond the "Counter-Majoritarian Difficulty": Lessons from Contemporary Democratic Theory' (2009) 41 *Polity* 30.
20 Waldron (n. 17).
21 D. Kennedy, 'The Critique of Rights in Critical Legal Studies' in W. Brown and J. Halley, *Left Legalism/Left Critique* (Duke UP, 2002).
22 See generally J. H. Merryman and R. Pérez-Perdomo, *The Civil Law Tradition: An Introduction to the Legal Systems of Europe and Latin America* (3rd edn, Stanford UP, 2007).
23 R. Unger 'The Critical Legal Studies Movement' (1983) 96 *Harvard Law Review* 561.
24 For further discussion of the republican perspective, see E. Daly and T. Hickey, *The Political Theory of the Irish Constitution: Republicanism and the Basic Law* (Manchester UP, 2015).
25 *Citizens United v. Federal Election Commission*, 558 US 310 (2010).
26 Waldron (n. 17).
27 *Ibid.*, 1376.
28 *Ibid.*
29 Bellamy (n. 1); A. Tomkins, *Our Republican Constitution* (Hart, 2005).
30 See generally P. Pettit, *Republicanism: A Theory of Freedom and Government* (Clarendon Press, 1997).
31 Bellamy (n. 1) p. 152.
32 Tom Hickey rethinks Bellamy's arguments, suggesting that the so-called 'new commonwealth model of constitutionalism' does better on republican lights than either undiluted legislative supremacy or judicial supremacy, in T. Hickey, 'The Republican Virtues of the New Commonwealth Model of Constitutionalism' (2016) 14(4) *International Journal of Constitutional Law* 794.
33 [1994] 3 IR 1.
34 *Ibid.*, 47.
35 *Fleming v. Ireland* [2013] IESC 19 (emphasis added).
36 *Heaney v. Ireland* [1994] 3 IR 593.
37 [1965] IR 294, 312.
38 [2009] IESC 82.
39 [1974] IR 284.
40 Fiona de Londras makes this general argument in her chapter in this volume (see Chapter 1, p. 21). See also G. Whyte, 'The Role of the Supreme Court in our Democracy: A Response to Mr. Justice Hardiman' (2006) 28 *Dublin University Law Review* 1; more generally, see J. Goldsworthy, 'Judicial Review, Legislative Override, and Democracy' (2003) 38 *Wake Forest Law Review* 451.
41 Waldron (n. 17).
42 See, for example, J. Hendy, 'McGowan & collective bargaining in Ireland',

lecture in conjunction with Irish Congress of Trade Unions, Trinity College Dublin, 30 January, 2014 (copy on file with author).
43 See *TD v. Minister for Education* [2000] 3 IR 62.
44 Thus, in her chapter in this volume, de Londras – making an argument essentially in favour of judicial supremacy – says: 'In Ireland ... rights are politically conceptualised as legal instruments; the domain of law and lawyers and not easily amenable to political contestation on their own terms' (Chapter 1, p. 14). Although she concedes throughout her chapter that the meaning of constitutional provisions (including rights provisions) are not static or self-evident, she does not seem perturbed by the idea that judges, in systems of supremacy, may effectively stifle political contestation on their meaning in this way.
45 Dáil Debates 1980, vol. 321 No. 3.
46 See, for example, E. Daly and T. Hickey, 'Religious Freedom and the "Right to Discriminate" in the School Admissions Context: A Neo-Republican Critique' (2011) 31 *Legal Studies* 615.
47 Houses of the Oireachtas Joint Committee on Education and Social Protection *Report on the Draft General Scheme of an Education (Admissions to School) Bill 2013* (Houses of the Oireachtas, 2013).
48 Hickey discusses other examples in the Irish setting, on issues such as same-sex marriage, abortion in cases of fatal foetal abnormality, and the running of constitutional referendums, see Hickey (n.7), pp. 143–149.
49 C. Barry, 'Church is prepared to mount constitutional challenge if stripped of ethos rights' *Irish Catholic* (25 September 2014).
50 K. Whittington, 'Presidential Challenges to Judicial Supremacy and the Politics of Constitutional Meaning' (2001) 33 *Polity* 365.
51 See generally Bourdieu (n. 9).
52 S. Gardbaum, 'The New Commonwealth Model of Constitutionalism' (2001) 49 *American Journal of Comparative Law* 707.
53 This idea is elaborated in Daly and Hickey (n. 24) ch. 5, and in Hickey (n. 32).
54 Bourdieu (n. 9).
55 Common J. Jaconelli, 'Reference of Bills to the Supreme Court: A Comparative Perspective' (1983) 18 *Irish Jurist* 322.
56 Constitution of the Fifth French Republic, 1958.
57 Waldron (n. 17).
58 For example, in 2015 the Fine Gael–Labour government held a referendum to remove a perceived constitutional barrier to same-sex marriage, but this proves the exception rather than the rule.

3

Unenumerated personal rights: the legacy of *Ryan v. Attorney General*

The Hon. Mr Justice Gerard Hogan

The 31 July 2013 saw the fiftieth anniversary of Justice Kenny's judgment in *Ryan v. Attorney General*.[1] While the anniversary passed unnoticed, it is undoubtedly the case that the decision ushered in the era of unenumerated personal rights. While this era is still with us, the judicial ardour for unenumerated rights, which repose solely in the imaginative mind of the judiciary, has been cooling for some two decades or so. While I offer a critique of the reasoning in *Ryan* in this chapter, it is only appropriate to record that the judgment nonetheless represents an impressive response to what was then a novel constitutional issue of some difficulty.

I do not suggest that Justice Kenny was necessarily wrong as a matter of either constitutional history or constitutional construction, still less that there is no room for a doctrine of implied constitutional rights. On the contrary, given the generality of the language of the Constitution and the fact that these rights are of necessity open textured, some form of implied rights is absolutely necessary in order to make the Constitution function.[2] As Professor Gerard Casey has put it:

> Implicit rights are, of necessity, unenumerated and the process of making them explicit is perfectly legitimate. However, it is one thing for the courts to render the implicit explicit: it is quite another thing for them to reserve the right to discover rights not only not enumerated in the text but also logically necessitated by the text save by the exercise of hermeneutical somersaults.[3]

I nevertheless contend that the *Ryan* doctrine brought about certain imbalances in constitutional law. Specifically, it deflected attention from the actual text of the Constitution. It is, I think, quite difficult to understand why, for example, Justice Kenny found it necessary to resort to ascertaining the existence of an implied right to bodily integrity when Article 40.3.2° expressly protects the 'person'. Is not the integrity of the body a key dimension of any meaningful protection of the person? A better way really to say all of this perhaps is to have acknowledged that there are indeed implied constitutional rights but that they derive principally from the actual text of the Constitution itself. Here one may agree with the comments of Justice White in *Bowers v. Hardwick*[4] – even if disagreeing with the actual result in that case[5] – when he observed that:

> The Court is most vulnerable and comes nearest to illegitimacy when it deals with judge-made constitutional law *having little or no cognizable roots in the language or design of the Constitution*. That this is so was painfully demonstrated by the face-off between the Executive and the Court in the 1930's, which resulted in the repudiation of much of the substantive gloss that the Court had placed on the Due Process Clauses of the Fifth and Fourteenth Amendments. There should be, therefore, great resistance to expand the substantive reach of those Clauses, particularly if it requires redefining the category of rights deemed to be fundamental. Otherwise, the Judiciary necessarily takes to itself further authority to govern the country without express constitutional authority. The claimed right pressed on us today falls far short of overcoming this resistance.[6]

This passage really highlights the difficulties with the open-ended nature of the *Ryan* doctrine. How can one determine what these implied rights are or whether they should be identified by reference to external sources such as natural law or the 'Christian and democratic nature of the State'?[7] Here it must be recalled that Justice Kenny resorted to a papal encyclical, *Pacem in terris* – which had itself been published during the course of the hearing in April 1963 – for this very purpose. He quoted from the following passage from the encyclical:

> Beginning our discussion of the rights of man, we see that every man has the right to life, to bodily integrity and to the means which are necessary and suitable for the proper development of life; these are primarily food, clothing, shelter, rest, medical care and finally the necessary social services.

Resort to such external sources raised eyebrows, even in an era which – measured by modern standards – was enormously deferential to church teaching. Professor Kelly was an early critic:

> No one, Christian or not, would find fault with the humane inspiration of a declaration like this; but its use as a ground for judicial invalidation of legislation in the context of our Constitution, which must after all be looked at as a whole [seems questionable]. The ideas set out in the Encyclical are very similar to those contained in Article 45 ... If Papal Encyclicals such as *Pacem in Terris* are going to be relied on as a source for ascertaining the personal

rights guaranteed by Article 40 so as to test the validity of legislation, the situation will have been reached that the general ideals of Article 45 will have been introduced into the machinery of judicial review by the back door.[8]

There has been a tacit judicial acknowledgment of these difficulties in the last two decades or so[9] and it may be significant that there has been no – or, at least, almost no – overt reference to natural law in any significant decision since the Supreme Court's decision on the *Abortion Information Bill* reference in 1995.[10] It may be accordingly suggested that the discretion to identify implied constitutional rights needs to be bounded by the key factors of text, history and tradition and of these the actual text is by far and away the most important. As Lazarus puts it:

> In many respects, this process resembles the childhood game of connect the dots. Constitutional provisions, common law traditions, the Court's own precedents: these were the dots or reference points that when connected created the rough outline – what Harlan called the 'continuum' – of due process liberty.[11]

Indeed, the Constitution Review Group had said something similar in 1996 when it expressed concern about the lack of objective criteria deployed in relation to Article 40.3.1°, even if it also recognised that implied rights were to some degree inevitable:

> While it is certainly arguable that it is both inevitable and necessary that the interpretation of the Constitution should develop over time and that in the future some rights should properly be recognised as existing even though they arise by implication only, it is less clear that new rights should be recognised where they lack any textual basis.[12]

Is there a sound historical basis for the implied rights doctrine?

It was fashionable for many years to suppose that the *Ryan* doctrine had never actually been intended by the drafters.[13] A consideration of the drafting documents has in some respects proved disappointing on this particular score, because while many drafting decisions are meticulously documented, in other cases one is just left to guess as to what was in the minds of the Constitution's drafters. The drafting of Article 40.3.1° and Article 40.3.2° is one such example. A mid-February 1937 draft nevertheless gives some clue, since it provided that: 'The State guarantees to respect and defend the personal rights of each citizen [including] those that are inalienable, indefeasible and antecedent to positive law, as well as those that have been by law granted and defined.'[14]

It is of some interest that Hearne[15] prepared an *OED* definition of the word 'vindicate' in Article 40.3 for de Valera[16] and as it happens that by a remarkable coincidence the very self-same *OED* definition was used by the Supreme Court to elucidate the meaning of Article 40.3.2° in *Grant v. Roche Products Ltd*.[17] We also know that the Department of Justice and the Department of Finance objected to these provisions. The Secretary of the Department of Justice, Stephen Roche – a noted sceptic of the draft Constitution – thought that the guarantees in Article 40.3.2° 'were very widely worded and may have unexpected results'. Finance thought that Article 40.3.1° was 'dangerous' and that there still remains 'obscurity as to what practical obligations they impose on the State'.[18] The drafting committees simply noted these comments, adding tantalisingly that the 'Law Officers were satisfied'. Hearne *et al.* presumably discussed these objections among themselves. But why were the comments ignored? Was it because the drafters were happy that Article 40 might have these results or because they thought these objections far-fetched? Given the conservatism of the 1930s one might suppose that the latter explanation is more tenable, but on the other hand as the drafters responded quickly to other objections – for example, accommodated the Department of Finance by moving the nascent socio-economic rights from the property rights section of Article 43 to a newly created Article 45[19] in a relatively last-minute change in April 1937 – and thus the other possibility cannot be at all excluded. Unless new documentary materials concerning the drafting of Article 40.3 are unearthed we shall probably never know what exactly the drafters had in mind.

Is the implied rights doctrine correct as a matter of constitutional construction?

Justice Kenny based his conclusion that Article 40.3 was intended to safeguard a category of unenumerated rights on a comparison of the language of Article 40.3.1° with that of Article 40.3.2°:[20]

> The words 'in particular' show that sub-section 2 is a detailed statement of something which is already contained in sub-section 1 which is the general guarantee. But sub-section 2 refers to rights in connection with life and good name and there are no rights in connection with these specified in Article 40. It follows, I think, that the general guarantee in sub-section 1 must extend to rights specified in Article 40.[21]

Professor Kelly agreed that this analysis was 'logically faultless'.[22] But not everyone is so sure and Professor Gerard Casey has argued that the absence of a clause approximating to the 9th Amendment of the US Constitution might suggest that no such power was ever intended.[23]

For my part, I think that Kelly is correct. But my difficulty with the *Ryan* doctrine as articulated in this chapter is an altogether different one, since I contend that it is has contributed to a situation where the courts have been deflected from looking at the express language of the Constitution itself and that it has distorted the proper understanding of the Constitution in the process.

At its most basic, the drafters of the Constitution intended that the fundamental rights of the individual and the family would be protected against legislative and executive intrusion, if necessary by a form of dialogue between the courts and the other branches of government, even if, subject to the ultimate possibility of constitutional amendments by way of referendum, the courts would have the last word on the protection of these rights. At the heart of this were notions of human dignity, personal freedom, the protection of life and the person, the inviolability of the dwelling and the inalienable rights of the family. Much of this thinking and wording was drawn liberally by Hearne from various nineteenth-century and interwar continental constitutions, even if the extent to which this borrowing was appreciated by others (such as de Valera) was either limited[24] or, in the case of both the (then) unicameral Oireachtas and the People, virtually non-existent. It was, I think, a failure to appreciate this fact that led Justice Kenny to make the following observations:

> Not one of the counsel in this case has attempted to state what the inalienable and imprescriptible rights of the Family are and as the Constitution gives little help on this I am in some difficulty in dealing with this argument. 'Inalienable' means that which cannot be transferred or given away, while 'imprescriptible' means that which cannot be lost by the passage of time or abandoned by non-exercise.[25]

This passage must be regarded as an example of where essentially civilian terms were read through the prism of the common law and their import was accordingly distorted in this translation. These terms were originally conceived by Paine and others – and the continental constitution drafters who followed them such as Hugo Preuss[26] – in a general philosophical, rhetorical and even lyrical sense. Neither the political scientists, jurists, or even drafters who used these often high-sounding phrases, meant that these words were to be taken absolutely literally. Rights so described could, of necessity, sometimes be breached, taken away, or lost through passage of time. It was never intended, for example, that a parent who abused or abandoned a child could not lose access or custody in respect of that child, even if these parental rights were described as 'inalienable',[27] just as much as it could not plausibly be argued that a home built without planning permission could never be demolished or (subject to important safeguards) a house repossessed by a bank, no matter what Article 40.5 said about the 'inviolability' of the dwelling.[28]

Accordingly, even if these phrases were not meant to be taken absolutely literally, their underlying purpose cannot be discounted or ignored. The drafters clearly intended thereby to secure the maximum possible degree of protection which might realistically be secured in a modern society. This *is* relevant when assessing comparable ECHR Article 8 jurisprudence in cases presenting under Article 40.5, Article 41 and Article 42 of the Constitution in respect of the dwelling, family and education. After all, the original draft of Article 8 ECHR prepared by the French rapporteur, M. Teitgen, for the Consultative Assembly of the Council of Europe in 1949 sought to protect the 'inviolability' of private life, the home and the family. The (hugely influential) British delegation objected to the term 'inviolability' as too all-encompassing and the drafting Committee then adopted the words 'immunity from arbitrary interference' in its place. That was then changed – again at the behest of the British delegation – to 'freedom from governmental interference with his privacy, family, house or correspondence'. Finally, following a conference of senior officials in June 1950, this was changed again to the present wording used in Article 8(1): 'Everyone has the right to respect for his private and family life, his home and his correspondence.'[29]

Quite apart, therefore, from the fact that as a matter of drafting history the drafters of ECHR rejected the use of terms such as 'inviolable'– preferring the more modest term 'respect' for the family home – it is clear that, rightly or wrongly, the Constitution does in fact use the more all-encompassing language favoured in the continental constitutional tradition ('inviolable', 'inalienable and imprescriptible' and 'antecedent and superior to all positive law') and some weight, it is suggested, must be given to this more emphatic language.

The heart of the objection to *Ryan* remains: the distorting effect of the unenumerated rights doctrine surely contributed to a situation where a generation of judges and lawyers failed to make proper use of key provisions of the Constitution, among them the Preamble's commitment to the protection of the 'dignity and freedom of the individual', Article 40.1's guarantee of equality of all human persons before the law, Article 40.3.2°'s protection of the person and the guarantee of the inviolability of the dwelling in Article 40.5. This may be contrasted with the approach of the German Constitutional Court where Article 1 (human dignity), Article 2 (right to life and freedom of the person), Article 3 (equality) and Article 13 (inviolability of the dwelling) of the Basic Law have been at the heart of the Karlsruhe jurisprudence.[30] (Incidentally, any Irish lawyer reading these sections of the Basic Law cannot but be struck by the similarity of concepts and language between these provisions of the Constitution and the Basic Law.[31] Is this a pure coincidence? Or is it possible that those constitutional experts who attended the Herrenchiemsee Convention in August 1948[32] may have borrowed phrases and language from the Preamble and Article 40?)[33]

Indeed, so pervasive has been the effect of the *Ryan* doctrine that almost no Irish court has been required to ask itself what the object and effect of these express constitutional provisions actually is. Perhaps we can hesitatingly venture where juristic angels have heretofore feared to tread and attempt to answer these questions.

The dignity of the individual presupposes that the state will treat its citizens with respect and honour,[34] and that the essence of their privacy will be safeguarded.[35] That notion of respect implies that due allowance will be made where possible for human frailties and imperfections. Special regard will be had to the needs of those vulnerable persons who clearly need the support of the state and community. The state accordingly 'violates human dignity when it treats persons as mere objects' by officiously piercing the protected sphere of privacy, as it must leave the individual 'with a personal/private sphere for the purpose of the free and responsible development of his or her personality'.[36]

So far as the protection of the person is concerned,[37] this presupposes the physical integrity of the body, so that, for example, an assault would be an open attack on that right. Medical autonomy is clearly a dimension of that right.[38] It likewise protects the integrity of the human mind and personality, so that, for example, prisoners cannot be detained in conditions which would expose them to the risk of psychiatric disturbance.[39]

The inviolability of the dwelling implies that the dwelling is a private place where the individual is, generally speaking, permitted to engage in private activities free from the glare of state interference and intrusion. As Hardiman J. put it in *The People v. O'Brien*[40]:

> This constitutional guarantee presupposes that in a free society the dwelling is set apart as a place of repose from the cares of the world. In so doing, Article 40.5 complements and re-inforces other constitutional guarantees and values, such as assuring the dignity of the individual (as per the Preamble to the Constitution), the protection of the person (Article 40.3.2), the protection of family life (Article 41) and the education and protection of children (Article 42). Article 40.5 thereby assures the citizen that his or her privacy, person and security will be protected against all comers, save in the exceptional circumstances presupposed by the saver to this guarantee.

Against that background, let us examine a number of venerable examples from well-known constitutional cases to see how they might have been reworked in the light of this analysis.

McGee v. Attorney General

In this celebrated case a majority of the Supreme Court held that s. 17 of the Criminal law (Amendment) Act 1935 (which prohibited the importation of contraceptives) was unconstitutional. The plaintiff was a young mother who had a medical condition which made further child-bearing dangerous.[41] While the majority judgments[42] rely to varying degrees on the unenumerated personal right to marital privacy, this seems to have been an obvious case where the protection of the person in Article 40.3.2° might also have come into play. It is also interesting to note that at least three members of the Court sought to ground their conclusions in the express text of the Constitution while also referring (to admittedly varying degrees) to the unenumerated rights doctrine. Justice Walsh referred to the autonomy of spousal decision-making under Article 41 and Justice Budd invoked the dignity and freedom of the individual contained in the Preamble. While Justice Henchy also invoked these provisions of the Preamble, he alone also mentioned Article 40.3.2° in the context of the state's duty to vindicate the 'life and person' of every person.[43]

Justice Griffin was accordingly the only judge of the majority to invoke *Ryan* in terms and he was also the only member of the majority to rest his decision exclusively[44] on the unenumerated rights doctrine. Yet in the course of arriving at that conclusion, Justice Griffin asked rhetorically: 'Would we allow the police to search the sacred precincts of marital bedrooms for tell-tale signs of the use of contraceptives? The very idea is repulsive to the notions of privacy surrounding the marriage relationship?'[45]

But is this not at the heart of what Article 40.5 is all about? Why does the Constitution describe the dwelling as 'inviolable'? What are these words trying to tell us about the heart of the relationship between the state and the individual? Is it not that the individual is free to make private choices in respect of the home and the family? Might that not have another alternative basis by which the (de facto) prohibition on the use of contraceptives could have been invalidated?

Draper v. Attorney General

In *Draper v. Attorney General*,[46] the plaintiff suffered from multiple sclerosis and was confined to her house. This meant that, 'she could not be taken to a polling station now by any means without suffering physical discomfort and exposing her health to a risk which she has been medically advised to avoid'.[47] As the law then stood, however, no provision was made for postal voting, so that she could not exercise the franchise.

The Supreme Court rejected a challenge to the constitutionality of the electoral law on the ground that the Oireachtas had to weigh the balance between access to the franchise and the risk of abuse which the Court thought was inherent in any system of postal voting. There was no mention in the judgments of either Justice McMahon in the High Court or Chief Justice O'Higgins in the Supreme Court of the dignity of the individual or the protection of the person. But it requires only a little imagination to say that the sense of dignity of the individual means that the state must make necessary accommodations for those who through illness cannot otherwise exercise a fundamental right. One might add: how was the person of the plaintiff adequately protected by law if the Oireachtas did not endeavour to enable her to exercise that fundamental right as guaranteed in Article 16, her pervasive disability notwithstanding?

Kennedy v. Ireland

Our next example involves the right to privacy in a non-sexual intimacy context: *Kennedy v. Ireland*.[48] In this case, state agents had recorded the private home telephones of two journalists without any legal authorisation. Justice Hamilton used the *Ryan* 'Christian and democratic nature of the State' formula to conclude that the plaintiff's constitutional right to privacy had been violated. But would it not have been open to him to have concluded that this right really derived from the guarantee in Article 40.5 of 'inviolability' of the dwelling?

Given that telephone communication is an established feature of home life, surely the easiest way of approaching this matter is to say that the occupier of any dwelling has an expectation of privacy when using a telephone at home and that unlawful interception of the telephone is just as much a breach of that right as if state agents had secreted themselves in a dwelling and illegally listened to the conversations of the occupiers.[49]

Article 13(1) of the German Basic Law provides that 'the dwelling [*Wohnung*] is inviolable [*unverletzlich*]', while Article 13(2) provides for certain exceptions for searches. Of course, Article 40.5 is couched in exactly the same terms because Article 7 of the 1922 Constitution borrowed almost word for word the corresponding provisions of Article 115 of the Weimar Constitution of 1919. The two new Constitutions (i.e. 1937 and 1949 respectively) borrowed in turn from this earlier version. But it may be observed that in the *Second Telephone Tapping* case[50] the German Constitutional Court drew on Article 13(1) (as well, of course, as the more specific guarantee of the 'inviolability' of privacy of communications in Article 10(1) of the Basic Law) to say that these provisions: 'guarantee the free development of personality through the private exchange, free from the eyes of the public, of news, thoughts and opinions (information) and thereby guarantees the dignity of the thinking and freely acting human person'.

Is this not an altogether sounder and more satisfactory basis for a right to privacy in a domestic context than simply references to the Christian and democratic nature of the state? Does the Sermon on the Mount say anything about privacy of communications? And while I fully agree that Article 5 – describing the democratic nature of the state – is another underused constitutional provision, it possibly requires a long stretch of this provision to say that it embraces a right to privacy. Guarantees bearing on the autonomy and dignity of the individual in the Preamble (dignity and freedom of the individual), Article 40.5 and Article 40.3.2° (protection of the person) would seem rather to provide a better fit.

In this context Lazarus's critique of *Roe v. Wade* also seems apposite. He thought that in that case the US Supreme Court had exercised:

> the greatest measure of judicial power on the least defensible justification. This was Justice Black's nightmare come to life: a Court unrestrained by constitutional text, history, or Harlan's promised discipline of legal reasoning and judicial self-restraint ... . Simply put, the Court built the right house on the wrong land and put it up too quickly ... . [G]rounding the right to abortion in the Constitution's mandate of equality would have saved liberals – anxious to support the Court's expansion of civil liberties – from ignoring their better judgment in a stampede to defend a terribly vulnerable decision. And it would have avoided the incalculable damage that *Roe* inflicted on the idea that there is such a thing as constitutional law ruled by neither the hands of long-dead Framers nor the personal biases of sitting Justices. Soft but essential notions such as trusting in discretion and reasoned judgment melt away quickly, and *Roe* was a very hot flame.[51]

Leaving the debate on the underlying merits of *Roe* aside, something similar can probably be said about *Ryan*: it was the right house on the wrong land, and was put up too quickly. And to continue with the metaphor: there was, in any event no need to go around the back door to put up the new house, because many forgot – and still forget – that if you go through the already open front door of the old house and ignore some of the dated furniture in the front room you will pass through to a gleaming modern kitchen which to date has still not been properly used.

And I thus close with the point on which I started. My basic criticism of *Ryan* is that it went too far too quickly and thus distorted the entire body of constitutional jurisprudence. A further disadvantage is that the development of the unenumerated rights doctrine was at the expense of a sufficiently careful analysis of the purposes, objects and meaning of the enumerated rights in the text itself. More fundamentally, it was also largely *unnecessary*:[52] the same results and more were there to be achieved through a greater focus and understanding of the text of the Constitution itself.

Notes

1 [1965] IR 294.
2 See generally, G. Hogan, 'Constitutional Interpretation' in F. Litton (ed.), *The Constitution of Ireland 1937–1987* (IPA, 1988), G. Hogan, 'Unenumerated Personal Rights: *Ryan*'s case Re-evaluated' (1990–92) 25–27 Irish Jurist 95. For a response, see R. Humphreys, 'Constitutional Interpretation' (1993) 15 *Dublin University Law Journal* 59 and R. Humphreys, 'Interpreting Natural Rights' (1993–95) 28–30 *Irish Jurist* 221.
3 'Are There Unenumerated Rights in the Irish Constitution?' http://researchrepository.ucd.ie/bitstream/handle/10197/5336/Are_There_Unenumerated_Rights_in_the_Irish_Constitution%3F.pdf?sequence=1 (last accessed 9 October 2014).
4 478 US 186 (1986).
5 In *Bowers* the constitutionality of legislation which criminalised consensual male homosexual acts was upheld by a majority of the US Supreme Court. *Bowers* was itself overruled by the US Supreme Court in *Lawrence v. Texas* 539 US 558 (2003).
6 478 US 186, 195 (1986). Emphasis supplied.
7 Note the comments of P. Sutherland in 'The Courts, the Constitution and the Legislature' (2014) 103 *Studies* 20, 23, where he said that the various methods ('worthy as they are') of determining what unenumerated rights were protected which have been judicially mentioned simply 'individually underline how uncertain the limitation of judicial discretion actually are'. He continued: 'They also demonstrate that on difficult moral and ethical issues in particular, where attitudes are changing, the superior courts may be drawn into making decisions that may not merely have profound consequences but on which the courts are not particularly well qualified to make judgments. Where are judges to seek the essence of the values to be upheld in the determinations related, for example, to the commencement of life or the right to terminate one's own life.'
8 J. M. Kelly, *Fundamental Rights in the Irish Law and Constitution* (2nd edn, Figgis, 1967) pp. 44–45.
9 See for example, the comments of Chief Justice Keane in *TD v. Minister for Education* [2001] 4 IR 259, p. 281.
10 [1995] 1 IR 1. Note the comments of A. Kavanagh, 'Natural Law, Christian

Values and the Ideal of Justice' (2012) 48 *Irish Jurist* 71, 91: 'The *Abortion Information* case marked a shift away from Justice Kenny's touchstone of the "Christian and democratic nature of the State" towards an emphasis on the democratic nature of the State. And it represented a shift away from a judicial emphasis on a higher law or divine law, towards a greater emphasis on a higher law or divine law, towards a greater emphasis on the text of the Constitution itself and what could be "reasonably implied" therefrom.'

11 E. Lazarus, *Closed Chambers* (Penguin, 2005) p. 363. The internal reference is to Justice Harlan's famous judgment in *Griswold v. Connecticut* 381 US 479 (1965).

12 *Report of the Constitution Review Group* (Dublin, 1996) (Pn. 2632) p. 248. See also R. Humphreys, 'Interpreting Natural Rights' (1993–95) *Irish Jurist* 221, J. W. Parker, 'Must Constitutional Rights Be Specified? Reflections on the Proposal to Amend Article 40.3.1' (1997) 32 *Irish Jurist* 102; A. Kavanagh, 'The Irish Constitution at 75 Years: Natural Law, Christian Values and the Ideals of Justice' (2012) 48 *Irish Jurist* 71.

13 See for example, the dissenting judgment of Justice Keane in *IOT v. B* [1998] 2 IR 321, 369–370. Note further the comments of the same judge as Chief Justice in *TD v. Minister for Education* [2001] 4 IR 259, 281: 'Whether the formulation adopted by Justice Kenny is an altogether satisfactory guide to the identification of such rights is at least debatable. Secondly, there was no discussion in the judgment of this [i.e. Supreme] Court [in *Ryan*] as to whether the duty of declaring the unenumerated rights, *assuming them to exist*, should be the function of the courts rather than the Oireachtas' (emphasis added). One distinguished former Attorney General has gone even further: see P. Sutherland, 'The Constitution, the Courts and the Legislature' (2014) 103 *Studies* 20, 22: 'I think that one may say with reasonable assurance that the unexpressed rights established by the Courts since *Ryan v. Attorney General* in 1965 were not intended to be justiciable by those whose who enacted the Constitution (namely, the People). In other words, the courts have elaborated and enforced various values or rights that have been found other than by an examination of the text which expresses the original intent of the People. It is, however, only fair to say that Sutherland also acknowledged in the same article (*ibid*., 24) that 'in many respects the activism of the courts has breathed life into the Constitution itself and has been profoundly beneficial'.

14 G. Hogan, *Origins of the Irish Constitution* (RIA, 2012) pp. 353–356.

15 John Hearne (1893–1969). Legal adviser, Department of External Affairs. Senior counsel, 1939, later Ambassador to Canada and subsequently to the United States. Principal drafter of the Constitution.

16 Hogan (n. 14) p. 312.

17 [2008] 4 IR 679.

18 Hogan (n. 14) pp. 355–356.

19 *Ibid*., pp. 326–332.The preamble to Article 45 declared that the principles of social policy 'set forth in this Article are intended for the general guidance of the Oireachtas' and further stated that they 'shall not be cognisable by any Court under any of the provisions of this Constitution'.

20 Article 40.3.1° provides: 'The State guarantees in its laws to respect, and, as far as practicable, by its laws to defend and vindicate the personal rights of the citizen.' Article 40.3.2° provides: 'The State shall, in particular, by its laws protect as best it may from unjust attack and, in the case of injustice done, vindicate the life, person, good name, and property rights of every citizen.'
21 [1965] IR 294.
22 Kelly (n. 8) p. 42.
23 J. Casey, 'The "logically faultless" argument for unenumerated rights in the Constitution' (2004) 22 *Irish Law Times* 246.
24 We can only guess at the extent of the discussions between de Valera and Hearne so far as this issue is concerned. The German Weimar Constitution of 1919 was certainly mentioned in the context of the presidency in the their first meeting concerning the drafting of a new Constitution in May 1935 (Hogan (n. 14) p. 163) and during the course of the drafting process Hearne prepared a series of memoranda both on the functioning of the continental constitutional courts and the substantive provisions of those constitutions: see Hogan (n. 14) pp. 189–191, 332–324.
25 [1965] IR 294, 308.
26 Liberal German (and Jewish) politician who was the principal drafter of the Weimar Constitution.
27 In any event, the (original) Article 42.5 provided that the state might intervene where the parents 'for physical or moral reasons fail in their duty towards their children'.
28 See, *Wicklow County Council v. Fortune* [2012] IEHC 406; *Irish Life and Permanent plc v. Duff* [2013] IEHC 43.
29 This is taken from a summary file note (DH (56) 12) entitled 'Preparatory Work on Article 8 of the European Convention of Human Rights' prepared by the Secretariat of the (then) European Commission of Human Rights in August 1956.
30 As D. P. Kommers and R. A. Miller, *The Constitutional Jurisprudence of the Federal Republic of Germany* (Duke UP, 2012) have commented: 'The Basic Law places human dignity at the center of its scheme of constitutional values ... the human dignity clause is ... a fertile source of constitutional litigation ... [The] human dignity, liberty and equality clauses inform the meaning of other constitutional value' (p. 355).
31 Of course, we can pass over the topics with no relevance to Ireland such as German federalism.
32 The meeting of constitutional lawyers from each of the German *Länder* who prepared the first draft of the Basic Law.
33 And not just Article 40. The language of Article 6(2) of the Basic Law is very similar to that of the ('old') Article 42.5.
34 Note that in *Garvey v. Ireland* [1981] IR 75, 101, Justice Henchy stressed that the preamble's concepts of the dignity and freedom of the individual required that individuals be treated honourably by the state, so that they could not be summarily removed from office: 'An office such as this, which provides its holder

with his livelihood, and in which he may reasonably hope to qualify for honourable retirement, is such an integral part of what goes to make up his dignity and freedom that his removal from it should have attached to it, at least the justification of a stated and examinable reason.'

35 From comments made by him earlier in his judgment in *McGee v. Attorney General* [1974] IR 287, 328 regarding the importance of the concept of dignity as informing the personal rights provisions of Article 40.3, Justice Henchy also considered that obliging the plaintiff to disclose the nature of her sexual relations violated that concept of dignity: 'If the plaintiff were prosecuted [for importing contraceptives] there would necessarily be a violation if intimate aspects of her marital life which ... ought not to be brought out and condemned as criminal under a glare of publicity in a courtroom.'

36 *Microcensus* Case (1969) 27 BVerfGE 1. Compare the comments of Justice Hardiman delivering the judgment of the Supreme Court in *CC v. Ireland* [2006] IESC 33, [2006] 4 IR 1: 'It appears to us that to criminalise in a serious way a person who is mentally innocent is indeed "to inflict a grave injury on that person's dignity and sense of worth" and to treat him as "little more than a means to an end", in the words of Wilson J. quoted earlier in this judgment. It appears to us that this, in turn, constitutes a failure by the State in its laws to respect, defend and vindicate the rights to liberty and to good name of the person so treated, contrary to the State's obligations under Article 40 of the Constitution.'

37 This, of course, is a very civilian concept and idea, with many civilian codes expressly drafted with concepts of the protection of the person in mind, which provisions often then lead to subsequent provisions dealing with the protection of personality (or, in the language of Article 40.3.2, 'good name'): see, e.g., Part 1 of the Swiss Civil Code (1907).

38 See, e.g., the comments of Justice Laffoy in *Fitzpatrick v. FK (No. 2)* [2009] 2 IR 7, 18–19. In *Fleming v. Ireland* [2013] IEHC 2, [2013] 2 ILRM 9 the right to bodily integrity was described by Justice Kearns ([2013] 2 ILRM 9, 23) as being an 'overlapping and ancillary' right to the protection of the person in Article 40.3.2°. This 'may reflect a nascent preference for a basing a decision upon a right in the text of the Constitution, where possible, rather than upon an unenumerated right': see Sutherland (n. 7) 23.

39 See, e.g., *Kinsella v. Governor of Mountjoy Prison* [2011] IEHC 235, [2012] 1 IR 467.

40 [2012] IECCA 68.

41 The matter was put starkly by Justice Henchy ([1974] IR 284, 325): 'The dominant feature of the plaintiff's dilemma is that she is a young married woman who is living, with a slender income, in the cramped quarters of a mobile home with her husband and four infant children and that she is faced with the risk of death or crippling paralysis if she becomes pregnant.'

42 Justices Walsh, Budd, Henchy and Griffin, Chief Justice Fitzgerald dissenting.

43 [1974] IR 284 at 326. Kavanagh's analysis of the reasoning in *McGee* (A. Kavanagh, 'The Irish Constitution at 75 years: Natural Law, Christian Values and the Ideals of Justice' (2012) 48 *Irish Jurist* 71, 74–82) is particularly insightful.

44 Or perhaps almost exclusively, because he also made reference in passing to the guarantees in respect of the family in Article 41.
45 [1974] IR 284, 335, quoting Justice Douglas in *Griswold v. Connecticut* 381 US 479, 485 (1965). Compare *Omar v. Governor of Cloverhill Prison* [2013] IEHC 254, [2014] 1 ILRM 254, 266–267 (night time entry by a Garda into the bedroom of a sleeping 7-year-old boy without warrant or true parental consent in order to wake him in represented 'an extremely serious breach of Article 40.5' which 'this court views with dismay').
46 [1984] IR 277.
47 *Ibid.*, 281, *per* Justice McMahon.
48 [1987] IR 587.
49 See *Schrems v. Data Protection Commissioner* [2014] IEHC 310, [2014] 2 ILRM 441; *Anti-Terrorism Database* Case (judgment of the German Constitutional Court of 24 April 2013). Note also the judgments in June and July 2014 of the Austrian and Romanian Constitutional Courts respectively in which data retention legislation was held to be unconstitutional as being contrary to the 'inviolability of the dwelling' clauses in their respective constitutions.
50 BVerfGE 67, 157 (1984).
51 Lazarus (n. 11) pp. 369, 371.
52 Of course, I acknowledge that it may not be completely unnecessary and that there may well be instances where the unenumerated rights doctrine will enable the courts to protect a right not otherwise safeguarded by the text of the Constitution. I am grateful to Dr Conor O'Mahony of University College Cork for making this point. There is, however, another way of looking at this issue. If the court is forced to revert to the unenumerated rights doctrine to in order to safeguard a right which has no textual links *whatever* with the express language of the Constitution, then the question arises as to the extent to which this is legitimate.

4

Judges and the idea of 'principle' in constitutional adjudication

Tom Hickey

In this chapter I explore the role of principle in constitutional adjudication. I attempt to reconcile the principles-oriented contribution that constitutional adjudication (or judicial review) can make to overall public deliberation with the fact of reasonable disagreement on rights. The chapter is in two sections. The first section assesses the school of 'legal constitutionalism' in the context of Irish constitutional law and experience. It suggests the pre-eminence of two strands of legal constitutionalism in that context, and assesses those strands with an eye on the role of principle. The second section introduces a distinctive way of understanding the role of principle in judicial review; one that works from a conception of deliberation that – in contrast to contemporary deliberative democracy theory – embraces disagreement and thus, it is argued, better accounts for the political and contestable nature of rights. The chapter then closes by combining the ideas in these parts to argue that the intuition shared by many to support outright judicial supremacy does not stand up to scrutiny, but that the primary cause of that intuition – the principled nature of judicial review – demands and justifies a more constrained form of judicial power.

'Legal constitutionalism' and courts as forums of principle

As Eoin Daly argues in his chapter in this volume (and, indeed, that chapter and this might be read in tandem, developing distinct, but complementary arguments), the desirability of judicial supremacy is rarely questioned in Irish political and legal culture.[1] Its value is apparently deemed self-evident, despite so much scholarly scepticism – usually rights-based and progressive-oriented scepticism – in the anglophone academy.[2] Although there are no doubt several reasons for this – and many are surely particular to Irish history and experience – it might be surmised that one among them is the influence of the school of 'legal constitutionalism' generally in the twentieth century.[3] Although a broad school, legal constitutionalist scholars (i.e. in contrast to 'political constitutionalist scholars') tend to present law as a distinctive enterprise to politics, and, indeed, as a higher, more principled, vocation. They suppose that law serves to contain and control politics, through the enforcement of certain principles of legality and fundamental rights. Very often, those principles and rights are understood as predetermined and mechanically identifiable. That is, that the job of judges is to set out the meaning and implications of a set of pre-existing, pre-political rights and to apply them against political actors, thereby upholding an essentially legally defined framework within which ordinary politics can occur.

I cannot hope to measure the influence of legal constitutionalism on Irish constitutional affairs, but, with a view to developing my overall argument, I suggest that two strands are broadly discernible. The first – perhaps a classical strand – is drawn from the 'state of nature' thinking associated with Hobbes and Locke and presents rights as inalienable, somehow absolute, and as pre-existing the political state.[4] It is associated with the contractualist image of a set of human beings consenting to the formation of the state, and to its overall authority, on condition that these 'natural rights' would remain sacrosanct. It tends to promote a minimalist conception of the state. The state is seen as an intrusive, yet necessary, evil: required to prevent outright anarchy, but inclined, as it interferes more in the lives of individuals, to undermine freedom (where freedom is similarly conceived in the natural, pre-political sense, informed by the image of the state of nature).[5] The role of law, on this analysis, is to block the state from becoming too powerful; law thus prevents the use of state power to achieve certain positive goals.

Much of the text of the Irish Constitution evokes this classical strand: the dwelling of every citizen is 'inviolable';[6] the family is an institution 'possessing inalienable and imprescriptible rights, antecedent and superior to all positive law';[7] there is a 'guarantee to respect the inalienable right ... of parents to provide ... for the ... education of their children';[8] and the state 'acknowledges that man ... has the natural right, antecedent to positive law ... to the private ownership of external goods'.[8] The same themes are in evidence in prominent judgments in the activist era of the 1970s and 1980s. In *McGee v. Attorney General*, for example, Justice Walsh insisted that there were rights 'over which the State has no authority' and which 'it could not control', before elaborating that the difficult task of identifying these rights was a matter for judges: 'in this country, it falls finally upon the judges ... as best they can from their training and their experience ... to interpret the Constitution and in doing so to determine, where necessary, the rights which are superior or antecedent to positive law or which are imprescriptible or inalienable'.[10]

Although, again, difficult to measure,[11] the overall thesis may be said to inform, at least to some extent, the work and approach of some contemporary Irish judges, including two who contribute to the current volume (albeit that it is surely not as prevalent nowadays, following the conscious ousting of natural rights justifications in the *Abortion Information Case* in 1995).[12] In his chapter, Justice Hogan, when referencing the aforementioned rights provisions, asserts:

> At its most basic, the drafters of the Constitution intended that the fundamental rights of the individual and family would be *protected against legislative and executive intrusion*, if necessary by a form of dialogue between the courts and the other branches of government. At the heart of this were notions of human dignity, personal freedom, the protection of life and the person, the inviolability of the dwelling and the inalienable rights of the family.[13]

Similarly, when considering the implausibly emphatic language used in the rights provisions (such as 'inalienable and imprescriptible' as well as 'antecedent to all positive law'), he argues that 'even if these phrases were not meant to be taken absolutely literally, nonetheless their underlying purpose cannot be discounted or ignored' and that 'the drafters clearly intended thereby to secure the *maximum possible degree* of protection which might realistically be secured in a modern society'.[14]

And the positions taken by Justice Hardiman in cases concerning gender discrimination[15] and socio-economic rights,[16] compared to those concerning police powers,[17] might also be reflected upon in light of this classical strand of legal constitutionalism. His conclusion in each case might be said to correspond with the 'freedom as non-interference' or minimal state thesis, with his positions on the nature and extent of judicial power varying accordingly. Thus judges do not have power to prevent golf clubs from discriminating against women: men can associate with whom they wish, free from government interference, based on a certain reading of equality legislation.[18] They do not have the power to prevent ministers from rowing back on commitments (made to a High Court judge in earlier proceedings) to fund particular social projects deemed necessary for the vindication of various social and economic rights: the vindication of these 'positive' rights cannot be compelled by judges in virtue of a certain account of the separation of powers, and a certain status afforded to that account within the overall constitutional system.[19] Yet judges do have the power to quash the convictions of individuals where evidence relied upon is obtained in inadvertent breach of due process-oriented rights: these are 'negative' rights recognised by the classical scholars and, based on a certain understanding of those rights and of the rule of law, interpreted as having been violated in the circumstances, albeit in technical ways.[20]

The second strand of legal constitutionalism – a more contemporary strand, associated with Ronald Dworkin and John Rawls – might seem to have superseded the classical strand in recent decades, since the embrace of the proportionality test and the tendency towards greater deference to the political branches. This approach presents constitutional courts as forums of principle, contrasting them with legislatures and other electoral settings which are characterised by political horse-trading.[21] In this thesis, rights are associated with moral principle: they are understood as corresponding with, or flowing from, an ideal conception of justice, where a democratic society is understood as assuming a kind of implied consensus among all citizens on essential principles of justice.[22] Judges are better placed to settle disputes concerning rights, because, immune from the populist influences that bedevil ordinary politics, they operate under conditions resembling Rawls's 'original position' (in which the deliberators are ignorant of their own real-life situations and so choose unbiased principles of justice). That is, judges in constitutional adjudication are not moved by concern to further their own personal worldview or to placate any powerful group. Accordingly, they are institutionally inclined towards deliberation based on principle and thus, in Dworkin's phrase, to identify the determinate 'right answer' in hard cases.[23]

Where the classical strand may be described as libertarian, this contemporary strand may be said to be liberal in the more progressive, modern, sense. It embraces the state, and conceives of freedom more in line with the republican sense of non-domination (and thus as intimately connected to equality) rather than with the minimal state or non-interference sense of Hobbes and his ilk.

Dworkin's account of adjudication warrants elaboration in the present context for its analysis of the ways in which the 'hard data' of legal doctrine alone (i.e. legislation, case law and 'law' emanating from other such recognised sources) is insufficient for judges to reach conclusions in cases that fall to be decided. As scholars of contemporary legal philosophy will recall, in the *Riggs v. Palmer* case which he made famous, the court found an ostensibly valid will invalid in circumstances where the primary beneficiary of the will had murdered the testator in order to expedite his inheritance.[24] There was no express statutory provision to justify the court's conclusion – no hard legal data governing the outcome – yet, in Dworkin's analysis, the judges did not go beyond the law. Rather they pursued their interpretative task, discovering principles implicit in the legal system that explained the 'black letter' legal rules that applied to the case. Various, and often competing, principles were at play (including one oriented around the idea that 'no person shall profit from his own wrong', and another around the idea that 'the enactments of the legislature should be enforced according to their clear wording').[25] The judges could not consult particular legal sources in order to identify the deeper principles, but neither could they make them up from thin air, or on the basis of their own preferences. Rather, judges in hard cases identify principles that best fit with and justify the 'black letter' legal rules: judges decide cases by 'trying to find, in some coherent set of principles about people's rights and duties, the best constructive interpretation of the legal doctrine of their community'.[26] They engage in an analysis and justification of legal doctrine in a particular domain and reconcile it with a broader analysis and justification of the entire legal system. In *Riggs*, this interpretative enterprise led them to clarify that the statutory rules on succession were subject to an implicit exception precluding a murderer from inheriting under his victim's will.

The *Doherty v. Government of Ireland* case similarly illuminates the ways in which judges necessarily rely on unexpressed, non-promulgated, moral principle – in conjunction with the hard data – in order to carry out their task (and also represents an example of the influence of this strand of legal constitutionalism in contemporary Irish constitutional law).[27] Here, the applicant sought an order compelling the then Fianna Fáil–Green coalition government to hold a by-election in the Donegal South West constituency, some eighteen months after the vacancy had arisen. The relevant legislative provision empowered the Dáil to cause by-elections but had no stipulation regarding timeframe. The government, holding a slender majority at a time of economic crisis, wanted to avoid a by-election it would inevitably lose, and so on three occasions over the period had used its majority to block Opposition by-election motions in the Dáil. Justice Kearns thus faced quite the task: on the one hand, the Constitution protected equal democratic representation; on the other, he could hardly hand down an order which would effectively dictate to TDs how to vote on a motion in parliament. In the end, he opted for a declaration (as distinct from a mandatory order) that the eighteen-month gap was inconsistent with the Constitution, and the by-election duly followed as the judicial encouragement prompted government to relent. Like *Riggs* or any other hard case, despite the fact that there was no clear text determining the outcome, there was no gap in the law (if we are to follow Dworkin's analysis). The judge's discretion was not of the un-bounded, extra-legal kind. Rather, on a Dworkinian reading, Justice Kearns discovered principles implicit in the constitutional text, and in the legal system more broadly – principles, for example, pertaining to the equal standing of citizens, equal democratic representation, the importance of dispersing, as distinct from concentrating, governmental power – within which the black letter legal rules were embedded. Those principles made sense of the rules, and in combination, led to Justice Kearns's ruling.

If legal constitutionalism, and its embrace of strong judicial power, may seem to have had a general influence on Irish constitutional law and adjudication, what initial ideas emerge from this analysis? On the one hand, there are certain reasons to be optimistic about judicial review. Taking just two cases already mentioned – *McGee* and *Doherty* – the judges seemed to get it broadly right in both instances, at least so far as outcomes are concerned.[28] Good riddance to laws banning contraceptives, and to governments exploiting their control of parliament for their own electoral ends. Not only that, but in both instances judicial review seemed to run counter to dominating or factional outputs that had emerged from vote-based processes. That is, in respect of *McGee*, a conservative society and political culture meant that it was unlikely that political actors would deliver reform of oppressive laws on contraception. And in respect of *Doherty*, the fact that political actors controlled a process that influenced their own fate made factional outcomes possible, if not probable. Thus we might provisionally conclude – noting the contingent nature of the conclusion – that vote-based processes *can* produce such outcomes, and that judicial review *can* counteract vote-based processes in such instances.[29]

One need not be persuaded by Dworkin's overall thesis to conclude further that rights-based judicial review can bring moral principle to bear on contested questions. It may be that the claim made by some critical scholars that judges subtly or subconsciously draw on their own political preferences, or on oppressive ideology, is persuasive. (The contempt for homosexuals in Chief Justice O'Higgins's judgment in *Norris v. Attorney General* is an example.)[30] But if it is, surely there is sometimes, even usually, at least an element of deliberative, principled engagement. Again, the two cases are illustrative. The near universal acclaim of *McGee* is hardly warranted insofar as the various judgments arbitrarily discriminate between married and non-married couples and are vaguely misogynistic.[31] But, just as moral ideas around equal democratic standing reverberate within Justice Kearns's judgment in *Doherty*, important moral ideas around bodily integrity, autonomy, and privacy in intimate relationships (or, as Dworkin would have it, moral independence for citizens from the collective will in respect of certain features of their lives) nevertheless reverberate within the various judgments in *McGee*.[32]

Competing with these potential advantages is a reason for caution that is, by my reckoning, both fairly obvious and quite significant. This is the fact that, much as we might *almost* all broadly agree on the particular outcomes in *McGee* and *Doherty*, we cannot escape the fact of general disagreement at the level of principle among reasonable citizens in free communities and the associated fact of reasonable disagreement on rights. This is not to surrender to the taking of unreasonable stances: we cannot equate, for instance, a claim that a particular racial group should enjoy exclusive access to public services, and a claim that hate speech should never be proscribed. Both claims, if made, would prompt disagreement. But the former can be dismissed as unreasonable insofar as it is premised on a thesis which holds that one racial group can lord it over others. The latter, by contrast, reflects ordinary political disagreement that defines democratic communities in which citizens can think freely. It happens to concern tension between freedom of expression and the dignity of individuals within particular racial groups, but comparable tensions apply in respect of, for example, freedom of religion and neutrality in respect of religion, or the right to education and other social rights that place competing demands on the public purse.

As political constitutionalists have argued, these kinds of disagreements can be explained by factors other than sheer ignorance or self-interest.[33] They necessarily follow from, among other factors, the difficulty of identifying and assessing often complicated empirical evidence with regard to a particular case; the vagueness and indeterminacy of concepts (such as what counts as 'speech' or 'privacy' or 'conscience' or 'equal democratic representation'); the effect of people's different life experiences on how they assess evidence and weigh political and moral values, etc.[34] And so, for any analyst who will broadly agree with the particular outcomes in the cases mentioned, there are several decisions of the Irish superior courts with which that analyst will substantively disagree. And, equally, between and among progressives, conservatives, libertarians, environmentalists, religious and non-religious minded citizens and everyone else, there will be reasonable disagreement over how to best resolve various quandaries in which rights clash among themselves, and against more general considerations. This is not to argue that objective right answers are not theoretically available in rights cases or generally; it is not to subscribe to a general sceptical school of thought. It is merely to step back and recognise the practical limitations of human reason.

The overriding objection to legal constitutionalism then, as the likes of

Richard Bellamy and Jeremy Waldron argue, is that it treats rights and law, implausibly, as beyond the 'circumstances of politics'.[35] It works from a premise that overlooks, or fails to take sufficient account of, the fact that rights are the subject of the very same kinds of disagreements that animate debate in ordinary political contexts. The classical strand, as Gerard Hogan implies in his chapter in the current volume, appears naive, or even absurd, to modern minds (although Hogan's conclusion is that we should not take the language so literally).[36] It makes for the absolutist and emphatic adjudication most starkly illustrated by Justice Walsh's judgment in *McGee* or Chief Justice Kennedy's famous dissent in *State (Ryan) v. Lennon*: it has judges casting themselves as God's philosophers, sitting beyond the democratic system, pointing their thumbs to signal to the mortals whether their sacred, pre-political, rights have been violated.[37] The contemporary strand makes for a more deliberative and conceptual judicial engagement with the relevant legal provisions and a drawing out of deeper principles implicit in those provisions, as illustrated in the skilful work of Justice Kearns in *Doherty*[38] or, indeed, that of Justice Denham in her dissent in *TD v. Minister for Education*.[39] But it too has judges as philosopher kings, somehow hunting out the determinate right answers, liberated, in their Herculean wisdom, from the intellectual limitations that burden the rest of us. Ultimately, both strands, in different ways, conceive of rights and constitutionalism as corresponding with a universal, impliedly agreed-upon, pre-political theory of justice that ought to govern liberal democratic communities. With that premise, it is inevitable that that the conceptions of adjudication will fail to adequately account for the fact of disagreement on rights.

Disagreement and the reconceptualising of judicial review

This theme of disagreement informs the political constitutionalists' claim that judicial supremacy is undemocratic, a claim that runs against the intuitions of contemporary legal scholars for whom the sceptical arguments prioritise abstract theory over common sense and potentially jeopardise the role of courts in lifting oppression and injustice. Although I argue against both stances, I take each to contribute valuable arguments to the overall debate on judicial power. I argue that judicial review can contribute to principled and democratic deliberation but that, to the extent that it draws on a pre-political conception of justice and rights, the legal constitutionalist account of that element is unsatisfactory. To conceptualise its contribution in a satisfactory way, I turn in this final section to an account of deliberative regulation developed in Philip Pettit's recent (republican) work but which has a pedigree in certain multiculturalist and liberal scholarship.[40] Although this account is reminiscent of Rawlsian ideas around public reason and deliberation, I argue that it is distinctive in ways that – when applied to judicial review – assuage concerns associated with principled disagreement and democratic legitimacy.[41]

To develop the account, we might think of two alternative modes of public debate.[42] In the first, interlocutors simply announce their preferred outcome on a particular matter, and pursue the debate by begrudgingly conceding to their opponents until an outcome is reached. This mode will be characterised by intransigence and factional power-plays. We might think of it as likely to engender a sense of exclusion among those defeated, and as at odds with ideas of civic virtue and patriotism. The alternative mode has interlocutors in public exchanges accompanying their preferred outcome with justifications that will render that outcome more amenable to fellow citizens who might prefer different, even diametrically opposed, outcomes. In this mode, the emphasis is on the deeper justifications that are presented in support of contested policy preferences. The idea is that these deeper justifications can be recognised by any reasonable citizen as at least relevant, regardless of one's deeper ethical or religious commitments. Others may continue to rail against the preferred outcome but, so long as such deeper justifications have been presented in its favour, they are likely to find any corresponding outcome more relatable. This mode relies on, but also promotes, civic virtue and patriotism. That is, once it prevails, it is likely to give rise to an expectation in the public culture that citizens owe one another such justifications. Almost everyone will comply, consciously or otherwise, but not only that: almost everyone will approve of compliance, and disapprove of non-compliance, such that compliance is more or less required in order to be taken seriously in public debate.[43] Gradually, more specific norms emerge and come to constitute points of reference in public debate. They come to be 'commonly avowable': they are recognised as manifestly relevant by all-comers, such that policy preferences, in order to pass muster, must correspond with them.

If this is to prevail in a political culture, we may think of politics as operating at two speeds.[44] On the one hand, there is the routine back-and-forth disagreement: the readily identifiable stuff of politics that makes for headlines and analysis in an everyday sense. But there is also the slower march of this body of commonly avowable norms. They develop and shift relentlessly, as they come to be considered in new contexts and are applied in different settings. As they do, they gradually impact on political outcomes. They will mean that certain deeply factional outcomes will come to be seen as more or less off the table. (How could formal apartheid, for instance, be justified with reference to norms that are commonly avowable in this way?)[45] But their real work is done more subtly in respect of outcomes generally: they make it more difficult for powerful or established groups to railroad their preferred outcomes through by sheer force of will, and they gently encourage outcomes that correspond with common goods.

Certain features of this understanding of deliberative regulation warrant particular attention in the context of my overall argument. First, unlike Rawlsian thought, it does not rely on the possibility of the reaching of a 'rational consensus'. And, unlike the deliberative democracy theory (which Rawls's work did much to inspire), it does not regard ultimate disagreement as a failure. It embraces disagreement, even thrives on it, insofar as it is disagreement that drives citizens towards the identification of new norms or to the scrutiny of previously established norms.[46] Thus, while these norms will encourage interlocutors towards certain kinds of outcomes, and away from others, they remain fluid and open to new interpretations; they do not dictate any particular 'right answer', but rather point to better, and away from worse, answers.

Second – and again unlike Rawls (as well as the contemporary strand of legal constitutionalism which his work did much to inspire and, indeed, the classical strand that preceded it) – the approach does not operate from any pre-political 'objective' idea of justice. It sees common norms as evolving from within the existing public culture, rather than as governed by a pre-political order, divinely ordained or otherwise. It is avowedly *political* in that sense and, insofar as it is 'of the people', avowedly *democratic*. Pettit's elaboration is worth setting out:

> The specific norms that emerge in any group ... will be subject to constant development, as deliberative innovators manage to gain acceptance for novel sorts of arguments, perhaps by extending the reach of recognised arguments to new domains, perhaps by coming up with new arguments that gain acceptance by others. Such innovations are likely to be triggered by changes in the dispositions of the existing membership and, of course, by changes of membership that occur at any time and across different times. As new norms evolve in this way, others may decay and lose potential, say because they are not acceptable to some members in the changed society. But in general we would expect the norms that are given countenance to increase in number and application, being laid down like a sediment deposited by the flow of debate and exchange.[47]

So, how does this relate to judicial review?[48] First, it should be clear that, no matter what particular powers judges have within the overall political and constitutional system, their role and contribution is quite modest. The thought is that the people, through their private reflection and their public exchanges, determine their own shared fate, albeit that it is necessarily mediated through particular institutional structures. Their attitudes towards themselves; their communities; their fellow citizens etc., contribute to an ever-evolving public morality that in turn sets the terms for public exchanges, which produce various, and ever-evolving, public outcomes: policies and laws, institutional arrangements, public facilities and goods, etc.[49] Shifts in these terms are prompted by the exchange of ideas across a vast range of settings: within families and across dinner tables; in parliamentary exchanges and branch meetings of social movements; in the tension between non-governmental bodies, or international human rights bodies, for instance, and government departments or government itself; in social media and through myriad forms of creative expression. Judicial engagement with public questions, through judicial review, is assuredly among these sites of contestation and exchange, but the characterisation of judges as ultimate guardians of a pre-determined set of public values, standing beyond the political system, is not persuasive. Rather, in line with Sunstein's characterisation, we might see them as following, rather than leading, the 'emerging moral commitments of "We the People"' and accordingly see the meaning of constitutional doctrine as a 'product not only of text and history, but also of social movement and struggles, dissents and sometimes deaths, changing hearts and minds'.[50] We might thus see judges, not as God's philosophers on earth, but as a set of actors who play a modest yet potentially valuable role within a vast system of inter-checking mechanisms.

In this light, whether judges enjoy supremacy (for instance, where their word on legislation is 'final', as in the Irish system) or whether their power is more constrained (as in the UK system) might seem of academic importance. Indeed, although it defends judicial supremacy and has a legal constitutionalist orientation, the overall argument presented by Fiona de Londras (Chapter 1 in this volume) might seem to have much in common with this line of thinking.[51] I take her notion of 'judicial innovation' as referring to ordinary judicial interpretation: to the ways in which judges, as Justice Kearns in *Doherty*, cannot but draw on deeper principle in order to make sense of, and give meaning to, vague constitutional principles (she also, notably, recognises the capacity of courts to 'savagely undermine liberty [and to] scathingly excoriate those who do not conform to the perceived "norm"').[52] And her thesis very much emphasises the iterative and collaborative nature of constitutional interpretation. That is, regardless of the particular details of the institutional arrangements, there is an 'eco-system' of constitutional interpretation: courts share the responsibility with the executive, the legislature, and with public bodies.[53] She presents what many would see as the 'final word' of judges under a legal constitution as merely the 'next word' (or, perhaps, the 'latest word') on the basis that every interpretation is contingent, and awaiting further interpretation.[54] Thus the role of courts under her account might be interpreted as contributing to the development and rethinking of commonly avowable norms.

But – although the primary aim of this chapter has been to scrutinise the philosophical underpinnings of legal constitutionalism and to reconceptualise the principled nature of judicial review – it might be instructive to set out what I think are some of the strong arguments, flowing from the idea of commonly avowable norms, against judicial supremacy and in favour of a more constrained form of judicial power. I have developed these arguments in other recent work, based on this and on other elements of neo-republican thought, specifically defending the 'new commonwealth model of constitutionalism' under which judges can hand down declarations of incompatibility regarding impugned legislation but do not have the final word that the outright invalidating power represents.[55] Although I cannot repeat the argument here comprehensively, I might close the chapter with reference to some aspects of it that pertain to the 'commonly avowable norms' element.

There are two related features of judicial review that recommend it, when assessed in light of this idea of deliberative regulation through public norms. First, whereas political actors engage with particular questions with factors other than rights in mind, judges in judicial review engage with rights as essential departure points in their deliberative assessments. To suggest this is not to fall into the Dworkinian bifurcation of law and politics – with law as a haven for moral principle and politics as a world of vice – as de Londras, arguably, along with most legal constitutionalists do.[56] We can recognise a strong correlation between popular interests and rights, and an accompanying capacity, even tendency, of political actors to bring rights to bear in their ordinary deliberation.[57] But we might also recognise that political actors do not approach their work with rights consciously to the fore as the pre-eminent consideration. They have (and *ought* to have) other, often related, factors in mind, such as popular interests and broader policy considerations. Although courts also have factors other than rights in mind, they nevertheless operate with rights front and centre. We can recognise the fact of reasonable disagreement on rights, particularly when it comes to engaging them in concrete contexts, and we can account for this fact in the detail of institutional design. But we can nevertheless conceive of rights as broadly corresponding with norms we take to be commonly avowable: thus, although there is deep disagreement about what the right to 'primary education' under the Irish Constitution might mean in practice, even it – as a socio-economic or 'second generation' right – might be said to correspond with a norm that all-comers in contemporary Irish society recognise as at least relevant.

The other feature of judicial review that might recommend it in this light is that it operates independently of populist pressures. Again, this is not to concede that populist pressures are invariably at odds with non-arbitrary government, or that judges, immune from those populist pressures, never act out of self-interest or based on oppressive or poorly-thought-out accounts of rights. (Or, as Eoin Daly, perhaps cuttingly, puts it in his chapter, to subscribe to the view which, 'in its most cliché form ... manifests itself as a lawyerly conceit that suggests that only the courts stand between "politics" and "rights"'.)[58] But we can nevertheless recognise certain more or less obvious ways in which unbridled electoral processes can make for the intervention of 'alien interests'.[59] The notion of gerrymandering is just one illustration; the inclination to appeal to interests of an influential media group another; indeed the factors referred to earlier, at play in *McGee* and *Doherty* respectively, bring out the idea: elected actors, if left entirely unconstrained, would have to be angelic not to be swayed by factors other than their sincere, carefully considered, assessment of common interests.

And so these factors suggest that we might embrace judicial review in at least some form. Its contribution though – certainly in respect of the first feature – might be in the more long-haul sense.[60] That is, we might conceive of judges grappling with concrete quandaries with rights-oriented principle at the heart of their assessments, and of thus contributing to the evolution of commonly avowable norms in that more gradual sense. Just as the principle sheds light on the particular quandary, the quandary reflects back on the principle, making for a more sophisticated and comprehensive understanding of the principle in question. Thus, in line with Máiréad Enright's idea, we might conceive of constitutional litigation as a formalised contestatory space (among several others, both formal and informal) which affords often marginalised individuals or groups the opportunity to speak their particular truth to power, forcing others to respond or to engage in an exchange of reasons.[61] With the prestige that a constitutional court potentially commands, its deliberations might be particularly influential; or might in some instances serve to rupture orthodoxy in particular domains, even if its characterisation by many lawyers as a nation's conscience might be dismissed on the basis of an understandable tendency of particular domains of expertise to unduly elevate their own importance.[62] This defence is certainly not premised on a conception of judicial review as producing a particular right answer. Indeed it would be less concerned with actual outcomes of litigation and more with its gradual role in prompting shifts in the understandings of what these norms might require, or exclude, in terms of particular political outcomes. Hence it seems to call for, or certainly be satisfied by, judicial review of the more constrained variety, as under the new commonwealth model of constitutionalism.

Conclusion

The idea of commonly avowable norms prompts several arguments in respect of the form that judicial review ought to take. One, for example, is that under systems of judicial supremacy, judicial rulings can in some instances be taken as conclusively settling a contested matter, or can have that practical effect, stifling ongoing deliberative assessment that might otherwise be open to new interpretations.[63] Or, relatedly, that the presence of strong form judicial review hovers over and diminishes political deliberation, such that 'political issues that would be otherwise regarded as open-ended political–moral considerations are divested from the political sphere to what is broadly perceived as the technocratic and expertised domain of constitutional law'.[64] These are concerning not only in respect of the particular contested questions themselves, but also in the longer haul sense insofar as it denies or stymies the development of shared norms that might otherwise emerge, were that further, or that less shackled, assessment to occur. Another is the fact that judges routinely reach different, often diametrically opposed, conclusions in the same case, reflecting the principled disagreement on rights across broader society, as referred to throughout the chapter. In those circumstances, whatever about its potential as a forum in which more sophisticated understandings of commonly avowable norms might develop, it is difficult to escape the conclusion that, under judicial supremacy, the resolution of society-wide disagreements on principle is determined in significant part by the happenstance of how many judges favour a particular litigant's claim. These and other arguments[65] suggest that the more constrained form integrates what is valuable about judicial review without the costs associated with outright supremacy.

But this chapter has been less about the argument around the form judicial review should take, and more about the dubious philosophical basis for the two strands of legal constitutionalism that I claim are broadly discernible in Irish constitutional law and practice. I hope it might contribute to a reconceptualisation of why and how judicial review is valuable in Ireland, and – if I may be so bold – beyond.

Notes

Thank you to Peter Malone and David Prendergast for their insightful comments on an earlier draft.

1 See Chapter 2. To suggest, as Daly does, that its desirability 'has almost gone unquestioned in political and intellectual circles', is perhaps too strong. Some questioning is provided in, for example, D. Gwynn Morgan, *A Judgment Too Far? Judicial Activism and The Constitution* (Cork UP, 2001).
2 Among the more prominent examples are J. Waldron, 'The Core of the Case against Judicial Review' (2006) 115 *Yale Law Journal* 1346; R. Bellamy, *Political Constitutionalism: A Republican Defence of the Constitutionality of Democracy* (CUP, 2007).
3 For an account of what he deems the 'six tenets of legal constitutionalism', see A. Tomkins, *Our Republican Constitution* (Hart, 2005) pp. 10–25.
4 See T. Hobbes, *Leviathan*, ed. C. B. MacPherson (Penguin, 1968 [1651]); J. Locke, *Two Treatises on Government* (CUP, 1960).
5 Hobbes insisted that freedom prevails only in the 'silence of the laws' and that 'the liberty of a subject, lyeth therefore only in those things, which in regulating their actions, the Sovereign hath pretermitted' (*ibid.*, pp. 143, 264).
6 Constitution of Ireland, Article 40.5.
7 Article 41.1.1°.
8 Article 42.1.
9 Article 43.1.1°.
10 *McGee v. Attorney General* [1974] IR 284, p. 310.
11 I acknowledge the somewhat conjectural nature of these characterisations of Justice Hogan's and Justice Hardiman's positions. It would be trite – not only because of the complexity of legal reasoning, with the myriad trade-offs and fact-specific dimensions, but also because of the similarly complex ideas pertaining to the notion of a 'classical strand of legal constitutionalism' – to rigidly categorise particular judges, or indeed scholars. I gesture towards the connections here in order to develop my overall argument.
12 Re Article 26 and the Regulation of Information (Services Outside the State for the Termination of Pregnancies) Bill 1995 [1995] 1 IR 1.
13 See Chapter 3, p. 53 (emphasis added). He later (p. 56) references the provision describing the dwelling as 'inviolable', asking: 'What are these words trying to tell us about the heart of the relationship between the state and the individual? Is it not that the individual is free to make private choices in respect of the home and the family?'
14 *Ibid.*, p. 54 (emphasis added). I take Justice Hogan's reference to the 'maximal possible degree of protection', not unjustifiably, I hope, to correspond with the Hobbesian/Benthamite notion that state interference, which itself undermines freedom (where freedom is understood as non-interference), is justified only to the extent that it counters greater interference than its itself represents. For a good account and critique of this idea, see Q. Skinner, *Liberty before Liberalism*

(CUP, 1998), especially the chapter entitled 'Free States and Individual Liberty'.
15 *Equality Authority v. Portmarnock Golf Club* [2010] 1 ILRM 237.
16 *TD v. Minister for Education* [2001] 4 IR 259, *Sinnott v. Minister for Education* [2001] 2 IR 545.
17 *DPP v. JC* [2015] IESC 31.
18 The case hinged on interpretation of section 9, Equal Status Act 2000, which provides an exemption for 'discriminating' clubs in circumstances where the 'principal purpose [of the club] is to cater only for the needs of ... ', in this instance, 'persons of a particular gender'.
19 In *TD v. Minister for Education* [2001] 4 IR 259, Justice Hardiman described the separation of powers as a 'high constitutional value' but also, more notably, as a constitutional doctrine which rigidly and precisely sets out the boundaries between the branches of government. The doctrine, he suggests, is 'not in any sense a porous one, still less that a court, or any other organ of government, can strike its own balance ... as to how [it] is to be observed'. The assertion seems to imply that the doctrine needs no interpretation, yet, on any analysis, he engages in an interpretation of it in order to reach the conclusion he reaches in the case (as, inescapably, does Justice Denham, in order to reach her dissenting conclusion). For an insightful critical analysis, see O. Doyle, *Constitutional Law: Texts, Cases and Materials* (Clarus Press, 2008) pp. 363–372.
20 For a general analysis of the case, see Y. Daly, 'Overruling the Protectionist Exclusionary Rule: *DPP v. JC*' (2015) 19 *International Journal of Evidence and Proof* 270.
21 Although she does not engage directly with Dworkin's work, this general thesis may be said to inform Fiona de Londras's chapter in the present volume, for example (see Chapter 1). Comparing judicial and political approaches, she asserts that courts are 'better positioned to make [certain decisions], simply because the infrastructure of the judicial administration of justice – the independence of the judiciary, the separation of powers, the security of tenure – allows space for a form of principled courage that is not facilitated by the structure of the political system' (p. 17). I consider de Londras's argument at more length later in the chapter.
22 Thus, for Rawls, a 'well-ordered society' is one in which 'everyone accepts, and knows that everyone accepts, the very same principles of justice' (*Political Liberalism* (Columbia UP, 1993) p. 35). For Dworkin, law rules by virtue of its 'fit' with 'a coherent set of principles about justice and fairness and procedural due process' (*Law's Empire* (Fontana, 1986) p. 265).
23 See the chapter entitled 'Hard Cases' in R. Dworkin, *Taking Rights Seriously* (Harvard UP, 1978).
24 *Riggs v. Palmer* 115 NY 506 (1889). See the chapter entitled 'The Model of Rules I' in Dworkin (n. 23).
25 For a useful account, see the chapter entitled 'Dworkin' in N. Simmonds, *Central Issues in Jurisprudence* (3rd edn, Thomson, Sweet & Maxwell, 2008).
26 R. Dworkin, *Law's Empire* (Fontana, 1986) p. 255.

27 *Doherty v. Government of Ireland* [2011] 2 IR 222. For a more comprehensive account of the facts of the case, as well as a critical take on Justice Kearns's judgment, see Prendergast, Chapter 16, this volume. See also D. Prendergast, 'By-elections and the Filling of Dáil Vacancies within a Reasonable Time – A Note on *Doherty v. Ireland*' (2011) 34 *Dublin University Law Journal* 242.
28 Although Prendergast notes the fact that a time-frame stipulation was considered by parliament during the debates on the legislation, but rejected, possibly on principled grounds (connected with the suitability of by-elections in proportional representation electoral systems). See Prendergast (n. 27) 251–252.
29 For an elaboration, see T. Hickey, 'The Republican Virtues of the New Commonwealth Model of Constitutionalism' (2016) 14(4) *International Journal of Constitutional Law* 794. I develop this point later in the chapter.
30 *Norris v. Attorney General* [1984] IR 36. Chief Justice O'Higgins insisted: 'It cannot be said … that no harm is done if it [buggery] is conducted in private by consenting males. Very serious harm may in fact be involved. Such conduct, although carried on with full consent, may lead a mildly homosexual person into a way of life from which he may never recover' (at 62).
31 Justice Hogan has claimed that the decision 'represented the finest hour in the entire history of the Supreme Court' and 'transformed the political landscape and set the country on a new course'. See G. Hogan, 'Elegantia Juris: Mr Justice Seamus Henchy, Some Thoughts on Two Leading Judgments', available online at www.ul.ie/law/news/00%5Bnid%5D-inaugural-justice-henchy-memorial-lecture-0 (accessed 15 July 2015). For an interesting feminist perspective, see the *McGee* judgment presented by Máiréad Enright in M. Enright, J. McAndless and A. O'Donoghue, *Northern/Irish Feminist Judgments: Judges' Troubles and the Gendered Politics of Identity* (Hart Publishing, 2017).
32 On Dworkin's idea of moral independence, see R. Dworkin, *Freedom's Law: The Moral Reading of the American Constitution* (Harvard UP, 1996) p. 25.
33 See for example, J. Waldron, *Law and Disagreement* (OUP, 1999) pp. 111–112; Bellamy (n. 2) pp. 20–26.
34 Bellamy (n. 2) p. 21.
35 *Ibid.*
36 Hogan (n. 13) p. 59.
37 On Chief Justice Kennedy's judgment in this context, see T. Hickey, 'Revisiting *Ryan v. Lennon* to Make the Case Against Judicial Supremacy (And for a New Model of Constitutionalism in Ireland)' (2015) 53 *Irish Jurist* 125.
38 Although Prendergast (n. 27) argues that the judgment presents as inevitable a constitutional reading that is in fact highly creative and castigates as absurd an analysis of the statute that actually informed its enactment.
39 For a good analysis of Justice Denham's judgment, see Doyle (n. 19) pp. 367–369.
40 See in particular, P. Pettit, *On the People's Terms: A Republican Theory and Model of Democracy* (CUP, 2012) pp. 252–279. See also I. M. Young, *Inclusion and Democracy* (OUP, 2000) pp. 16–51; Hickey (n. 29).
41 See, for example, J. Rawls, *The Law of Peoples: with 'The Idea of Public Reason*

Revisited' (Harvard UP, 2001); J. Habermas, *The Theory of Communicative Action* (Beacon Press, 1984).
42 Pettit (n. 40) pp. 252–259.
43 *Ibid.*, pp. 254, 256.
44 *Ibid.*, pp. 269–270.
45 Hickey (n. 29).
46 Pettit (n. 40) pp. 267–268.
47 *Ibid.*, pp. 257–258.
48 I develop this more comprehensively in Hickey (n. 29).
49 This idea that public morality is ever-evolving is reflected in Justice Kennedy's observation in *Obergefell v. Hodges*: 'The nature of injustice is that we may not always see it in our own times. The generations that wrote and ratified the Bill of Rights and the Fourteenth Amendment did not presume to know the extent of freedom in all of its dimensions, and so they entrusted to future generations a charter protecting the right of all persons to enjoy liberty as we learn its meaning. When new insight reveals discord between the Constitution's central protections and a received legal stricture, a claim to liberty must be addressed' (*Obergefell v. Hodges* 576 US____(2015) (Slip Opinion, 11)).
50 See C. Sunstein, 'Gay Marriage Shows Court at Its Best' (Bloomberg View, 26 June 2015) www.bloombergview.com/articles/2015–06–26/gay-marriage-shows-court-at-its-best (accessed 15 July 2015).
51 de Londras (n. 21).
52 *Ibid.*, p. 18.
53 *Ibid.*, pp. 12–16.
54 *Ibid.*, p. 22.
55 See Hickey (n. 29).
56 See a telling excerpt at de Londras (n. 21). Also, while she certainly acknowledges the ways in which judges can get it badly wrong, she does not engage with whether this might inform scrutiny of the *form* of judicial power required for her 'innovation'. She simply asserts: 'One can criticise the outcome and mechanism of reasoning deployed without deeming the judicial activity of innovation *per se* illegitimate, just as one can criticise dangerous driving without calling for roads to be shut down and private car ownership abolished' (*ibid.*, p. 18).
57 Think of the social and economic reforms (or the vindication of social and economic rights) brought about through ordinary electoral politics in Britain in the decades following the extension of the franchise in the mid and late-nineteenth century, for instance. See Bellamy (n. 2) p. 34.
58 Daly (n. 1) p. 32.
59 See Pettit (n. 40) pp. 232–238; Hickey (n. 29).
60 Hickey (n. 29).
61 In her account of 'meeting Mrs. McGee' (the main litigant in *McGee*), and her analysis of the limitations, and potential, of litigation in affecting social change, Máiréad Enright suggests: 'There is, in law, the litigious as well as the juridical, and the litigious can have its own political power. Litigation promises that the turn to law is not always depoliticising and incorporative, but can presage

an exchange of reasons. It can provide a space in which citizens can author new worlds together, and transgress the boundaries of older ones ... It [can] provide a framework within which agents can publicly justify their actions and demand some justification from those in power' ('Meeting Mrs. McGee: Reflections on Feminist Judgment as Critical Legal Practice' (Northern/Irish Feminist Judgments Project, 22 January 2015) www.feministjudging.ie/?p=1002 (accessed 15 July 2015)).

62 Thus Enright suggests that 'the illegal work' of various family planning and other such groups 'was much more important' than the *McGee* judgment to the transformation in women's access to contraception in the 1970s, and that 'generally ... litigation and high constitutional argument constitute only a very small part of the story' (*ibid.*).

63 This line conflicts with de Londras's overall argument. I elaborate on it (in the context of the decision of the Irish Supreme Court in *Coughlan v. Broadcasting Complaints Commission* [2000] 3 IR 1 and other cases) in Hickey (n. 37) pp. 147–149.

64 Daly (n. 1) p. 39.

65 See, for example, the analysis of Daly, Chapter 2, this volume.

Part II

Judging in the case of *O'Keeffe v. Hickey*: analysis and debate

5

O'Keeffe v. Ireland: overview and analysis

James Gallen

Introduction

In *O'Keeffe v. Ireland*, the European Court of Human Rights concluded that Ireland failed to protect Louise O'Keeffe from sexual abuse suffered as a child in an Irish National School and violated her rights under Article 3 (prohibition of inhuman and degrading treatment) and Article 13 (right to an effective remedy) of the European Convention on Human Rights (the Convention).[1] The decision clarifies the Court's jurisprudence on the positive obligations under Article 3 of the Convention in situations of child abuse where there was no knowledge of a 'real and immediate' risk to the applicant.

This brief introductory chapter reviews the case and the contributions of Adrian Hardiman and Conor O'Mahoney to this book (see Chapters 6 and 7). Their discussion reveals the tension between the principle of subsidiarity and the right to effective protection and an effective remedy in the Convention. The case also raises concerns about the Court's methodology for the historical application of the Convention and about the interaction of Article 3 positive obligations with vicarious liability in tort. A further section examines the impact of the decision for victims of child sexual abuse.

O'Keeffe v. Ireland

From 1968 Louise O'Keeffe attended Dunderrow National School, which was staffed primarily by lay teachers but managed by the local priest and owned by the local Catholic Bishop. She and her parents were unaware that the local priest had received an allegation in 1971 that a teacher, LH, had sexually abused a child, but had not acted upon that complaint. In 1973 the applicant was subjected to approximately twenty sexual assaults by LH in his classroom. Following a meeting of parents with school authorities in 1973 in which the sexual abuse of several children was alleged, LH resigned, but was later employed in another school until his retirement. In 1996, police contacted the applicant after complaints against LH by another former pupil. LH was charged with 386 criminal offences of sexual abuse involving twenty-one former pupils over a period of ten years. In 1998, he pleaded guilty to twenty-one sample charges and was imprisoned.

The same year, the applicant was awarded €53,962.24 by the Criminal Injuries Compensation Tribunal, which administers *ex gratia* compensation for criminally inflicted personal injuries. The applicant also commenced civil proceedings against LH and Ireland. She claimed Ireland was: (i) negligent in its failure to prevent ongoing abuse by LH; (ii) vicariously liable for the acts of LH based on its relationship with LH; and (iii) liable as the educational provider under Article 42 of the Irish Constitution. LH did not defend the civil action and the applicant was awarded €305,104 in damages. Ireland applied to strike out the case, arguing it had no prima facie liability.

The High Court accepted Ireland's application, being 'satisfied that the plaintiff had not established a case in negligence'.[2] It subsequently held that Ireland was not vicariously liable for the abuse by LH.[3] The applicant challenged the vicarious liability finding in the Irish Supreme Court. Mr Justice Hardiman rejected this claim, concluding that, having regard to the limited state control and management of schools, Ireland was not vicariously liable.[4] Mr Justice Fennelly concurred, concluding that Ireland was not vicariously liable as acting as school manager the local priest, not Ireland, employed LH.[5] The applicant appealed to the European Court of Human Rights, arguing that Ireland failed to protect her from sexual abuse by LH and left her without an effective remedy. A majority of the Court dismissed Ireland's preliminary objections as unfounded, found Ireland in breach of its positive obligations under Article 3 to prevent torture, inhuman and degrading treatment and under Article 13 to provide an effective remedy, and dismissed the other claims.

Ms O'Keeffe claimed that Ireland had violated Article 3 by failing to put in place an adequate legal framework of protection of children from a known or foreseeable risk of sexual abuse. The Court affirmed that Article 3's positive obligation to ensure protection against torture, and cruel, inhuman and degrading treatment was applicable in 1973. The Court concluded that Ireland must have been aware of the risk of sexual abuse of children in 1973, citing both pre-1970s government reports that revealed prosecution rates in Ireland for sexual offences against children and subsequent post-1973 commission of inquiry reports.[6] The Court considered that when relinquishing control of the education of children to non-state actors, Ireland should have been aware, given its inherent obligation to protect children, of potential risks to their safety if there was no appropriate framework of protection, including effective mechanisms for the detection and reporting of any ill-treatment.[7] The Court concluded that the mechanisms in place did not provide sufficient protection to children in 1973 and therefore Ireland had violated Article 3.

Under Article 13, the Court considered that an effective remedy should exist regardless of criminal remedies against the perpetrator of the sexual abuse, the limited civil remedies against church authorities or the applicant's inability to prove Ireland's vicarious liability. It noted that the Supreme Court rejected Ireland's vicarious liability for the sexual abuse and would be unlikely to accept its vicarious liability for church authorities' failure to prevent this abuse. Second, a claim against Ireland in negligence would require the recognition of a duty of care on its part to the applicant.[8] However, the exclusion of state control in national schools would preclude any such duty.[9] The Court also concluded that Ireland had not demonstrated how it could be held responsible for a breach of the right to bodily integrity, noting that Mr Justice Hardiman in the Supreme Court rejected this argument obiter. The Court concluded that there was a violation of Article 13.

In his contribution to this volume, Adrian Hardiman positions the European Convention on Human Rights in the context of the Irish domestic legal system and highlights the political motivations behind the decision to give effect to the Convention in Irish law at a sub-constitutional and interpretative level. He emphasises that this decision remains one predicated on the sovereignty of Ireland as a nation state and the supremacy, in its own legal system and jurisdiction, of its constitutional order. He cites the principle of subsidiarity and the attendant requirement for an applicant to the Strasbourg Court to exhaust domestic remedies, as reflecting the primacy of national sovereignty and domestic legal jurisdictions.[10] This principle is under threat in the decision in *O'Keeffe*, where, in his view, the Strasbourg Court dramatically expanded its jurisdiction and encroached upon national sovereignty.

Mr Justice Hardiman is particularly concerned that the Strasbourg Court entertained a claim that was not presented in the High Court or Supreme Court and that the judgment appeared to merge O'Keeffe's claims under direct state responsibility and vicarious liability. He argues that this reflects a departure from prior case law for the ECtHR. Mr Justice Hardiman's second concern centres on the use by the court of language of 'objective', 'core objective' and 'core grievance', suggesting that use of these terms implies that, at the discretion of the ECtHR, the simple word 'all' may mean 'some' or even 'at least one'.[11]

In response, Conor O'Mahony argues that several cases in ECHR jurisprudence support the proposition that where a remedy has been pursued, use of another remedy which has essentially the same objective is not required.[12] O'Mahony argues that the distinction between the vicarious liability and direct responsibility claims 'hinges on the question of how to separate out form and substance, and in particular, how narrowly to define the latter'.[13] Second, he observes that the Chamber judgment, cited and approved by the Grand Chamber, used the more normal formulation of 'essential grievance' and cited a lengthy list of decisions, which have developed this concept and clearly established that an applicant is free to choose between remedies. Additional case law not cited by the Chamber provides further support for this point, including case law involving Ireland.[14]

O'Mahony also notes that the decision of the Grand Chamber also rested on a separate and independent ground – the futility of domestic proceedings on the direct liability issue.[15] The ECtHR outlined in *Akdivar v. Turkey* that the rule that domestic remedies must be exhausted is 'based on the assumption, reflected in Article 13 of the Convention – with which it has close affinity – that there is an effective remedy available in respect of the alleged breach in the domestic system'.[16] O'Mahony's chapter notes that it is 'incumbent on the government claiming non-exhaustion to satisfy the Court that the remedy was an effective one available in theory and in practice at the relevant time, that is to say, that it was accessible, was one which was capable of providing redress in respect of the applicant's complaints and offered reasonable prospects of success'.[17] In *O'Keeffe*'s case, the Court concluded that Ireland had not demonstrated how it could be held directly responsible, noting that Mr Justice Hardiman in the Supreme Court rejected this argument *obiter* in the Supreme Court decision.[18] It will be interesting to see whether this decision impacts on the Irish Supreme Court's willingness to offer a remedy to victims of child sexual abuse, where the state is directly liable, through the avenue of constitutional torts or otherwise.

The Court's methodology in the historical application of the Convention

The contributions to this volume also discuss the Court's methodology. Mr Justice Hardiman is concerned that the court heard evidence from

Irish government reports not presented in argument before an Irish court.[19] O'Mahony counters that such evidence came in the form of the findings of state-established inquiries, namely the Carrigan Report and the Ryan Report, and can hardly be described as being of questionable provenance.[20] Indeed, the state relied on a number of passages from the Ryan Report to support its own case.[21]

It is also worth noting that the judgments of the Strasbourg Court disagreed more fundamentally on the appropriate method to apply Convention standards to the Irish legal system in 1973, the year of the relevant abuse.[22] The joint dissenting judgment criticised the majority's methodology, emphasising that Ireland's obligations should be assessed in the light of the facts and the Convention as understood in 1973 and as then in force. It concluded that there was no relevant case law in 1973 to support the majority's view of the positive obligation to protect, and prevent the ill-treatment of, children at school as requiring 'an appropriate framework of regulations encouraging complaints'. The joint dissent noted: '[i]t is Kafkaesque to blame the Irish authorities for not complying at the time with requirements and standards developed gradually by the case law of the Court only in subsequent decades'.[23]

The general interpretative methodology of the Court regarding the application of its evolutionary approach to historical cases thus remains unresolved. It is possible to agree with Mr Justice Charleton that 'the standards of today based on experience up to today are not necessarily how conduct in the past is fairly to be judged'.[24] However it does not necessarily follow that 'the Irish authorities could not reasonably have anticipated that the origin of such behaviour would be a head teacher with a mandated duty to protect children under his care'.[25] The triangular system between school, church and state provided no meaningful state oversight of children in church-run schools and presumed a high level of trust of church authorities and teachers. Mr Justice Charleton's judgment neglects to acknowledge that the need for potential state intervention was envisaged by the system of school inspectors, but this was not directed at all to the issue of abuse by a teacher towards his pupils. Even granting historical ignorance of the prevalence of such abuse in the 1970s, it seems unreasonable for Ireland to ignore oversight and regulation of the possibility of any physical or sexual abuse by teachers of pupils. While the court was unlikely to articulate a comprehensive interpretative methodology some broader guidance is welcome to avoid suggestions of ad hoc and ideological judicial activism.[26] In *O'Keeffe*, Judge Ziemele correctly concluded 'it is indeed high time that the Court acknowledged the issue of time and took care to explain clearly its methodology as regards the application of the Convention over time'.[27]

Government compensation scheme

One concern motivating Mr Justice Hardiman's criticism of the decision in *O'Keeffe v. Ireland* is the extent of the state's financial liability for the child sexual abuse committed by actors allegedly beyond the control of the state, in this instance, a primary school teacher in a church administered case.[28] The state has sought to narrow the extent of its liability arising out of the decision. In December 2014 the government authorised the State Claims Agency (SCA) to offer 'out of court' settlements to persons taking cases of school child sexual abuse against the state where their cases come within the terms of the ECHR judgment and are not statute barred.[29] The SCA has identified 210 cases of alleged child sexual abuse in schools, which are eligible for compensation Under the terms of the scheme, survivors of child sexual abuse will be offered up to €84,000, plus legal costs, to settle their claims but only where it is shown that the school authorities failed to take action in response to a complaint of abuse.[30] The scheme will also only apply to abuse that took place prior to 1991, when child protection measures were introduced, subject to the statute of limitations.

Louise O'Keeffe has since criticised the response of the government to the decision of the Strasbourg Court.[31] The primary limitation of the scheme is its arrangements 'only concern those cases of school child sexual abuse where there was a prior complaint about the teacher concerned to school authorities as these were the circumstances on which the ECtHR judgment was based'.[32] This approach seems contrary to the tenor of the decision in *O'Keeffe*. The Court determined that Ireland must have been aware of the risk of sexual abuse of children in 1973.[33] The Court considered that when relinquishing control of the education of children to non-state actors, Ireland should have been aware, given its inherent obligation to protect children, of potential risks to their safety if there was no appropriate framework of protection, including effective mechanisms for the detection and reporting of any ill-treatment.[34] It seems hard to reconcile this conclusion with a prerequisite for a victim to register a complaint before an obligation on the state to protect exists.

In addition, the scheme continues to be *ex gratia* in nature, such that the state does not accept its responsibility at a general or systemic level for the historical obligation to protection children from sexual or physical abuse. In discussing the scheme, Minister for Education Jan O'Sullivan said: 'While there is no legal obligation on the State to address the situation of these survivors, I believe that the approach adopted is fair and balanced in addressing the position of these survivors.'[35] Such an approach is adopted despite the apology from the minister 'to all those who were sexually abused as school children for the horrific abuse which was inflicted upon them, and for our collective failure to protect them'.[36]

Potential impact of the decision

The *O'Keeffe* case has the potential to impact the role of the ECtHR generally and make a specific impact on the prospects of litigation from victims and survivors of child abuse. As noted by Mr Justice Hardiman, the debate on the United Kingdom on the role of the Strasbourg Court has become fraught and dramatic, with suggestions that the United Kingdom may revise its involvement and interaction with that body.[37] It is hoped that the impact of the *O'Keeffe* case does not contribute to a further retrenchment of states' interaction with the court, but rather merely represents a further evolution of the interpretation of the Convention as the Court begins to address the historical application of the Convention and continues to clarify the positive obligations of states under Article 3. Mr Justice Hardiman raises concern that 'human rights law has not become too big, too boundless and above all too unitary'.[38] In regards to other Convention rights, the Strasbourg Court has been at pains to ensure an effective balance between the margin of appreciation of individual member states to the Convention and the evolving consensus around Convention rights and obligations.[39] The Court's approach to the issues raised in *O'Keeffe* should continue this trend to best maintain the Court's legitimacy and effectiveness in the view of as many member states as possible.

A second potential consequence to this decision is that it may provide an alternative to the challenging use of vicarious liability in Irish law for child sexual abuse.[40] Conor O'Mahony notes in this volume that while analogous case law both in England and Wales and in Canada had recently allowed victims of sexual abuse to recover against the employers of the abuser, Irish case law had not yet developed in this direction.[41] The state's liability in international human rights or constitutional law remains conceptually distinct from its vicarious liability for the control of a particular employee in tort law. A clear delineation of these bases of liability remains necessary. The potential benefit of the development in *O'Keeffe* may be that a human rights approach under Article 3 of the Convention provides redress where the state failed to implement sufficient measures to protect children in primary education, while the state's narrower vicarious liability remains unengaged. It may be that after the Strasbourg court's decision, plaintiffs may be encouraged to assert the state's positive obligations to provide a system of protection against the physical and sexual abuse of children through domestic constitutional law and seek to develop the state's obligations through constitutional tort.[42]

Conclusion

The decision in *O'Keeffe* imposed a positive duty on Ireland to protect children from abuse in primary education. Its impact may extend to the Magdalene laundries or other similar cases of child abuse going to Strasbourg.[43] While those contexts are distinguishable, any such applications may nevertheless involve a similar historical analysis of the application of the Convention standards, so the methodology employed by the Court and level of knowledge of harm imputed to Ireland in *O'Keeffe* will be relevant and remains in need of clarification. It may be that the impact of *O'Keeffe* will extend beyond situations of child sexual abuse and shape the methodology and positive obligations jurisprudence of the Court. The discussion by Mr Justice Hardiman and Conor O'Mahony demonstrates that any such impact may well be contentious.

Notes

1 *O'Keeffe v. Ireland* [2014] ECHR 96.
2 *Ibid.*, at [26].
3 *L.O'K v. LH & Ors* [2006] IEHC 13.
4 *O'Keeffe v. Hickey* [2009] 2 IR 302 at 343.
5 *Ibid.*, 373–378.
6 *O'Keeffe v. Ireland* (n. 1) at [69]–[74].
7 *Ibid.*, at [162]; J. Gallen, 'O'Keeffe v. Ireland: The Liability of States for Failure to Provide an Effective System for the Detection and Prevention of Child Sexual Abuse in Education' (2015) 78(1) *Modern Law Review* 151–163.
8 *O'Keeffe v. Ireland* (n. 1) at [66].
9 *Ibid.* at [185].
10 Hardiman, Chapter 6, this volume.
11 *Ibid.*
12 Cases cited in support of this finding included *O'Reilly v. Ireland*, 24196/94, 22 January 1996; *TW v. Malta*, 25644/94, 29 April 1999 at [34]; *Moreira Barbosa v. Portugal*, 65681/01, 29 April 2004; *Jelicic v. Bosnia and Herzegovina*, 41183/02, 15 November 2005; *Shkalla v. Albania*, 26866/05, 10 May 2011 at [61]; *Leja v. Latvia*, 71072/01, 14 June 2011 at [46].
13 O'Mahony, Chapter 7, this volume.
14 *Ibid.*; *O'Keeffe v. Ireland*, 28 January 2014 (Grand Chamber) at [109]; see, e.g., *Airey v. Ireland*, 6289/73, 9 October 1979 at [23]; *Croke v. Ireland*, 33267/96, 15 June 1999.

15 O'Mahony (n. 13).
16 *Akdivar v. Turkey*, 21893/93, 16 September 1996, at [65].
17 *Selmouni v. France* 25803/94, 28 July 1999 at [76].
18 [2009] 2 IR 344.
19 Hardiman (n. 10).
20 O'Mahony (n. 13).
21 *O'Keeffe v. Ireland* (n. 1) at [133]
22 Gallen (n. 7).
23 Joint partly dissenting opinion of Judges Zupancic, Gyulumyan, Kalaydjieva, De Gaetano and Wojtyczek at [9].
24 Partly dissenting opinion of Charleton J. at [36].
25 *Ibid.*
26 A. Mowbray, 'The Creativity of the European Court of Human Rights' (2005) 5(1) *Human Rights Law Review* 57–79, 71.
27 Concurring opinion of Judge Ziemele at [1].
28 Hardiman (n. 10).
29 Action Plan, Information submitted by the Government of Ireland 28 July 2015, para. 17.
30 *Ibid.*
31 'School abuse survivors offered up to €84,000 in cases against State', *Irish Times* (16 December 2014).
32 '28 July, 2015 – Government approves approach for those who discontinued their legal proceedings but who come within the terms of the ECtHR Judgment in Louise O'Keeffe' available at www.education.ie/en/Press-Events/Press-Releases/2015–Press-Releases/PR-%202015–%2007–%2028.html (accessed 18 August 2015).
33 *O'Keeffe v. Ireland* (n. 1) at [69]–[74]
34 *Ibid.* at [162]; *E and Others v. the United Kingdom* [2002] ECHR 769 at [99].
35 '210 cases of sexual abuse in schools eligible for compensation', *Irish Times* (28 July 2015).
36 *Ibid.*
37 'Tories plan to withdraw UK from European convention on human rights', *The Guardian* (3 October 2014).
38 Hardiman (n. 10).
39 P. van Dijk et al. (eds), *Theory and Practice of the European Convention on Human Rights* (4th edn) (Intersentia, 2006) pp. 1055–1056
40 Gallen (n. 7) 161–162.
41 O'Mahony (n. 13).
42 *Ibid.*; C. O'Mahony 'State Liability for Abuse in Primary Schools: Systemic Failure and O'Keeffe v. Hickey' (2009) 28(3) *Irish Educational Studies* 315–331
43 'Magdalene survivors are still waiting for restorative justice', *Irish Times* (6 February 2014).

6

The jurisdiction of the European Court of Human Rights and the case of *O'Keeffe v. Hickey*

The Hon. Mr Justice Adrian Hardiman

Introduction

The law school of Dublin City University is described as the School of 'Law and Government'. This brings into focus two things, which are obviously closely connected but which the practitioners of both law and government, and the Constitution itself, regard as radically contrasted. Article 6 of the Constitution provides:

6.1 All powers of government, legislative, executive and judicial derive, under God, from the people ...
6.2 These powers of government are exercisable *only* by or on the authority of the organs of State established by this Constitution.

These provisions establish a quite rigid separation of powers, closely modelled on the American precedent. There is extensive discussion of the incidents and consequences of this separation in the judgments of the Supreme Court in both the *Sinnott* and *TD* cases, which I need not repeat here.[1]

Nevertheless, the great and perhaps the very first, political scientist, Alexis de Tocqueville, in his ground-breaking study of the United States published almost one hundred and eighty years ago, gave pride of place to the aspect of the new Nation which fascinated Europeans: it was, or appeared to them to be, a pure democracy. Nevertheless, de Tocqueville observed: 'Scarcely any political question arises in the United States that is not resolved sooner or later into a judicial question.'[2]

I think this observation is at least as true nowadays as it was when first made. But the point has to be emphasised that in Ireland the courts have firmly rejected such a role. This rejection takes two complimentary forms. First, the Courts have rejected interference in the judicial function by the political arms of government. This is seen in cases such as the *Sinn Féin Funds* case and *McMahon v. The Attorney General*.³ On the other hand, the Courts have resisted the temptation to discharge the functions reserved to the other organs of government, even in circumstances where to extend their powers in this way might have attracted widespread popular endorsement. This is illustrated, *inter alia* by the *Sinnott* and *T.D.* cases. The Courts have also rejected attempts to create zones of non-justiciability in which gravely adverse findings can be made about individuals without their having recourse to the Courts, as in *Maguire v. Ardagh*.⁴

I have sketched in very broad brush terms the Irish view of the separation of powers as a necessity of a democratic society by way of background to some remarks about a recent development in the jurisprudence of the European Court of Human Rights. Since the Convention has been given a particular domestic role in Irish law by a statute of 2003, this raises the intrinsically political question of the content of the law, which the Courts are to enforce.

The Strasbourg Court interprets implements and enforces the European Convention for the Protection of Human Rights and Fundamental Freedoms.⁵ The Convention was, at its origins in 1950, a treaty between the non-Communist countries of Europe. It reflected the concern of European nations to ensure that the despotic systems of the Third Reich and of Stalin's Russia were never extended into post-war Europe. In all countries – about fifty – of the Council of Europe, the Convention now has some, but varying, domestic legal status. It is not just a part of the international obligations of each such state but is actually part of their own domestic legal order in one way or another. In Ireland, domestic effect has been given to the Convention since 2003 by the Human Rights Act of that year.⁶

As has often been observed, notably by Lord Sumption of the United Kingdom Supreme Court last year, the Convention is unique among the many national and international declarations of human rights in providing for its enforcement by an international court.⁷ This Court has the right to hear individual petitions, and not merely state complaints, and to make decisions, which the contracting states have bound themselves to put into effect. In Ireland, this obligation is met by the European Convention on Human Rights Act, 2003 which is:

> An Act to enable *further effect* to be given, *subject to the Constitution*, to certain provisions of the Convention for the protection of human rights and fundamental freedoms done at Rome on the 4th day of November, 1950 and certain protocols thereto.⁸

Ireland ratified the Convention in 1953, which did not involve giving it binding legal effect in Ireland. It was, however, frequently referred to and followed as in the leading tort case of *Ó Domhnaill v. Merrick*.[9]

The need to give the Convention domestic effect arose not from anything within the Convention itself, or any development of a case law, but from the Good Friday Agreement of 1998, a political instrument. There, in the year the United Kingdom passed the Human Rights Act, 1998, the Irish government agreed to 'ensure at least an equivalent level of protection of human rights as will pertain in Northern Ireland'.[10] This is a political and not a legal, imperative.

It is technically incorrect to say that the Convention has been 'incorporated into Irish law'. Instead the statute provides, only for 'further effect' to be given to the Convention in Ireland 'to the Constitution'.[11] (For a critique of this form of domestication of the Convention, see *Kelly on the Constitution*.[12]) It is therefore said that Ireland has given effect to the Convention in a sub-constitutional and interpretative fashion.

It is easy to see why this was done. At one level, this particular and somewhat limited form of incorporation avoided the need for a constitutional amendment by referendum. There is no prospect of conflict with the Constitution because where there is dissonance between that instrument and the Convention, the Constitution will take precedence. Equally, by s. 5(2) of the Act, the operation of it cannot affect the validity of a statutory provision. By s. 4 of the Act, the courts must take judicial notice of the Convention itself and of any declaration, decision, advisory opinion or judgment of the Court of Human Rights, and certain other bodies.

The Courts, in interpreting and applying any statutory provision or rule of law shall 'insofar as is possible' do so in a manner consistent with the state's Convention obligations. Every organ of state, is obliged to perform its functions in a manner compatible with those obligations 'subject to any statutory provision or rule of law'. It would be unfair to say that the form of the 2003 Act is referable exclusively to a desire to avoid a referendum. In the debate on the Bill, which became the Act of 2003, on 18 February 2003, the Minister for Justice of the day made it clear that the Convention could not simply be incorporated into Irish law for a number of reasons, which he described as follows:

> First, Ireland has a Constitution and constitutional jurisprudence which, are in most respects far more affirmative of the rights of the individual than the European Convention on Human Rights.[13]

This view is based on a report for the Law Commission of a committee under the chairmanship of Mr Justice Gerard Hogan.

Second, the European Convention was not designed to be a constitution of any country but an international agreement to which countries would subscribe. This was not to be a constitutional document. Third, in our proceedings in this House and Irish society generally, we proceed on the basis that *this country is a sovereign, constitutional, independent republic and that our rights are those determined by the people through the Constitution and not otherwise*. It would be as impermissible for the Irish Legislature without recourse to the people to delegate the exposition of human rights in Ireland to the court in Strasbourg (without a constitutional amendment) as it would have been, for instance, for a pious Government in the 1930s to defer, say, to the Vatican, to Papal encyclicals or to the decisions of the Roman curia on such matters. ... it would be as impermissible for the Irish Legislature to bring forward in Ireland an authoritative source of human rights which had the effect of invalidating Irish legislation or overriding the function of the courts under the Constitution to interpret it or apply it amongst the citizens as that scenario would have been impermissible in retrospect.

The State only has the capacity to subscribe to the Strasbourg convention because it is compatible with the Constitution. ... The State and the organs of Government have no right to accede to an international agreement at variance with the Constitution. Once one starts from this, much becomes obvious. Once one starts from the error that seems to infuse most of the criticism of this Bill, that the Strasbourg convention is up there, that down the pecking order comes the Constitution, and further down is legislation, one falls into the error into which two Deputies have fallen, namely, that this is in some sense an inadequate incorporation of the Convention. It is not.[14]

What the minister said derives support from the jurisprudence of the Convention itself. The Convention is based on the principles of subsidiarity and solidarity. The leading textbook, *Jacobs, White & Ovey* said as follows in 2010:

> Subsidiarity refers to the role of the Strasbourg Court as *secondary* to the institutions of the national legal systems in adjudicating claims that convention rights have been violated. It is partly for this reason that a complaint cannot be made to the Strasbourg Court until *all* efforts to resolve the dispute have been undertaken *within the national legal order*. This principle also explains why the Strasbourg Court does not regard itself as a Court of Appeal from decisions of institutions within the national order.[15]

Interestingly, a very similar emphasis on the need for the Convention to coexist with national sovereignty, and for that coexistence to find a legal expression, is contained in Lord Justice Laws Hamlyn lectures of November 2013.[16]

This principle, at least until recently, was key to the powers of the Strasbourg Court and to the incorporation in various ways of the Convention by the different states of the Council of Europe. The view of the learned authors is based, almost inevitably, on Article 35.1 of the Convention which, stating the powers of the Court, lays down: 'The Court may *only* deal with the matter after *all* domestic remedies have been exhausted, according to the generally recognised principles of international law.'[17]

Accordingly, the textbook already cited concludes: 'Applicants *must* have raised before the national authorities, if it is possible to do so, the *particular* complaints which they wish to make before the Court. If they raise only some of their complaints, *only* those will be admissible.'[18] It will be noted that the requirement that *all* domestic remedies be exhausted is an essential requirement of the 'only' jurisdiction of the Court to deal with a particular matter. Moreover, apart from this jurisdictional requirement set out in Article 35.1 of the Convention, Article 35.4 provides: 'The Court *shall* reject any application which it considers inadmissible under this Article. It may do so at any stage of the proceedings.'

This is manifestly a mandatory requirement. An application in relation to which *all* domestic remedies have not been exhausted *must* be rejected by the Strasbourg Court. That Court, to quote a 2009 case, simply *cannot* examine a complaint in relation to which all domestic remedies have not been exhausted.[19] These provisions are of the greatest importance in considering the nature of the Strasbourg jurisdiction, and are the basis of the academic remarks about its secondary and subsidiary nature, quoted above.

Relevant case law

This view of the Strasbourg jurisdiction was strongly reaffirmed in a case called *A v. The United Kingdom*, in 2009.[20] There, a number of detained persons complained both of the fact of their detention and of the conditions in which they were detained. But they had made no attempt to raise the latter point before any domestic tribunals. While time does not permit extensive citation of the decisions, the Court noted that each applicant 'had at his disposal' remedies under administrative and civil law to challenge his conditions of detention. But the applicants did not make use of these remedies 'and did not therefore comply with the requirement under Article 35 to exhaust domestic remedies'.[21] The Court continued:

It follows that the Court *cannot* examine the applicants' complaints about their conditions of detention nor can it, in consequence, state the conditions of detention into account in forming a global assessment of the applicant's treatment for the purposes of Article 3.[22]

But the Court significantly departed from this approach, which appears to be mandatory, in dealing with a recent Irish case, *O'Keeffe v. Ireland*.[23] In discussing the implications of the procedures adopted in this case for the Strasbourg jurisdiction, I am making no comment one way or the other on the merits of the plaintiff's case. I am simply concerned with the light the case throws on what appears to me to be a considerable expansion of the Strasbourg Court's jurisdiction.

O'Keeffe v. Hickey was a case where the plaintiff had contended that she had been abused by a teacher in a Catholic run national school while she was a child. By 'Catholic run' I mean a school which, pursuant to the scheme operated in Ireland since national education was established in the 1830s, the state paid for the delivery of primary education, and paid the teachers in particular, but schools were under the management of the local Catholic clergyman and the patronage of the local Catholic Bishop. Similar arrangements exist in relation to other denominations. The abusing teacher was not himself a cleric. This peculiar system whereby the state paid for national education but resigned any control of it to clerical bodies is fully discussed in the Supreme Court judgments of Fennelly J. and myself in *O'Keeffe v. Hickey*.[24]

The plaintiff brought proceedings alleging that the state was directly liable in negligence for her abuse. She also separately claimed that they were vicariously responsible for the acts of the teacher. Her claim relating to direct state liability was dismissed by the High Court in 2005 as was the claim based on vicariously liability. The plaintiff appealed the latter decision – the dismissal of the claim in vicarious liability – but did not appeal the dismissal of her claim based on direct state responsibility. This aspect was, accordingly never dealt with by the Supreme Court. That Court did however dismiss her claim against the state based on vicarious liability.[25]

It is noteworthy that the plaintiff never sued the clerical manager of the school, or the Episcopal patron, or any church body. If they had been sued together with the state, the latter on behalf of the taxpayers might have claimed contribution or indemnity but if damages for the abuse are awarded against the state then, by reason of s.16 of the Civil Liability Act, 1961, satisfaction by the state of any damages awarded for the original tort 'shall discharge the others [i.e. the current wrongdoers] whether such others have been sued to judgment or not'. In other words, there is a significant risk, by reason of the nature of the plaintiff's proceedings that the taxpayer will, alone, have to discharge the damages by reason of the exclusion of the liability of other possible wrongdoers. The same risk would arise in any other case similarly constituted.

When the plaintiff lost her appeal based on vicarious liability, she made a complaint to the Strasbourg Court. She claimed direct state responsibility, the cause of action, which had been dismissed in 2005 and not appealed. The case was declared admissible on 26 June 2012 and a hearing took place on 6 March 2013. Having considered the plaintiff's claim, including the deployment of a considerable body of material, which had not been referred to before the High Court, the state took an objection under Article 35, discussed above. They asked the Court to revisit the decision that the case was admissible, on the basis of non-exhaustion of domestic remedies. They failed in this application by a majority decision.[26]

Accordingly, the Court was prepared to entertain a claim which had never been taken by the applicant, who was represented at all times, to the Supreme Court. It thus assumed a jurisdiction, and made a finding adverse to the state, in a case where domestic remedies have not even been attempted to be exhausted. The applicant's claim before the Strasbourg Court was the same claim as was dismissed by the High Court for no evidence. That ruling was not appealed to the Supreme Court. Moreover, in the majority judgment at Strasbourg, at paragraph 69–90, references made to evidence, which was presented in argument before the Strasbourg Court, but never referred before the domestic tribunal.[27]

It is of course not in accordance with established practice that novel evidence, not referenced before a domestic tribunal, is introduced before the Strasbourg Court with a view to establishing a claim, which the applicant pleaded without deploying the new material, lost, and did not appeal to the Supreme Court. In the course of the dissenting judgments, it was pointed out that the law which binds the Strasbourg Court through Article 35 has been:

> elided in favour of the Court now being asked to decide an issue of negligence which was abandoned by the applicant. On advice, the applicant appealed only on vicarious responsibility. The Court should not take on the task of analysing facts which were not but could have been presented before the domestic tribunals. Every government has the entitlement to debate such evidence before the domestic forums of justice. That debate would necessarily have been through the examination of witnesses and the scrutiny of any reports on which the founded opinions. That entitlement is central to Article 35. It has been by-passed.[28]

New thinking at Strasbourg

The majority of the Court proceeded on the basis that the applicant had only a single grievance: the assaults perpetrated many years before, and the state's direct responsibility for them. However, Mr Justice Charlton was surely correct in suggesting that there was nothing essentially similar about a state defendant being liable for its *own* failure and a state defendant being liable despite carefully training employees because the wrong of the employee is within the scope of the employment relationship.[29] But the decision appears also at odds with the long-established jurisprudence of the Strasbourg Court itself. Apart from the English case already cited one might refer to *Akdivar v. Turkey*:

> The Court recalls that the rule of exhaustion of domestic remedies referred to in the Convention *obliges those seeking to bring their case against the State before an international judicial or arbiter organ to use first the remedies provided by the national legal system.* Consequently, States are dispensed from answering before an international body further acts before they have had an opportunity to put matters right through their own legal system. This rule is based on the assumption, reflected in the Convention ... that there is an effective remedy available in respect of the alleged breach in the domestic system whether or not the provisions of the Convention are incorporated in national law. *In this way it is an important aspect of the principle that the machinery of protection established by the Convention is subsidiary to the national systems of protecting human rights.*[30]

An earlier example of the same principle is *Handyside v. UK*.[31] It is worth paying close attention to how precisely the Court avoided the consequences of its own longstanding jurisprudence. It held, at paragraph 110 that 'the applicants' core grievances' concerned the state's responsibility for the sexual assaults as well the availability of a civil remedy against the state in that respect. It held that it was 'reasonable' to pursue a remedy for this grievance on the basis of vicarious liability only. It did concede that: '[t]he basis of State responsibility invoked domestically *was* different to that pursued before the [Strasbourg] Court'.[32]

This concession in itself seems to me fatally to undermine the ECHR's jurisdiction and it understates the position. The plaintiff did claim direct state liability in the High Court. She was non-suited and did not appeal that. As Mr Justice Charlton said she abandoned that claim. The Strasbourg Court said that she was entitled to pursue the vicarious liability action: 'without being required when the route reasonably chosen proved unsuccessful to exhaust another remedy with essentially the same objective'.[33]

Article 35 does not appear to me to speak of 'objectives' or 'core objectives'. It speaks of remedies and requires that 'all' of those should be exhausted. Accordingly, the passage thus quoted appears to me to amount to an attempted amendment of the Charter. Article 35 does not speak exhausting one reasonable remedy: it speaks in terms of exhausting 'all' domestic remedies. Equally, the amorphous concept of 'core grievance' destroys the rigour of the Convention, and empties Article 35 of any specific meaning: there must be specific complaints and once these are formulated in specific terms the question of whether 'all' domestic remedies have been exhausted can be examined.

This seems to me to be saying that, at the discretion of the Strasbourg Court, the simple word 'all' may mean 'some' or even 'at least one'. That is manifestly false but it represents a form of forensic thinking which is not uncommon. Whenever I come across such an argument I am reminded of the well-known passage from Lord Atkin's judgment in *Liversidge v. Anderson*.[34] There, a statute permitted the Home Secretary to intern a person if he had reason to believe certain things. The Crown submitted that that form of words meant 'if the Home Secretary thought he had reason to believe'. The House of Lords upheld this very odd view and Lord Atkin alone dissented. He said:

> I know of only one authority which might justify the suggested method of construction: 'when I use a word' Humpty Dumpty said in rather a scornful tone, 'it means just what I choose it to mean, neither more nor less'. 'The question is' said Alice, 'whether you can make words mean so many different things'. 'The question is' said Humpty Dumpty, 'which is to be master – that's all' (*Alice through the Looking Glass*, Chapter 6). After all this long discussion the question is whether the words 'if a man has' can mean 'if a man thinks he has' I am of the opinion that they cannot, and that the case should be decided accordingly.[35]

Nor is the foregoing merely a technical or verbal exercise. The question of whether state liability, if any, is direct or vicarious may have many consequences, which are all too real. The centre on the question of whether the tax payer alone has to discharge any damages awarded or whether other responsible persons or bodies can be compelled to contribute in the case of mass claims, this question, so far from being merely technical, may be very significant indeed to the public finances.

As far as I have been able to discover the term 'core grievance', which was key to the Strasbourg Court departing from the previous jurisprudence, was used for the first time in *O'Keeffe*'s case. It has no jurisprudential basis that I can find in the Courts output. Moreover, it does not feature in the Courts own 2011 'Guide on admissibility criteria'.[36] This points out that the obligation to exhaust domestic remedies is part of general international law and applies to all other human rights conventions. It also acknowledges that the Court is intended to be subsidiary to the national systems so that it is appropriate that the national courts should initially have the opportunity to determine questions regarding the compatibility of domestic law with the Convention.[37] It acknowledges in the same paragraph that if the case goes to Strasbourg 'the Court should have the benefit of the views of the national courts, as being in direct and continuous contact with the vital forces of their countries'.

At paragraph 51 it is pointed out that a convention right need not be raised explicitly in domestic proceedings provided that it is raised 'at least in substance'. That is 'he must have raised arguments to the same or like effect on the basis of domestic law in order to have given the national courts the opportunity to address the alleged breach in the first place'. This, of course, was precisely what did not happen in O'Keeffe.

The end of subsidiarity?

If the Strasbourg Court assumes the responsibility for making direct findings against the state, where there has been no exhaustion of domestic remedies, then the Convention will have changed in a radical and indeed a revolutionary way. The Convention the subject of the 2003 Act was undoubtedly a secondary and subsidiary instrument, which in strong and mandatory terms required an exhaustion of domestic remedies before it could be resorted too. If there is now to be a right simply to *bypass* national courts or any of them, then having regard to the role of those Courts in *Bunreacht na hÉreann*, very serious questions might arise.

There is no doubt that, in many areas, the Strasbourg Convention has had very desirable affects. It is very much to be hoped that difficulties such as the one I have outlined can be resolved with mutual respect and dialogue. But it is necessary to emphasise that respect must be mutual and that dialogue involves listening as well as declaiming. One would wish to avoid the somewhat fraught debate about the utility of the Convention, which takes place in the United Kingdom. At a legal level this is represented by the tensions between the views of such luminaries as Lord Bingham and Lord Neuberger on the one hand and Lord Justice Laws in his well-known 2013 lectures on the other. One would also wish to avoid such extreme circumstances as were found in the English case of *Chester*.[38] There, the Attorney General of England and Wales, on behalf of the government very dramatically, invited the UK Supreme

Court not to apply the principles in two Strasbourg decisions, *Hirst* (2005) and *Scappola* (2013), relating to prisoners' voting rights.[39]

But difficulties of the sort that led to these notorious conflicts in a neighbouring and quite similar jurisdiction will not be avoided without discretion, deep thought, and a large measure of restraint on the part of all relevant parties. The very remarkable American Supreme Court Justice Antonin Scalia famously remarked that any judge who takes his or her oath of office seriously will find himself deciding cases against his personal preferences very frequently. The law is the law and the judges generally do not have power to repeal or amend it. But one is not quite sure if this truism holds sway in Strasbourg. Certainly, the judges there seem to me to have succeeded in sucking the meaning out of Article 35(1) and 35(4) of the Convention. It would not be a proper proceeding for a national judge to amend national law and I cannot see that it is proper for a group of international judges to amend an essentially political agreement by which they themselves are bound either.

Reading certain Strasbourg judgments one wonders if human rights law has not become too big, too boundless and above all too unitary. Much of the difficulty that arises with Strasbourg decisions is that Court's tendency to assume that 'one size fits all'. The Convention is now subscribed to by forty-seven countries ranging from Ireland in the West to the other side of the Black Sea and to the Urals in the East. These countries are very diverse in history and tradition and in particular in how solidly the rule of law is established. It is perhaps not often enough stated that Ireland is the Republic among the Council of Europe countries in which the rule of law has been the longest established without tragic intervals caused by the Nazi and Stalinist Terrors and other historical events. The Convention is, as its wording plainly establishes, a statement of general principles. If one attempts to build on this foundation an identical, detailed legal and administrative framework, to apply to utterly disparate countries, the effort will almost certainly be in vain.

It would be good to hear from the Strasbourg Court that it embraces and upholds the principle that the jurisdiction it exercises is subsidiary to the national systems and secondary to them. This would merely involve the repetition of what has been said on several occasions in the cases I have referred to and others. If that does not prove possible, then we have to adapt, slowly, discretely and with great thought, to the fact that the basis on which we incorporated the Convention seems to have been based on the misunderstanding that the Convention was of the nature described in *Jacobs and Ovey,* and that role of the member states was fully acknowledged. One very much hopes that such extreme events as a national government asking a court not to follow Strasbourg decisions, or an Irish person aggrieved by a Strasbourg decision claiming that the Act of 2003 was enacted on a false basis and that only a referendum could incorporate the Strasbourg jurisdiction. With patience, diplomacy and respect, which must be, *and be expressed to be*, mutual, such extreme circumstances will be avoided.

Domestic thinking on human rights

I have to say that there are aspects of our domestic thinking on human rights which are not at all clear to me. For example, some time subsequent to June 2012 (when the *O'Keeffe* case was found to be admissible) the Irish government took their Article 35 objection to the admissibility of the case and argued it trenchantly. The state was represented by solicitor and counsel and by an official of the Attorney General's office. But when the eventual judgment, adverse to the Irish State, was handed down, it was publicly adopted by important officials of the very state who had objected to the Court's jurisdiction, and in particular by a then member of the Cabinet.

This reaction suggested that Ireland had succeeded in a case rather than having an apparently soundly based objection to the Strasbourg Court's jurisdiction dismissed out of hand for reasons which do not appear coherent. It was for this reason, I believe, that the radical nature of the expansion of the Strasbourg Court's jurisdiction did not emerge as a topic for public discussion. It is obviously in the interest of the state that there should be a greater measure of consistency among its various representatives. One would not like to think that the state might raise a similar objection in another case and be met by a citation of the official reactions I have mentioned.

Second, the state possesses a Public Service unit to deal with human rights. As I understand it, it is located in the Department of Foreign Affairs. It is simply not clear to me what that unit's function is and whether it operates to defend the state against claims made against it in an international forum, or to assist persons making such claims or complaints, or both. It seems desirable to have some transparency in this regard.

I view the proceedings of the Strasbourg Court, in general, with an admiring and respectful eye but that is not a reason for failing to take appropriate notice of what it appears to me to be, on the face of it, a unilateral expansion of that Court's jurisdiction *vis-a-vis* members of the Council of Europe from whom it derives its only jurisdiction. It appears to me that the effect of what has been done is to amend, or deprive of meaning, the very Articles of the Convention from which the 'secondary and subsidiary' nature of the Strasbourg jurisdiction derives. But this instrument to which our 2003 Statute relates is the Convention as it then stood without any form of judicial amendment or elision.

Perhaps for the reasons I have suggested, the development I have discussed has largely escaped discussion in Ireland. This is ironic because, of course, the Strasbourg Court's new departure took place in addressing an objection raised by the Irish State. I have no doubt that that objection was properly taken and was competently argued on the instructions of the Attorney General. Its rejection, on what appeared to me to be very inadequate grounds, and the consequence of that rejection, appear to me to require more discussion than they have received. In this discussion, one must always remember the truism that, as in all human affairs, we are much more likely to be dealing with confusion, or ambiguities in expression, than with any form of conspiracy at illegitimate and revolutionary change.

Notes

This chapter was presented as the keynote address at the inaugural School of Law and Government conference Judges, Politics and the Irish Constitution, 4 September 2014.

1 *Sinnott v. Minister for Education* [2001] 2 IR 505; *TD v. Minister for Education* [2001] 4 IR 259.
2 A. de Tocqueville, *Democracy in America and Two Essays on America* (Penguin, 2003 [1835]) p. 315.
3 *Buckley v. Attorney General* [1950] IR 67; *McMahon v. Attorney General* [1972] IR 69; (1972) 106 ILTR 89.
4 *Maguire v. Ardagh* [2002] 1 IR 385.
5 Convention for the Protection of Human Rights and Fundamental Freedoms, 213 UNTS 222, entered into force 3 September 1953, as amended by Protocols Nos 3, 5, 8 and 11 which entered into force on 21 September 1970, 20 December 1971, 1 January 1990 and 1 November 1998 respectively.
6 European Convention on Human Rights Act, 2003.
7 Lord Sumpton, 'The Limits of Law' 27th Sultan Azlan Shah Lecture, Kuala Lumpur, 20 November 2013, 7.
8 European Convention on Human Rights Act 2003.
9 *Ó Domhnaill v. Merrick* [1984] IR 151.
10 The Northern Ireland Peace Agreement (the Good Friday Agreement) 10 April 1998, Human Rights, section 10.
11 European Convention on Human Rights Act 2003.
12 G. W. Hogan and G. F. Whyte, *JM Kelly: The Irish Constitution* (4th edn, LexisNexis Butterworths, 2004) pp. 797–801.
13 Select Committee on Justice, Equality, Defence and Women's Rights Debate,

European Convention on Human Rights Bill, 2001: Committee Stage, 18 February 2003, Minister for Justice, Equality and Law Reform (Mr McDowell).
14 *Ibid.*
15 R. White and C. Ovey, *Jacobs, White & Ovey: The European Convention on Human Rights* (OUP, 2010) p. 84.
16 J. Laws, *The Common Law Constitution* (Hamlyn Lectures) (CUP, 2014).
17 Convention for the Protection of Human Rights and Fundamental Freedoms (n. 5).
18 White and Ovey (n. 15) p. 35.
19 *A v. United Kingdom* [2009] ECHR 301, at [133].
20 *Ibid.*
21 *Ibid.*, at [133].
22 *Ibid.*
23 *O'Keeffe v. Ireland* [2014] ECHR 96.
24 *O'Keeffe v. Hickey* [2009] 2 IR 302.
25 *Ibid.*, 310.
26 Decision on admissibility delivered by a Chamber, *O'Keeffe v. Ireland*, 35810/09, 26 June 2012; *O'Keeffe v. Ireland* (n. 23) at [99]–[103].
27 The evidence included the report of the Carrigan Committee, 1931; the Cussen (1936) and Kennedy (1970) reports on reformatory and industrial schools; the Report of the Commission to Inquire into Child Abuse (the Ryan Report 2009); the Ferns Report (2005); the Murphy Report (2009); the Cloynes Report (2011).
28 Partly Dissenting Opinion of Judge Charleton, at [9].
29 *Ibid.*, at [10].
30 *Akdivar v. Turkey* (1997) 23 EHRR 143.
31 *Handyside v. United Kingdom* [1976] ECHR 5.
32 *O'Keeffe v. Ireland* (n. 23) at [110].
33 *Ibid.*
34 *Liversidge v. Anderson* (1941) 33 AER 207 at 245.
35 *Ibid.*
36 Council of Europe & European Court of Human Rights, *Practical Guide on Admissibility Criteria* (2011).
37 *Ibid.*, para. 45.
38 *R (Chester) v. Secretary of State for Justice* [2013] UKSC 63.
39 *Hirst v. United Kingdom (No. 2)* (2005) 42 EHRR 41; *Scoppola v. Italy (No. 3)* (2013) 56 EHRR 19.

7

Subsidiarity of ECHR and *O'Keeffe v. Ireland*: a response to Mr Justice Hardiman

Conor O'Mahony

Introduction

Mr Justice Hardiman has written a detailed and searching critique of the judgment of the Grand Chamber of the European Court of Human Rights (ECtHR) in *O'Keeffe v. Ireland*.[1] Essentially, his argument is that the ECtHR should never have adjudicated on the merits of the case at all, but should have declared it inadmissible for failure to exhaust domestic remedies. The reason given is that the basis on which the Grand Chamber decided the case (i.e. direct state liability for failure to implement child protection mechanisms in primary schools) differed from the matter pursued to the Irish Supreme Court (i.e. vicarious liability of the state for the tortious conduct of the school principal). The former issue, while raised in the High Court, was not appealed; thus, it is argued that domestic remedies were not exhausted. Mr Justice Hardiman takes issue with the notion of 'essential grievance' that was relied on by both the Chamber and Grand Chamber in declaring the decision admissible. In this brief reply, I will respectfully submit that 'essential grievance', while well developed in the jurisprudence of the ECtHR, is only one route to admissibility. The decision of the Grand Chamber also rested on a separate and independent ground – namely the futility of domestic proceedings on the direct liability issue. I will argue, *contra* Mr Justice Hardiman, that the reasons given by the Chamber and Grand Chamber were each sufficient in themselves to declare the case admissible, and that the decision was entirely in line with the jurisprudence of the ECtHR on admissibility.

Sufficient to have raised the 'essential grievance'

From the outset of her litigation, Louise O'Keeffe had a simple aim in mind: to prove that responsibility for her abuse did not rest solely with her abuser. He had been allowed to remain in a teaching post over a period of several years during which he committed at least 386 counts of abuse on at least twenty-one girls. Louise O'Keeffe was one of the later victims, and her abuse occurred after complaints had been made against the abuser by the parents of another victim. In these circumstances, Louise O'Keeffe passionately believed that the state bore partial responsibility by virtue of its failure to control the abuser or detect or prevent the abuse.

As in any litigation, an end goal must be translated into a cause of action. In the domestic proceedings, three causes of action were raised. The first was an action for vicarious liability: the state, as the school principal's employer, should bear vicarious liability for his tortious action in assaulting the girls. Analogous case law both in England and Wales[2] and in Canada[3] had recently allowed victims of sexual abuse to recover against the employers of the abuser, but Irish case law had not yet developed in this direction. This action was rejected by the High Court[4] and Supreme Court[5] on the basis that although the state paid his salary, the principal was employed by the local school manager. Although this finding was sufficient to dispose of the case in itself, Hardiman J. (with whom Murray CJ agreed) expressed the view in the Supreme Court that the conduct of the school principal was outside the scope of his employment – an unauthorised act rather than an unauthorised mode of performing an authorised act – and that accordingly his employer would not be held liable for it in any event.[6]

Two other arguments were presented in the High Court that focused on direct rather than vicarious liability of the state. First, it was argued that the state was guilty of negligence for failing to put in place measures that would have prevented and detected the abuse in Dunderrow National School. As a matter of domestic law, this ground was more tenuous, since no previous case law had clearly established either a duty of care or relevant standard of care in this context. Moreover, as noted by the Grand Chamber in its judgment in *O'Keeffe*, the interposition of the school manager to the exclusion of state control in national schools appeared to be incompatible with the existence of any duty of care existing on the part of the state in Irish negligence law, since the necessary proximity would not have existed.[7] In the event, the claim was nonsuited by the High Court.

An additional ground referred in broad terms to '[t]he constitutional role and responsibility of the state defendants in the provision of primary education arising under Article 42 of the Constitution and the measures which the second-named defendant, the minister, had adopted and the steps put in place to discharge those responsibilities'. In essence, this was a different version of the negligence claim, albeit relying on the Constitution rather than the law of torts. The High Court rejected this constitutional claim on the basis that an adequate remedy for any breach of a constitutional right was provided in this case by the law of torts.[8] This rather missed the point that the claim was not necessarily for a breach of a constitutional right of the child as such, but rather one of liability of the state for failing to fully discharge its duties under Article 42.4 by virtue of its failure to implement effective measures to prevent and detect sexual abuse in the primary school system. Even so, it was an entirely novel claim, and could not point to any previous analogous case law interpreting Article 42. Neither the negligence claim nor the constitutional claim was pursued on appeal to the Supreme Court, although in the event, the Supreme Court did pass comment on them (as will be seen below).

When the case proceeded to the ECtHR, the applicant's argument focused entirely on the direct liability of the state for failing to implement effective measures to detect and prevent abuse rather than on vicarious liability for the actions of the school principal. More than anything else, this was a function of the relevant case law available to support a claim for state liability for failing to prevent the abuse. In domestic law, vicarious liability offered the most advantageous route for the plaintiff, since it involves a significant body of Irish case law as well as analogous case law from other common law jurisdictions. The direct negligence claim and the constitutional claim would both have required a domestic court to break new ground. By contrast, the jurisprudence of the ECtHR provided ample support for the direct liability claim. A number of previous cases had established that the state has a positive obligation under Article 3 (read together with Article 1) of the ECHR to take measures to detect and prevent child abuse, and moreover, that domestic law should provide a remedy for victims in cases where the state fails to do so. The circumstances of Louise O'Keeffe's case and legal issues arising therefrom were strikingly analogous to *Z v. United Kingdom*[9] in particular.

When the application was made to the ECtHR, the government immediately contested admissibility by reason of failure to exhaust domestic remedies, on the basis that the issue of direct liability had not been appealed to the Supreme Court. It was argued that these were separate and distinct claims, and that it was not tenable to suggest that exhausting a remedy on one issue (vicarious liability) amounted to exhaustion on another (negligence).[10] The Chamber recalled a substantial body of previous ECtHR jurisprudence that established the principle that 'if there are a number of domestic remedies which an individual can pursue, that person is entitled to choose a remedy which addresses his or her essential grievance. In other words, when a remedy has been pursued, use of another remedy which has essentially the same objective is not required.'[11] It held that 'the applicant's essential grievances concerned the state's responsibility for the abuse suffered by her as well as the availability of a civil remedy against the State in that respect' and that the vicarious liability action was a 'reasonable choice' in pursuit of that grievance; the applicant 'was not required when ultimately unsuccessful with the reasonable route chosen, to take another remedial route with essentially the same objective'.[12] Thus, while the government's argument was that the claims of vicarious or direct liability were entirely distinct, the Chamber rejected this characterisation, finding that they were essentially two different routes of arriving at the same place – namely, a finding that the state bore civil liability for failing to prevent the abuse suffered by Louise O'Keeffe.

Mr Justice Hardiman criticises the 'essential grievance' decision as being 'at odds with the long-established jurisprudence of the Strasbourg Court itself', and states that '[a]s far as I have been able to discover the term "core grievance", which was key to the Strasbourg Court departing from the previous jurisprudence, was used for the first time in *O'Keeffe's* case. It has no jurisprudential basis that I can find in the Court's output.' It is true that the term 'core grievance' did appear in the Grand Chamber judgment,[13] and is not the normal formulation of this concept in Strasbourg case law. The Chamber judgment, cited and approved by the Grand Chamber,[14] used the more normal formulation of 'essential grievance'. As observed above, the Chamber judgment cited a lengthy list of decisions which have developed this concept and clearly established that an applicant is free to choose between remedies. Additional case law not cited by the Chamber provides further support for this point, including case law involving Ireland.[15] While Mr Justice Hardiman's paper refers to the text of Article 35 itself and the obligation to exhaust 'all' reasonable remedies, it does not engage with any of the substantial body of jurisprudence that has developed the application of this provision over the decades in which the Convention has been in force. Mr Justice Hardiman argues that 'the amorphous concept of 'core grievance' destroys the rigour of the Convention, and empties Article 35 of any specific meaning'. This may or not may not be so, but it is an entirely separate point to the unsustainable argument that the concept was 'at odds with the long-established jurisprudence of the Strasbourg Court itself' and was 'used for the first time in O'Keeffe's case'.

Finally, Mr Justice Hardiman states that the dissenting opinion of Judge Charleton was 'surely correct in suggesting that there was nothing essentially similar about a State defendant being liable for its *own* failure and a State defendant being liable despite carefully training employees because the wrong of the employee is within the scope of the employment relationship'.[16] This is a point of substantive disagreement as to whether the vicarious and direct liability claims were, in fact, the same claim. It hinges on the question of how to separate out form and substance, and in particular, how narrowly to define the latter. The approach of the ECtHR has been to define substance relatively broadly and allow for a range of forms.[17] Was Louise O'Keeffe's 'essential grievance' *whether* the state should be liable for the abuse, or *on what basis* the state should be liable for the abuse? The latter view would surely seem semantic to any applicant in similar circumstances. Should the state be liable because it failed to supervise an employee in the course of his employment, or because it failed to supervise the activities of teachers in private schools in which children were vulnerable to sexual abuse? In any event, even if the majority of the ECtHR had agreed with Judge Charleton and Mr Justice Hardiman that domestic remedies had not been exhausted on the essential grievance, the next section will demonstrate that this would not have been decisive on the question of admissibility.

Futile domestic remedies need not be pursued

Having declared the case admissible, the Chamber relinquished jurisdiction on the merits to the Grand Chamber. However, that did not end the discussion of admissibility; Article 35(4) and associated case law makes it clear that a case may be declared inadmissible at any point in the proceedings,[18] and the government continued to contest admissibility. Indeed, in oral argument before the Grand Chamber, admissibility constituted the main focus of the government's submissions.[19] In its judgment, the Grand Chamber reaffirmed the Chamber's finding that the domestic proceedings had addressed the applicant's 'essential grievance', holding that 'the applicant was entitled to devote resources to pursue one feasible appeal (vicarious liability) over another (a claim in negligence and/or a constitutional tort)'.[20]

The only issue around admissibility addressed in Mr Justice Hardiman's paper is the distinction between vicarious and direct liability and the concept of 'essential grievance'. Admittedly, it is the only issue raised in the section of the Grand Chamber judgment addressing the preliminary objection relating to failure to exhaust domestic remedies. However, the arguments advanced by the applicant before the Grand Chamber raised a further, independent reason why non-exhaustion of domestic remedies could not justify a finding of inadmissibility – namely, the futility of domestic remedies on the question of direct liability. The argument advanced on behalf of Louise O'Keeffe, and accepted by the ECtHR, was that an appeal against the High Court's dismissal of the direct liability claim had no prospect of success. This issue became blurred into other aspects of the Grand Chamber's judgment because of the overlap between the issue of the futility of domestic remedies (as it pertains to admissibility) and the issue of the availability of an effective remedy (as it pertains to the Article 13 issue in the merits of the case). As the ECtHR outlined in *Akdivar v. Turkey*, the rule that domestic remedies must be exhausted is 'based on the assumption, reflected in Article 13 of the Convention – with which it has close affinity – that there is an effective remedy available in respect of the alleged breach in the domestic system'.[21] Thus, it can be difficult to properly separate out the two issues, for which reason the ECtHR will often direct that the question of the effectiveness of other remedies should be joined to the merits of the applicant's complaint under Article 13. This is precisely what happened in the Chamber decision in *O'Keeffe*.[22] The relevance of this aspect of the Grand Chamber's decision would certainly have been more apparent if it had featured in the section dedicated to admissibility; but nonetheless, it is clear from the judgment as a whole that the Court did not believe that there was a realistic prospect of success in domestic proceedings on direct liability. The case law of the ECtHR demonstrates that this provides ample justification for a decision to declare a case admissible.

While the principle that domestic remedies must be exhausted before applying to Strasbourg is expressly stated in the Convention itself, it is well established that an applicant is not required to exhaust remedies that would be futile. A key authority on this point is *Selmouni v. France*, in which the Grand Chamber held:

> the only remedies which Article 35 of the Convention requires to be exhausted are those that relate to the breaches alleged and at the same time are available and sufficient. The existence of such remedies must be sufficiently certain not only in theory but also in practice, failing which they will lack the requisite accessibility and effectiveness; it falls to the respondent State to establish that these various conditions are satisfied.
>
> It is incumbent on the Government claiming non-exhaustion to satisfy the Court that the remedy was an effective one available in theory and in practice at the relevant time, that is to say, that it was accessible, was one

which was capable of providing redress in respect of the applicant's complaints and offered reasonable prospects of success.

The Court would emphasise that the application of this rule must make due allowance for the [Convention] context. Accordingly, it has recognised that Article 35 must be applied with some degree of flexibility and without excessive formalism ... .[23]

Accordingly, where domestic proceedings would be futile, applicants may proceed directly to Strasbourg without first exhausting domestic remedies. This issue has featured prominently in two previous cases before the ECtHR involving Ireland. In *D v. Ireland*,[24] the applicant claimed that the absence of an exception to the prohibition of abortion in cases of fatal foetal abnormality violated her rights under Articles 3, 8 and 10 of the ECHR. She sought to take her claim directly to Strasbourg, without first pursuing any litigation in the domestic courts, on the basis that the protection accorded to unborn life by Article 40.3.3° of the Irish Constitution precluded the possibility of a successful outcome to such litigation.[25] The government argued that it was ultimately a matter for the Irish courts to determine whether the applicant had a valid claim, and that cases like *Attorney General v. X*[26] had illustrated the potential for judicial development of Article 40.3.3°. For this reason, the government argued that it was it was impossible to foresee that Article 40.3.3° clearly excluded an abortion in the applicant's situation.[27] Ultimately, the ECtHR held that the uncertainty in the law was such that it was reasonable to have expected the applicant to have at least instructed a lawyer and issued a plenary summons, even if the pressure of time involved for a woman seeking an abortion meant that it would have unreasonable to have expected her to have pursued that litigation to a conclusion. In the absence of any steps having been taken in the domestic legal arena, the Court declared the case inadmissible.[28]

D v. Ireland can be contrasted with the more recent and well-known case of *A, B and C v. Ireland*,[29] which concerned three women who had sought to have an abortion in Ireland on health and wellbeing grounds. Irish law only allows for abortion in cases of a real and substantial threat to life (as distinct from health), and at the time, no legal framework existed for determining which cases fell within the exception. As a result, all three women travelled to the UK to have their abortions, and complained that the trauma, expense and medical complications associated with being forced to travel violated a number of provisions of the ECHR. Crucially, in the current context, the ECtHR declared the case admissible even though no domestic litigation of any sort had taken place. In contesting admissibility, the government referred back to *D v.*

Ireland and again argued that the precise interpretation and application of domestic law to the situation of the applicants was an open question. In particular, it was argued that the applicants could have sought a declaration that the relevant legislative provisions were unconstitutional.[30] The Grand Chamber of the ECtHR rejected this argument, holding that it had not been demonstrated that such an action would have had any chance of success, 'going against, as it would, the history, text and judicial interpretation of Article 40.3.3° of the Constitution'. Accordingly, the argument that a declaration of unconstitutionality might have provided the applicants with a remedy in domestic law was rejected, and the application was ultimately declared admissible.[31]

The *O'Keeffe* case, of course, did not go directly to Strasbourg; the issue of vicarious liability was pursued all the way to the Irish Supreme Court. The issue of direct liability was pursued in the High Court, although its dismissal was not appealed to the Supreme Court. The Chamber did not see this as important, since the essential grievance had been appealed, albeit in a different form. Mr Justice Hardiman has expressed his disagreement with this finding, and I have defended it above. However, that particular argument is not decisive on the question of admissibility. Even if direct liability differs from vicarious liability as a matter of substance rather than form, the rule in *Selmouni*, as applied in *A, B and C*, makes it clear that the direct liability claim could have been brought directly to Strasbourg, without any domestic litigation whatsoever, if it had no reasonable prospect of success in domestic courts. As outlined in *Selmouni*, it is 'incumbent on the Government claiming non-exhaustion to satisfy the Court that the remedy was an effective one available in theory and in practice at the relevant time, that is to say, that it was accessible, was one which was capable of providing redress in respect of the applicant's complaints and offered reasonable prospects of success'.[32]

In Louise O'Keeffe's case, there were multiple factors that suggested that the direct liability claim did not offer reasonable prospects of success. First, it was non-suited by the High Court; her argument was that an appeal would have been futile, since it is essentially unheard of for the Supreme Court to reverse a decision made on this basis.[33] Jacobs and White, described by Mr Justice Hardiman as authors of the 'leading textbook' on the ECHR, state that the approach of the ECtHR is to accept an opinion of Counsel that an appeal is futile.[34] Second, notwithstanding the failure to appeal, Hardiman J. (with whom Murray CJ agreed) proceeded to address the direct liability claim in the final paragraphs of his Supreme Court decision. The possibility of success for such an appeal was summarily dismissed:

I would comment as follows on the other two headings under which the plaintiff's claim was put, though neither was proceeded with. The first was negligence in failing to put in place appropriate measures and procedures 'to protect and cease the systematic abuse which the first defendant on the evidence embarked upon ...'. In my view this is a claim which could more appropriately be made against the manager. It was he who had the power to put in place appropriate measures and procedures governing the running of the school. The Minister can hardly be responsible for a failure to 'cease' a course of action of whose existence he was quite unaware.

It is also claimed that by reason of the constitutional provisions of Article 42, cited above, he had a responsibility, presumably, to put measures described in the first paragraph in place. ...

I do not read the provisions of Article 42.4 as requiring more than that the Minister shall 'endeavour to supplement and give reasonable aid to private and corporate educational initiative', to 'provide for free primary education'... In my view the Constitution specifically envisages, not indeed a delegation but a ceding of the actual running of schools to the interests represented by the patron and the manager.[35]

These *obiter* remarks provide a strong indication that an appeal, if pursued, would have been unsuccessful, and they did not escape the attention of the ECtHR.[36] Coming as they did from the Supreme Court bench in the very same set of proceedings, it would be reasonable to speculate that they were the nail in the coffin of the government's admissibility argument. They demonstrate not only the futility of an appeal to the Supreme Court in the case at hand, but also the futility of a direct liability claim more generally. The direct liability claim did not fit into any pre-existing and recognised cause of action in Irish law. Success on this claim would have required the Irish courts to fashion a novel remedy, and as the ECtHR observed, the government (who bore the burden of proving the availability of a remedy with a reasonable prospect of success) had not been able to demonstrate, with relevant case law, how this might occur.[37] Accordingly, Louise O'Keeffe was not obliged to appeal the point to the Supreme Court. In fact, if direct liability differs from vicarious liability as a matter of substance rather than form, ECtHR jurisprudence indicates she would not have been obliged to pursue any domestic litigation at all. She would have been entitled to go directly to Strasbourg when she first instituted proceedings against the state in 1998 rather than spending the next eleven years engaged in protracted and contentious litigation during which the state consistently sought to pursue her for costs. Viewed in this light, the argument that her direct liability claim should have been declared inadmissible irrespective of her domestic litigation seems clearly out of line with the

Grand Chamber's statement in *Selmouni* that the admissibility criteria should be 'applied with some degree of flexibility and without excessive formalism'.[38]

Finally, a key part of Mr Justice Hardiman's objection to the decision to declare *O'Keeffe* admissible is based on a point made in the dissenting judgment of Judge Charleton, namely that the ECtHR found itself examining evidence not previously raised and scrutinised before a national tribunal.[39] However, since the ECtHR retains the right to hear cases directly where domestic remedies are futile, it must (by definition) retain the right to make a first-instance assessment of the evidence in such cases. The Rules of Court make provision for the use of documentary evidence and expert witnesses before the Court, while Article 38 of the ECHR even provides for the conduct of investigations in cases brought before the court.[40] Therefore, it is clearly permissible for the ECtHR to assess evidence not previously raised before a national tribunal.

Even so, this can scarcely even be said to have occurred in *O'Keeffe*. The vast majority of the evidence of Louise O'Keeffe's particular circumstances had been before the domestic courts; the first-instance assessment carried out by the ECtHR related only to broader systemic evidence relating to the general approach towards child protection in Ireland at the time. Even here, this evidence relied on by the ECtHR came in the form of the findings of state-established inquiries, namely the Carrigan Report[41] and the Ryan Report,[42] and can hardly be described as being of questionable provenance. While the government did contest the relevance of the Ryan Report outside of the context of residential institutions, it did not contest the accuracy of its overall findings; on the contrary, in its written submissions, the government sought to rely on a number of passages from the Ryan Report to support its own case. The ECtHR was careful to filter out other evidentiary sources relied on by the parties, such as letters written by Professor Ferguson and Professor Rollison, that it deemed not to be sufficiently reliable or relevant.[43] The manner in which evidence is dealt with before the ECtHR may seem unfamiliar to Irish lawyers, but that does not mean that the decision in *O'Keeffe* went outside of the Court's own powers in this regard.

Conclusion

The key concern of Mr Justice Hardiman's paper is that '[i]f the Strasbourg Court assumes the responsibility for making direct findings against the State, where there has been no exhaustion of domestic remedies, then the Convention will have changed in a radical and indeed a revolutionary way'. He points to the decision in *O'Keeffe* as a potential touchstone for such a revolutionary shift. As I have argued above, this misrepresents the true nature of the *O'Keeffe* decision. Quite to the contrary, the Grand Chamber's judgment, insofar as it addressed admissibility, was entirely in line with previous jurisprudence of the ECtHR. The decision to declare the case admissible on the basis that the vicarious liability claim had addressed the applicant's 'essential grievance' finds ample support in the case law of the Court and was in no way revolutionary. Any disagreement with this finding must be reduced to the question of whether the vicarious liability claim did in fact address the same essential grievance as the direct liability claim. Even if (unlike the ECtHR) one concludes that it did not, the government bore the burden of proof of demonstrating that the direct liability claim was available and sufficient and had a reasonable chance of success in domestic courts. It was not able to discharge this burden, and the *obiter* remarks at the conclusion of Mr Justice Hardiman's Supreme Court judgment in *O'Keeffe* gave the ECtHR strong support for its conclusion that the direct liability claim would have been futile. For this reason alone, Strasbourg jurisprudence indicates that the Grand Chamber was entirely within its rights to declare the case admissible and proceed to the merits.

Notes

The author, along with Professor Ursula Kilkelly and their students in the Child Law Clinic, collaborated with Louise O'Keeffe's legal team in the preparation of the case before the European Court of Human Rights.

1 *O'Keeffe v. Ireland*, 35810/09, 26 June 2012 (Chamber); 28 January 2014 (Grand Chamber).
2 *Lister v. Hesley Hall Ltd* [2002] 1 AC 215.
3 *Bazley v. Curry* (1999) 174 DLR (4th) 45 and *Jacobi v. Griffiths* (1999) 174 DLR (4th) 71.
4 *LO'K v. LH* [2006] IEHC 13.
5 *O'Keeffe v. Hickey* [2009] 2 IR 302 at 343–344 (*per* Hardiman J.) and 379–380 (*per* Fennelly J.).
6 *Ibid.*, at 328 (*per* Hardiman J.).
7 35810/09, 28 January 2014 (Grand Chamber) at [185]. Proximity is a key element of the test for establishing the existence of a duty of care as set out in *Glencar Exploration plc v. Mayo County Council* [2002] 1 IR 84.
8 *LO'K v. LH* [2006] IEHC 13.
9 29392/95, 10 May 2001.
10 *O'Keeffe v. Ireland*, 35810/09, 26 June 2012 (Chamber) at [65].
11 *Ibid.*, at [85]. Cases cited in support of this finding included *O'Reilly v. Ireland*, 24196/94, 22 January 1996; *TW v. Malta*, 25644/94, 29 April 1999 at [34]; *Moreira Barbosa v. Portugal*, 65681/01, 29 April 2004; *Jelicic v. Bosnia and*

Herzegovina, 41183/02, 15 November 2005; *Shkalla v. Albania*, 26866/05, 10 May 2011 at [61], and *Leja v. Latvia*, 71072/01, 14 June 2011 at [46].
12 *O'Keeffe v. Ireland*, 35810/09, 26 June 2012 (Chamber) at [86].
13 *O'Keeffe v. Ireland*, 28 January 2014 (Grand Chamber) at [110].
14 *Ibid.*, at [109].
15 See, e.g., *Airey v. Ireland*, 6289/73, 9 October 1979 at [23]; *Croke v. Ireland*, 33267/96, 15 June 1999.
16 Emphasis provided by Mr Justice Hardiman, when referring to *O'Keeffe v. Ireland*, 28 January 2014 (Grand Chamber), Dissenting Opinion of Judge Charleton at [10].
17 For example, in *O'Reilly v. Ireland*, 24196/94, the applicant was detained under s. 184, Mental Treatment Act 1945, but later released when it was found that she was not suffering from mental illness. She sought to bring proceedings against the doctor who certified her illness on the basis that he had not acted with reasonable care. Pursuant to s. 260 of the Act, the High Court and Supreme Court refused leave for such proceedings on the basis that substantial grounds did not exist to support them. When the applicant brought her case to the European Commission on Human Rights, the government argued that it would have been open to her to have challenged the constitutionality of s. 184, and that her failure to do so constituted a failure to exhaust domestic remedies. Although a challenge to the detention under s. 260 was very different in form to a challenge to the constitutionality of s. 184, the Commission held that both remedies would have been directed towards the same essential grievance – i.e. securing compensation for having been detained in the absence of mental illness – and that the choice she made was a reasonable one. The reverse approach was taken by the applicant in *Croke v. Ireland*, 33267/96, 15 June 1999, who challenged the constitutionality of the 1945 Act, but did not invoke various provisions of the Act which could have allowed him to challenge his detention. Again, the ECtHR held that this was a reasonable choice, and rejected the government's claim of non-exhaustion.
18 See, e.g., *Odièvre v. France*, 42326/98, 13 February 2003.
19 Video of the oral argument can be viewed in full online at www.echr.coe.int/Pages/home.aspx?p=hearings&w=3581009_06032013&language=lang (accessed 18 August 2015).
20 *O'Keeffe v. Ireland*, 28 January 2014 (Grand Chamber) at [110]–[111].
21 21893/93, September 16, 1996, at [65].
22 *O'Keeffe v. Ireland*, 35810/09, 26 June 2012 (Chamber) at [87].
23 25803/94, 28 July 1999 at [74]–[77].
24 26499/02, 27 June 2006.
25 *Ibid.*, at [77].
26 [1992] 1 IR 1.
27 26499/02, 27 June 2006 at [65]–[69].
28 *Ibid.*, at [102]–[103].
29 25579/05, 16 December 2010.
30 *Ibid.*, at [134]–[136].

31 *Ibid.*, at [145]–[149].
32 25803/94, 28 July 1999 at [76].
33 *O'Keeffe v. Ireland*, 28 January 2014 (Grand Chamber) at [181].
34 C. Ovey and R. White, *Jacobs and White: The European Convention on Human Rights* (4th edn, OUP, 2006) p. 486.
35 *O'Keeffe v. Hickey* [2009] 2 IR 302 at 344.
36 *O'Keeffe v. Ireland*, 28 January 2014 (Grand Chamber) at [40] and, more particularly [186]: 'Whether or not this ground was properly pleaded before the Supreme Court, it remains relevant to note that Hardiman J. of the Supreme Court rejected it.'
37 *Ibid.*, at [186].
38 25803/94, 28 July 1999 at [77].
39 *O'Keeffe v. Ireland*, 28 January 2014 (Grand Chamber), Dissenting Opinion of Judge Charleton at [9].
40 See further Ovey and White (n. 34) pp. 480–482.
41 W. Carrigan, *Report of the Committee on the Criminal Law Amendment Acts (1880–1885) and Juvenile Prostitution* (Stationery Office, 1931).
42 S. Ryan, *Commission to Inquire into Child Abuse Report* (Stationery Office, 2009), available at www.childabusecommission.ie/rpt/pdfs (accessed 18 August 2015).
43 *O'Keeffe v. Ireland*, 28 January 2014 (Grand Chamber) at [167].

Part III
Judges and the political sphere: appointments and dialogue

8

Judicial appointments in Ireland: the potential for reform

Laura Cahillane

In January 2014, the Department of Justice in Ireland initiated a consultation process, calling on members of the public to suggest ways in which the procedure for appointing judges could be improved. It specified a number of areas for consideration: eligibility for appointment; the need to ensure and protect the principle of judicial independence; promoting equality and diversity and the role of the Judicial Appointments Advisory Board, including its membership and its procedures. This was in response to criticisms, made over a number of years, that the procedure for appointing judges in Ireland was not fit for purpose. The aim of this paper is to consider the current procedure and put forward some tentative suggestions for reform in an attempt to begin a debate on this area.

The current position on judicial appointments

Article 35.1 of Bunreacht na hÉireann states that: 'The judges of the Supreme Court, the High Court and all other Courts established in pursuance of Article 34 hereof shall be appointed by the President.' However, the role of the President is only a ceremonial one, as in accordance with Article 13.9, this function is to be exercised 'only on the advice of the Government'. Thus, judges in Ireland are appointed by the government.

In the past, the process was quite informal. Indeed, the All Party Oireachtas Committee on the Constitution described how 'successive Governments were seen to appoint, almost invariably, their own supporters to judicial office'.[1] Then in 1995, in response to the fallout from the attempted appointment of the then Attorney General to the post of President of the High Court,[2] the Judicial Appointments Advisory Board

(JAAB) was established under the Courts and Court Officers Act 1995 in order to provide a fair and impartial system for appointing judges.

Section 16(2) of the Act, requires the JAAB to recommend to the minister at least seven persons for appointment to a particular post. Although the 1995 Act empowers the JAAB to arrange for interviewing candidates, the JAAB has chosen not to exercise this power. Section 14(2)(f) also provides that the Board can do such other things as it considers necessary to enable it to discharge its functions under this Act. While the Act does allow for quite wide powers for the JAAB, that body has been overly cautious in exercising its functions. Besides refusing to interview candidates or using the potential of section 14(2)(f) to expand its functions, it has actually diminished its role. For fear of falling foul of the Constitution, which requires the government to appoint judges, it was decided that rather than presenting the government with a list of at least seven names, distilled from the original list of applications, the JAAB should simply remove any unqualified or undesirable candidates and present all other applicants to the government.[3] This means the government could be presented with a list of 20 or so names for a High Court appointment or up to 90 names for a District Court appointment. This practice has further weakened the already dubious purpose of the JAAB.

The government then usually selects a name from the list presented by the JAAB but is not actually required to do so. Section 6 of the Act specifies that: 'In advising the President in relation to the appointment of a person to a judicial office the Government shall *firstly* consider for appointment those persons whose names have been recommended to the Minister pursuant to this section.'[4]

Problems with this system

Some might argue that there is no need for reform since Irish judges have never shown any deference to the government which has appointed them and they have an excellent record in terms of independence.[5] This is all very true but there are problems with the current system. These issues will first be briefly outlined before some potential solutions are then considered.

Political appointments
The first problem is one that appears obvious considering the amount of attention it has received in the media and by Opposition politicians – that of appointments being or being seen to be political.[6] Judges themselves have admitted using political influence to ensure their appointment. Retired Judge Michael Patwell told Charlie Bird a few years ago

that such an approach was 'common'.[7] In an interview in 2012, Mr Justice Peter Kelly, President of the Association of Judges in Ireland stated that the JAAB does not work: 'We all know cases of people who would be excellent judicial appointments and are passed over in favour of people who are not so well qualified.'[8] Thus it would seem that political favouritism is still a problem and the current system does nothing to prevent this. A study of the Irish judiciary carried out in 2004 which involved interviewing superior court judges, concluded that the general view among members of the judiciary was that the JAAB was good in theory but in practice it had made little difference to the political patronage system of appointments in Ireland.[9] This view is hardly surprising given the limited role played by the JAAB and the level of unscrutinised discretion which is still left to the government.

Thus it is uncontroversial to say that this is an issue which needs to be addressed.

Lack of transparency

Another issue, related to problem of political appointments, is the lack of transparency in the process. As noted above, when making a judicial appointment, the government may select from the list of seven or more names but it is not required to do so.[10] Whether or not the successful candidate has been chosen from the list, the government is not required to provide reasons for its decision. This lack of transparency is certainly problematic. Perhaps we need to consider whether it should be a necessary part of the process to provide reasons – particularly if candidates are not being interviewed or assessed in any way and especially if it happened that a name which did not appear on the list was chosen by the government.

Lack of diversity[11]

While the gender balance of the courts has improved in recent years, there is still some way to go in order to ensure an appropriate balance in terms of gender, background and ethnicity on the bench. In the 2004 study mentioned above, an interesting conclusion was reached on the profile of superior court judges in Ireland:

> The person who is most likely to be a judge of the Superior Courts in Ireland in 2004 is male, was born in Dublin and grew up in an urban setting. He lived in Dublin and was a practising Senior Counsel at the time of his appointment. He did not necessarily come from a legal family background. He attended a private secondary school and studied at University College Dublin ... He was appointed after he was forty-five, but most likely after he was fifty. He describes himself as middle class but believes that it is very difficult to define or apply a social class structure to the Irish context.[12]

Eleven years later, this description is still very familiar. At the time of writing, the number of sitting judges is 161.[13] Of the total number of sitting judges, 33.5% are women: female representation in the Supreme Court is 30%, 20% in the Court of Appeal, 28.5% in the High Court, 44% in the Circuit Court, and 32% of the District Court. Thus, it is clear that significant progress has been made, even in the last year, in the attempt to secure an appropriate gender balance.[14] However, the percentage of female judges is still too low.

Many people appear to be satisfied with these figures and having raised this issue in a number of different forums recently, the main response was that progress had been made and this was fine. It is interesting to compare this with the situation in France in 2003, when 80% of those entering the judiciary were women and the Minister for Justice threatened to introduce quotas in order to restore gender balance and maintain public confidence.[15] If the Irish figures were reversed and if we had less than 30% male judges, I wonder would we have the same level of complacency? However, the Irish judiciary themselves do not seem to see diversity as an issue which needs to be addressed.[16]

This issue is one which deserves more depth of analysis than can be accorded to it here but the central point is that this issue also needs to be considered and just because the current government have made a point of selecting outstanding women to judicial office does not mean that the diversity issue has been solved.

Limitations

There are two more issues then with the JAAB itself: First, the board has no role if the post in question is the presidency of any court or if a vacancy is being filled by the promotion of a lower judge by the government. The second problem is that while it is clearly intended to be an advisory body, the JAAB is in fact nothing more than a filtering mechanism or short-listing process whereby undesirable or unqualified candidates are excluded. The requirement that at least seven names be recommended means that in reality, there is nothing 'advisory' about the process and the more recent practice of the JAAB in recommending all suitable candidates simply exemplifies this.

Possible reforms

The previous section has outlined briefly the central problems inherent in the current process for the appointment of judges in Ireland. We can now move to consider possible actions which could be considered in order to address these issues.

Reduce the number of names which the board can recommend

Starting which the last issue mentioned above, if the requirement to produce a list of at least seven names was amended to provide that only two or three names can be recommended, this would go some way towards eliminating the possibility of appointments being political. It would also give the JAAB a more advisory role and remove the appearance that it is simply a short-listing body. Such an amendment would be compatible with the Constitution, as the final choice is still left with the government. By allowing the government to choose from, let's say, three candidates, the JAAB would not be usurping the role of the government. It would simply be fulfilling its duty as an advisory body. As David Gwynn Morgan has noted, this procedure is something the government has applied in relation to other sensitive appointments, for example the DPP and the chairperson of An Bórd Pleanála.[17] Furthermore in order to make sure that this would not offend the Constitution, it could still be specified in the legislation that, as is the case now, the government is not *required* to choose from the names put forward by the JAAB. While in practice, it would be envisaged that the government would choose from the list, as it does now, by allowing for the possibility of a departure, this ensures compatibility with the Constitution.

Interview candidates

Section 14(e) of the 1995 Act allows for arrangements to be made for interviewing candidates. However, the JAAB has never availed of this possibility and has expressly declined to do so. Interviewing the candidates would provide a better means of providing a suitable list to the government, especially in the event that the list of names is reduced. There is no obvious reason why candidates should not be interviewed – as long as the process is fair, there is no threat to judicial independence – it is a practice which is carried out in many other jurisdictions. Judicial candidates in England and Wales may be required to take part in either panel interviews, interview and role play, interview and presentation or interview and situational questioning.[18] This is a much more rigorous process and ensures that a candidate can be assessed as to their suitability in a practical manner.

Rank candidates

It has been suggested that the JAAB should be empowered to rank candidates in order of preference. However, there is potentially an argument that this runs the risk of unconstitutionality, as it effectively removes the choice from the government and places it into the hands of a body not officially recognised by the Constitution. However, this is a matter of interpretation and it has also been argued that allowing the JAAB to indicate its own order of preference would be constitutionally valid.[19] The principal argument in favour of ranking, which maintains constitutional validity of this idea, is that mentioned above – that the government would still have the choice not to accept the preferred ranking of the JAAB. This ensures the ultimate choice still lies with the government.

Publish reasons

In relation to the complaint that the current system lacks transparency, one simple solution would be to require the government to publish reasons for its choice. Whether it would have to publish reasons in every case or simply in cases where it decided to depart from the names (or the ranking, if this was introduced) given to it by the JAAB, would be a matter for further discussion.

Many other jurisdictions have reformed their practices in order to provide for more transparency. For example, in England and Wales, the Judicial Appointments Commission selects a candidate on the basis of established criteria and submits one name to the appropriate authority (Lord Chancellor, Lord Chief Justice or Senior President of Tribunals), who invariably accepts the recommendation. In fact, she/he can only reject the recommendation on the basis that the person is not suitable for the office concerned and the reasons for this decision must be provided in writing.[20]

Involve opposition parties

As another possibility to avoid political patronage, it would be possible to provide for the involvement of members of opposition parties in the selection process. This is something which currently happens in South Africa. The Judicial Service Commission, which is the body which recommends candidates for appointment to judicial office to the President, comprises twenty-three members, including six politicians, at least three of whom must be members of opposition parties.[21] While allowing for the participation of opposition members of parliament would certainly reduce the possibility of the government party blatantly appointing someone seen as friendly to their own ideals, such a move might also turn out to be more problematic and possibly even more political. A more suitable route would be to look at reforming the JAAB itself.

Reform membership of the JAAB

One possible option would be to consider reforming the membership of the JAAB. Current membership of the Board comprises:

(i)   the Chief Justice, who shall be the chairperson of the Board,
(ii) the President of the High Court,
(iii) the President of the Circuit Court,
(iv) the President of the District Court,
(v)   the Attorney General,
(vi) a practising barrister,
(vii) a practising solicitor who shall be nominated by the President for the time being of the Law Society of Ireland,

And

(viii) not more than three persons appointed by the Minister who shall be persons engaged in, or having knowledge or experience ... of commerce, finance, administration or persons who have experience as consumers of the services provided by the courts that the Minister considers appropriate.

Thus, there is an overwhelming majority of lawyers on the Board. In order to preserve judicial independence, it is appropriate that judges should be involved in the selection process but it is submitted that increasing the lay members on the committee would help to ensure that issues such as diversity are considered. It would also help to avoid the appearance of self-perpetuation by the judiciary (and would help reduce claims of political bias, provided that the role of the JAAB is strengthened and the list of names reduced). Some jurisdictions, such as Ontario, have tackled this issue by providing for a majority of lay members. Others, such as Scotland have provided for equal representation among lay and legal members. In England and Wales, the chair of the Judicial Appointments Commission is a layperson.

Given the manner in which the board is currently set up, it is hard to imagine that the lay contingent has any real sway and is likely to feel it should defer to the judicial and legal members. Increasing the lay representation would help to combat this.

Amend eligibility criteria

Another major reform would be to amend the eligibility criteria for appointment to judicial office. Section 16(7) specifies the selection criteria to be applied by the JAAB. It provides that the Board shall not recommend a candidate unless she/he:

(a) has displayed in his or her practice as a barrister or solicitor, as the case may be, a degree of competence and a degree

of probity appropriate to and consistent with the appointment concerned,
(b) is suitable on grounds of character and temperament,
(c) is otherwise suitable, and
(d) complies with the requirements of section 19 of this Act. (This involves an undertaking to take courses or training.)

These requirements are unacceptably vague and need to be refined. Various other jurisdictions provide for more precise guidelines. Scotland is one example where selection criteria have been drawn up to match the various judicial offices. The detailed criteria required are measured under various headings: 'knowledge of the law, skills and competence in the interpretation and application of the law, court experience and skills, intellectual capacity and powers of reasoning, personal characteristics, case management skills and efficiency and communication skills'. These are further broken down into subheadings.[22]

In England and Wales, candidates are assessed based on merit, which is measured by six core qualities:

Intellectual capacity
- Expertise in your chosen area of profession
- Ability to quickly absorb and analyse information
- Appropriate knowledge of the law and its underlying principles, or the ability to acquire this knowledge where necessary

Personal qualities
- Integrity and independence of mind
- Sound judgement
- Decisiveness
- Objectivity
- Ability and willingness to learn and develop professionally

An ability to understand and deal fairly
- An awareness of the diversity of the communities which the courts and tribunals serve and an understanding of differing needs
- Commitment to justice, independence, public service and fair treatment
- Willingness to listen with patience and courtesy

Authority and communication skills
- Ability to explain the procedure and any decisions reached clearly and succinctly to all those involved

- Ability to inspire respect and confidence
- Ability to maintain authority when challenged

Efficiency
- Ability to work at speed and under pressure
- Ability to organise time effectively and produce clear reasoned judgments expeditiously
- Ability to work constructively with others

Leadership and management skills
- Ability to form strategic objectives and to provide leadership to implement them effectively
- Ability to motivate, support and encourage the professional development of those for whom you are responsible
- Ability to engage constructively with judicial colleagues and the administration, and to manage change effectively
- Ability to organise own and others time and manage available resources.[23]

A more comprehensive set of eligibility criteria, against which to measure candidates, such as those listed above, would facilitate in the short-listing process and help to ensure the most suitable candidates are put forward.

A further issue in relation to eligibility is the question of appointing academics. The system in England and Wales allows for the appointment of academic lawyers to judicial office. Section 50 of the Tribunals, Courts and Enforcement Act, 2007 creates a judicial-appointment eligibility condition that a person must hold a relevant qualification and have gained 'experience in law' for a specified period while holding that qualification. Section 52 defines 'experience in law' to include 'teaching or researching law'. Such a system, has allowed for the appointment of Supreme Court Justice Lady Hale and Mr Justice Beatson to the Bench in England and a similar system in Canada led to the appointment of Chief Justice Bora Laskin.

An approach which includes the appointment of academic lawyers should be considered in Ireland. Arguments against this approach include the fact that many academic lawyers will not have the requisite knowledge of court procedure. However, such concerns were also expressed in relation to appointment of solicitors but yet the extension of the qualification criteria of the superior courts to include practising solicitors has not proved to be a problem. Furthermore, Section 19 of the 1995 Act already specifies that an individual must agree to undergo training, which could easily be provided in order to equip the successful candidate with the requisite knowledge of court procedure. Furthermore, it could be argued that academic lawyers are naturally suited to the types of cases that arise in the Supreme Court, which require detailed analyses of legislation and constitutional provisions. Such a move would also open up more opportunities for women and other minorities interested in judicial office.

This may be a controversial suggestion but it is one which should at least be considered.

Require JAAB to consider diversity

In relation to the problems with diversity, there is certainly a need for more work to be carried out in order to find the best way of achieving a fair system. While in many ways, the issue of diversity of applications is dependent on equality in the legal professions generally, there are still actions which could be taken in order to encourage applications from women and minorities.

One simple step here would be to provide feedback so as to encourage unsuccessful applicants to apply again in the future and so as to ensure that unsuccessful candidates understand why they have not been chosen (and that the choice has been based on objective criteria and not on qualities such as political allegiance or gender).

Another step which could be taken would be to draw up a diversity strategy. In Scotland, the Judicial Appointments Board has adopted a diversity strategy in order to ensure recruitment is from the widest possible pool. The strategy involves ensuring that the selection process is fair and non-discriminatory, monitoring the diversity profile of applicants, the holding of information sessions about the selection process, and working with the legal profession and judiciary to help them to become more active in promoting judicial office among those who are currently not coming forward.[24]

In England and Wales, the Judicial Appointments Commission has conducted a 'Barriers to Entry' survey in order to discover reasons which would discourage people from applying for judicial office.[25] A similar study in Ireland would be welcome.

As mentioned above, in order to provide for diversity among members of the judiciary, it is also necessary that there is diversity among the legal professions in Ireland. In England and Wales, a Judicial Diversity Taskforce was established in order to implement the 53 recommendations of the 'Report of the Advisory Panel on Judicial Diversity 2010' and to work with the Bar Council, the Law Society and the Judicial Appointments Commission in order to remove barriers and promote diversity. Some similar action is needed in Ireland because it is very clear from reports like Gender InJustice[26] that there are major problems, particularly at the Bar, and especially with women being promoted to Senior Counsel and so these need to be tackled in the first place.

Furthermore, judicial diversity should involve more than just gender and ethnicity considerations; it should be concerned with providing a true representation of the population of Ireland. Issues such as geographic spread, cultural and socio-economic backgrounds, education, and age should also be taken into consideration. The judiciary needs to be one which is representative of the whole population of Ireland and not just one section of it. A diverse judiciary is one which can bring different perspectives to bear on various matters and issues around representativeness and how the public perceives the judiciary are directly related to public confidence in the administration of justice. There is no quick fix for this issue but perhaps following the lead of our neighbours in setting up a taskforce or at least implementing a diversity strategy are options which should be considered. At the very least, we need to recognise that a diverse judiciary is a worthwhile goal.

Conclusion

The options outlined above are some concise and tentative suggestions – ideas which could be examined in further detail in order to improve the system which currently exists. The review of the procedures for appointing judges which has been initiated by the Department of Justice is to be welcomed and as legal academics, we need to engage with this process in a meaningful way. An attempt was made in 1995 to provide for a suitable judicial appointments process in Ireland but as we have seen, it has not brought about much change, something which makes the current reform process all the more significant. Perhaps others will disagree with these suggestions but the aim of this piece was to start a conversation on this very important issue. I hope it has provided some food for thought.

Notes

1 *Fourth Progress Report: The Courts and the Judiciary* (Stationery Office, 1999) p. 7.
2 For more on this, see D. G. Morgan, 'Selection of Superior Judges' (2004) 22 *Irish Law Times* 42.
3 J. Carroll, unpublished paper from UCD Garret Fitzgerald Summer School 2014. See also www.irishtimes.com/news/crime-and-law/judicial-appointments-board-gave-discretion-back-to-politicians-1.1841679 (last accessed 18 August 2015).
4 Emphasis added.

5 See M. Hilliard, 'Ireland scores well on perceptions of judicial independence', *Irish Times* (14 April 2014).
6 In 2014, there were two separate bills published which proposed to remove the political influence from the judicial appointments process; one by Independent TD Shane Ross and one by Sinn Féin. See also Kenny, Chapter 9, this volume.
7 RTE Radio One interview, 25 August 2012.
8 S. Gilhooly, 'The Peter Principles' Autumn 2012 *The Parchment* 30.
9 J. Carroll, 'You Be the Judge Part II – The Politics and Processes of Judicial Appointments in Ireland' (2005) 11 *Bar Review* 186.
10 Although there was an incident in 1998, when the government was about to appoint a candidate whom the Board did not consider suitable. The Board threatened to resign and the Government climbed down. See Morgan (n. 2).
11 While the issue of gender diversity is focused upon in particular, diversity more generally also needs to be addressed.
12 J. Carroll, 'You Be the Judge Part II – The Politics and Processes of Judicial Appointments in Ireland' (2005) 11 *Bar Review* 186.
13 At the time of writing, there is currently one vacancy in the High Court, one vacancy in the Circuit Court and one vacancy in the District Court. These figures are from the 'Judicial Gender Balance 2015' Courts Service statistics from April 2015.
14 Of course, one significant problem in relation to gender, particularly with the appointment of more senior judges is that the pool from which many appointees are drawn, the inner Bar, contains shockingly few women. Of the 166 silks appointed since 2003, only 41 have been women. While women represent 43% of the entire bar the inner Bar is a different matter, where men make up over 83% of members. This issue was flagged by the Gender inJustice report; see I. Bacik, C. Costello and E. Drew, 'Women in Law – Gender InJustice Report' (Trinity College Law School, 2003). More recently, Conor Gallagher and Elizabeth Fitzgerald wrote separate pieces in the *Irish Times* on this issue and it is clear that where women are concerned, there are barriers to becoming senior counsel (Gallagher, 'Why are so few women becoming senior counsel?', *Irish Times* (9 December 2013); Fitzgerald, 'Barrister fee records reveal scale of gender inequality', *Irish Times* (20 January 2014)). This is certainly another area where the lack of diversity should be considered.
15 T. Rubens, 'France has plenty of women judges – why don't we?', *The Times* (9 March 2004); also quoted in E. Rackley, *Women, Judging and the Judiciary: From Difference to Diversity* (Routledge, 2013) p. 19.
16 While the Judges' Report to the Department on Reform to the Appointments Process stated that a Commission should be set up to take evidence on issues around diversity, the tenor of the report was that progress had been made and in the absence of any evidence of a problem, the focus should be on judicial education. The report also stated that 'any such alteration is complex to devise and operate and creates a difficult intersection with the principle of appointment on the basis of demonstrable merit' (Judicial Appointments Review Committee, Preliminary Submission to the Department of Justice and Equality's Public

Consultation on the Judicial Appointments Process, 30 January 2014, pp. 21–22, www.supremecourt.ie/SupremeCourt/sclibrary3.nsf/(WebFiles)/51E71A71B9 961BD680257C70005CCE2D/$FILE/A%20Preliminary%20Submission%20 of%20J.A.R.C.%2030.01.2014.pdf (last accessed 18 August 2015)). The issue of reconciling merit and diversity has been considered elsewhere: e.g. Lady B. Hale, 'Equality in the Judiciary', Kuttan Menon Memorial Lecture, 21 February 2013, www.supremecourt.uk/docs/speech-130221.pdf (last accessed 18 August 2015); K. Malleson, 'Diversity in the Judiciary: The Case for Positive Action' (2009) 36(3) *Journal of Law and Society* 27; Rackley (n. 15).

17 See D. G. Morgan, 'Powerful superior courts in urgent need of reform', *Irish Times* (24 May 2010).
18 See overview of the selection process of the Judicial Appointments Commission of England and Wales, https://jac.judiciary.gov.uk/overview-selection-process (last accessed 18 August 2015).
19 See Morgan (n. 2).
20 See selection policy of the Judicial Appointments Commission of England and Wales, at https://jac.judiciary.gov.uk/about-us (last accessed 18 August 2015).
21 Constitution of the Republic of South Africa 1996, Chapter 8, Section 178.
22 See Judicial Appointments Board for Scotland Guide to the Appointment Process, at www.judicialappointmentsscotland.org.uk/Guide_to_Appointment_Process/index (last accessed 18 August 2015).
23 Although these are currently in the process of being revised. See Judicial Appointments Commission Annual Report 2014 https://jac.judiciary.gov.uk/sites/default/files/sync/basic_page/jac_annualreport_2014–15_print_version.pdf (last accessed 18 August 2015).
24 See www.judicialappointmentsscotland.org.uk/Diversity_Strategy (last accessed 18 August 2015).
25 See Judicial Appointments Commission Annual Report 2012/2013.
26 Bacik et al. (n. 14).

9

Merit, diversity and interpretative communities: the (non-party) politics of judicial appointments and constitutional adjudication

David Kenny

Judicial appointments in Ireland are again under scrutiny as senior judges have frankly criticised the role of party-political patronage in the selection of candidates for judicial office.[1] However, attempts to avoid partisan politics expose problems of politics more broadly defined that inhere in judicial appointments in a constitutional democracy such as ours. It is this politics that I explore in the course of this chapter, arguing that, contrary to the ambitions of some, we could never avoid political considerations in judicial appointments.

In the first section, I examine a recent report written by senior judges that proposes eliminating politics from appointments with a system based on solely on 'merit'. Merit, however, is an 'empty vessel for substantive norms'[2] – it is filled with content that is invariably political. In Ireland, it is given political content in the focus on professional experience of litigation as the indicator of merit: this selects judges from a small 'interpretive community'[3] of lawyers that are fairly homogeneous in terms of legal thought, having been inculcated into the particular values and suppositions that come with traditional legal practice. In the second section, I argue that the composition of the judiciary in Ireland probably lacks diversity in terms of personal and educational background, and this compounds the homogeneity of judicial viewpoints. Especially in constitutional adjudication, political viewpoints and experience inevitably shape our views on what the Constitution is for, and what the Constitution means, and therefore the diversity of our judiciary matters.

Finally, in the third section, I advance three suggestions in light of my conclusion that there are irreducible political considerations in judicial appointments: that we abandon the language of merit, along with any aspiration to nominate judges in a manner that expresses no political viewpoint about what judging should be; that, however we might reform judicial appointments to excise political patronage, we should not delegate this function from government to an independent body; and that we should increase the diversity of our judiciary, in terms of both professional and personal background. The way forward lies in admitting, rather than concealing, the politics at play in judicial appointments.

This chapter draws on the anti-foundationalist and conventionalist writings of Stanley Fish and on the pragmatist jurisprudence of Richard Posner,[4] which have received little attention in Ireland. I use the term 'politics' in the broad sense used by Fish: a political stance is one that is angled, partial, biased towards a particular ideology or vision of society.[5] It is not based on neutral, procedural, or universal standards, but on a contestable and contested vision of society and social life, angled towards one idea of the good and away from others. Such a politics can be 'enterprise specific' – you can have a judicial politics that will be in some ways different from other political views.[6] But enterprise specific politics is still politics. There are many who dispute that even politics in this broad sense should feature in judging and judicial appointments; it is this formalist, technocratic position with which I take issue in this paper.

Merit and politics

Party political judicial appointments and the merit principle

Judicial appointments in Ireland are made by government, and they are frequently made based on party political considerations: appointing those who had earned the government's favour.[7] In 2014, a Report authored by the Chief Justice and other senior judges affirmed the persistence of party political preference in appointments, and maintained that '[i]t is simply wrong in principle that consideration of political considerations should form any part of the decision process'.[8] It called on the government to declare that, in future, political allegiance 'would play no part in the selection for appointment of the judiciary'.[9] The objection to politics seems to be deeper than just patronage; when the Report stated that 'political considerations should be irrelevant',[10] it seemed to disclaim *any* role for politics in appointments. As a solution, it called for merit to be the only determining factor in choosing judges.[11] This 'merit principle' is endorsed by many important international bodies.[12] However, merit, of itself, has no content; and any content it is given, by the outlining of a vision of the judicial role, will invariably be political.

As Fish puts it, 'merit is just a word for whatever qualifications are deemed desirable for the performance of a particular task, and there is nothing fixed about those qualifications'.[13] Merit does not *identify* the qualifications and characteristics that are desirable. In the Judges' Report, it is first used to oppose something regarded by almost all as an irreverent consideration – party political allegiance. However, it is then used as a supposedly apolitical and neutral adjudicative principle for selecting judges. While merit is unobjectionable in the former role, it is highly problematic in the latter. Unless merit is combined with a view of what judging *is*, what it is *for*, and when it is *good*, it has no content, and agreeing to the merit principle is an agreement so general as to be meaningless. As soon as it has been given that content by specifying what one thinks makes a good judge and what the value of judging is, it ceases to be a neutral adjudicative principle and instead becomes the battleground for contested concepts of the good we are seeking to achieve in the judicial process. The debate, then, is not about 'merit' and 'not merit'; it is about different versions and visions of merit and what judging should be.[14] Every such vision will have within it a political outlook, because it must answer questions about the nature and purpose of judging that will be partial, partisan, and angled towards a particular social outlook.

The politics of experience in practice
Little in the Judges' Report elaborates a vision of what merit, in this context, actually entails. It offers only one firm indicator of merit: practical experience (and lots of it) in the conduct of litigation:[15]

> An essential element of merit to which particular weight should be given is that of practical experience in the conduct of litigation and advocacy. There is no substitute for this and no amount of formal academic training in judicial skills or experience in other branches of the law can equate with actual practical experience of the conduct of litigation in court.[16]

Although this is presented as a neutral vision of merit, it is, in fact, political.

The Report offers no clear reason for why experience in litigation is the watchword of merit; perhaps it is taken to be self-evident. It is implied that since our current judges were all practitioners, and are well regarded, change from past practice would risk that reputation.[17] This is a false syllogism: the fact that we have had good judges drawn from the practice of litigation says little about how well other candidates would do.[18] Mr Justice Kevin Cross, writing extra-judicially, recently set out a more elaborate version of the objection: those without substantial practice in litigation will not know how to run a courtroom, deal with witnesses, know the rules of evidence etc.[19] But this concern is less acute in the context of appellate courts, where judges do not oversee the conduct of trials, and given the advent of the Court of Appeal, the force of this argument is lessening. Additionally, while running a courtroom and knowing one's way around the rules of evidence are valuable skills, surely this is not rocket science.[20] Some activities might be more challenging than others – perhaps we will always want a general practitioner of long-standing on a motions list, say – but do the basic skills require decades at the bar to acquire? Could we not train people in this art with judicial education?

I suspect that behind these objections lies a deeper concern. Discomfort with the idea of a judge who has 'not learned the way things work' is not merely about procedure and technicality. A person who has not practiced at or near the bar would not know the way things should be done; they would not be fully inculcated into the customary practices and unwritten conventions of the Irish judiciary. They would not, in other words, have been inducted into the right interpretative community.

The interpretative community of judging
Though explored in American law by Fish and Posner, among others, the role of customary practice and convention in judging has received little attention in Ireland.[21] Judicial conduct, like any practice, is influenced by a set of conventions and suppositions that are gradually acquired, largely subconsciously, from experience. Judging is guided by intuitions acquired over time – intuitions, Posner says, 'that lie so deep that we don't know how to question them'.[22] In the language of Fish, judges exist inside an 'interpretative community', a set of assumptions, beliefs, and suppositions that are shared by those who are within it.[23] Membership of this community will influence the way one acts, guiding the exercise of judgment with 'an ever-changing collection of rules of thumb, doctrines, proverbs, precedents, folk-tales, prejudices, aspirations, goals, fears, and above all, beliefs'.[24] Once in place, these are so deeply embedded that they are part of the constitution of our professional selves.[25] We don't *have* the beliefs so much as the beliefs have *us*.[26]

The intuitions and beliefs that constitute the interpretative community of judging begin to accrue long before one's time on the bench; they '[come] with the territory, with the experience of law school, of practice, of a life in the courts, etc.'.[27] Training for judging – for the mindset that judging is thought to require – begins long before appointment. This explains our judges' fixation with legal practice as the only appropriate training for judging: practice at the bar is, to them, the most crucial stage of inculcation into the interpretative community. One learns which arguments will earn the favour of judges (and colleagues) and which will earn their derision. One learns what one is supposed to be doing in legal practice, and what a judge is supposed to be doing in judging. One learns a vision of the core purpose of the enterprise.

From this comes a set of beliefs about what one should and should not do – the arguments one should make as a practitioner, the arguments one should accept as a judge.[28] Because this necessarily requires a conception of the limits and purpose of the judicial role, the values of the community are not neutral; they are political. They advance some agendas and they reject others; they treat some matters as cognisable and some as not. Over the course of a life in practice, this vision of judging is internalised; when one becomes a judge, these suppositions are as much a part of oneself as any fundamental constitutive belief. It would be, in Fish's words, 'unthinkable' to depart from these practices and beliefs, because conforming to them is now nothing more than doing what comes naturally, 'comporting oneself in ways inseparable from one's position in a field of institutional activity'.[29] They will greatly influence the manner in which one judges.

If judges are selected solely from a small group of litigators, only those who have internalised the values, practices, and precepts of the current interpretative community of the bar and the bench will join the judicial ranks. This ensures a level of conformity, and homogeneity, in judicial thought. It propagates particular beliefs and practices that will have a substantive impact on judicial conduct. Those from different interpretative communities – those who had experience more distant from the practice of litigation – might see things differently, but few if any of these voices – voices that might reject the dominant, prevailing ideology – would ever reach the bench and articulate a contrary vision.

Of course, there would be degrees of acceptance of the precepts of the interpretative community: depending on temperament, background, intellectual disposition, etc. different people in practice could take very differently to this training. This is what gives us difference even within a homogeneous interpretative community – the relatively interventionist judge in a highly restrained legal community. But, if the precepts of the community are mostly internalised, these will be small variations along a narrow spectrum. The more homogeneous the group, the smaller this spectrum will be; the rarer the individual who is at its fringes; the more likely that this individual will be regarded as perverse. A small, geographically condensed, and tightly bound legal community such as ours will likely have a more homogeneous interpretative community than a larger and more diffuse one.

This is, at least in Ireland, a radical suggestion to make about judicial conduct. However, recent extrajudicial writing of Mr Justice Cross seems to support my thesis. Justice Cross argues against non-practitioners becoming judges because of their lack of experience in dealing with arguments and evidence. His specific target is academics, having found disturbing the pragmatist and realist positions articulated by Posner, an American academic turned judge. His argument seems to be about technical rules of evidence, etc., but it is in fact broader: 'Academics, however learned, can never surpass the practitioner's experience in litigating cases. A practitioner soon learns what will and will not succeed in the common law court.'[30] A practitioner does not just learn technical rules; she learns what will and will not *succeed* before a judge. She learns how judges think; what judges want to hear; how they will be persuaded; what they are ultimately willing to hold. She learns a philosophy of judging.

Justice Cross describes his judicial philosophy as a 'practically based idealism born from decades of litigation in the courts'.[31] The judge seeks 'justice and fairness. These are objective ideals and the judge will apply the law with that objective in mind.'[32] Judges' understanding of these objective goods may be imperfect, but they will strive towards them nonetheless.[33] He is clear that these ideas do not come from a personal worldview, and are not political even in the broad sense that I use the term: 'Decisions should be as objective as possible, based on where the legal evidence leads and not based on a judge's view of how society ought to work. Society rightly expects a judge to set his own bias and prejudices and views aside and apply the rules.'[34] How did Justice Cross acquire this philosophy? He learned it in the King's Inns, from John A. Costello, then father of the bar and former Taoiseach.[35] He learned it from a practitioner while training for practice. Justice Cross speaks only for himself, and not every judge would adopt his view. However, his statements support my thesis: practitioners are likely to adopt a particular judicial philosophy having been inculcated into it in practice. That is why he is so wary of appointing non-practitioners: they might think differently, as Posner does, and this would endanger the prevalent and, in his view, objectively correct approach that we currently adopt in Ireland.

However, Justice Cross's confidence that there is an objective notion of justice or fairness to which all judges should strive results in part from the homogeneity of Irish judges. Something contestable can *appear* to be objective because of broad agreement among those discussing it – that is, because of a homogeneous interpretative community.[36] Posner calls this 'conversational objectivity';[37] it exists within a particular discourse, but outside of it, dissent would immediately spring up and the appearance of objectivity would collapse. The objectivity that Justice Cross perceives in the judicial enterprise is, in part, a product of the largely homogeneous philosophy of Irish judges, which is itself a product of the restrictive view of who would make a good judge that he advocates.

Viewed this way, the professional focus in appointments is not a neutral mechanism that objectively selects the best candidates, but a political mechanism that selects those most likely to agree with the prevailing (but contestable and contested) judicial ideology.

The politics of restraint

It has been put to me that what is internalised in this process is not politics, but a sense of 'restraint', a principle endorsed by Justice Cross.[38] Restraint is presented as apolitical, but it is no such thing.[39] First, restraint cannot decide cases unless combined with a political outlook on the purpose of judging. Restraint might mean 'that a judge should decide as little as necessary',[40] but as little as necessary *to do what*? To decide cases *correctly, fairly, justly* etc. Second, one's level of restraint has political implications because there is politics in doing nothing. One is doing nothing, or little, because one thinks that things are generally acceptable as they are; because other arms of the state, left to their own devices, do a reasonable (if not perfect) job. One leaves in place what has been done in the past – by government and the legislature (refusing to intervene) or by other judges (adhering to precedent) – because one is broadly happy with it, or believes it will work itself clear.[41] This is my sense of the prevailing politics of the Irish judiciary (though the full content of this politics is impossible to know):[42] a liberal judicial conservatism – a Burkean conservatism, motivated by a general commitment to enlightenment liberalism, manifesting in a sense that things will get gradually better if left alone.[43]

The political content of restraint is clearly seen when restraint inevitably runs out. Justice Cross is very clear on the need to stay within well-established judicial boundaries: 'We cannot ignore what has been established law for generations merely because we disagree with it.'[44] But he has a line:

> Should, at some future date, a rogue government utilise some apparently constitutionally legitimate means, say, Article 28(3)(iii), to abolish liberties … it is to be hoped that some brave judge will try to avoid evil and to do good by evoking a higher natural law to decree the state's actions as unlawful.[45]

Some future judge should set aside restraint and break with precedent and long-held understanding of Article 28(3) (that is what it means for the action to be 'apparently constitutionally legitimate') in order to uphold what Justice Cross sees as the higher value of liberty. To be clear, my criticism is not that Justice Cross is unfaithful to the ideal of restraint, because restraint is not an ideal one can be faithful to all the way down. Rather, he illustrates what restraint is: not acting – unless and until the fundamental principles that you believe underwrite the project are jeopardised. What those principles are depends on your political vision of what the constitutional project is for, and what it can tolerate. Restraint is thus a political stance, just one that usually has some leeway before intervention is required.

Diversity and politics

The homogeneous professional backgrounds of our judges result in a narrow interpretative community, which is compounded by homogeneous social, cultural, educational and intellectual backgrounds. Because part of the interpretative community will be influenced by life experiences outside of professional background, a lack of diversity further narrows the views within the community.

The Judges' Report disputes that a lack of diversity exists,[46] suggesting an empirical study, which would be worthwhile. However, Carroll's relatively recent research shows that Irish judges are drawn from a small sector of society: they are largely male former barristers with middle class backgrounds.[47] In terms of ethnicity,[48] sex,[49] professional experience,[50] geographical situation[51] and educational background,[52] there is a level of sameness in the ranks of Superior Court judges. Little in the interceding decade would suggest that this has changed. The gender balance of the courts generally has improved, but it is far from optimal, and may have reached a limit in terms of progress at Superior Court level.[53] The question of class/socio-economic status is difficult; judges show reluctance to engage with it.[54] However, since the overwhelming majority of Superior Court judges were Senior Counsel at the Irish bar before appointment, one sympathises with the participant in Carroll's study who commented: 'I can't think of how much upper [class] you could go beyond being a Senior Counsel.'[55] The ranks of the senior judiciary are filled with those who have had excellent (and similar) educational opportunities and substantial career success. It would be hard to argue that this group of people is representative of society as a whole.

While stating that '[d]iversity is an important consideration in shaping a judiciary which reflects the society it serves',[56] the Judges' Report is emphatic that diversity is irrelevant to the practice of judging.[57] But diversity is irrelevant to judging only if there exist technical and mechanical skills that allow someone to judge without any regard to social, educational, cultural or intellectual experience. This is Justice Cross's claim: personal background plays no role.[58] However, in a constitutional democracy such as ours, judges cannot view disputes completely severed from their experiences and outlook. I do not suggest that the traditional bases for judging – legal texts, precedents and principles – are irrelevant, but that the interpretation of those legal materials is unavoidably influenced by background, education, intellectual and professional experience. Nor do I mean that judges decide cases based on pure personal preference for the outcome; rather, I suggest that *all* preferences for particular interpretations or outcomes are necessarily a function of conventions that are themselves a function of experiences and politics.[59]

To read the Constitution differently – say, to see the separation of powers as rigid on the one hand or flexible on the other – is to have a different conception of what a constitution, or our Constitution, is *for*.[60] Constitutional adjudication, in particular,[61] requires a conception of its purpose that must involve a vision of social life in our community. This is not a distortion of textual interpretation, but a *necessity* in textual interpretation: texts, especially vague texts like the Constitution, can never tell us the whole story.[62] The Constitution is dependent for its meaning on what we understand it to be doing, what its goals and objectives are. These understandings are our politics, and without them, the Constitution would be mired in ambiguities. It is the politics that we have – and the sense of direction and purpose that it gives us – that grounds our understanding and gives indeterminate text determinate meaning.[63]

Views on these matters could, and almost certainly do, vary across different groups in society, and while there is probably a significant commonality between them, the differences are important. The proper role of judges; the meaning and extent of personal rights; the extent (if any) of the deference courts owe to the Oireachtas, the executive, and administrative bodies – all these matters (and many more) might be viewed differently from a different perspective in terms of education, upbringing, life experience, intellectual experience, etc. The constitutional text does not resolve them; any textual answer raises equally significant questions not answerable by reference to text.[64] Nor can legal training tell us what the Constitution means.[65] It may tell us what it meant to judges in the past; what it meant to its drafters; what it means to academics. But it cannot tell us whether we should reject/endorse/alter/adopt those meanings. Constitutional meaning can and does change. Precedent does not bind completely.[66] It is, ultimately, for us to decide, through the lens of our education, experience, and judgment, what the Constitution means. This will be shaped by our human experiences, and since difference is part of the human condition, our different experiences will, in major and minor ways, alter our understanding.

There was a time in our constitutional history where we acknowledged this. Justice Walsh famously said that judges had to look to their own conceptions of prudence, justice, and charity, shaped by their experiences, to understand elements of the Constitution.[67] Extra-judicially, he said that, expounding vague constitutional concepts, a judge 'must rely upon instinct or intuition, which, in short, means on his own moral sense and his own intelligence'.[68] We seem to run from this now, but denying that our experiences shape our understandings does not make it so. The proposition that we should avoid bringing our own views into constitutional interpretation is a function and a product of those views, even as it renounces that this should be so.

Constitutional interpretation cannot be divorced from life experience. If the experience of our judges is very similar, then the range of possible conceptions of the Constitution that our judiciary will consider is smaller. That is not to say that there will be no difference between judges: similar is not identical, and different experiences will lead to different views on what the Constitution means. However, these differences will exist within a narrow range, and no voices that might express anything outside that range will be appointed to positions where they could express them as part of the relevant discourse. In the absence of those voices, conversational objectivity will once again occur, buttressing dominant ideologies, and insulating them from challenge – insulating them, indeed, from the challenge that they are ideologies at all and not objective truth.

The future of judicial appointments

I have three suggestions that follow from the insight that political considerations, broadly defined, are unavoidable in judicial appointments. First, we should disclaim supposedly neutral standards for judicial appointment and instead argue about what makes a good judge on political grounds. There is no sense in using terms such as merit to imply a neutrality that cannot exist. Instead, argue for professional experience/ restraint/formalism on the grounds that it produces the results that are, from your perspective, good. I can see why a proponent of these virtues might be loath to give up this ground; claiming that preferred values are objective and apolitical is a great rhetorical strategy if you can make it work. However, if these virtues are worthwhile, why not, in the interests of openness, test them plainly against the contrary political assertions, and see which prevails?

Second, since politics is unavoidable, we should not devolve the power to appoint judges to an independent body. Though not expressly set out, the Judges' Report suggested obliquely that the power might be removed from government altogether.[69] This would be a mistake: while it might hide the politics involved behind a veil of independence and neutrality, it could never remove them, and would simply transfer the political questions onto that independent body. We should be willing to leave the power of appointments in the hands of elected representatives – political agents who are used to political questions, and who are notionally responsive and accountable to the people. The downside of the government retaining control of the process is that political patronage appointments may remain. However, there are other ways to end this practice. A declaration of intent from the government to do just that, as suggested by the Judges' Report, would be a start.[70] Oireachtas committee hearings on appointments might help, though these are contentious.[71] It is said that this would make judging more political,[72] but politics in appointments is unavoidable; the choice is to acknowledge the politics that is always and already at play, or to hide it.[73] Whatever the solution, excising the elected branches completely should not be entertained.

Finally, I want to make my own (openly political) case for diversity in judicial appointments. Since professionalised judicial appointment leads to a homogeneity of judicial viewpoints, we should increase the diversity of our judges, both in terms of professional background and in terms of socio-economic, educational and intellectual background, sex, etc. How we might achieve this diversity is an interesting and challenging question, but must await another occasion.

Diversity could change the shape of the interpretative community of the Irish judiciary, albeit slowly and in an undirected way, to make it more representative of society as a whole. Disagreement about the meaning of the Constitution is a disagreement between people: people who approach the act of interpretation with different goals, priorities, suppositions, and beliefs.[74] These background factors are determined to a significant degree by professional and life experience. If the professional and life experiences of judges differed more, the shape of the interpretative community would change, and more interpretations would be heard as potentially reasonable. The content and nature of an interpretative community can change, but in the ordinary course of that community's activity, change is not entirely predictable; no sequence of steps will definitely bring about particular alterations.[75] However, if a community maintains great homogeneity, change will be less likely and much slower. In a closed interpretative community like judging, only the views of its members need be taken seriously; external voices can be ignored. The appointments power is, ultimately, a prerogative to decide who should be permitted to join, and therefore to shape, the interpretative community of judging.

Diversity in judicial personnel could broaden – to some degree – the range of acceptable legal outcomes that judges would consider. I could not deny, based on the analysis above, that this is a political argument; I find this outcome politically desirable, thinking the prevailing formalism rather narrow, and would like an array of viewpoints to be aired in the judicial process to see which might win out. My case for a broader discourse might be unappealing if your judicial politics is well reflected in our current judiciary. But it is important to set out the limits of my claim to placate potential opponents.

First, this change is not directed towards the results of specific cases, but towards the consideration of different ideas in the judicial process. Some read diversity as a demand for judges with particular backgrounds to decide particular cases.[76] This misses the point. If people from different social, intellectual or cultural backgrounds see the world – or the meaning of a constitutional provision – in a somewhat different way, and they are not well represented in the judiciary, then these views are not aired, considered, or debated within the judicial discourse. They will not take hold because they will never be taken seriously as *judicial* points of view. Diversity is not about altering the results of particular cases, but about how ideas and viewpoints are included within the interpretative community of judging. Over time, inclusion of new views may change the results of cases, or may not. Whether these viewpoints ultimately take hold and alter the common understanding of what the Constitution means will depend on whether or not they gain broader acceptance, whether or not they can persuade others to accept them. However, to even have a chance to do this, they have to be aired in a judicial context. Having those viewpoints articulated and considered – rather than necessarily having them prevail – is my goal.

Second, the proposal is not designed to use appointments to alter radically or undermine the conduct of judging; I think this would be neither desirable nor possible, and so there is little to fear in this proposal. Nothing in my proposal suggests that we should appoint *anyone* to be a judge, regardless of the content of her politics. If people existed in our society that thought that the continuity of the state, the Constitution, and the rule of law were not a good thing, I would strongly oppose appointing them to the bench. The nature of politics is that you favour some things and dislike others, and our prevailing common politics will keep out those very rare individuals (should they actually exist)[77] that would attempt to subvert the entire judicial enterprise. Imagining we did appoint such a person, she would not accomplish much, except setting new records for getting overturned on appeal, or issuing fringe dissents. I propose only that we should have more viewpoints in judicial discourse; if those viewpoints are heard as being[78] completely unreasonable and receive negligible support, little will come of them. This is not particularly dangerous.

Conclusion

Politics in judicial appointments is inevitable and irreducible in our constitutional democracy. I have set out suggestions for what we might do in light of this, including making diversity a consideration in appointments. There are many possible objections to my proposals: that appointees without a background in litigation would not manage a courtroom as well as we would wish; that they would not command the respect of barristers; that it might lower international regard of our judiciary; that we are better off with a reserved and restrained judiciary; that we should stick with what we have rather than rock the boat. These are political arguments, many of which I disagree with, but which I will acquiesce to if, at the end of the day, I am outnumbered. But these are the arguments we should be having – putting aside the myth of apolitical judicial appointment, and arguing instead on pragmatic and political grounds. We should admit that merit is just what we think is best, and what we think is best is always political and subject to dispute. We should allow the debate about judicial appointments to visibly take on the political characteristics it will, in any event, have. We should take our politics out into the light. Even if nothing else were to follow from it, this would be no small thing.

Notes

1 Judicial Appointments Review Committee, 'Preliminary Submission to the Department of Justice and Equality's Public Consultation on the Judicial Appointments Process', 30 January 2014 (hereafter 'the Judges' Report').
2 L. Alexander, 'Liberalism, Religion, and the Unity of Epistemology' (1993) 30 *San Diego Law Review* 763, 776.
3 See S. Fish, *Is There a Text in this Class?* (Harvard UP, 1980) for the origin of the idea in literary theory.
4 The views of these writers are not entirely compatible. More of the particulars in this chapter align with Fish's account.
5 S. Fish, *A Matter of Principle* (Harvard UP, 1999) p. 94.
6 S. Fish, 'Fish v Fiss' (1984) 36 *Stanford Law Review* 1325, 1336. One can be judicially conservative while being, say, generally politically liberal: one might

favour a liberal result, but be unwilling to reach it judicially. That does not mean judicial politics are neutral; it just means that one's broad political views favour restraint in the specific context of judging.
7 J. Carroll, 'You Be the Judge, Part I' (2005) 10(5) *Bar Review* 153; Cahillane, Chapter 8, this volume.
8 Judges' Report (n. 1) p. 16.
9 *Ibid.*, p. 18.
10 *Ibid.*, p. 59.
11 *Ibid.*, p. 56.
12 *Ibid.*, pp. 58–60.
13 Fish (n. 5) p. 30.
14 *Ibid.* Compare R. Davis and G. Williams, 'Reform of the Judicial Appointments Process: Gender and the Bench of the High Court of Australia' (2003) 27 *Melbourne University Law Review* 819.
15 Other desiderata for merit mentioned briefly were subjective and vague: 'ability, work ethic, education, legal writing, decision making capabilities, leadership, professional development, and personal characteristics' (*ibid.*, pp. 56–57).
16 Judges' Report (n. 1) p. 56.
17 *Ibid.*, pp. 9, 16, 66.
18 Moreover, 'the appointment of a judge [is] a largely unknown entity in that a person's performance at the Bar did not necessarily indicate how they might perform as a judge' (Carroll (n. 7) p. 168).
19 K. Cross, 'Fiat Justicia' (54) *Dublin Review of Books*, 22 April 2014, at www.drb.ie/essays/fiat-justitia (last accessed 18 August 2015).
20 Legal academia is, similarly, not rocket science; P. Schlag, 'Spam Jurisprudence, Air Law, and the Rank Anxiety of Nothing Happening' (2009) 97 *Georgetown Law Journal* 803, 809.
21 See, however, O. Doyle, 'The Judicial Protection of Human Rights in Ireland: The Interaction of the Constitution and the European Convention on Human Rights'. Four Jurisdictions Conference, Middle Temple, London, 12 May 2012; O. Doyle, 'Conventional Constitutional Law', Symposium on Constitutionalism and Conventions, Trinity College Dublin, 15 November 2014.
22 R. Posner, *The Problems of Jurisprudence* (Harvard UP, 1990) p. 73.
23 See Fish (n. 3). The product of these interpretative guides/constraints issues without need for conscious recourse to them; it 'will issue from you as naturally as breathing' (Fish, *Doing What Comes Naturally* (Duke UP, 1989) p. ix).
24 S. Fish, 'Almost Pragmatism: The Jurisprudence of Richard Posner, Richard Rorty, and Ronald Dworkin' in *There's No Such Thing as Free Speech* (OUP, 1994) pp. 200, 203.
25 *Ibid.*, p. 214.
26 Fish (n. 23) p. 127.
27 *Ibid.*; cf. Doyle (n. 21).
28 *Ibid.*, p. 225.
29 Fish (n. 24) p. 225.
30 Cross (n. 19).

31 *Ibid.*
32 *Ibid.*
33 *Ibid.* In law, ontological problems can always be made to seem like epistemological problems, and even these can then be used to supposedly disprove alleged ontological deficits. See P. Schlag, 'Hiding the Ball' (1996) 71 *NYU Law Review* 1681, 1692.
34 Cross (n. 19).
35 *Ibid.*
36 Fish (n. 24) p. 201; cf. Posner (n. 22) p. 32.
37 Posner (n. 22) p. 31.
38 Cross (n. 19).
39 See N. Cox, 'Passive Judicial Activism' (2000) 22 *Dublin University Law Journal* 201; O. Doyle, *Constitutional Equality Law* (Round Hall, 2004) 25. A similar critique can be levelled at other supposedly apolitical restraints, such as text, advocated by Mr Justice Hogan, see Chapter 3 in this volume, or disciplining rules of interpretation. See Fish (n. 6).
40 Cross (n. 19).
41 Fish (n. 6) p. 1339.
42 Even a judge fully immersed in this politics could not fully elaborate it, as she would already be formed and influenced by the ideas she is trying to explicate. See D. Kenny, Conventional Constitutional Law and the Limits of Critical Self Consciousness', Symposium on Constitutionalism and Conventions, Trinity College Dublin, 15 November 2014.
43 This is not an oxymoron: the broad political goals are those of enlightenment liberalism (freedom of rational agents, etc.) but the means for judges to achieve them is Burkean non-interventionism. See D. Kennedy, *A Critique of Adjudication (fin de siècle)* (Harvard UP, 1997) pp. 54–56.
44 Cross (n. 19).
45 *Ibid.*
46 Judges' Report (n. 1) p. 21.
47 See Carroll (n. 7); J. Carroll, 'You Be the Judge, Part II' (2005) 10(6) *Bar Review* 182.
48 The 2004 study of the composition of the Irish Superior Courts found that over 93% of Superior Court judges were of wholly Irish ethnicity (*ibid.*, p. 170).
49 Judges' Report (n. 1) p. 62.
50 As of 2014, there were six former solicitors sitting as Superior Court judges, representing about 14% of the Superior Court Bench. The rest are barristers (*ibid.*, pp. 62–63).
51 Of Superior Court judges, 83% in the 2004 study were born and raised in an urban setting (Carroll (n. 7) p. 154). They were all living in Dublin or an adjacent county at the time of appointment (*ibid.*, p. 167).
52 In 2004, 79% of the Superior Court judiciary were educated in University College Dublin, and 15% attended Trinity College Dublin (*ibid.*, p. 168); 92% obtained their professional legal qualification at the King's Inns (*ibid.*, p. 169).
53 The gender balance of the Circuit Court bench is close to equal, but the disparity

at Superior Court level will be difficult to address: the number of women being called to the inner Bar, from where most Superior Court judges are appointed, still fails to reach more than 30% of those called (being as low 13% in recent years) (C. Gallagher, 'Why are so few women becoming senior counsel?', *Irish Times* (9 December 2013).
54 Carroll (n. 7) p. 172.
55 *Ibid.*
56 Judges' Report (n. 1) p. 65.
57 *Ibid.*, p. 22.
58 See (n. 34).
59 Critiques of legal realism that allege that the realist judge is a radically unconstrained actor are misplaced; we are always and already constrained by the suppositions and conventions of our interpretative community (Fish (n. 23) p. 5; Fish (n. 6) p. 1346).
60 Fish (n. 6) pp. 1335–1336; cf. Posner (n. 22) p. 148: 'political factors, and sometimes social vision, are decisive in the most difficult cases'; Schlag (n. 33).
61 This may in fact be true for all law (Fish (n.6) p. 1337) but in constitutional law the political considerations are particularly obvious and acute.
62 It is here, again, that I diverge from Mr Justice Hogan, Chapter 3, this volume; text is only meaningful when combined with a range of assumptions and suppositions not apparent from the text nor derived from it (S. Fish, 'There Is No Textualist Position' (2005) 42 *San Diego Law Review* 629; Fish (n. 23) p. 4).
63 See R. Posner, 'A Political Court' (2005) 119 *Harvard Law Review* 32, 34, 40.
64 To take an example: we can, as the text instructs, restrict property rights in 'the exigencies of the common good' by reference to 'the principles of social justice'. Any elaboration on those textual concepts will take us outside of the text: to context, to history, to precedent, to moral philosophy, to common sense. Which of these external reference points we go to, and what we find when we get there, will be a function of our politics.
65 This applies equally to rules of interpretation, or disciplining rules, which themselves must be chosen between and interpreted. See Fish (n. 6).
66 Deciding to cleave to precedent would, just like restraint, be a political decision. See Posner (n. 59) 43–45; Fish (n. 23) 109–111.
67 *McGee v. Attorney General* [1974] IR 284, 318–319.
68 B. Walsh, 'The Constitution and Constitutional Rights' in Frank Litton (ed.), *The Constitution of Ireland 1937–1987* (IPA, 1988) p. 106.
69 See Judges' Report (n. 1) pp. 13, 48–49.
70 *Ibid.*, p. 18.
71 P. K. McMorrow, 'Judicial nominees should have to attend Oireachtas hearings', *Irish Times* (9 June 2014).
72 In the United States, bitter, partisan confirmation hearings are common; Justice Cross (n. 19) thinks 'a more blatant politicisation of judges could not be envisaged'.
73 As Fish would say, it just seems more 'obviously political; but in fact the entire system is political' (Fish (n. 6) p. 1338).

74 *Ibid.*, p. 1335.
75 'Almost anything and nothing in particular' brings about change. Fish (n. 24) 207; see also Posner (n. 22) 148–151.
76 The Judges' Report seems to adopt this view; see above (n. 57). Justices Ginsberg and Sotomayor of the US Supreme Court have had statements on gender and racial diversity read this way. See 'The compelling Judge Sotomayor', *Seattle Times* (28 May 2009).
77 I doubt we could find such a candidate; undergoing any legal training probably indicates/results in broad agreement that the enterprise of judging is worthwhile. One could not appoint those with no legal training or experience because, having no idea what to do, they would have to replicate judicial practice as it stands. Fish (n. 6) pp. 1328–1330.
78 Things are *heard as being* reasonable rather than simply *being* reasonable in a vacuum: 'the state of the culture, of what it will hear as reasonable (not the force of reason itself) bars [particular outcomes]' (Fish (n. 24) p. 204). See also P. Schlag, *The Enchantment of Reason* (Duke UP, 1998); S. Fish, 'Liberalism Doesn't Exist' (1987) *Duke Law Journal* 997.

10

Speaking to power:
mechanisms for judicial–executive dialogue

John O'Dowd

Introduction

Several recent episodes in Ireland have highlighted how judges collectively communicate with the executive concerning the judiciary's constitutional functions and conditions of service, often a politically sensitive matter. Three main models may be proposed based on this experience: presidential – where the Chief Justice (or equivalent) speaks to government on behalf of her court; associational – where judges establish a professional association to speak on their behalf and conciliar – in which a judicial council established by law performs representational (as well as regulatory) functions for the judiciary. There have been prominent recent Irish examples of the first two options. Both have seen the judiciary entangled in potentially rebarbative exchanges with ministers. The Association of Judges of Ireland has combatively represented judges' interests in relation to salaries, pensions and other matters.[1] In parallel, the judiciary has been unprecedentedly open in commenting on salary reductions and reform of the judicial appointments system (this latter submission being itself a hybrid of the presidential and associational types of representation, which calls for a move to a judicial council and an associated system of de-politicised judicial appointments).[2]

A brief background

Developments in Ireland since 2011 have highlighted the increasing salience of relations between the executive and the judiciary in relation to the terms and conditions on which the judges themselves hold office. This is distinct from with the broader 'dialogue' between the two branches – in which the public may be involved to a greater or lesser degree – in relation to broad questions arising out of the content of the courts' decisions or changes to the law or legal system generally promoted by a particular government.[3] The most spectacular example was the debate on the ultimately successful proposal for an amendment of the Constitution to allow for a reduction in judicial salaries.[4] The question of reduction of judicial salaries – and the introduction of a lower starting scale for newly appointed judges is – however – only one facet of this ongoing interaction. If anything, the preservation of the value of judges' pensions in the face of potentially detrimental changes in the determination of public sector pensions seems to have been a greater point of tension.[5] At the other end of the scale, there have been well-publicised clashes over judges' travel and subsistence expenses.[6]

In April 2013, such tensions led to a highly publicised clash between the president (Mr Justice Peter Kelly) and at least one prominent member (Mr Justice Adrian Hardiman) of the Association of Judges of Ireland and the then Minister for Justice and Equality, Mr Alan Shatter TD, in the course of which judicial resentment at perceived attacks on their independence came to the fore.[7] Subsequently, some greater element of détente was achieved in relations between the judiciary and the executive, notably through the establishment of a Working Group to facilitate discussions between the two 'sides' and some accommodation over the length of the courts' summer vacation.[8] A key concern for the judges, which has drawn them all together (whether personally involved in the Association of Judges of Ireland or not) is the need for a reform of the system of judicial appointments, as evidence by the trenchant submission they collectively made in January 2014 to the Minister for Justice and Equality's consultation on that topic.[9] The reform of the system of judicial appointments is not a topic with which this paper deals with particularly, but this document is noteworthy in several respects, which as will be highlighted below. Above all, there appears to be profound judicial unease that the constitutional guarantee against reductions in their remuneration was removed without any countervailing steps being taken to remove decisions on that issue from direct political control or to depoliticise the system for appointing judges in the first place.[10]

Since 2011, disagreements and tensions between the executive and the judiciary have emerged into the glare of media attention more often and more spectacularly than ever before. Nevertheless, the general relationship between the two remains largely a collaborative one, in which the judiciary have considerable influence over the government in the pursuit of the judges' own priorities for the reform and development of the legal system. Two noteworthy examples are the General Scheme for the Judicial Council Bill, for which the corresponding Bill is still awaited at the time of writing and the Thirty-Third Amendment of the

Constitution (Court of Appeal) Act 2013. In each case, the argument for major institutional changes made by the judiciary – and notably by the present Chief Justice, Ms Justice Denham – persuaded the government, to the point putting the second to a referendum, something, which generally requires some considerable force to outweigh the instinctive caution that politicians have developed in relation to such an undertaking.[11]

Three models of judicial representation

As a way of making sense of recent Irish experience it is useful to adopt three different models for how communications take place between the judiciary and the executive, particularly in relation to topics where the later has most control over the working conditions of the former. One is where the interests of judges are represented by the president of court of which they are members or, more generally, by the Chief Justice, acting alone or in concert with the other court presidents. The second is where judges establish an association or union to defend their interests, especially by attempting to engage in dialogue with the relevant government bodies and by putting their grievances into the public domain. The third is where a statutory judicial council, established by law, discharges these representational functions, as well as performing disciplinary functions in relation to the judiciary.

The first we may call the presidential model, in that it is the president of each court and, in a special sense, the Chief Justice – as spokesperson for the entire judiciary – who takes on the role of representing their collective views and interests to the political branches. Traditionally, this dialogue has not attracted, or been open to, any degree of public scrutiny. In recent years, with the increasing openness of clashes between members of the two branches, a greater degree of attention has been drawn to this role. The general role of court presidents and especially of the Chief Justice as a conduit for communication between the judiciary and the executive has many international parallels, especially in other common law countries, and it forms the background, for example, for the International Commission of Jurists' vindication of the actions of Chief Justice McLachlin in the *Nadon* matter.[12] That controversy in Canada in 2014 over the communications between the Chief Justice and the executive in relation to judicial appointments process shows that even the existence of a long-established and relatively sophisticated national and provincial judicial council has not eliminated the role of the Chief Justice (or of the presidents of other courts) in making representations to the executive in relation to matters of concern to the judiciary as a whole. The representational function of the court president parallels the role that he or she has traditionally placed in dealing with questions of judicial misconduct or incapacity, where informal means of resolution typically involved the president of each court engaging personally with the judge concerned to deal with whatever kind of problem had been disclosed. Attachment to this system seems to have been one important source of judicial resistance to the formalisation of investigations of judicial misconduct. As a result, the General Scheme for the Judicial Council Bill reflects a desire to preserve as much of the court presidents' role in this regard as is consistent with a new more formal, transparent and inclusive system of investigation.

Since 2011, more light has been shed on the representational role that a court president (and the Chief Justice, in particular) may be expected to play, although the role that Ms Justice Denham has been called on to play has been complicated by the fact that the Association of Judges of Ireland has come into existence with the explicit role of representing the judges' professional interests. Almost all the judges in Ireland are members of this association and are publicly identified as such. In that respect, the role of the court presidents and especially the Chief Justice has often seemed to be one of conciliating or mediating between the government and the judges' association. At the very least, the Chief Justice is called upon to create, renew and keep open channels of communication between the two branches. The same function can be seen in the role of chief justices and court presidents in other common law systems, as the *Nadon* controversy in Canada shows.[13]

The second way in which the judiciary may represent their interests to the government collectively is through some kind of professional association, such as the Association of Judges of Ireland. As already noted, a very high proportion of Irish judges are members of this body. The Association was established at the end of 2011, as a direct result of the enactment of the Twenty-Ninth Amendment of the Constitution (in relation to the reduction in remuneration of judges) and the precarious situation in which most judges felt this placed them. More profoundly, it reflected judicial disquiet at the political mind-set, which many of the judges felt that the amendment reflected.[14] Since its establishment the Association has had mixed success in persuading the government of its case that the quality and the international reputation of the Irish judiciary was put at risk by the many cost-saving measures that the government applied to judges. To some extent, the Association's dialogue with the government has been maintained only by the deft intervention of the Chief Justice and not before public disclosure of vehement criticism of the government's policies by the Association's President, with, it seems, the full backing of his members.

Mechanisms for judicial–executive dialogue

As is discussed in greater detail below, the *Bangalore Principles of Judicial Conduct* – a widely accepted statement of proper standards of judicial behaviour – recognises that 'a judge may form or join associations of judges or participate in other organizations representing the interests of judges'.[15] Nevertheless, this type of 'trade union' organisation by judges has not escaped criticism. Professor David Gwynn Morgan, for example, underlined the difficulties posed by such a new departure, such as the danger of a loss of public confidence in the judiciary if they engage in acrimonious public disputes over their terms and conditions and the problem of a perceived lack of impartiality in cases involving the government, especially when virtually every judge in the country belongs to the Association.[16] Equally, in developing the Canadian constitutional law framework for the determination of judicial remuneration, it was considered axiomatic, that 'under no circumstances is it permissible for the judiciary – not only collectively through representative organizations, but also as individuals – to engage in negotiations over remuneration with the executive or representatives of the legislature. Any such negotiations would be fundamentally at odds with judicial independence.'[17]

Even a commentator with more sympathy than Professor Morgan for the position of the judges, who recognised their legitimate sense of grievance at the lack of communication and consultation on the part of the Minister for Public Expenditure and Reform, detected a certain element of 'over-pleading' in the claims made by the Association (such as a 'brick by brick' demolition of judicial independence).[18] As there is an obvious tension between the role of the judiciary as a coordinate branch of government and their self-interest as an elite professional group, it is obviously desirable to have resort to some general principles by which to assess any particular contribution by judges to the public debate about their terms and conditions. The *Bangalore Principles of Judicial Conduct* may provide some useful guidance, especially as they are relied upon, as far as related issues are concerned, both by the open letter by the International Commission of Jurists commenting on the public clash in 2014 between the Chief Justice of Canada and the Prime Minister calls[19] and by the Judicial Appointments Review Committee's *Preliminary Submission to the Department of Justice and Equality's Public Consultation on the Judicial Appointments Process*.[20] It is clear from the Bangalore Principles that a body such as the Association of Judges of Ireland is compatible with internationally recognised principles of good judicial conduct (which is unsurprising, as associations or trade unions representing judges are relatively common around the world): '4.13. A judge may form or join associations of judges or participate in other organizations representing the interests of judges.'[21]

How such an association should be conducted is, however, potentially affected by the gloss which the official *Commentary on the Bangalore Principles of Judicial Conduct* places on the requirement that judges should always exercise their human rights to expression, belief, association and assembly 'in such a manner as to preserve the dignity of the judicial office and the impartiality and independence of the judiciary'.[22]

A judge may speak out on matters that affect the judiciary

There are limited circumstances in which a judge may properly speak out about a matter that is politically controversial, namely, when the matter directly affects the operation of the courts, the independence of the judiciary (which may include judicial salaries and benefits), fundamental aspects of the administration of justice or the personal integrity of the judge. However, even on these matters, a judge should act with great restraint. While a judge may properly make public representations to the government on these matters, the judge must not be seen as 'lobbying' government or as indicating how he or she would rule if particular situations were to come before the court. Moreover, a judge must remember that his or her public comments may be taken as reflecting the views of the judiciary; it may sometimes be difficult for a judge to express an opinion that will be taken as purely personal and not that of the judiciary in general.[23]

The often fraught relationship between the judiciary and the executive over the last few years in Ireland has placed in the spotlight the issue of how far the 'great restraint' mentioned here should extend. A complicating factor seems to be the increasing tendency, across the world, of many politicians (and those who manage their interactions with the media) to place their side of such arguments in the media spotlight in a hasty and unsubtle fashion, of a piece with the hectic 'news cycle' in which they are caught up. In the Irish case, the difficulty of deciding how far judges should respond in kind is heightened by the fact that the appears to be a remarkably high degree of agreement across the judiciary as a whole on the basic demands that the Association puts forward on their behalf, so that the group can with considerable justification put itself forward as expressing the opinion of the judiciary as a whole, at least on these matters.

Against this background, it is not surprising that there is also apparent unanimity among the judiciary, on the need for the establishment of a statutory judicial council, which would enable representational, disciplinary and educational functions to be discharged in a less confrontational (and less precarious) manner. When the Association of Judges of Ireland was first established there was a strong suggestion (though no explicit public statement) that it was provisional in character, pending the establishment of such a body, which might then subsume the Association's role on a more satisfactory basis.[24] At that time, the General Scheme of the Judicial Council Bill (2010) represented the government's response to the judiciary's long-standing call for the creation of such a body, an enterprise with which the current Chief Justice has long been associated.[25] A representational role could be extracted from wide reading of the functions of the proposed Judicial Council – particularly maintaining and promoting '(a) excellence in the exercise by judges of their judicial functions ... (c) the efficient and effective use of judicial resources ... and (e) respect for the independence of the judiciary'.[26] Nevertheless, the General Scheme does not specifically give the proposed Council the function of making representations to the executive concerning the salaries, benefits, terms and conditions of judges. Accordingly, we may expect that the position of the Association will be to wait and see how any new Council performs its functions in practice before the Association reassesses its own role. The Judicial Appointments Review Committee's submission on judicial appointments was particularly insistent on the need to establish a council of this kind forthwith and explicitly mentioned its representational function: 'The foregoing discussion only illustrates the damage caused by the absence of a judicial council with powers in relation to judicial representation, appointments, discipline, and responsibility for supervising judicial education.'[27] At the same time, the submission conceded that the appointments function could also be exercised by a properly constituted separate body.[28]

A better model for judicial conduct investigations?

One of the key elements of the General Scheme for the Judicial Council Bill deals with the investigation of allegations of judicial misconduct.[29] Under the General Scheme, the Judicial Conduct Committee would have a general responsibility for maintaining and promoting high standards of judicial conduct and for the investigation of complaints of judicial misconduct. It would consist of eight judges (the Presidents of the four courts then in existence and one judge elected by the members of each) and three lay members.[30] On the other hand, formal investigations of complaints of misconduct against a judge would be entrusted to a Panel of Inquiry – consisting of two judges and one lay person (none of whom could be members of the Judicial Conduct Committee).[31]

Given that Canada is sometimes cited as a significant influence on the Judicial Council which it is proposed should be established in Ireland, it is interesting to see how the debate about the nature of investigations of judicial conduct, particularly at the federal level, has developed in that country in recent years. Between 2010 and 2015, much additional attention was focused on that debate by the long-drawn-out inquiry into the conduct of Associate Chief Justice of Manitoba, Lori Douglas. This episode was unedifying both on account of the salacious nature of some of the allegations and the tortuous and acrimonious course of the proceedings in the matter, which was complicated by litigation or the threat of litigation at several points.[32]

Some interesting suggestions can be found in the Canadian Bar Association response to the Canadian Judicial Council's call for submissions on the reform of the judicial conduct process.[33] The desire to avoid some of the problems highlighted by the Lori Douglas controversy is obvious, even though that case is not mentioned specifically anywhere in the submission. Among the notable recommendations made by the CBA are that the inquisitorial nature of proceedings for the investigation should be retained,[34] that the complainant should have the status of a witness and not a party[35] and that the inquiry committee's counsel should have an essentially administrative role (not including the examination of witnesses or the drawing up of reasons for decision).[36] In a broader context, the CBA recommended greater involvement of lay people at all stages of the judicial conduct process.[37] The inquiry committee in the *Douglas* case consisted, for example, of three judges and two lawyers. As the CBA point out:

> Lay participation has been a prominent and increasingly important feature in complaints and professional discipline processes of regulated professions for many years. Self-governing professions are vulnerable to public suspicion that their governing bodies act in the interest of members of the profession rather than in the public interest. Lay participation in the complaints and discipline process tends to alleviate this suspicion and increase public confidence in the process. Laypersons frequently bring a valuable outside perspective to complaints about professionals and can serve to enhance the transparency and objectiveness of the proceeding.[38]

Such extensive lay involvement in inquiries is already a feature of the judicial conduct system at a provincial rather than a federal level in Canada.[39]

It is also interesting to note a different aspect of the Canadian Bar Association submissions to the Canadian Judicial Council's review of the judicial conduct process. The CBA recommends the CJC should be empowered, on a non-consensual basis 'to issue warnings and reprimands, to suspend the judge with or without pay for any period, or to order such specified measures as apologizing to a complainant, receiving continuing education, or undergoing treatment as a condition of continuing to preside as a judge'.[40] At the moment, all the only disciplinary action that the CJC can take is to recommend that a judge be removed from office. As the CBA points out, this restriction may mean that judges escape any disciplinary action for their misconduct, as the CJC feels that it does not meet the threshold for removal, or it may result in judges being removed in cases where a lesser sanction would have been appropriate.[41] Once again, this greater flexibility is found at a provincial level in Canada.[42]

The need for a graduated response in relation to judicial misconduct highlights some overlap between a conciliar model – which is now proposed for Ireland and calls for a higher degree of formality in the process than now exists – and a presidential model – in which the president of the relevant court exercises a general supervisory role over his or her colleagues. The latter approach, which is traditional in Ireland, does have the merit of allowing flexible and pragmatic responses to judicial misconduct or incapacity, particularly where ill-health or substance abuse is at the root of the problem. It is to be hoped that the conciliar model will not mean the sacrifice of that flexibility, in favour of an overly adversarial and legalistic process.

Under the General Scheme it is envisaged that a Panel of Inquiry's recommendations could include giving advice to the judge, recommending a specific course of action (such as receiving training of some particular kind), making a recommendation to the Chief Justice or the President of the relevant court, recommending procedural change, practice directions, redistribution of work or related matters and issuing a reprimand to the judge under investigation.[43] On receipt of the Panel of Inquiry's report, it would be for the Judicial Conduct Committee to make a determination as to which if any of the recommendations made should be accepted.[44] Somewhat cryptically, the Scheme provides:

> (6) Where the Judicial Conduct Committee considers that a particular course of action should be taken following its consideration of the report of the Panel of Inquiry, it shall be for the Committee itself to initiate the taking of such action.

This must certainly include, at the very least, communicating to the minister or the government, a recommendation that a judge should be removed from office under Article 35 of the Constitution.[45] Without a constitutional amendment underpinning a new system for judicial conduct, it seems unlikely that the sanction of suspension without pay could be introduced by law. On the other hand, it would seem that, acting in conjunction with the Presidents of the various courts there would be no objection to the Judicial Conduct Committee disposing of cases in the manner on which the CBA and the General Scheme broadly concur. This is, after all, to some extent merely a formalisation of long-standing practice as far as the role of the President of each court is concerned.

In summary, the recent debate over the federal judicial misconduct process in Canada confirms some of the main features of the model which has commanded broad consensus in Ireland for the last decade or more and which is embodied in the General Scheme for the Judicial Council Bill. On each of these points – notably, the retention of the lay element in both the Judicial Conduct Committee and the Panels of Inquiry and the full use of the range of disciplinary measures that the Scheme envisages – it seems appropriate to draw the lesson from recent Canadian experience that what is proposed in the General Scheme ought to be made law.

Conclusion

The Irish judiciary finds itself in something of a hiatus in terms of its relationship with the executive branch at present. The old method of communicating judges' concerns to politicians (and civil servants) in which the Chief Justice and the Attorney General acted as discreet and uncontroversial conduits for an exchange of views has come under considerable strain in recent years, if not broken down entirely. It is interesting to note that a common complaint in Canada during the controversy over the attempted Nadon appointment was that the dysfunction in the relationship between the Supreme Court and the executive arose partly from the failure of the Attorney General (an office there combined with that of Minister of Justice) to play his traditional role as the guardian of the legal system's integrity. Instead, it is claimed, the Attorney General now acts as a member of a highly partisan and combative government, in which the lead is increasingly taken by the Prime Minister's Office rather than the relevant department. This criticism has been made both in relation to the specific criticisms made of the Chief Justice's role in the case and of the handling of the Nadon appointment more generally.[46] In Ireland, there are also signs of politicians being aware that old ways of bridging the differences between the two branches are no longer as effective as they once were and that the only lasting solution to this is the establishment of a judicial council along the lines of the General Scheme of 2010.[47]

The expedient to which Irish judges have currently resorted – a professional association to represent their interests – does not appear to be one that can long be maintained. We have already seen too many examples of the potential for confrontation between the two sides to escalate into acrimonious public exchanges, which, if long continued, would be damaging to the authority of the judiciary. The establishment of the Working Group in 2013 seems to have been part of a détente facilitated by the Chief Justice among others that has avoided any further escalation of tension and enabled progress to be made on some of the issues in dispute. In addition, there have been some signs of the two methods of representing judges – what have been called here the associational and presidential models – being run together, most notably in the composition of the Judicial Appointments Review Committee. There is a broad equivalence between bringing these two strands of representation together in that context and what would be secured by establishing a judicial council. The only long-term solution would appear to be to establish the Judicial Council envisaged in the General Scheme. However, as we have seen, there is some ambiguity in the Scheme concerning the nature of the Council's representational role. This is a function, which the judges clear seek for it, as evidenced by the Judicial Appointments Review Committee's submission on judicial appointments.[48]

Canadian experience suggests that the establishment of a judicial council is no panacea for the ills that can afflict the relationship between politicians and judges. Individual judges (and especially the Chief Justice and other court presidents) will retain a role in bringing the concerns of the judiciary to the executive's attention and sometimes also to the attention of the public and this inevitably runs the risk of cutting across politicians' own priorities and sensitivities. Similarly, in relation to the investigation and sanctioning of judicial misconduct, there are lessons to be learned from some of the failings of the Canadian system. It encouraging that many of these appear to have been noted already in the design of the General Scheme, especially in relation to the importance of lay involvement and flexibility of outcomes of the disciplinary process.

Behind a great deal of the judicial unease about the power of the executive over them there lies a fundamental concern about the nature of the judicial appointments system, described in the Canadian case as 'an opaque, executive-centred procedure' by the International Commission of Jurists.[49] The courts have constitutional instruments for establishing some limits to the power of politicians to shape the bench in whatever way they desire, although only sporadically and not so as to bring into being an alternative, more generally legitimate, system. Both the ICJ and the Judicial Appointments Review Committee stress the importance of independent appointments bodies and clearly prescribed consultation procedures. The Committee's submission is particularly striking in terms of its insistence on a purely merit-based system of appointment and the exclusion of political preferment as a factor. Whether or not the full potential of a judicial council to establish new, more stable conventions for interactions between the judiciary and the executive may depend to a great extent on whether the parallel issue of reform of judicial appointments can be solved in a manner that satisfies the two groups.

Notes

The author is grateful to the anonymous reviewer for his or her comments and suggestions.

1. C. Coulter, 'Judges form association to represent interests', *Irish Times* (24 December 2011), 1.
2. Judicial Appointments Review Committee, Preliminary Submission to the Department of Justice and Equality's Public Consultation on the Judicial Appointments Process (January 2014) (hereafter the Judges' Report).
3. N. Olivetti Rason and P. Luigi Petrillo, 'The Dialogue among Constitutional Judges, Parliaments and Executives' in G. Franco Ferrari and J. O'Dowd (eds), *75 Years of the Constitution of Ireland: An Irish–Italian Dialogue* (Clarus Press, 2014) pp. 133–152.
4. For a general account, see J. O'Dowd, 'Judges in Whose Cause? The Irish Bench after the Judges' Pay Referendum' (2012) 48 *Irish Jurist* 102.
5. R. Mac Cormaic, 'Take-home pay down by a third since 2009', *Irish Times* (10 July 2013), 6.
6. Editorial: 'Ignoring the judges', *Irish Times* (26 February 2014), 15.
7. R. Mac Cormaic, 'Shatter defends government's handling of judicial independence', *Irish Times* (15 April 2013), 1; R. Mac Cormaic, 'Judges concerned at erosion of autonomy: Judges' association gives "full support" to comments by Mr Justice Peter Kelly', *Irish Times* (16 April 2013), 1; R. Mac Cormaic, 'Judge made speech after failed efforts to engage with Howlin', *Irish Times* (25 February 2014), 4.
8. R. Mac Cormaic, 'New forum has been created for judges and Government, says Chief Justice: Mrs Justice Susan Denham pays tribute to "energy and commitment" of colleagues', *Irish Times* (18 April 2013), 9; R. Mac Cormaic, 'High Court to extend sittings into summer holidays: Plan will be seen as gesture after public row with Government', *Irish Times* (27 April 2013), 1.
9. Judges' Report (n. 2).
10. Mac Cormaic, 'Judges concerned at erosion of autonomy' (n. 7), 1.
11. S. Denham, 'Proposal for a Court of Appeal' (2006) 6 *Judicial Studies Institute Journal* 1; Report of the Working Group on a Court of Appeal (Prn. A8/0153, May 2009), at www.courts.ie/Courts.ie/library3.nsf/(WebFiles)/D3E9CCA7BA

AB5F868025760B0032EA4E/$FILE/Report%20of%20the%20Working%20 Group%20on%20a%20Court%20of%20Appeal.pdf (last accessed 27 August 2015).

12 International Commission of Jurists, *ICJ responds to concerns about interference with integrity and independence of the judiciary in Canada* Geneva, 23 July 2014, at http://icj.wpengine.netdna-cdn.com/wp-content/uploads/2014/07/Canada-JudicialIndependenceAndIntegrity-CIJL-OpenLetter-2014.pdf (last accessed 27 August 2015).

13 'Canadian Law Deans worried about Government's statements regarding Chief Justice' Montreal, 7 May 2014, at www.newswire.ca/en/story/1350835/canadian-law-deans-worried-about-government-s-statements-regarding-chief-justice (last accessed 27 August 2015); S. Fine, 'Law-school deans join critics of Harper's attack on top judge', *National Post* 7 May 2014, at www.theglobeandmail.com/news/national/law-school-deans-join-critics-of-harpers-attack-on-top-judge/article18510787 (last accessed 27 August 2015).

14 O'Dowd (n. 4), 129.

15 *Bangalore Principles of Judicial Conduct* (2002) para. 4.23, at www.unodc.org/pdf/crime/corruption/judicial_group/Bangalore_principles.pdf (last accessed 27 August 2015)

16 D. G. Morgan, 'Trade union for judges in no one's interest', *Irish Times* (6 December 2012), 14.

17 *Reference re Remuneration of Judges of the Provincial Court (PEI)* [1997] 3 SCR 3 at para. 134, Lamer CJ. For further discussion, see O'Dowd (n. 4), 129.

18 C. Brady, 'The case for and against an angry judiciary: Do the judges have genuine grievances and who exactly should they be angry with?', *Irish Times* (17 April 2014), 14.

19 ICJ responds to concerns about interference with integrity and independence of the judiciary in Canada 4–6 citing ECOSOC 2006/23, Strengthening basic principles of judicial conduct, at www.unodc.org/pdf/corruption/corruption_judicial_res_e.pdf (last accessed 27 August 2015).

20 Judges' Report (n. 2), pp. 59 and 61.

21 *Bangalore Principles of Judicial Conduct* (n. 15), para. 4.23.

22 *Ibid.*, para. 4.6.

23 United Nations Office on Drugs and Crime, *Commentary on the Bangalore Principles of Judicial Conduct* (2007), 96, at www.unodc.org/documents/corruption/publications_unodc_commentary-e.pdf (last accessed 27 August 2015). This commentary is cited in *ICJ responds to concerns about interference with integrity and independence of the judiciary in Canada* (ibid., 5–6).

24 Coulter (n. 1).

25 Department of Justice, Equality and Law Reform, *General Scheme of the Judicial Council Bill* (Stationery Office, 2010), at www.inis.gov.ie/en/JELR/General%20Scheme%20Judicial%20Bill.pdf/Files/General%20Scheme%20Judicial%20Bill.pdf (last accessed 27 August 2015).

26 *Ibid.*, p. 10 (head 5).

27 Judges' Report (n. 2) p. 23 (para. 53).

28 *Ibid.*, p. 25 (para. 61).
29 Scheme of Bill (n. 25).
30 *Ibid.*, p. 31 (head 20).
31 *Ibid.*, pp. 51–52 (head 28).
32 See A. Roussy, 'The Continuing Saga of the Douglas Inquiry in Canada' (2014) 17 *Legal Ethics* 442; S. Lautens, 'Light through the Window' *Canadian Lawyer* 2 March 2015, at www.canadianlawyermag.com/5492/Light-through-the-window.html (last accessed 27 August 2015).
33 Canadian Bar Association, *Review of Judicial Conduct Process of the Canadian Judicial Council* (Ottawa, July 2014), at www.cba.org/CBA/submissions/pdf/14-44-eng.pdf (last accessed 27 August 2015). For the call for submissions, see *Consulting Canadians on Judicial Conduct* (Canadian Judicial Council, March 2014), at www.cjcccm.ca/cmslib/general/CJC%20Discussion%20Paper%20on%20Judicial%20Conduct%202014-03-18.pdf (last accessed 27 August 2015).
34 *Ibid.*, pp. 3–6.
35 *Ibid.*, pp. 9–11.
36 *Ibid.*, pp. 6–9.
37 *Ibid.*, pp. 11–12.
38 *Ibid.*, pp. 11.
39 *Ibid.*
40 Canadian Bar Association (n. 33), 12.
41 *Ibid.*
42 *Ibid.*
43 Scheme of Bill (n. 25).
44 *Ibid.*, p. 62 (head 31).
45 Head 31(8) (*ibid* 63) makes it clear that (8) nothing in this Scheme affects the power of any member of the Oireachtas to table a motion calling for a resolution in accordance with Article 35 of the Constitution.
46 M. Bryant, 'By politicizing judicial appointments, Harper risks constitutional crisis', *Globe and Mail* (19 May 2014), at www.theglobeandmail.com/globe-debate/by-politicizing-judge-appointments-harper-risks-constitutional-crisis/article18722354 (last accessed 27 August 2015).
47 For example, Alan Shatter Speech to be delivered by Alan Shatter TD, Minister for Justice, Equality and Defence, at Law Society Annual Conference 11 May 2013, at http://justice.ie/en/JELR/Pages/SP13000187 (last accessed 27 August 2015). At the same time, it is notable that in this speech the former minister also strongly challenged what he saw as an overly broad claim for the scope of judicial independence on the part of judges, at the expense of the government's legitimate role in introducing changes to reduce costs and improve efficiencies in the judicial system.
48 Judges' Report (n. 2) p. 23 (para. 53).
49 International Commission of Jurists (n. 12), 6.

Part IV

Judges and the Constitution in historical perspective

11

The Irish Constitution 'from below': squatting families versus property rights in Dublin, 1967–71

Thomas Murray

Distinguished by a strong focus on the state and a curious neglect of society, Irish constitutional studies have not yet attempted to see Bunreacht na hÉireann from the perspective of those constitutionalised. This omission is surprising, not least because people in Ireland, on occasion, have taken the law into their own hands. Seeing a constitution 'from below' denotes tracing this two-fold social phenomenon whereby participants in a conflict both challenge received interpretations of a constitution and create new forms of justice. Minimally, this might involve people lobbying government and media to draw attention to the gap between a constitution's expressed ideals and existing state practices. Maximally, people can take direct action to realise their aims themselves, including boycotting, striking or squatting vacant property.[1] In the Irish context, people have interpreted all manner of rights into the 1937 Irish Constitution, challenging the highly regulated space of the courtroom and the law's ideological prerequisites, and, in some cases, forming or constituting entirely new spaces, senses and practices of justice.

The present chapter draws on a critical social theory of law and a range of qualitatively rich primary sources to incorporate heretofore neglected social movement voices into a more complex account of constitutional development in Ireland. What follows, however, is not a complete survey of every popular invocation of the 1937 Constitution. Instead, I concentrate here on the political practices and discourses at stake in a single moment of conflict when property rights were contested from below, specifically the squatting campaigns of the Dublin Housing Action Committee (DHAC) in the late 1960s and early 1970s. In doing so, I aim to open up a broader terrain of debate about constitutional development and judicial power in Ireland than conventional studies of case law, legislation or parliamentary politics would suggest.

The conflicts examined here highlight a crucial tension in capitalist societies between housing as a commodity and housing as a social need. In the wake of the global economic crisis of 2008 and the bursting of associated property bubbles in several countries, including Ireland, this tension is once more readily apparent.[2] Ireland's current crisis, moreover, has deep-rooted origins. Historically, its political economy has facilitated various forms of rent extraction.[3] Arguably, the 1937 Irish Constitution and associated formal legal processes, notably when utilised by landlords to strike down rent controls or when deployed against squatters or when used as a justification for failing to implement state controls on property speculation, played a small but significant role in reproducing this political economy.[4]

For present purposes, however, the squatters' actions examined here are most important because they demonstrate how the Irish constitutional framework for property relationships has worked in practice, including its human consequences. These conflicts also demonstrate how people can contest private property rights and create new social relations. The means they adopted were important. While these conflicts broadly emerged from the needs of homeless families, participants followed distinct trajectories of meeting those needs, varying along a spectrum between direct action or legal-political representation, between an oppositional understanding of the state as dominated by powerful interests or a ruling class and a value-consensus understanding of the state as a neutral site of contestation for competing interests.[5] Before comparing these two trajectories, however, it is necessary to outline the intellectual politics at stake in doing so.

Recuperating the Constitution 'from below'

Recent international scholarship has advanced the possibility of considering seriously the politics of law and rights as experienced by dominated groups. The work of Balakrishnan Rajagopal and Boaventura de Sousa Santos, in particular, has attempted to foreground the voices and actions of those attempting to challenge the relationship between law, state and society 'from below'.[6] More generally, the recent postmodern turn in socio-legal analysis, away from Marxist and Weberian foundational theories towards law's 'formative contexts', sustains this reorientation. Socio-legal inquiry has increasingly opened up intersectional structures of law and oppression for critique, prompting a much closer consideration of the politics of gender, race, sexual orientation and class among multiple 'other' identities, as well as of the symbolic systems or discourses implicated in the reproduction of law and legality.[7]

Importantly, the recuperation of lived experiences of rights contestation and constitutional development challenges the extent to which established socio-legal analysis may privilege expert knowledge or theory over the popular experience of history as life. This reorientation has decidedly ethico-political implications. Antonio Gramsci, for instance, explicitly located the possibility of emancipatory social transformation in the genuine elaboration of working class experience through political organisation, as opposed to political actors' distorting this experience for narrower, instrumental purposes.[8] Moreover, as John Holloway argues, this reorientation offers hope of overcoming the tendency of left-wing projects of social transformation to accentuate categorisations of domination to the detriment of ways of talking about liberation.[9]

These debates and perspectives, so vibrant in the study of international law, have yet to impact on the relatively short shelf space occupied by Irish constitutional studies. The first wave of such studies, led by Brian Farrell, Basil Chubb, Alan Ward and John Kelly, primarily concentrated on the Irish 'state tradition' as a liberal legacy of British rule as well as on the nationalist or confessional aspects of the 1922 and 1937 Constitutions.[10] While recent scholarship, notably by Gerard Hogan and Bill Kissane, has usefully contextualised Irish constitutionalism within wider European and Transatlantic traditions of constitution-making, the focus of this research continues to centre on the shifting intersection of liberal institutions and norms with nationalist and Catholic ones.[11] In comparative constitutional studies, similarly, the Irish case is most readily forwarded as an example of a socio-legal order deeply expressive of and divided by questions of national identity and values.[12] In terms of the subsequent usage and development of the 1937 Constitution, Chubb's cultural contextualist thesis on the 'normative force' of the Irish constitutional tradition, a basic law gradually adjusting to changing societal norms, remains the standard explanatory account of change.[13]

Yet, to paraphrase Franz Neumann, constitutions do not simply demand loyalty to an externally valid value system; they also embody decisions about the future structure of society.[14] Scholarship on the Irish Constitution has yet to consider seriously how constitutionalism intersects with economic institutions or class interests, narrowly or broadly understood. In existing studies, the acceptance of property rights or the rejection of socio-economic rights is mentioned only in passing. These decisions, their wider societal significance and the politics underpinning them are unnamed or understood simply in cultural terms as products of framers' 'innate conservatism'.[15] Similarly, subsequent judges' defence of property rights or opposition to recognising socio-economic rights is deemed to stem from common law traditions of judicial deference to property rights and to the principle of the separation of powers. In both instances, however, we do not explain anything with an appeal to tradition: rather we must ask why tradition persists.

The striking absence of critical sociological research in Irish constitutional studies owes something to its absence in Irish legal studies more generally. A generation ago, Nial Osborough observed how sociology had 'almost totally been ignored' in legal education and research.[16] Jurists have since recorded a whole series of associated deficiencies. These included a lack of elementary data on the workings of the criminal justice system;[17] on the social, legal and economic effects of the absence of divorce or the removal of rent control;[18] and on the socio-legal consequences of European Community membership.[19] The most striking absence, perhaps, has been the neglect of labour law: even the law reports have failed to record the courts' use of labour injunctions to curtail strikes.[20] In general, legal research in Ireland has consistently overlooked law-as-process by failing to examine either 'the policy which underlies, or is claimed to underlie, the particular bloc of law under consideration' or 'the "delivery" of the law, i.e. the impact which it actually makes on the individuals affected and the wider society'.[21] Nor would it appear that sociological blindness will be addressed in the near future.[22]

In these circumstances, scholars have tended to focus their analyses of the Irish Constitution on norms, elites and institutions and to absent a broader consideration of the experience of those constitutionalised. Their studies thus conclude somewhat prematurely, often with a number of jarring assertions concerning the Constitution's contribution to democracy in Ireland. Hence, we have Brian Farrell's argument that judicial review has enabled 'de Valera's Constitution' to become 'ours' or John Kelly's endorsement of the courts' handling of constitutional issues as 'beneficial, rational, progressive and fair'.[23] More recently, Bill Kissane has claimed that 'any enduring reconciliation of constitutionalism and democracy is worthy of respect'.[24] Appeals to longevity seem a particularly dubious basis for celebration, however, not least because one constitution's longevity is another, potentially better one's delay.[25] More basically, when evaluating a constitution, it seems necessary to take into account the substantive well-being and opinions of those constitutionalised. The social movement perspective forwarded here thus seeks to develop a wider consideration of the Irish 'demos' and its relationship to the Constitution. The analysis of the Dublin Housing Action Committee's squatting campaign demonstrates the plausibility and necessity of this reorientation in Irish constitutional scholarship.

The Dublin Housing Action Committee (1968–71)

Historically, the political economy of Dublin's housing combined a minimal welfare effort with state-assisted slum landlordism, resulting in poor housing conditions for much of the twentieth century. In the 1960s, however, a number of factors combined to make the chronic acute. Austerity cutbacks on housing provision in the 1950s combined with population increases in the 1960s to pressure the state's available housing resources. Some 10,000 applicants waited on Dublin Corporation's 'approved' housing list; an equivalent number waited off it. At the same time, the collapse of inner-city tenements resulted in four fatalities, including two children.[26] The Fianna Fáil government's immediate response was to condemn the buildings and to compel several hundred families to be rehoused in suburbs without social amenities or public transportation. This fitted a broader urbanisation process whereby Dublin's working class were to be suburbanised and the city centre adapted for offices, services and car parking spaces.[27] This urbanisation process in turn would centre on private home-ownership with the state reducing and privatising its stock of social housing, thereby generating payoffs for property speculators as well as political actors responsible for planning and rezoning. Given the extent of housing waiting lists, however, the government's attempts to clear tenement residents triggered an intense political campaign.

In May, 1967, left-leaning members of Sinn Féin established the Dublin Housing Action Committee (DHAC). Although Irish Republican Army (IRA) members participated, the DHAC was not simply an 'IRA offshoot'.[28] The Committee maintained an ostensibly independent structure and soon expanded to include a diverse range of left-wing organisations, including the Irish Communist Organisation, Labour party branches, the Worker's Party, Connolly Youth, as well as trade unionists and a variety of local housing groups such as the Ballymun Tenants' Association and the Dublin Flat-dwellers' Association. Members pledged to fight for '(1) Adequate housing for the citizens of Dublin (2) Fair rents for proper homes (3) Protection from eviction by unscrupulous landlords (4) An end to the scandal of empty homes (5) Protection for squatting families'.[29] The DHAC combined building voluntary networks of the homeless with holding prominent, public demonstrations aimed at publicising demands for social housing.

Initially, the DHAC picketed Dublin Corporation meetings to call for more housing. By September 1968, however, the Committee had moved to direct action, organising homeless families to squat vacant property. Throughout 1968 and 1969 the DHAC contested office block developments such as those in Mount Street, disseminated information on suitable locations for squatting and helped people to resist evictions.[30] Similar organising models were adopted by Housing Action Committees in Derry and Cork.[31] In addition to direct action, the DHAC appealed to a combination of civil disobedience and moral force. When the legal system continued to serve injunctions against the DHAC, it responded by challenging the existing sites and values of state justice. Alternative interpretations of the Constitution featured prominently in their legal and public defence.

The most prominent squatter to be taken to court was Dennis Dennehy, Secretary of the DHAC and member of the Irish Communist Organisation. During the summer of 1968, Dennehy squatted with his wife, Máire, and children at no. 20, Mountjoy Square, the property of landlord, Ivor Underwood. From the 1960s onwards, Underwood had built up a portfolio of Dublin properties, including some 70 Georgian houses, leaving an estate of some €69m on his death in the 2000s.[32] Prior to squatting, the Dennehy family had been living in a leaking caravan, the children 'shivering at the side of the road'.[33] Local residents had previously signed a petition demanding that the square be rebuilt as working-class housing (not as offices or gentrified, single-family dwellings), and marched to the Custom House to raise awareness of the city's housing shortages. When Underwood sold a number of houses on Mountjoy Square to a development company, slogans denouncing the sale were painted on the walls of his Dalkey residence and his car was damaged by a home-made pipe-bomb.[34] Although the Dennehys offered to pay rent, the landlord refused and subsequently sought an injunction to restrain them from occupying the premises.

Subsequent High Court hearings suggested a tension between law and justice. Dennehy, representing himself in court, explained to the judge that he could see two crimes – 'the crime of empty houses and the crime of people homeless' – and he thought it was the lesser crime to go into empty houses. He had nowhere else to go. If the Corporation provided a place for his family, however, he would be in a position to leave.

> *Judge Butler*: Did you get in touch with the Relieving Officer of the Dublin Corporation and tell him there was an order of this court, that you were to leave the house?
> *Dennehy*: The official told me – and I quote his words – he said: 'High Court judges know as much about Corporation houses as the birds in the sky'.[35]

The judge replied that he had sworn to uphold the Constitution, had no choice but to do so, and held that squatters had no right to be on the premises. In response, Dennehy appealed to an alternative understanding of the 1937 Constitution:

> *Judge Butler*: You see, there must be some social order. People cannot take the law into their own hands and what I am here for is to see that does not happen. It is distasteful for me and I am sure it is distasteful for Mr. Mackey [Underwood's counsel] to have to make decisions like this but I have no option.
> *Dennehy*: Can I ask for your advice on one thing before I reply? There appears to be a contradiction between the Constitution and what this injunction is asking me to do. The State has a duty to protect the family, according to the Constitution, and this injunction means the family is going to be broken up.[36]

Judge Butler replied that the Constitution also required people to respect private property and that this was being flouted, as was the authority of the court. Dennehy responded, 'I think the family is more important than the rights of private property'.[37] By January, after a number of hearings, it was clear that the Dennehy family had no intention of leaving No. 20. Rex Mackey, counsel for Ivor Underwood, insisted on the Dennehys being involved in a 'criminal conspiracy' against his client, against 'your lordship' and against 'the Constitution which this gentleman has had the temerity to invoke'.[38] While professing his sympathies for Dennehy, Judge Butler issued an order for his committal to Mountjoy Prison.

In a number of subsequent cases, the DHAC raised similar interpretations of the 1937 Constitution to challenge injunctions against their squatting.[39] Foregrounding the 'sanctity of the family' to support housing demands was a deliberate means of revealing the 'contradiction' between constitutional theory and state practice. The court cases attracted publicity and the DHAC subsequently forwarded these alternative interpretations at public demonstrations in support of jailed squatters. Bernard Brown, chairman of the DHAC, cited Article 41 in defence of three men jailed for refusing to obey a High Court order to vacate their squat at the Carlton Hotel, Harcourt Street: 'The State recognises the Family as the natural primary and fundamental unit group of society, and as a moral institution, possessing inalienable and imprescriptible right, antecedent and superior, to all positive law'; yet, despite this, he said, 'three men who wanted nothing more than accommodation for their families had been sent to jail'.[40] Similarly, Con Lehane, a solicitor for the DHAC, pointed to the contradiction between the Constitution's property rights and Directive Principles of Social Policy, concluding that the government considered 'the rights and profits of the property speculators and developers ... more important than the misery of the homeless parents who seek the shelter of the empty houses of the speculators'.[41]

The imprisonment of DHAC members focused media attention on the state's housing policy and ignited popular discontent at housing shortages. When Denis Dennehy went on hunger strike, a wave of protests erupted across Dublin. Public meetings took place outside the GPO where nightly marches would set off for Mountjoy prison to show support for imprisoned squatters. Hundreds also took part in regular sit-down protests at O'Connell Bridge. Joseph Clarke, a veteran of the 1916 Rising, interrupted state celebrations in the Mansion House commemorating the fiftieth anniversary of the First Dáil to protest Dennehy's treatment. As security guards carried Clarke outside, students greeted them with banners proclaiming 'Evictions: English landlords, 1868; Irish landlords, 1968–69'.[42] People's Democracy, en route from Belfast to the GPO as part of its campaign for civil rights in Northern Ireland, held a meeting of 800 people outside Dennis Dennehy's squat at No. 20 Mountjoy Square to protest about the housing situation on both sides of the border. The Dublin Trades Council passed a resolution calling for street demonstrations by trade unionists. Dennehy was eventually released and found housing. Undeterred, he supported a more extensive campaign of squatting.

Subsequent protests aimed at foregrounding the judiciary's complicity with the property-owning class. In September 1969, three women and two men from the DHAC occupied the Four Courts in Dublin.[43] The group arrived at 11am and announced that they had an appointment to see a senior counsel. When they found the Master's Court vacant, they barricaded the door with furniture and then painted a sign on a window blind overlooking Inn's Quay proclaiming: 'D.H.A.C. We are occupying the Four Courts to demand the release of jailed homeless.' The object of the demonstration was to protest at the imprisonment of Patrick Brady and Patrick Geraghty for refusing to vacate a squat at the Carlton Hotel, Harcourt Street. Seán Dunne, vice-chairman of the DHAC, claimed that Brady and Geraghty were being treated as criminals and that their food had been cut off when they complained about the prison's 'atrocious conditions'. At 1 p.m. a force of twenty Gardaí arrived, cleared photographers and reporters from the corridors and broke down the barricade. According to activists Eric Fleming and Isolda Byrne, the Gardaí ignored claims that their protest was peaceful, compelled them to sit on the floor and kicked them in the head and mouth.[44] The DHAC insisted it was not 'anti-police', citing as proof their helping a Garda widow threatened with eviction from her home of thirty-five years.[45]

Various squats and protest marches across the country typically met with a violent state response. Hilary Boyle, a 70-year-old social justice campaigner, described how the Gardaí charged at one such march 'like mad bulls ... They hit out with their batons, they kicked and punched and generally acted as agents provocateurs'. Meanwhile, as the conflict in Northern Ireland escalated, the government introduced a raft of 'law and order' measures, some of which aimed at breaking the DHAC. The Prohibition of Forcible Entry and Occupation Act (1971) changed squatting from a civil to a criminal offence and, furthermore, made its public endorsement illegal. Throughout 1971, a diverse coalition attempted to oppose the legislation as unjust and unconstitutional, including Citizens for Civil Liberties, the National Association of Tenant Organisations, the Union of Students of Ireland, Labour party branches and the Irish Congress of Trade Unions.[46]

By this stage, however, the anti-squat legislation was almost unnecessary: Dublin Corporation's 'crowbar brigades' were ejecting people daily without recourse to the law. These evictions came as the DHAC was fracturing under the pressures of its own internal politics, largely centring on how members interpreted and responded to the escalation of paramilitarism and state coercion on the island of Ireland.[47] In a large number of cases, however, the group had succeeded in negotiating on behalf of tenants with Dublin Corporation and private landlords, a number of whom, unwilling to be publicly shamed by protests, accepted squatters as legal tenants.[48] Members of the DHAC identified their primary achievement as one of deeper politicisation. Speaking of the thirty or so families she had personally encouraged to occupy empty houses, the feminist organiser Máirín de Búrca observed: 'They won't ever lie down again and accept whatever the law says if they think the law is unjust.'[49]

Conclusion

By focusing on resistance to the Irish Constitution's property rights framework, this chapter has drawn attention to the human consequences of constitutional development and social movements' capacities to critique and challenge such developments. The Dublin Housing Action Committee and associated squatting families relied on direct action to meet their housing needs. Members claimed public and private spaces, including roads, state buildings and speculators' properties, and transformed them into generative sites of participation where grievances and demands came to be aired. In doing so, they articulated a contradiction between constitutional ideology and state practice. They questioned whether, in fact, the state prioritised the family, workers and social justice ahead of the rights of speculators and landlords. In short, they made clear the ambiguity of the 1937 Irish Constitution's rights provisions and the politics or power relations at stake in terms of determining which understanding was to be superior.

To be clear, what is at stake here is not the particular legal challenge raised by the DHAC, namely whether the 1937 Irish Constitution could or should be interpreted so as to prioritise family rights over private property rights to the extent of loss of property rights. Rather, the more fundamental point is that the direct actions of the DHAC and various squatting families challenged the legitimacy of the state to decide such matters. The Constitution contains a myriad of provisions that could reasonably be interpreted to help the disadvantaged, notably concerning equality, free speech and the common good. Arguably, the judiciary has, on the whole, protected rights that ultimately benefit the advantaged more, including rights to reputation, privacy and property.[50] The real power of judges, however, does not so much concern the quality of their adjudication as their capacity to adjudicate. This authoritative capacity is far from natural but rather based on the state ensuring that people do not take the law into their own hands, whether through concessions, coercion or a combination of both.

The experience of Dublin's squatters outlined here is thus in keeping with contemporary social movements that characteristically see the state differently to how judges see it, as something other than a neutral site of contestation between competing interests.[51] Ideologically, the DHAC advanced an oppositional understanding of the state as dominated by powerful interests or a ruling class. Squatters not only attacked the Constitution's value system for upholding property and capital to the detriment of families, workers and communities, but insisted that people change their loyalty to a different value system and start acting for it. When challenged through the legal system, the DHAC subverted its legitimacy by occupying the Four Courts and by transforming court appearances, traditionally associated with criminality, into causes for celebration and wider publicity. Confidence in the success of alternative forms of justice did not reside in the power of mere suggestion but rather in housing activists' patient organising of networks of trust, participation and solidarity among the discontented and the dispossessed.

There are contemporary lessons to be drawn from these struggles. In the wake of the recent property bubble and crash, the extent to which successive Irish governments have prioritised the commodification of housing ahead of housing as a social need has never been more apparent. In terms of challenging these political priorities and market logics, the experiences presented here should caution contemporary social movements and social justice advocates from expecting too much from the courts. Faced with appealing to the Four Courts and occupying them to secure social justice, the respective merits of representational and direct action strategies require more elaboration than is possible here. At the very least, however, it can be argued that people need to think and to act differently if they want different outcomes in the future.

One area where we can change our mode of thinking is in Irish constitutional studies. The conflicts examined in this article point towards the necessity of a much broader understanding of the 1937 Constitution's role in social life than formal legal ideology would permit. The perspective that I have tried to advance here, seeing the Constitution 'from below', at least challenges some of the more laudatory celebrations of the 1937 Irish Constitution that pepper the existing literature. More than that, recuperating the voices of squatters and social justice campaigners in past struggles allows us to imagine a potential path towards a more democratic, more egalitarian society. For those who would bring some imagination to power, it is their voices and actions that will provide most inspiration.

Notes

I would like to thank the organisers of the Judges, Politics and the Irish Constitution conference at DCU and, in particular, all participants in the panel on Equality and the Irish Constitution for their questions and suggestions. Thanks also to Dr Graham Finlay, UCD School of Politics and International Relations, for comments on an early draft of this chapter. The usual disclaimer applies.

1 D. Graeber, *Direct Action: An Ethnography* (AK Press, 2009).
2 See D. Harvey, *Rebel Cities* (Verso, 2012).
3 C. McCabe, *Sins of the Father: Tracing the Decisions that Shaped the Irish Economy* (History Press, 2012).
4 R. Keane, 'Land Use, Compensation and the Community' (1983) 18(1) *Irish Jurist* 23.
5 P. Hillyard, 'Public Attitudes towards the Police in a Medium-sized Town in Northern Ireland' (1972) 7 *Irish Jurist* 62.
6 B. Rajagopal *International Law from Below* (CUP, 2003); B. de Sousa Santos and C. A. Rodríguez-Garavito, *Law and Globalisation from Below* (CUP, 2005).
7 R. Unger, 'Legal Analysis as Institutional Imagination' (1996) 59(1) *Modern Law Review* 1, 20; C. A. MacKinnon, 'Feminism, Marxism, Method, and the State: An Agenda for Theory' (1982) 7(3) *Signs* 515; R. Fine, *Democracy and the Rule of Law* (Pluto, 1985).
8 D. Kennedy, 'Antonio Gramsci and the Legal System' (1982) 6(1) *American Legal Studies Forum* 36.
9 J. Holloway, *Crack Capitalism* (Pluto, 2010).

10 B. Farrell, 'The Drafting of the Irish Free State Constitution: I, II, III and IV' (1970–71) 5–6 *Irish Jurist* 115, 343, 111 and 345; B. Farrell, 'From First Dáil through Irish Free State' in B. Farrell, *De Valera's Constitution and Ours* (Gill & Macmillan, 1988); B. Chubb, *The Politics of the Irish Constitution* (IPA, 1991); B. Chubb, *The Constitution and Constitutional Change in Ireland* (IPA, 1978); J. Kelly, *Fundamental Rights in the Irish Law and Constitution* (2nd edn, Allen Figgis, 1967); J. Kelly, 'The Constitution: Law and Manifesto' in F. Litton (ed.), *The Constitution of Ireland 1937–1987* (IPA, 1988); G. Hogan and G. Whyte, *J. M. Kelly: The Irish Constitution* (4th edn, Butterworths, 2003); A. Ward, *The Irish Constitutional Tradition: Representative Government in Modern Ireland* (Catholic University of America Press, 1994).

11 G. Hogan, 'De Valera, the Constitution and the Historians' (2005) 40(2) *Irish Jurist* 293; G. Hogan, *The Origins of the Irish Constitution: 1928–41* (Royal Irish Academy, 2012). B. Kissane, *New Beginnings: Constitutionalism and Democracy in Modern Ireland* (UCD Press, 2011). Recent research has opened new lines of normative questioning. See T. Hickey and E. Daly, *The Political Theory of the Irish Constitution: Republicanism and the Basic Law* (Manchester UP, 2015).

12 H. Lerner, *Making Constitutions in Deeply Divided Societies* (CUP, 2011) pp. 152–192, 48; M. Tushnet, *Weak Courts, Strong Rights: Judicial Review and Social Welfare Rights in Comparative Constitutional Law* (Princeton UP, 2009) p. 12.

13 Chubb (n. 10) p. 117; Kissane (n. 11) p. xii.

14 F. Neumann, *Behemoth: The Structure and Practice of National Socialism* (Harper, 1942) p. 17.

15 Farrell (n. 10) p. 18; Kissane (n. 11) p. 37.

16 N. Osborough, 'Irish Legal Scholarship' (1976) 11(1) *Irish Jurist* 1.

17 *Ibid.*, 2.

18 D. G. Morgan, 'Review' (1985) 20(2) *Irish Jurist* 445, 446.

19 I. Maher, 'Review' (1989) 24(2) *Irish Jurist* 309, 312.

20 F. von Prondzynski, 'The Problem of the Labour Injunction' (1981) 16(2) *Irish Jurist* 228; T. Kerr, 'Trade Disputes, Economic Torts and the Constitution' (1980) 16(2) *Irish Jurist* 241.

21 Morgan (n. 18) p. 446.

22 D. G. Morgan, 'Review' (2006) 41(1) *Irish Jurist* 137, 139; J. Stannard, 'Review' (2010) 45(1) *Irish Jurist* 254–255.

23 Farrell (n. 10); Hogan and Whyte (n. 10); '[T]hose concerned with property rights, homosexuality and abortion may have dissented from [Kelly's] view' (D. Ferriter, *The Transformation of Ireland* (Profile, 2005) p. 731).

24 Kissane (n. 11) pp. i, 148.

25 See T. Murray, 'Where we are: Review of Bill Kissane's *New Beginnings*' (Dublin Review of Books, 2012), at www.drb.ie/essays/where-we-are (accessed 3 September 2014).

26 See E. Hanna, *Modern Dublin: Urban Change and the Irish Past, 1957–1973* (OUP, 2013) p. 124.

27 McCabe (n. 3) pp. 31–32.
28 B. O Cathaoir, 'Government urged to encourage split in IRA', *Irish Times* (Dublin, 3 January 2000).
29 Dublin Housing Action Committee, 'Crisis Bulletin: Aims and Objectives' (Irish Election Literature Blog, 1 July 2014), at https://irishelectionliterature.wordpress.com/tag/dublin-housing-action-committee (accessed 1 July 2014).
30 See Dublin Housing Action Committee, 'The Squatter' (Cedar Lounge Revolution Blog, 10 October 2011), http://cedarlounge.files.wordpress.com/2008/06/D.H.A.C.-1969 (accessed 10 October 2011).
31 'Gardai hurt in street row in Cork', *Irish Times* (Dublin, 17 February 1969).
32 'Ireland's Rich List: No. 176', *Irish Independent* (Dublin, 31 March 2010).
33 'Judge orders family to leave house', *Irish Times* (Dublin, 26 November 1968).
34 'Explosion damages car outside home', *Irish Times* (Dublin, 9 October 1968).
35 'Judge orders family to leave house', *Irish Times* (Dublin, 26 November 1968).
36 *Ibid*.
37 'Family who occupied room in Dublin house must go', *Irish Times* (Dublin, 17 December 1968).
38 'Room squatter to be imprisoned', *Irish Times* (Dublin, 4 January 1969).
39 'Another court order to squatters', *Irish Times* (Dublin, 14 August 1969).
40 'Protest march over jailed squatters', *Irish Times* (Dublin, 24 September 1969).
41 C. Lehane, 'Letter to the editor', *Irish Times* (Dublin, 29 January 1971).
42 Hanna (n. 26) p. 139.
43 'Protestors forced from Four Courts', *Irish Times* (Dublin, 26 September 1969).
44 'Housing Group seeks inquiry into police attitude at Four Courts', *Irish Times* (Dublin, 27 September 1969).
45 *Ibid*.
46 'Demand for axing Anti-Squat Bill', *Irish Times* (Dublin, 2 March 1971).
47 B. Hanley and S. Millar, *The Lost Revolution: The Story of the Official IRA and the Workers' Party* (Penguin, 2010).
48 M. Maher, 'The making of a revolutionary', *Irish Times* (Dublin, 19 January 1970).
49 *Ibid*.
50 D. G. Morgan, 'Review: Whyte, Social Inclusion and the Legal System' (2002) 37 *Irish Jurist* 344.
51 Rajagopal (n. 6).

12

'The union makes us strong': *National Union of Railwaymen v. Sullivan* and the demise of vocationalism in Ireland

Donal Coffey

The 1940s are not regarded as a time of particular judicial innovation in Ireland. The honourable exceptions to this tradition are the justly celebrated decisions in *Buckley and Others v. Attorney General*[1] (more commonly known as the 'Sinn Féin Funds case')[2] and the decision of Justice Gavan Duffy in *The State (Burke) v. Lennon*.[3] A case which has been undervalued in terms of its historical importance is *National Union of Railwaymen v. Sullivan* which held part III of the Trade Union Act 1941 unconstitutional.[4] The importance of this case is related to the manner in which it undermined the vocational project in Ireland, which was an ongoing concern in 1945 when the decision was handed down. It also marks a decisive turn in the development of judicial review in Ireland.

As a preliminary issue, it is worth canvassing why the opinion has been overlooked. The reason is relatively simple: it is not a well-reasoned opinion. The legal consensus about the decision has been consistent and critical. It incorporates leading academics in Ireland; J.M. Kelly,[5] Gerry Whyte,[6] and James Casey.[7] It also applies to two governmental reports on the Constitution.[8,9] Moreover, commentators have strongly predicted that the decision would be overruled if it was to be reconsidered.[10] Finally, the decision itself makes no reference to vocationalism or corporatism and it is therefore not obvious what role the decision plays in relation to these concepts. Instead the decision is viewed historically in terms of the conflict between the Irish Trade Union Congress and the Congress of Irish Unions.[11] This chapter seeks to show that the decision, although poor, played an important role in the failure of the vocational project in Ireland.

Vocationalism

Article 15.3 of the 1937 Constitution contains an unused power which conferred on the Oireachtas the power to establish or recognise 'vocational councils'. Article 19 of the 1937 Constitution provides for the possibility, also unexercised, of direct election by functional or vocational groups to the Senate.[12] This lack of constitutional implementation belies the vitality of the concept of vocationalism in the 1930s.

Keogh and McCarthy date the influence of corporatism in Irish political life to the publication of *Quadragesimo Anno* in 1931.[13] This encyclical declared: '[t]he aim of social legislation must ... be the re-establishment of vocational groups'.[14] These groups were to be organised on the lines of profession or industry and would include representatives from all strata of members involved in the industry.[15] This meant that both employers and employees would be represented on the same council. The council would be responsible for promulgating:

> regulations binding all who are engaged in the profession. To determine working conditions, wages, interest, dividends and prices; to settle industrial disputes; to look to the technical training of future members, to arrange social insurance; in a word to care for everything which pertains directly to the prosperity of its own profession would be the work of each vocational group.[16]

The nexus between group recognition, authoritative determinations, and compulsory application to all members of that group were the key to the vocational organisation of the state.[17]

The encyclical was marked with a distrust of the centralisation of power in the hands of the state and sought instead to encourage governance on the basis of subsidiarity. The Pope believed that 'it is an injustice and at the same time a grave evil and disturbance of right order to assign to a greater and higher association what lesser and subordinate organisations can do'.[18] The basic thrust of the movement was to locate decision-making as close as possible to those the decision applied to.

Vocationalism was a key element of Irish social and political life of the time, although it was never implemented practically. Given the close links between Catholicism and the early state, each of the major parties of the state were committed, at least on paper, to the vocational organisation of the state. It provided political ammunition with which to criticise political schemes.[19] The link between the constitutional development of the state and Catholic social teaching was marked in the new state. On the inauguration of the new Constitution in 1937, the *Irish Press* published an editorial which claimed:

[I]t can be said that *Bunreacht na hEireann* is rooted in and derived from the Encyclicals of two of the greatest Popes who have ever sat in the Chair of Peter – Leo XIII and Pius XI. In all its clauses concerning social subjects, the inspiration, the intention, the very phraseology, follow the doctrines laid down for the guidance of men by these two great Pontiffs.[20]

Nonetheless, while de Valera declared himself to be in favour of vocational organisation, he believed that such organisation had to be voluntary and without state support. State recognition would be forthcoming in the event that such an organisation was successfully set up.[21]

This scepticism about the utility of vocationalism may be seen in de Valera's decidedly non-committal view on the establishment of the Commission on Vocational Organisation: 'So far as I am concerned, it is simply a question of saying that I am in favour of the motion, because ... I cannot see that any harm can be done in having a commission set up to examine the question.'[22] De Valera was convincible but not committed on the issue of the vocational organisation of the state.[23] It was in light of this background that the Committee on Vocational Organisation was established in 1939.

As the Committee conducted interviews for its report, the reorganisation of civil society continued apace in the Oireachtas, including the Act which was ultimately challenged in *National Union of Railwaymen v. Sullivan* – the Trade Union Act 1941.

Trade Union Act 1941

Justice Gavan Duffy had called for legislation in relation to industrial affairs in the 1938 case of *Cooper v. Millea* in order to remedy a situation where judges had to decide the lawfulness of industrial disputes 'in the milky way of the common law'.[24] More pressing again from the point of view of the government was the manner in which the proliferation of trade unions made industrial life in Ireland difficult.[25] As a result, the Trade Union Act 1941 sought to reduce the number of trade unions operating in different areas.[26] The most controversial element of the Act was Part III which was ultimately held to be unconstitutional. This part provided for the establishment of a Trade Union Tribunal which could determine that if the majority of members in an area had organised 'for the purpose of carrying on of negotiations for the fixing of wages and other conditions of employment' that the union would have the sole right to so negotiate.[27] The Tribunal could determine that two or more unions, or none, would have this power.[28] The Department of Industry and Commerce specifically proposed this provision on a centripetal basis, arguing that it would gradually lead to large areas of industry in which only one registered union would represent organised labour.[29] Moreover, it was a nationalist measure, for it provided in s. 26(2) that trade unions registered and headquartered outside the state could jointly or severally organise any particular class of workmen.

The opposition of the Dublin Trades Union Council was expressed in existential terms. It was, in their view, the thin end of the wedge which would end with:

> the transformation of the Unions, or rather their submersion, in corporative organisations made up of both workers and employers and directly under the control of the Government. Thus, the final realisation of the dreams and struggles of the pioneers of Irish Trade Unionism will be the subjection of Irish workers to the employers and the Government in so-called Corporations similar to those existing in totalitarian and fascist countries.[30]

Opposition to the Bill was seen as opposition to the corporate experiment generally.[31] The Dublin Trades Union Council called a march for 23 June 1941 to oppose the Bill, and up to 20,000 people took part.[32] At the march, James Larkin Senior burned a copy of the Bill.[33] Questions as to the constitutionality of the Bill were raised in a number of different arenas. De Valera and MacEntee met a deputation of the Dublin Trades Union Council on 19 June 1941, and representations were made that the Bill 'interfered with the fundamental rights of trade unionists to associate freely and to strike'.[34] MacEntee and de Valera disagreed with this prognosis. Similarly, in the Oireachtas, Opposition Deputies questioned the constitutionality of the Bill.[35]

An Article 26 reference?

The Irish Women Workers' Union took the step of securing counsel's opinion from Sean MacBride about the constitutionality of the Bill and forwarded extracts from the opinion to the President in the hope of securing an Article 26 reference on the basis of the prohibition on class discrimination contained in Article 40.6.2°.[36] Michael McDunphy, Secretary of the Department of the President, brought the correspondence to the attention of the Department of the Taoiseach. De Valera indicated that the Council of State should only be convened if, in the opinion of the President, a *prima facie* case had been made out for an Article 26 referral.[37] In 1941, however, this did not occur. In part, this may have been as a result of the deliberations which had occurred in the first Council of State in 1940. In that deliberation, Douglas Hyde had specifically asked the attendees not to refer to 'political considerations' or 'legal arguments'.[38] The result of this was that the attendees simply expressed their opinion as to whether or not a reference was desirable.[39] The utility of such meetings was questionable. It is noteworthy that in the event of the second meeting of the Council of State, to discuss the School Attendance Bill in 1943, de Valera indicted to McDunphy that a similar direction 'would tend unduly to restrict discussion', which was best left to the judgment of the members.[40] As a result, in 1943, the restriction was lifted which meant that 'the discussion was much freer, fuller and more informative'.[41]

In 1941, therefore, the utility of a Council of State meeting may have appeared negligible given that a *prima facie* case had not been made out and the procedure at the time was to simply record the views of attendees. The 1941 Bill was duly signed into law and the chance for an Article 26 reference was missed.

However, the success of the opposition to the Act served to redeem James Larkin in the eyes of the Labour leadership. As a result of this détente, Larkin was chosen as a local candidate in 1942 and subsequently a national election candidate in 1943. This action was taken in the face of sustained and bitter reaction from the ITGWU due to the acrimonious nature of the relationship between William O'Brien and Larkin.[42] This resulted in the ITGWU leaving the ITUC and forming a new body, the Congress of Irish Unions (CIU), and some of the ITGWU members of the parliamentary Labour party forming National Labour. Charles McCarthy has noted the importance of the 1941 Act, and particularly section 26(2), in the growth of the CIU, which gave their Irish-based unions 'so considerable [an advantage] that a number of the amalgamated unions themselves began to feel that their days were numbered'.[43] Ultimately section 26(2) was struck down by the Supreme Court which removed this advantage.

Commission on vocational organisation

The 1943 Report of the Commission on Vocational Organisation[44] was a comprehensive review of the possibility of vocational organisation in Ireland which ran to over 500 pages.[45] The Report was particularly concerned to argue against any perception, as the Dublin Trades Union Council had in relation to the 1941 Act, that it was advocating a totalitarian view of the state:

> It has been suggested again and again that the introduction of vocational organisation is equivalent to the introduction of 'fascism' or 'totalitarian-

ism' or 'dictatorship', or is at least the first steps towards such forms of government. Such an opinion is unfounded since the evidence shows that vocational organisation exists under democratic forms of government, or under communistic forms.[46]

The report advocated the reorganisation of different sectors of society, e.g. agriculture, industry, on vocational lines. The reorganisation would place the responsibility for those sectors in the hands of bodies organised locally, with an administrative apex in each sector. So, in industry, there would be employers' and workers' associations[47] which would then coordinate in Joint Industrial Boards representative of a particular industry, and the industries generally would meet in the National Industrial Conference.[48] In the organisation of each of the different sectors of society, the Report recommended a coordinating national body with power over the wages and working conditions for each sector.[49]

In light of this organisational structure, it is clear that something similar to the Trade Union Act 1941 was necessary in each sector. In fact, the Report of the Commission on Vocational Organisation specifically averted to the potential constitutional pitfalls of the 1941 Act and rejected them: 'Some trade unionists have expressed opposition in principle to the right of the State to legislate for the reorganisation of trade unions, but we think that there can be no doubt whatever of the constitutional right of parliament to make a law on this matter in defence of the common good.'[50]

The report was critical of the public service in Ireland, which provoked a furious response when it was circulated.[51] During the operation of the Commission, the civil service had not always complied in preferring information to the Commission.[52] In the aftermath of the completion of the work of the Commission, governmental departments were asked for their views on the Report and, as Don O'Leary points out, were 'eager to retaliate' against the criticisms levelled against 'bureaucracy' in the report.[53]

In public, the report was criticised by Sean Lemass.[54] Ministerial opposition to the vocationalist ideal hardened – Sean Lemass, Sean MacEntee, and James Ryan were vocal in their criticisms of both the commission report and the Duignan proposal for organisation of the health service on the basis of vocational methods. The 1942 local elections and 1943 general election showed a galvanised Labour party which stimulated in part by opposition to the Trade Union Act.[55] Subsequently, the Larkin/O'Brien rift resulted in the formation of the National Labour party which split the Labour vote. However, the general suspicion of the trade union movement to the vocationalist ideal meant that it was unlikely that the government would endorse a report which would result in a loss of vote share.

The official, both governmental and bureaucratic, opposition to the report made implementation impossible in the short term. However, it was still possible in 1945 that a change in government would prove capable of changing official policy in the area, leading to the implementation of the report. It is in this light that the Supreme Court case should be considered.

Court proceedings

J. H. Whyte's account of church–state relations highlights two key episodes in relation to vocationalism: these were the Report of the Commission and the Duignan plan for national health insurance which did not end until Duignan's failure to be reappointed in August 1945.[56] The High Court case relating to the 1941 Act commenced before Justice Gavan Duffy in July 1945. The High Court action proceeded with a remarkable degree of speed; it was heard on 3 and 4 July, and the judgment was delivered on 6 July. This was all the more noteworthy as the general academic consensus is that Justice Gavan Duffy produced a much stronger judgment than the Supreme Court in this short period of time.[57] Gavan Duffy indicated from the outset of his judgment that he believed the 'attack on the statute by the N.U.R. is really intended to defeat a legislative policy which it mislikes'.[58] Moreover, Gavan Duffy, relying on US precedent as persuasive authority, argued that the power to 'regulate' included 'such a ... prohibitory provision as that for which the plaintiffs seek to have this enactment declared unconstitutional'.[59]

In the Supreme Court, the argument led by Lavery SC against the 1941 Act also echoed with the struggle against corporatism, although this was not reflected in the decision of the Court. Lavery SC argued:

> [I]f the Tribunal granted the sole right to organise workers to the I.T. and G.W.U., it would be exercising political discrimination in favour of a body with a declared political object, and putting a certain political section in a privileged position. That would be a law for which a precedent came from the Italian Fascist decree of April 3, 1926, and would be unlike American and Canadian legislation which was careful to protect the right of free association.[60]

This Italian law laid down sole recognition to the Fascist trade unions, effectively undermining the Catholic and Socialist unions.[61] However, Louis Franck's analysis of the law in the 1930s drew exactly the opposite conclusion to that of Lavery SC. He argued that while the law indulged in corporatism:

> no particular attention was paid to this because majority representation is in force in many countries which are not Fascist, in France and Belgium for instance, while the efforts of the American Federation of Labour to obtain it in the United States under Roosevelt are well known.[62]

Allowances must, naturally, be made for the tendency in counsel's arguments to use an example which is injurious to the opposing side's case. Nonetheless, the argument advanced by Lavery SC did not explain how exactly Title III differed from the provisions relating to exclusive bargaining under the National Labor Relations Act 1935.[63] Instead, Lavery chose to take aim at a statute which provided a major legislative underpinning to the corporative state in Italy. Moreover, Lavery's example gave a hint as to the stakes that were in play in the case. If the ITGWU were to succeed, then the groundwork for the corporative state would exist.

From the point of view of the decision eventually handed down by the court, the most important interjection was perhaps that of Justice O'Byrne. He questioned whether the legislature could provide 'that people who wanted to play Soccer, for instance, must join only Shamrock Rovers'. According to the *Irish Independent*, John A. Costello replied 'that it was a matter of degree although, he added, he did not think their lordships would have much difficulty in deciding that question'. This salvo elucidated laughter in the court.[64] This is a particularly interesting element of the court proceedings given that the point which was treated with such brevity and humour by Costello and the audience in the Court, was ultimately upheld by the Court as 'both logically and practically' the correct interpretation of the Constitution.[65]

Decision of the Court

The decision of the Supreme Court was read by Justice Murnaghan.[66] J. M. Kelly called the judgment 'colourless' and contended that it 'scarcely did justice to the opinions of Justice Gavan Duffy in overruling them'.[67] The decision turned on whether the power to 'regulate' included the power to 'prohibit'. The Supreme Court ruled that it did not. Casey has demonstrated that this reading introduces a large inconsistency into Article 40.6. Under Article 40.6.2°, laws 'regulating' the rights to associate and assembly must be free of discrimination. However, the right to assemble in Article 40.6.1(ii) can be 'prevent[ed]' by law. As Casey argues, if the Supreme Court is correct, this would mean that these laws could be discriminatory, as the prohibition of discrimination only applies to regulatory laws, and not to prohibitory laws.[68] While the decision was not a convincing one, there are a number of interesting elements of the judgment from a constitutional point of view.

First, the decision may be regarded as making the decisive contribution to the debate about the role of the Oireachtas in relation to the Constitution. J.M. Kelly famously advanced an argument based on the Dáil Debates in relation to the Constitution that de Valera intended that the fundamental rights provisions would act simply as 'headlines' to the legislature and would not involve a substantial amount of judicial review.[69] In *Re Article 26 and the Offences Against the State (Amendment) Bill, 1940* the Supreme Court had struck a conservative note in relation to judicial review. The Court had established the presumption of constitutionality.[70] However, the decision went further and developed an argument in relation to Article 40.3 which would have deprived the Article of effective force:

> The guarantee in [Article 40.3] is not in respect of any particular citizen, or class of citizens, but extends to all the citizens of the State, and the duty of determining the extent to which the rights of any particular citizen, or class of citizens, can properly be harmonised with the rights of the citizens as a whole seems to us to be a matter which is peculiarly within the province of the Oireachtas, and any attempt by this Court to control the Oireachtas in the exercise of this function, would, in our opinion, be a usurpation of its authority.[71]

Similarly, Justice Hanna in *The Pigs Marketing Board v. Donnelly* believed that the delineation of the concept of 'social justice' in Article 43.2 was a matter for the Oireachtas, and not the Courts, to determine.[72] In 1941, Patrick McGilligan, Professor of Constitutional Law in University College Dublin, had specifically ruled out the possibility of judicial review of the Trade Union Act as a result of this line of jurisprudence:

> Nobody cares at the moment as to what guarantee is given by the Constitution because the courts have already decided that all the fundamental rights are in the grip of the law. If we pass that measure people need not trouble to go to the courts in order to get their rights established there. The Dáil is supreme and if you pass this, the Constitution is at an end as far as the right of association is concerned.[73]

This interpretation of the role of the Oireachtas was put into some relief in the Article 26 reference of the School Attendance Bill where the Supreme Court considered what the meaning of 'certain minimum education' under Article 42 entailed. The Court provided an autonomous meaning of this phrase ('a minimum standard of elementary education of general application') but stressed the wide interpretative vista open to the legislature ('we are of opinion that the State, acting in its legislative capacity through the Oireachtas has power to define it').[74] Moreover, that Article 26 reference proceeded after the Council of State meeting where de Valera once again advanced a very expansive view of legislative authority:

> That the Constitution should not be construed narrowly as if it were an ordinary Act of Parliament; that, except for the rules providing for the establishment and maintenance of the fundamental State institutions, it should be regarded rather as a statement of general directive principles to which legislation should conform.[75]

Chief Justice Sullivan was present at the meeting of the Council of State and would have been aware, as a result, of de Valera's views on the matter.[76] *National Union of Railwaymen* was, however, the first comprehensive dismissal of de Valera's view. Justice Murnaghan held:

> Constitutions frequently embody, within their framework, important principles of polity expressed in general language. In some Constitutions it is left to the Legislature to interpret the meaning of these principles, but in other types of Constitutions, of which ours is one, an authority is chosen which is clothed with the power and burdened with the duty of seeing that the Legislature shall not transgress the limits set upon its powers.[77]

This argument clearly builds on the holding in the *School Attendance Bill* case, but it is notable for the manner in which it frames a view of the Constitution in lines extremely similar to that advocated by de Valera, which it then proceeds to discard. This dismissal of de Valera's idea of the fundamental rights provisions was more famously dismissed in *Buckley v. Attorney General*.[78] That justly celebrated case dismissed the argument that the legislature alone could determine what were the exigencies of the common good capable of limiting rights under the Constitution.[79] The really decisive turn had occurred, in this regard, the previous year in *National Union of Railwaymen*.

One other element of *Buckley* is explicable solely against the backdrop of *National Union of Railwaymen*. In the course of oral argument, counsel for the state argued that the right to private property under Article 43 only protected the general right to property. One's individual right to property could be regulated by the state. This was robustly rejected by the Supreme Court and is regarded by Hogan as a key element in the construction of the decision.[80] Richard McLoughlin

SC's opinion appears to have been based on the fact that Article 43 allowed the state to 'regulate' the right in question; *pace National Union of Railwaymen*, this allowed anything short of extinguishing the right. This overly literal reading of the Constitution might have appeared a misstep by counsel, but it was based on the poor precedent of *National Union of Railwaymen*.

More significant again, however, was the effect of the decision on the vocational project. We have seen how the concept of group organisation was a key element of vocationalism. The decision, by striking down Part III, as inconsistent with Article 40.6.1(iii), which provided for majority representation, eliminated any possibility of group organisation on vocational lines advocated by the Commission on Vocational Organisation. Any such proposal would now have to amend the Constitution in order to bring in implementing legislation to secure the vocational ideal. The court judgment therefore placed a constitutional bar in front of a project which already lacked the support of the civil service and Fianna Fáil administration. The fact that these powerful bodies were opposed to the Report of the Commission on Vocational Organisation may have obscured the importance of the constitutional bar. However, a coalition truly committed to the vocational ideal, as the Opposition parties ostensibly were, may have been in a position to try and implement it by statute. They would, however, face an extremely high burden of a constitutional amendment in face of trade union and Fianna Fáil opposition, particularly given the electoral response to the introduction to the 1941 Act, if they attempted to amend the Constitution. In point of fact, despite their opposition to bureaucracy and their support of vocationalism when in opposition, the first inter-party government did not proceed to operate on the vocationalist ideal when in charge of the machinery of bureaucracy.[81]

There appears to have been some confusion about the operation of the decision. Seán MacBride, who acted as Senior Counsel for the National Union of Railwaymen, argued in 1947 both in favour of the adoption of the Report of the Commission on Vocational Organisation and the decision in *National Union of Railwaymen*.[82] It is not clear how he believed the Report could be implemented absent the legislative underpinnings which had been so important in terms of the overall scheme advocated by the Commission.

Conclusion

Whyte argues that by the 1940s, a rift had opened up between two philosophies of government in Ireland: 'One could be labelled "vocationalist" and called for the diffusion of responsibility among vocational groups. The other could be called "bureaucratic", and defended the centralisation of authority in government departments.'[83] Despite the usefulness of this analytical method, the *National Union of Railwaymen* case demonstrates that it does not accurately reflect the conflict in the 1940s. The Report of the Commission on Vocational Organisation certainly argues for the debate in those terms, and particularly sets itself against the bureaucratic mindset. However, it is clear from the powers which it sought to arrogate to itself that the vocational state would centralise authority in areas where the state did not regulate in a parallel power structure, which could not but increase central authority. As J.J. Lee has pointed out: '[t]he commission envisaged sweeping social and economic changes that would require a degree of activism – "vocational" rather than "state", but still activism – far exceeding anything contemplated before the war, or implemented during the war'.[84] Moreover Lee points out that the report failed to adequately confront the possibility that any new administrative system would itself become bureaucratic.[85]

From a trade unionist point of view, this was the key problem with the vocational project – it would give rise to a centralised state architecture which would undermine the trade unions' ability to engage in independent action. This view was not without justification. Commentators such as Cornelius Lucey argued that the trade unions' ability to strike should be greatly restricted and certain types of strike action should be banned completely.[86] Moreover, the trade unions were, at the time, concerned to resist any attempts at compulsory arbitration of disputes, and successfully did so in regard of the Industrial Relations Act 1946.[87]

In fact, Anthony Whelan's analysis of the influence of corporatism on the political life of the state draws attention to two different models of corporatism – one based on a private sector in which subsidiary organisations can nonetheless rely on the ultimate sanction of state support, and a second consensual model based on pragmatic conflict resolution in which state goods are traded with private goods.[88] Whelan links the latter conception of corporatism with the industrial policy pursued by Seán Lemass and exemplified in the Industrial Relations Act 1946.[89] Despite referring to *National Union of Railwaymen v. Sullivan* and considering the liberalism inherent in the decision, Whelan appears not to recognise that it essentially closed the door on the former model of corporatism.[90]

In terms of judicial rigor, therefore, we may rightfully say that the decision in *National Union of Railwaymen v. Sullivan* is not of the highest standard. In terms of its historical importance in shaping a key debate about the future political and civic development of the state, however, it is clear that it was a constitutional case of the first rank.

Notes

1 [1950] IR 67.
2 See R. Keane, 'Across the Cherokee Frontier of Irish Constitutional Jurisprudence: The *Sinn Féin Funds* Case: *Buckley v. Attorney General* (1950)' in E. O'Dell (ed.), *Leading Cases of the Twentieth Century* (Round Hall Sweet & Maxwell, 2000); G. Hogan, 'The Sinn Fein Funds Judgment Fifty Years on' (1997) 2(9) *Bar Review* 375.
3 [1940] IR 136. See G. Hogan, 'The Supreme Court and the Reference of the Offences against the State (Amendment) Bill 1940' (2000) *Irish Jurist* 238, 244–250. An honourable mention here must go to the decision of Justice Kingsmill Moore in the High Court in *Comyn v. Attorney General* [1950] IR 142, 144–161 for an exceptional judgment.
4 [1947] IR 77.
5 J. M. Kelly, *Fundamental Rights in the Irish Law and Constitution* (Allen Figgis, 1961) pp. 120–121.
6 G. Whyte, 'Industrial Relations and the Irish Constitution' 16 *Irish Jurist* (1981) 35, 67.
7 J. P. Casey, 'Reform of Collective Bargaining Law: Some Constitutional Implications' (1972) 7 *Irish Jurist* 1, 13–14. This article presents perhaps the most compelling demonstration of the weakness of the Supreme Court's reasoning. See also, J. Casey, *Constitutional Law in Ireland* (3rd edn, Round Hall Sweet & Maxwell, 2000) p. 602.
8 *Report of the Constitution Review Group* (Government of Ireland, 1996) p. 312; *Report of the Committee on the Constitution* (Stationery Office, 1967) p. 42. The 1967 report précised the decision of the Supreme Court in a wonderful example of bureaucratic sarcasm: 'The Supreme Court held, apparently, that Part III went beyond regulation and control …'. The use of the word 'apparently' is superfluous unless the author is disbelieving of the Court's rationale.
9 *Report of the Committee on the Constitution* (n. 8) p. 42.
10 See, e.g., J. M. Kelly, *The Irish Constitution* (Jurist Publishing, 1980) p. 471; *Report of the Constitution Review Group* (n. 8) p. 314.
11 See e.g. C. McCarthy, *Trade Unions in Ireland 1894–1960* (IPA, 1977) pp. 279–280.
12 See further A. Whelan, 'Constitutional Democracy, Community and Corporatism in Ireland' in G. Quinn (ed.), *Irish Human Rights Yearbook 1995* (Round Hall Sweet and Maxwell, 1995) pp. 105–108.
13 D. Keogh and A. McCarthy, *The Making of the Irish Constitution 1937: Bunreacht na hÉireann* (Mercier Press, 2007) pp. 57–58.
14 See M. J. Ahern, 'What Is the Corporative State?' (1941) 69 *Irish Monthly* 572, 572.

15 W. Drummond, 'Papal Encyclicals and Vocational Order' (1944) 72 *Irish Monthly* 101, 101.
16 *Ibid.*, 104. See also C. Lucey, 'The Vocational Group Movement' (1938) 66 *Irish Monthly* 221, 229.
17 L. R. Franck, 'Fascism and the Corporate State' (1935) 6 *Political Quarterly* 355, 365. See also D. O'Leary, *Vocationalism and Social Catholicism in Twentieth-Century Ireland: The Search for a Christian Social Order* (Irish Academic Press, 2000) pp. xi–xiii.
18 See Ahern (n. 14).
19 Alfred O'Rahilly expressed doubts about Fianna Fáil's belief in vocationalism when considering the drafting of the 1937 Constitution (*Thoughts on the Constitution* (Browne and Nolan, 1937) p. 43).
20 *Irish Press* (29 December 1937).
21 See *Irish Independent* (29 January 1938); Keogh and McCarthy (n. 13) pp. 58–59.
22 21 *Seanad Debates* 438 (21 July 1938).
23 See further on de Valera's motivation, O'Leary (n. 17) p. 72; J. J. Lee 'Aspects of Corporatist Thought in Ireland: The Commission on Vocational Organisation, 1939–43' in A. Cosgrove and D. McCartney (eds), *Studies in Irish History: Presented to R. Dudley Edwards* (UCD Press, 1979) p. 325.
24 [1938] IR 749, 755.
25 NAI: Taois/s. 12279A 'Memorandum explanatory of Draft Heads of a Bill Relating to Changes in Trade Union Law and Organisation' (30 January 1941).
26 See C. McCarthy, *Trade Unions in Ireland 1894–1960* (IPA, 1977) pp. 201–202; K. Allen, 'Forging the Links: Fianna Fáil, the Trade Unions and the Emergency' (1991) 16 *Saothar* 48, p. 52. On the Act generally, see McCarthy (*ibid.*, ch. 5).
27 s. 26(1).
28 s. 26(1)(c).
29 NAI: Taois/s. 12279A.
30 NAI: Taois/s. 12279A 'Dublin Trades Union Council: Trades Union Bill 1931' (5 June 1941).
31 See D. Ó Drisceoil, '"Whose Emergency Is It?" Wartime Politics and the Irish Working Class, 1939–45' in F. Lane and D. Ó Drisceoil (eds), *Politics and the Irish Working Class, 1830–1945* (Palgrave MacMillan, 2005) p. 270.
32 *Ibid.*
33 *Irish Press* (23 June 1941). Larkin was a member of the Commission on Vocational Organisation which was holding meetings at the time, but he failed to sign the final report. See O'Leary (n. 17) pp. 95–96, 101 for Larkin's views of the Commission.
34 NAI: Taois/s. 12279A (19 June 1941).
35 See Dáil Debates, vol. 83, col. 1657 (5 June 1941).
36 NAI: Taois/s. 12279A, McDowell to President (25 June 1941). The arguments track those later published in the *Irish Law Times and Solicitor's Journal*; 'The Constitutionality of the Trade Union Act, 1941' (1942) *ILT & SJ* 15.
37 NAI: Taois/s. 12279A (19 August 1941).

38 NAI: Pres/P1488. On the 1940 meeting, see G. Hogan, *The Origins of the Irish Constitution, 1928–1941* (Royal Irish Academy, 2012) pp. 684–687.
39 NAI: Pres/1/P3041 (1 March 1943).
40 NAI: Taois/ s. 12337(22 February 1943). The note is recorded in G. Hogan, 'The Supreme Court and the Reference of the Offences Against the State (Amendment) Bill 1940' (2000) *Irish Jurist* 238, 258.
41 NAI: Pres/1/P3041 (1 March 1943).
42 See N. Puirséil, *The Irish Labour Party 1922–73* (UCD Press, 2007) pp. 86–99, 101–103; E. O'Connor, *A Labour History of Ireland 1824–2000* (2nd edn, UCD Press, 2011) pp. 164–169; McCarthy (n. 26) ch. 6.
43 McCarthy (n. 26) p. 279.
44 The most complete consideration of the Report remains Joseph Lee's excellent and acerbic analysis in 'Aspects of Corporatist Thought in Ireland: The Commission on Vocational Organisation, 1939–43' in A. Cosgrove and D. McCartney (eds), *Studies in Irish History: Present to R. Dudley Edwards* (UCD Press, 1979) p. 324.
45 The length was criticised by Brian O'Nolan for 'the tax-payer paying for these unnecessary and ill-worded passages, a farrago of repetition, pomposity and prolixity occupied with solicitude for the tax-payer' (*Irish Times* (18 September 1944)).
46 Report of the Commission on Vocational Organisation (Stationery Office, 1943) p. 11.
47 *Ibid.*, pp. 355–359.
48 *Ibid.*, pp. 360–362.
49 See, e.g., pp. 346 (agriculture), 360 (industry), 386–387 and 389 (commerce) and 396 (transport).
50 *Ibid.*, pp. 364.
51 See, e.g. *ibid.*, pp. 425–427.
52 O'Leary (n. 17) p. 88.
53 *Ibid.*, p. 106.
54 Brian O'Nolan also satirised the report (*Irish Times* (18 September 1944, 6 November 1944)).
55 B. Girvin, *The Emergency: Neutral Ireland 1939–45* (MacMillan, 2006) pp. 240, 243.
56 See J. H. Whyte, *Church and State in Modern Ireland 1923–1979* (2nd edn, Gill & Macmillan, 1980) pp. 96–119.
57 See, e.g., Kelly (n. 5) pp. 120–121.
58 [1947] IR 77, at 86.
59 *Ibid.*, pp. 87–88.
60 *Irish Independent* (6 June 1946); *Irish Press* (6 June 1946). The coverage of the *Irish Press* and *Irish Independent* appear to be based on the same original source; the *Irish Times* report from that day makes no mention of this argument.
61 See, e.g. P. Morgan, *Italian Fascism 1915–1945* (2nd edn, Palgrave MacMillan, 2004) p. 106.

62 L. R. Franck, 'Fascism and the Corporate State' (1935) 6 *Political Quarterly* 355, 366.
63 See 29 US Code s. 159(a). Presumably, he believed the fact that the individual right to bring a grievance was preserved was sufficient. However, this right was trammelled by the fact that any changes had to be consistent with the collective bargaining agreement in the area.
64 *Irish Independent* (8 June 1946). The laughter is not recorded in the *Irish Press* report of the same day.
65 [1947] IR 77, 102.
66 On Justice Murnaghan, see H. Geoghegan, 'The Three Judges of the Supreme Court of the Irish Free State, 1925–36: Their Backgrounds, Personalities and Mindsets' in F. Larkin and N. Dawson (eds), *Lawyers, the Law and History* (Four Courts Press, 2013) pp. 41–43. See also, D. K. Coffey 'The Judiciary of the Irish Free State' (2011) 18(1) *Dublin University Law Journal* 61.
67 Kelly (n. 5) p. 120.
68 J. P. Casey, 'Reform of Collective Bargaining Law: Some Constitutional Implications' (1972) 7 *Irish Jurist* 1, 13–14.
69 Kelly (n. 5) pp. 17–19.
70 [1940] IR 470, 478.
71 *Ibid.*, 481; Hogan (n. 3) p. 267.
72 [1939] IR 413, 417–418.
73 Dáil Debates, vol. 83, col. 1657 (5 June 1941).
74 [1943] IR 334, 345.
75 NAI: Taois/s. 12337. This was the first meeting of the Council of State where substantive points were made, see above.
76 See *Irish Independent* (26 February 1943).
77 [1946] IR 77, 99.
78 Hogan (n. 3) p. 267.
79 [1950] IR 67, 83.
80 Hogan (n. 3) p. 381.
81 O'Leary (n. 17) pp. 156–161.
82 S. MacBride, *Civil Liberty* (Irish People Co-Operative Society) pp. 3, 12.
83 Whyte (n. 56.) p. 117. Whyte continued this analysis elsewhere; 'To the Declaration of the Republic and the Ireland Act, 1945–9' in J. R. Hill (ed.), *A New History of Ireland: VII Ireland, 1921–84* (OUP, 2003) p. 266.
84 J. J. Lee, *Ireland 1912–1985: Politics and Society* (CUP, 2006) p. 276.
85 *Ibid*. The Report briefly addresses this criticism in one page, see (n. 50) pp. 450–451. See also Lee (n. 44) pp. 341–344 for further critical reflection on the report.
86 C. Lucey, 'Strikes and the Labour Court' (1947) 36 *Studies* 385, 393.
87 s. 68. On the history of the 1946 Act, see J. Hendy, 'McGowan & Collective Bargaining in Ireland', pp. 4–15, at www.ictu.ie/download/pdf/collective_bargaining_ireland_jan_30.pdf (last accessed 18 August 2015). My thanks to Dr Eoin Daly for bringing this to my attention.
88 Whelan (n. 12) pp. 108–110.

89 *Ibid.*
90 *Ibid.*, pp. 110–113, 120. A similar point in relation to liberalism is made by C. McCarthy; *Trade Unions in Ireland 1894–1960* (IPA, 1977) pp. 505–507.

13

Ulster unionism and the Irish Constitution, 1970–85

Rory Milhench

Introduction

This chapter seeks to analyse the nuances in the relationship between Ulster Unionists and successive Irish governments, with particular emphasis on how certain Articles of the Irish Constitution helped form the Unionist image of the Irish Republic and how this conditioned the relationship between the two parties. Particular scrutiny is devoted to the question of constitutional reform and the ways in which Irish governments considered amendments to improve relations with Unionists and secure their consent for a potential unity arrangement. The cause of Unionist hostility towards the Republic, their concept of Irish unity and their forecasted social station within an arrangement of unification are explored. A selection of constitutional Articles, including those relating to extradition, the territorial claim over Northern Ireland and the special position of the Catholic Church in the Republic are examined for this purpose. The contention is made that what particularly distressed Unionists about the Irish Constitution was the apparent convictions the document made about the type of state Ireland was and how it seemed to predict the realities of its unified future.

Northern Protestants and the Roman Catholic Church

In September 1972, Dr Gerard Benedict Newe, the Catholic Unionist politician, decried to the Chairman of the Inter-Party Committee of Dáil Éireann on the Constitution of the Republic of Ireland, Paddy Harte, that 'for fifty years, the Parliament, Government and people of the Republic of Ireland have made no sincerely honest or effective effort to understand the way of life and thought, traditions, attitudes and fears of the people of Northern Ireland'.[1] On the contrary, Newe surmised, the intention had been to denigrate Northern Ireland with constant references to the 'wee six', 'the six counties' and 'British occupied Ireland'.

The first attempt by southern politicians to adapt their own state for northern Protestants came with the Fifth Amendment of the Constitution Act, 1972, which removed the special position of the Catholic Church from the Irish Constitution.[2] Constitutional de-Catholicisation took its roots from the *Report of the Committee on the Constitution* of December 1967, a body established by Seán Lemass after his meeting with the Northern Premier Captain Terence O'Neill.

In its original state, Article 44 recognised 'the special position of the Holy Catholic Apostolic and Roman Church as the guardian of the Faith professed by the great majority of the citizens'. The report noted that 'there seems, however, to be no doubt that these provisions give offence to non-Catholics', before advocating its deletion to 'dispel any doubts and suspicions which may linger in the minds of non-Catholcs [*sic*], North and South of the Border, and remove an unnecessary source of mischievous and specious criticism'.[3] The provision was removed from the Irish Constitution after a referendum on 7 December 1972, with 84% of the turnout voting in favour of its deletion.[4] Among other intentions, it was an attempt to deconfessionalise the Irish state, remove a social charter which was no longer considered necessary and help Ireland appear less pious and sectarian to Ulster Unionists.

This invitation failed because it was viewed by Ulster Unionists as a superficial act of edition; it may have removed the ornament of the legal recognition of the church's exalted position, but it altered neither its ascendancy in matters of social dilemma nor the core religious fabric of the state. What remained essential for Ulster Protestants was not that the clause no longer existed, but what it had conveyed about Ireland while it was alive. To Unionists, the Constitution was not an agent or an umpire of devotionalism, but a response to public piety. Article 44 had decreed what had already become an assured social reality.

Such a view had not moderated almost a decade after the Article's excision. On 8 October 1981, Robert McCartney QC, later leader of the UK Unionist Party, met with an Taoiseach Garret FitzGerald to protest again the church's dignified position within Irish society and its knowing supremacy. McCartney claimed Unionist opposition to the Catholic Church in Ireland was because it was able to

> [d]ictate policy to the state on matters which the Church considers essential to the maintenance of its position. Such is the extent of this power that conflict between State and Church barely arises, and the power is so effective

in real terms that the badges of it such as the special position of the church in the Constitution are no longer necessary and can be dispensed with.[5]

What was particularly troubling to these members of the legal profession was how Catholic religious observance within Ireland had apparently fashioned the personality of Irish public law. The statute was Catholic to service its Catholic populace. This made them ponder what religious allowances might be granted to Unionists within a unified scenario. It also contravened a budding libertarianism among some Protestants which objected to the legal endorsement or state patronage of any religion.[6]

Irish officials speculated on a way to counter these anxieties, as shown in a Martin Mansergh paper on Irish unity.[7] Mansergh, himself a Protestant, speculated that:

> Article 44 might be revived, which while recognising the special position of the Catholic Church of the great majority in the island as a whole, recognises the special position of the Protestant churches in Northern Ireland, and guaranteeing that no law which in the opinion of the majority of Northern Ireland representatives or the leaders of at least three principal Churches infringes existing religious liberties or freedom of conscience shall have effect in Northern Ireland.[8]

It was thus the authoritarian impulse that Ulster Protestants feared about the Catholic Church and its influence over public law in Ireland, about which the deletion of Article 44 did little to subdue, and which Mansergh here seemed inclined to resurrect.

As early as October 1969, Taoiseach Jack Lynch saw the disposal of Article 44 as a potential formula through which to attain Unionist support for Irish unity. He said in Dáil Éireann that when the point is reached at which 'we can see clearly the various changes needed in our Constitution to facilitate a reunification settlement, I am sure that both Dáil and Seanad and our people generally will not be reluctant to consider and approve the necessary changes'.[9] The purpose of altering the Irish Constitution in this instance was to concoct an algorithm for unity in cold, clinical terms, not because reform was required for its own sake.

A Department of External Affairs paper written a month after Lynch's speech on Northern Ireland urged that 'Dublin should consider taking steps which would tend to convince Northern Protestants that they would enjoy full civil rights and equality in a United Ireland'.[10] It suggested organising a study into areas like divorce, birth control and questioned whether 'any reforms in the educational system are desirable, bearing in mind that a United Ireland would be pluralistic rather than a confessional society'.[11] The paper's author appeared more interested in how to persuade Unionists of a certain apparition of Ireland than the innate virtues of that vision for Irish citizenry.

Divorce

Like the special position of the Catholic Church, the injunction on divorce, enshrined in the Irish Constitution under Article 41.3.2°, had been reviewed in 1967 in the *Report of the Committee on the Constitution*. It noted that the offending Article, which provided that 'no law shall be enacted providing for the grant of a dissolution of marriage' had received criticism because 'it takes no heed of the wishes of a certain minority of the population who would wish to have divorce facilities and who are not prevented from securing divorce by the tenets of the religious denominations to which they belong'.[12] The Committee suggested that marriages should be permitted dissolution so long as the religion which granted it allowed for this. Divorce could be granted for those protestant denominations which were willing to facilitate divorce, while Catholic spouses would remain bound by their church's rejection of it.

The Department of External Affairs assumed that divorce was not a trophy Protestant churches would campaign too strongly for, its capture being virtually pyrrhic in nature. In late 1969, it acknowledged that the various Protestant denominations did not 'approve of divorce, but accept it as a fact of life. Embarrassment might, however be felt by them if divorce legislation was proposed on the grounds that they, the Protestant community, had been or were being denied their rights'.[13] A markedly similar view was communicated to Taoiseach Liam Cosgrave in April 1973 by the Presbyterian Church in Ireland, a submission which was passed on to a body titled the Inter-Party Committee on the Implications of Irish Unity (IPCIIU).

Its purpose was to examine the legal, economic, and constitutional implications of Irish unity and to make recommendations on the steps required to create the conditions conducive to such unity. It operated under the assumption that unification was inevitable and that Protestant and Unionist objections were its greatest fund of resistance. The Presbyterian submission reported a resolution made by its Dublin Synod. It generally advocated marriage as a contract of permanence, but also acknowledged the realities of marital breakdown and that much suffering could be upheld by their protraction, so urged 'the removal of the prohibition of divorce in the Constitution'.[14]

The IPCIIU itself discussed the Article prohibiting divorce in September 1972, and it was considered 'inappropriate to the Constitution and should be removed simply to empower parliament to entertain divorce legislation and without prejudice as to the merits or otherwise of such legislation'.[15] Rather than accept the disposal of certain constitutional Articles as important for Ireland's social renovation, most members of the committee saw it as a useful enticement to lure Unionists towards Irish unity. The Committee's chairman Paddy Harte sought to renounce such incentivising, asserting that 'the question should be approached not from the point of view of bargaining with Northern Unionists but in an attempt to creat [sic.] a society which Northern Unionists could accept'.[16] Only several of the coalition's members appeared willing to acknowledge that Unionist antipathy to unity was unlikely to be eased by several tantalising erasures to the Constitution.

In a letter to Monsignor Casoroli, Secretary of the Council for the Public Affairs of the Catholic Church, Garret FitzGerald wrote that the divorce prohibition appeared to 'threaten the existing divorce provisions in Northern Ireland and has suggested to many Northern Protestants an intention on our part, within a united Ireland, to require them to eliminate these provisions'.[17] FitzGerald added that in the event of a new Constitution being written for the Republic, there was a compelling case for the clause's deletion, given that it was offensive to Protestants in Ireland. A removal of distasteful constitutional Articles would also redirect Unionists from a convenient position of obduracy. If the Republic was no longer under-reformed, or inhospitably Catholic, Unionists would be compelled to change their argument as to why they would refuse Irish unity.[18] Typecasting the South as culturally introverted reassured Unionists, because it could strengthen their opposition to national unity for Ireland.

Articles 2 and 3 and the territory of Ulster

Other clauses existed within the Irish Constitution which threatened not only the survival of Ulster Protestantism within the bounds of the Republic, but the Northern Irish State itself. Article 2 claimed the six counties of Northern Ireland to be territory of the Irish State, while Article 3 assumed legislative sovereignty over that area. The IPCIIU considered 'that, in the context 32–County State, Article 3 was superfluous and were of the opinion that, in the event of a general revision of the Constitution, the amendment of Article 3 could be considered'.[19] It even suggested that in the event of unity, an entirely new Constitution would be required and that the current Articles 1 to 3 were not conducive to unity by consent.

To allay Unionist fears over the suspected march towards Irish unity, the Irish government claimed to be willing to sacrifice Articles 2 and 3. In a meeting with Brian Faulkner[20] shortly after the signing of the Sunningdale Agreement, Liam Cosgrave[21] stated that 'any referendum to change Articles 2 and 3 of the constitution might fail, but there would be better prospects for an entirely new constitution which could drop the unacceptable assertions'.[22] This was also a tacit acknowledgement that the Articles retained an important nationalist resonance for the Irish public, who would interpret their deletion as a restraint on the heights of their nationalist ambition. This awareness attended the Irish government's thinking when negotiating the Sunningdale Agreement, since they assumed it was vital to 'have regard to the body of sentiment in the Republic which attaches importance to the "claim" inherent in Articles 2 and 3 of the Constitution'.[23]

This was borne out by the attitudinal study of southern public opinion towards Northern Ireland by Davis and Sinnott. In their study, compiled in 1979, they found that of the 1758 persons they surveyed, 'there is a substantial body of opinion (50 per cent) opposed to removal of Articles 2 and 3 and only a small minority (16 per cent) in favour of outright deletion'.[24] They continued that

> [t]here is only limited support in the Republic of Ireland for changes in the 1937 Constitution which are frequently regarded as relevant to a solution of the Northern Ireland problem. This support is particularly low (24 per cent) in the case of the proposal to remove the claim to Northern Ireland from the Constitution.[25]

Gerard Hogan made the compelling argument that the Irish Constitution of 1937 shared the interior instincts of other Catholic constitutions, but conceded the most telling point that when it came to engendering cooperation in Ireland, it 'was unlikely, to put it mildly, to contribute to such an accommodation'.[26]

Brian Faulkner testified that it was the symbolic encroachment of the Irish State through these Articles that disconcerted Unionists the most. He told Cosgrave that it was 'open to doubt whether our Protestant community at large will ever be satisfied with anything less than an amendment to your constitution'.[27] This was because, to accept the Irish State's involvement in Northern Ireland through the vehicle of the Council of Ireland, Unionists had to be convinced that the Irish State was committed to repairing communal division there, not priming the conditions for unity.

Kevin Boland, a former Fianna Fáil Minister, brought a case to the High Court in Ireland in January 1974.[28] He alleged that the Sunningdale Agreement was unconstitutional because it surrendered and was adversarial to the sovereignty claim of Articles 2 and 3 of the Irish Constitution over the territory of Northern Ireland. This he attributed to article 5 of the British government's declaration on the agreement, which recognised Northern Ireland's continued position as a constituent member of the United Kingdom and the Irish government's refusal to rebut this. Instead, the Irish government asserted that 'there could be no change in the status of Northern Ireland until a majority of the people of Northern Ireland desired a change in that status'.[29]

The Irish government did not specify the reality of this status, that Northern Ireland was a member of the United Kingdom, only that it would not change without the expressed will of its majority. Brian Faulkner implored the Irish government to make a public declaration on this point, given that 'unionists would have to be sure that the Irish government accepted that NI would remain part of the UK until a majority of people wished otherwise'.[30] Faulkner's contention was that a failure to do so would make a Council of Ireland untenable, because it would be too challenging to convince the Unionist population that the Irish government's intentions were simply to redeem cross-border cooperation. The Irish High Court ruled in favour of the Irish government, judging that the Agreement did not contravene the Irish Constitution, but Unionist fears did not lose their surety.

This fear controlled Unionist views of the Irish State, despite their recognition that the Irish government was trying to limit the violence of the Provisional Irish Republican Army (PIRA). A Department of Foreign Affairs report from 1976 relayed the genuine sense of grievance among northern Protestants that these Articles still existed and that 'a change of the Constitution in this area is probably the one subject that is raised most frequently by Unionist contacts' and that 'while Articles 2 and 3 remain there will always be a residue of distrust about Dublin's ultimate intentions'.[31] However, they also provided Unionists with a repeating and convenient defence against participating in initiatives which had the Irish dimension preserved in them. Unionists could thus spoil new Anglo-Irish manoeuvres and do little to broker progress themselves, indulging in their pronouncements of 'Britishness'.

In January 1980, Democratic Unionist Party (DUP) Leader Ian Paisley told a session of the Conference on government in Northern Ireland that 'any solution which had the seal of approval of the Republic's government – which claimed sovereignty in the North – would be totally unacceptable to the majority in the North'.[32] Yet in October 1981, after Taoiseach Garret FitzGerald had suggested removing Articles 2 and 3 of the Irish Constitution to relieve concern over the Irish claim to jurisdiction, Unionists were slow to applaud, when before they had made it seem their central objection. FitzGerald explained to Margaret Thatcher his rationale that 'while the aspiration to unity remained, the Republic no longer claimed jurisdiction in Northern Ireland'.[33] Now Paisley remarked that it was an

> attempt to show the acceptable face of Dublin at the next Anglo-Irish talks: nothing would alter Northern Ireland's determination to remain British. By dropping the claim to the North, Dublin would merely normalise relations between the UK and the Republic, as between two foreign countries.[34]

UUP MP Martin Smyth was reviewed by Liam Hourican, Irish government press secretary, as exhibiting the same tendency. Of the proposed Anglo-Irish Council of 1981, Smyth said that 'Unionists could not contemplate recognising such a Council as long as Articles 2 and 3 existed. He became coy when asked whether recognition would follow their deletion'.[35] Articles 2 and 3 were a valuable propaganda weapon to Unionists because they seemed to testify to the invidious character of the Irish State; losing them would confiscate artillery from the armoury. Thus, there was unquestionably a tactical dimension to the Unionist revulsion of Irish unity, and the controversial Articles 2 and 3.

It should be emphasised that Unionists had a genuine and affecting fear of the idea of a thirty-two-county Republic because of their uncertain role within it. Thus they had a vested interest in not recognising the validity of the 'Irish dimension' debate, never mind conceive of an answer to its leading question.[36] The direct consequence of that would have been to acknowledge the right of the South to intervene in the political affairs of the North. Unionist representatives like Harold McCusker of the UUP might have been content to meet with southern politicians, and develop placid diplomatic relations with them, but would not 'tolerate anything which smacks of supra-national arrangements or which might give Southern politicians a standing to interfere in the affairs of the North'.[37]

It should also be added that the Irish government made a distinction between Articles 2 and 3 and the confessional elements of the Irish Constitution, like Article 44. The former were less suitable for reform, because, unlike the latter, there was no satisfactory argument which could claim them to be socially redundant. An Irish government could sell the reform of certain constitutional Articles to the Irish public under the logic that they were outdated, even if in private, alteration was only considered necessary to make unity appear attractive to Unionists. However, there was less latitude to apply the same rationale to Articles 2 and 3, because this would be to denounce the Irish claim of jurisdiction over Northern Ireland as improper, fictitious or irrelevant. This would be less acceptable to the Irish electorate.

In a meeting with a Unionist delegation, Tánaiste Michael O'Leary, referring to matters like divorce, admitted that there was scope to argue that 'the constitution needed change for its own sake'.[38] However, he qualified, the same was not applicable to Articles 2 and 3, which the Irish government would not abandon. Unionists may have seen them as a legal fiction, but to Irish nationalists they were a lament that the Irish nation had not yet been completed.[39]

It was not until an Irish High Court ruling by Justice Donal Barrington[40] in 1989 that Article 2 was interpreted as a political aim and not a legal right to jurisdiction over Northern Ireland.[41] Barrington also concluded that Article 3 gave the Irish government no authority to enact laws with an area of application in the counties of Northern Ireland. The judgment was in response to a case brought by Christopher and Michael McGimpsey of the UUP. The plaintiffs sought a declaration that the Anglo-Irish Agreement of 1985 was contrary to the provisions of the Constitution of Ireland. In particular, they argued that, in recognising the legitimacy of the present status of Northern Ireland, the agreement violated Articles 2 and 3 of the Irish Constitution.

This peculiar use of the Irish Constitution against the Anglo-Irish Agreement demonstrated the breathless desperation within Unionism to prevent its application. Until that point, Unionists could occasionally mispronounce the intention of the Articles, like Robert McCartney QC, who alleged that '[t]hese two articles gave political legitimacy to the terrorist campaign of the Provisional I.R.A'.[42] This was antithetical to the purpose of their creation, which was meant to act as a restraint on IRA militancy, not a license for its pollination. The Ulster Defence Association, the largest loyalist paramilitary group, considered the Irish Republic a potentially hostile nation because the mechanism of Articles 2 and 3 seemed to encourage the militancy of the PIRA. They believed that if Northern Ireland had been declared a possession of the South, it was inevitable that some of its citizens would seek to guarantee this exchange through violence and further, that the Articles would act as a receipt of this transaction: 'The U.D.A. believes that the existence of the territorial claim is the mainstay of the Provos and all other para-military Republican organisations. The claim supports the political philosophy of these groups.'[43]

Extradition

The other key loyalist grievance about the Irish Constitution, and one which became a highly publicised topic of Anglo-Irish friction, was the Irish State's inability to extradite Irish citizens to Northern Ireland courts for the trying of terrorist offences committed on Northern Irish territory. Republican activists would commit offences in the North and then escape to the Republic, from where they could not be extradited. Irish government efforts to secure the extradition of alleged Republican terrorists invariably failed in court because Article 29 of the Irish Constitution was interpreted as including a prohibition on the extradition of anyone sought for a political offence.

The basis for such an opinion, ironically grounded in a principle of international law established by a British court early in the twentieth century, was that a terrorist offence constituted a political act or could be said to have been borne of political motives. A 1981 report by the Ulster Young Unionist Council entitled *Ways of Strengthening the Law to more Effectively Fight Terrorism* argued that:

> In our view there is no single measure that would handicap the terrorist activities of the Irish Republican Army more than the introduction by the Irish Republic of extradition of terrorists to Northern Ireland from the Republic of Ireland for offences which they have committed within Northern Ireland.[44]

It went on to claim that the Criminal Jurisdiction Act, 1975, which was introduced in the Republic of Ireland to ensure that persons who had committed crimes in Northern Ireland be tried by the Courts of the Republic, had been a comprehensive failure. Up to that date, only two people had been brought to trial before the Republic's courts for murders they were alleged to have committed in the North, and in both these cases the persons were acquitted.

Unionists wondered how committed the South was to nullifying Republican violence and if it wished to sanctify it. The Unionist report stated that Northern Ireland's courts had been willing to deport suspects to the country of their citizenship. Further, that the Law Enforcement Commission, which was established to discuss the ramifications of an All-Ireland Court, contended that extradition for the Republic of Ireland would not be a breach of its Constitution, as was continually claimed by the South, nor an infringement of international law, since it had tended to no longer regard offences of a political nature as including crimes of terrorism.[45]

The British Home Office held that the view that international law 'precludes surrender in respect of political offence is not one shared by the United Kingdom government, and it is evidently not held by the other states which have ratified or signed the European Convention on the Suppression of Terrorism'.[46] In 1977, this Convention declared which offences would not be regarded as political; these included bombings, kidnappings and unlawful detention. Signatories included the United Kingdom, France, Germany and Ireland itself. It was also noted that Irish courts had created a broad definition of what constituted a political offence; if the fugitive could show that he was politically motivated in committing the offence of which he was accused, then the offence was said to be 'of political character'.[47]

The Irish government cited clauses 1 and 3 of Article 29 of the Irish Constitution, which professed a desire to adhere to the conduct of generally accepted principles of international law, as the interdiction to extradition.[48] The Irish government emphasised that it was not common for countries like France, Denmark and Belgium to extradite their own citizens. This was however, as Hogan and Walker explained, becoming a less convincing argument upon which to rely: 'whatever scope for argument there may have been in 1974, events since then – most notably the European Convention on the Suppression of Terrorism, 1977 – show that international law and practice does not preclude the extradition of politically motivated offenders'.[49]

The unsteadiness of this defence was compounded by the judgment of the Irish Supreme Court in the Dominic McGlinchey case in 1983.[50] It held that only what 'reasonable, civilised people would regard as political activity' could be used to interpret an offence as political.[51] This would preclude offences like hijackings, bombings and kidnappings. The Irish government understood that even if a failure to extradite fugitive suspects disturbed Ulster Protestants, its accommodation would have been equated by Irish nationalists as a wilful submission to the British government, permitting their police force unfettered interrogation of Irish suspects.

In a paper on new ideas for a settlement by Noel Dorr, Irish Ambassador to the United Nations, the main reason for opposing extradition was thusly admitted; 'though less openly stressed than the constitutional argument, much of our objection to extradition really related to interrogation and police procedures in the North'.[52] The reason this was not publicised was the injury it was expected to inflict on Anglo-Irish relations. The paper took the territorial imperative imported in Article 2 to its logical conclusion; treating Northern Ireland legally as another part of the Republic. It asked: 'Why not treat crimes of violence in th [*sic*.] other jurisdiction in Ireland similarly especially since Article 2 itself is based on the concept that it is the "national territory"'.[53] It also suggested a long-term strategy to include considering, because their outright deletion might be too challenging, a 'Constitutional amendment to de-fuse Articles 2 and 3 by adding the Sunningdale "consent" formula to Article 3'.[54]

An All-Ireland Court was the Irish government's preferred route around extradition, because it could be established without surgery to the Constitution. Another paper by Dorr on the idea explained its viability within the context of constitutional prohibition. He explained that despite Article 34.3.1° of the Constitution enshrining full and original jurisdiction with the High Court,

> [j]urisdiction may be given, also, to other tribunals over 'limited functions and powers of judicial nature, in matters other than criminal matters' [Art. 37] and other than 'the question of the validity of any law having regard to the provisions of this Constitution [Art. 34.3.2°]. Special courts may be established by law for the trial of offences in cases where it may be determined in accordance with such law that the ordinary courts are inadequate to secure the effective administration of justice' [Art. 38.3.1°].[55]

An All-Ireland Court could thus be set up as a special court, designated for a particular set of legal scenarios and all without requiring a change of the Irish Constitution. The report also remarked, tellingly, that this was a solution which had not hitherto received exploration. It was not pursued; Unionists made it clear that such a development would be appraised in the climate of unity. Ian Paisley told Margaret Thatcher that 'the suggested All-Ireland Court would be equally anathema to my people as they would see it as an overt and giant step towards the creation of an All-Ireland state'.[56] As an added indignity, Paisley feared it would threaten the constitutional sovereignty of Northern Ireland as part of the United Kingdom.

It was two judgments of the Irish Supreme Court which determined a change in the legislative practice of extradition. *Quinn v. Wren* [1985] held that members of illegal organisations committed to the overthrowing of the state, and thus the Constitution, could not claim protection under the 'political offence' exception.[57] This led to the extradition of persons belonging to illegal organisations dedicated to the destruction of the state. This ruling was followed by the Supreme Court decision in *Russell v. Fanning* [1988], where the Court refused the benefit of the political offences exception to an escaped prisoner from the Maze Prison, convicted of the attempted murder of an RUC officer.[58] This was because he was a member of an illegal organisation whose activities subverted the Constitution.[59]

There was even transiently an attempt to settle the question of fugitive offenders by making the Irish Constitution more resilient to extradition for political offences. Martin Mansergh drafted a constitutional amendment which would devote a stronger legal defence to the Irish refusal to permit extradition. It read: 'No Irish citizen may be extradited outside the jurisdiction of the laws of the State. Persons being persecuted for reasons of race, religion or politics shall enjoy a right of asylum.'[60] It was discounted because of the questionable objectivity of Irish courts, which might widen their interpretation of political offence and pledge total protection to IRA suspects.[61] In addition to the problem of defining what constituted Irish citizenship, it was feared that an anti-Irish prejudice 'would receive free and pungent expression if we were to prescribe in the Constitution that Irish citizens could not be extradited in any circumstances'.[62]

This was prescient, for even if the matter of extradition would receive some manner of closure through the 1987 Extradition Act, until then it poisoned and crippled relations between Unionists and the Irish State, as a report in December 1981 recognised:

> In all our contacts with Unionist opinion, extradition continues to be cited as an area in which our credibility and good faith is questioned. Although appreciation is expressed for the Taoiseach's understanding and sympathy by Unionist contacts there is no sign at present of any willingness on the part on Unionists to change fundamental attitudes to the South.[63]

Mansergh's attempt to strengthen the Irish government's constitutional defence against extradition implies not only that he knew it was weak in the context of international law, and the questionable veil of Article 29, but also that the Irish government did not want to allow extradition, and only did so because the Irish Supreme Court invalidated their oft-repeated defence. The episode confirmed that the Irish government was aware their refusal to extradite inflamed British and Unionist public opinion, as it could claim they were seeking to protect the men who were actually their gravest adversaries. However, the Irish government was more willing to exacerbate this, and help preserve an untruth about their sympathy for the Provisionals, than incite general public opinion by permitting the British government unrestricted access to Irish suspects.

To avoid asking turbulent questions about its Republican loyalties, the Irish government preferred that extradition remain shrouded in ambivalence. However, it should also be emphasised that the Irish government did not evaluate extradition with the same gravity or toxic symbolism as the British government did; problems with applying evidence and securing prosecution would remain more profound uncertainties. Recalling the instance when Secretary of State for Northern Ireland Jim Prior argued that extradition was 'a matter of supreme importance in view of the Unionist sensitivities', a Department of Foreign Affairs report replied that: 'While the granting of extradition for political offences could well be seen as a gesture of political goodwill to both the British and the Unionists, it is unlikely to make any significant difference to the security situation in Northern Ireland and its practical effects would be minimal.'[64]

The Irish government also well understood what extradition was to some Unionists; an accessory with which to personify the Irish Republic as being in concert with vicious terrorists, to whom they would quietly give sanctuary. There was great profit to be had from this profane caricature, and Eamon Kennedy, then Irish Ambassador to Great Britain, speculated that some Unionists would not want to relinquish this device, because it gratified a key Unionist ideological motive; established distance from the Republic. Kennedy wrote of the *McGlinchey* judgment that it will 'disappoint those extreme Unionists in the North who have used the Extradition issue to vilify successive Irish Governments'.[65]

This is precisely what Harold McCusker, UUP MP for Armagh, had done in March 1982. He petitioned the Economic and Social Council of the UN Division of Human Rights, accusing the Irish and British governments of human rights violations in Northern Ireland. The case against Ireland was based on their non-practice of extradition, which was indicted as having made Ireland a safe haven for Republican terrorists, of denying the right to self-determination of the people of Northern Ireland because of the claims enshrined in Articles 2 and 3 of the Irish Constitution and of failing to act in a manner compatible with various international instruments, including the Genocide Convention.

McCusker was petitioning on behalf of his constituents and collected Protestant victims of violence from Armagh, Tyrone and Fermanagh, whom he claimed were 'the victims of a sustained and calculated campaign of genocide against them and their community on account of their political opinion and/or religious belief'.[66] The Irish government questioned the admissibility of the petition on the grounds that it had manifestly political motivations, which is disallowed under UN charter, and that its claims were wildly overstated. The petition was not successful, rejected at the first stage by the Communications Working Group of the Sub-Commission for the Protection of Minorities and Prevention of Discrimination.

Conclusion

This has only been a cursory inspection into how certain fixtures of the Irish Constitution helped summon and entrench Unionist views of the Irish Republic, because of how they seemed to predict the obscured or withdrawn role of Unionists within a unified state. Just as crucial is the task of understanding the response of Irish governments to Unionist concerns about their station in a future united Ireland. Scrutiny should of course not be limited solely to the constitutional Articles discussed here; debates over abortion, adoption and the role of the Irish language can also elucidate the relationship between Irish governments and Unionist politicians during the years of the Northern Irish conflict.

The exchanges that have been offered for examination demonstrate that Unionists tried to use constitutional Articles to make their opposition to Irish national unity more credible and understandable to Irish officials. If the Irish Constitution acted as a document of the nation's intended character, the most important area to which research can now be directed is the general locus of Ulster Unionists/Ulster Protestants within the psyche of the Irish public, Irish judiciary and Irish government during the years of the Northern Irish conflict.

Notes

1. Letter from Newe dated Sep. 1972, Public Records Office of Northern Ireland (hereafter PRONI) D/3687/1/42/1. Newe was the close personal adviser to Brian Faulkner, leader of the Ulster Unionist Party (UUP).
2. Garret FitzGerald expressed concerns on the seemingly ecclesiastic nature of the Republic of Ireland as early as 1972. He wrote that, in order to correct Ireland for cooperative unity, the changes required included 'the repeal by referendum on the special position of the Catholic Church and divorce; amendment of the law banning the import and sale of contraceptives; a modification of the system of dealing with obscene printed matter'. He added that the removal of the Irish language as a requisite for entry into Irish public sector was also desirable (*Towards a New Ireland* (Charles Knight, 1972) p. 155).
3. *Report of the Committee on the Constitution* (Dublin Stationery Office, 1967) pp. 47–48.
4. See J. Whyte, *Church and State in Modern Ireland 1923–1979* (2nd edn, Gill & Macmillan, 1980) p. 389.
5. Report dated 8 October 1981, National Archives of Ireland, Department of Taoiseach (TAOIS) 2011/127/1015.
6. See for example M. Elliott, *Watchmen in Sion: The Protestant Idea of Liberty* (Field Day Theatre, 1985).
7. Mansergh served as a special adviser to Taoiseach Charlie Haughey.
8. Paper dated 22 April 1981, TAOIS 2011/127/1021
9. Jack Lynch speech in Dáil Éireann on 30 October 1969, Patrick Hillery Papers, P205/35, University College Dublin (UCD) Archives.
10. Report dated 28 November 1969, Patrick Hillery Papers, P205/35, UCD Archives.
11. *Ibid.*
12. *Report of the Committee on the Constitution* (n. 2) p. 43.

13 Draft paper entitled 'Provisions relating to Marriage in the Irish Constitution', October 1969, Irish Department of Foreign Affairs (DFA) 2001/43/1387.
14 Letter from Reverend A. J. Weir, Clerk of Assembly and General Secretary to the Presbyterian Church in Ireland, to Liam Cosgrave dated 17 April 1973, TAOIS 2004/21/505.
15 Minutes of a meeting of the IPCIIU on 19 September 1972, TAOIS 2003/16/539.
16 Ibid.
17 Letter dated 14 August 1973, National Archives of Ireland, JUSTICE 2004/27/12.
18 B. Chubb, *The Politics of the Irish Constitution* (IPA, 1991) pp. 55–56.
19 Meeting of IPCIIU on 28 June 1972, TAOIS 2003/16/539.
20 Faulkner (1921–77), holds the distinction of being the last prime minister of Northern Ireland. He held the position from 23 March 1971 to 31 March 1972. He was leader of the UUP from 31 March 1971 to 22 January 1974 and chief executive of Northern Ireland from 1 January 1974 to 28 May 1974.
21 Cosgrave (1920–) is the son of W. T. Cosgrave, one of the founders of the Irish Free State and was famous for voting against his own government's attempts to liberalise contraception policy in the Republic in 1974. He was Taoiseach of the Fine Gael–Labour coalition government during the UWC strike and the Constitutional Convention. He was also minister for foreign affairs, June 1954–March 1957 and Taoiseach, March 1973–July 1977.
22 Minutes dated 21 January 1974, PRONI OE/1/29.
23 The Agreement signed by the British and Irish governments in December 1973 which legislated for the establishment of a Council of Ireland. This would give the Irish Government a consultative role in the governance of Northern Ireland on certain policy issues (Seán Donlon brief dated September 1973, DFA 2013/27/1620).
24 E. E. Davis and R. Sinnott, *Attitudes in the Republic of Ireland relevant to the Northern Ireland Problem: Volume I* (ESRI, 1979) p. 68.
25 Ibid., p. 83
26 G. Hogan, *The Origins of the Irish Constitution, 1928–1941* (RIA, 2012) p. 214.
27 Letter from Faulkner to Cosgrave dated 31 March 1974, DFA 2013/27/1474.
28 *Boland v. An Taoiseach* [1974] IR 338.
29 Memorandum on the Sunningdale Communique, 18 January 1974, PRONI OE/2/4.
30 Meeting between Ministers of the Irish government and Northern Ireland Executive on 1 February 1974, DFA 2013/27/1474.
31 Brief dated 3 March 1976, DFA 2013/27/1483.
32 Minutes of the 33rd and 34th Sessions of the Conference on government in Northern Ireland, PRONI CENT/1/9/20.
33 Meeting between FitzGerald and Thatcher on 6 November 1981, PRONI CENT/1/10/93A.
34 Note on Northern Reactions to the Taoiseach's proposals for Constitutional Change by David Blatherwick, NIO, 7 October 1981, PRONI CENT/1/10/86A.

35 Letter from Hourican to Garret FitzGerald, 27 October 1981, TAOIS 2011/127/1015.
36 This was the notion that the Irish state ought to have a legally mandated role in the governance of Northern Ireland.
37 Report by David Blatherwick, NIO, dated 11 May 1981, PRONI CENT/1/10/36A.
38 Meeting with a Unionist Delegation of Lawyers dated 19 October 1981, TAOIS 2011/127/1015.
39 P. Hanafin, 'Legal Texts as Cultural Documents: Interpreting the Irish Constitution' in R. Ryan (ed.) *Writing in the Irish Republic: Literature, Culture, Politics 1949–1999* (Macmillan, 2000) p. 159.
40 See Finn, Chapter 14, this volume.
41 *McGimpsey v. Ireland* [1990] IESC 3.
42 Meeting between a Unionist delegation and the Irish government, 19 October 1981, TAOIS 2011/127/1015.
43 Draft minutes of a meeting between the New Ulster Movement (which dissolved in 1978 after most of its members left to form the Alliance Party in 1970) and the UDA dated 10 September 1974. Papers of the New Ulster Movement, PRONI, D/3159/1/10.
44 Report accessed via http://cain.ulst.ac.uk (last accessed 13 November 2014).
45 *Ibid.*
46 Letter from John Chilcot of the Home Office to Michael Alexander of FCO dated 18 September 1979, TNA FCO 87/1072.
47 *Ibid.*
48 Brief on Extradition dated 23 October 1981, DFA 2011/39/1830.
49 G. Hogan and C. Walker, *Political Violence and the Law in Ireland* (Manchester UP, 1989) p. 286.
50 *McGlinchey v. Wren* [1982] IR 154, [1983] ILRM 169.
51 Paper on the *McGlinchey* judgment dated 5 January 1983, DFA 2013/27/1520.
52 Paper dated 22 August 1981 by Noel Dorr, DFA 2011/53/11.
53 *Ibid.*
54 *Ibid.*
55 Report on matters of joint security by D. Quigley, Office of the Attorney General, 1981, TAOIS 2011/127/1109.
56 Letter from Paisley to Thatcher dated 6 November 1981, TNA PREM 19/509.
57 *Quinn v. Wren* [1985] IR 322.
58 *Russell v. Fanning* [1988] IR 505.
59 Hogan and Walker (n. 49) p. 181. For the conversation on whether it was the purpose of the IRA to overthrow the Republic and its Constitution, see M. Farrell, *Sheltering the Fugitive? The Extradition of Irish Political Offenders* (Mercier Press, 1985).
60 Report by Martin Mansergh on Northern Ireland, 16 July 1982, DFA 2012/59/1654.
61 *Ibid.*
62 Report dated 21 July 1982, DFA 2012/59/1654.
63 Report dated December 1981, DFA 2012/59/1756.

64 DFA report for an Anglo-Irish Official Level Meeting on 11 July 1983, DFA 2013/27/1612.
65 Report by Eamon Kennedy on British Conservative Policy on Northern Ireland, DFA 2013/27/1510.
66 Copy of *McCusker vs. Ireland and the UK*, DFA 2012/59/1673.

14

'Towards a better Ireland':[1] Donal Barrington and the Irish Constitution

Tomás Finn

Best known for his contribution to the debates that shaped Irish society and its politics, Donal Barrington's role in transforming the Irish Constitution into a 'living document' is less well understood.[2] This chapter is concerned with the consideration that Barrington, a public intellectual, gave to the Constitution, the basic law of the country, and the balance its Articles struck with regard to relations between church and state and Northern Ireland. It considers his vision for Ireland, how this changed and the extent to which he influenced attitudes towards the Constitution. Of particular interest is how from the 1950s to the 1970s his stance evolved on the Constitution and specifically on those Articles that related to moral issues and to the national question. From 1937, when it was enacted until the 1950s, when Barrington began to examine the Constitution's potential, the document reflected the central tenets of the Catholic nationalist tradition; this was a period when its role in providing protection for citizens' rights was rarely considered. On the other hand, the period from 1950s to the 1970s, which was before Barrington became a high-profile Judge and thus in some ways when he was freer to espouse radical views, is particularly significant in the transformation that took place in the Supreme Court's approach to the Constitution. This chapter examines Barrington's role in this change and the extent to which his views anticipated, but also reflected, the transition in the perception of the Constitution in legal circles as well as among the general public. Much of the new found interest in the Constitution followed the initial 'outburst of judicial creativity in the 1960s',[3] when the Constitution began 'to permeate all areas of Irish law'.[4] The protection the Constitution provided or perhaps more precisely, how judges interpreted it, for 'individual and minority rights in novel situations and changing conditions in society'[5] was central to Barrington's life. His views on the role judges should play in relation to the Constitution, and how it should be interpreted on moral issues and in seeking a resolution to the divisions between nationalism and unionism have helped define the nature of Ireland. These issues, church–state relations and Northern Ireland, each considered in turn, were connected as far as Barrington was concerned; the question as to whether the 1937 Constitution was appropriate in an all-island context became particularly important with the deteriorating security situation in Northern Ireland in the 1970s but also as liberal values became increasingly prevalent within southern society.

Barrington and the intellectual climate in Ireland

The Cearbhall Ó Dálaigh and Brian Walsh Supreme Courts in the 1960s played a leading role in the change to the way the Irish Constitution was interpreted. It was during this period, that a conservative society dominated by the Catholic Church, and a state and legal system which were inward-looking and distrustful of novelty, gradually opened up to fresh ideas about politics, the economy, society, law and religion. Broadly, the decades following the Second World War was a period in which the state faced huge challenges but as recent research has shown, it is one in which new thinking emerged and new policies were formulated.[6]

It is in that context that Barrington co-founded the society, *Tuairim* ('opinion' in Irish). Through the publication of pamphlets, *Tuairim* contributed to debates on Northern Ireland, administrative and political reform, education, childcare and censorship. Its first pamphlet, *Uniting Ireland*, was written by Barrington. A reaction to the IRA border campaign (1956–62), it argued for a more tolerant and inclusive approach to Northern Ireland and called for the adoption of the principle of consent. Partly as a result of this, Barrington, by the late 1950s, was already a well-known and influential figure in legal and political circles. He has more recently been praised by scholars, most notably Roy Foster, who described his pamphlet as 'prescient' and John Whyte who argued that in 'switching the thrust of nationalist policy from trying to induce the British to leave Ireland and trying to induce the Protestants to join in a united Ireland', Barrington was an 'innovator'.[7] Praised, in 2001, as possessing 'one of the most important intellectual voices in Modern Ireland',[8] Barrington, however, curiously, when compared to others such as Garret FitzGerald, David Thornley or Conor Cruise O'Brien,[9] has not been the subject of detailed historical analysis.

More broadly, there is a lack of literature on intellectuals in Ireland. Among the general histories of twentieth-century Ireland, only Joe Lee and Diarmaid Ferriter comment on the history of ideas and their impact; while Roy Foster has examined changing ideas since 1970.[10] Historians' more traditional preoccupation with political events, institutional structures and the founding fathers of the state was understandable given that during much of the 1920s, 1930s and 1940s, the national question permeated political thought and informed public policy. Political events, such as the 1921 Anglo-Irish treaty and its dismantling, the politically motivated economic war and the 1937 Constitution, had dominated the agenda. On the other hand, the fact that *Tuairim* existed and Barrington wrote *Uniting Ireland* is one indication that the post-Second World War period was different. These decades, from the 1950s through to the 1970s, witnessed a transformation in the state's approach to policy formulation and the legal establishment's attitude to the Constitution, much of which was the result of new ideas. The consequence was that Ireland evolved into a country which, in many ways, scarcely resembled the Ireland of the earlier decades.

Barrington's role in the Constitution's new found influence was significant; described as having 'led a revolution in constitutional law'[11] he was involved in some of the most significant constitutional cases in modern Ireland. During the 1970s, he acted as Senior Counsel for Kathleen Byrne on the right to sue the state, for Mrs McGee in her case on contraception and for Máirín de Búrca in hers on juries, while he also advised David Norris in his challenge to the constitutionality of the laws criminalising homosexual acts.[12] Important landmarks in the liberalisation of law and society, these cases resulted in an extension of individual rights which had not been specifically enumerated in the Constitution.[13] In 1979, Barrington was appointed to the High Court, where on Christmas Eve 1986, in a case which became a landmark in Irish law, he flouted the 'conventional wisdom of the political and legal establishment' and dramatically prevented the government from ratifying the Single European Act, the eventual effect of which was that the treaty had to be put to the people in a referendum.[14] He became Ireland's first member of the European Court of First Instance (1989–95), and finally a Supreme Court Judge in 1996 (1996–2000). His continued high standing was reflected in his appointment as the first President of the Human Rights Commission (2001–2), a body established as part of the Good Friday Agreement. It was this agreement and the approaches to peace on the island, which Barrington's own thinking had done much to anticipate.[15] More immediately, his role in the Human Rights Commission, where he argued that the European Convention on Human Rights should be incorporated into Irish law, has been seen as a culmination of his life's work in the area of human rights: not only was he an advocate of the removal from the Constitution of Articles banning divorce and the 'special position' of the Catholic Church as well as others which 'reflected exclusively the values of the Catholic Church' but he broke 'new ground in establishing rights through the courts';[16] in that light, his establishment in 1954 of *Tuairim*, as well as his early involvement in the Irish Council of Civil Liberties, the anti-apartheid movement and later Transparency International Ireland,[17] pointed to a determination throughout his life to speak and act in an independent and altruistic manner.

It was Barrington's publication of a series of articles in 1953 in the *Irish Monthly* and later in 1959 one on the church and state in a publication by the *Catholic Truth Society of Ireland* which first pointed to his interest in the Constitution. These articles, together with his other writings and speeches, illustrate the extent to which he challenged religious orthodoxy and irredentist nationalism – the two great pillars of modern Irish society, but also the extent to which his point of view evolved from the 1950s to the 1970s, particularly in relation to his view on how the Constitution should define the relationship between church and state. These changing opinions were informed by Barrington's background; as part of the first generation born since independence, he was imbued with idealism and a determination to ensure that Ireland would be a success. His sense of patriotism might in part have emanated from his parents' generation, those born in the pre-independence era. He was, however, also reacting against their politics and the issues surrounding the civil war, events around which Irish politics and society continued to turn. His priority was to move debate to the more immediate problems facing the country. Where previous generations needed to establish a state, Barrington and others were confronted with the state as it existed. Friendly with leading members of the main parties, Barrington was throughout his life interested in politics. In 1954, he stated that he was informed by a Christian Democratic approach, one which informed the 'political and social philosophy on which [the] constitution rested'.[18] It was, he believed, based on the 'idea that political freedom and moral responsibility are natural allies' and that man needed religion 'not only to emphasise his duties but to protect his rights'.[19] It followed that the state should 'aim at creating the kind of society in which the individual would be able to develop all his faculties to the highest degree of perfection of which they are capable'.[20] Far from being a radical, Barrington dismissed the concept of a modern secular state or a liberal political philosophy as one not based on religion and thus as a 'house built on sand'.[21] Equally he rejected clericalism or a confessional state but determined on a middle road where the 'State had a positive and very important role to play in the economic, the social, and the political field'.[22] That the state needed to act was underlined by the economic malaise which witnessed over 400,000 people emigrating from Ireland from 1952 to 1961.[23]

Barrington, nevertheless, recognised that his arguments during the 1950s for a greatly expanded role for the state in relation to the economy could be controversial, construed even as attacks on private enterprise. This, in turn, highlights the difficulties for those searching for a fresh approach to the nation's difficulties. Barrington's use of conciliatory language which was designed to persuade rather than to provoke those in positions of influence was his response to this intellectual climate. His ideas were, in the context of the 1950s, quite radical; he not only called for a new approach to Northern Ireland, reforms to education and an extension of the power of the state in relation to the economy but also for a new type of civil servant, one who would be equipped with the drive and enterprise necessary for modern economic life. While he maintained that the new context would also require increased legal and constitutional checks, he criticised as outmoded recent arguments with regard to the role of the state. Following the failure to implement the Mother and Child scheme in 1951, this discourse stressed that the role of the state should be limited, often identifying a more active state or those who advocated the same with communism and therefore, anti-Catholicism.[24]

The rights of church and state and the proper balance between the two authorities became a topic for consideration partly due to the rhetoric of the early 1950s. Connected to demands from a sizeable section of the population to make the country a truly Catholic state, the international context of the Cold War increased the difficulty of finding solutions to the country's problems. The pervasive influence of the Catholic Church throughout Irish life meant, to put it mildly, that it was not easy to dissent from orthodoxy. Similarly, traditional attitudes informed the legal profession's approach to the Constitution. Since its enactment, experience at court suggested that the Constitution provided minimal protection for human rights. This seemed particularly the case following the Supreme Court's apparent inability to invoke the fundamental rights Articles (Articles 40–44, specifically, Article 40.3 that the 'State guarantees in its laws to respect and ... defend the personal rights of the citizen') against the Offences Against the State Bill during the Second World War. The Irish legal profession would continue to follow British constitutional practice. Judges, according to Barrington, stressed the primacy of parliament and were not receptive to original arguments based on the Constitution while barristers were, understandably, unlikely to refer to it in support of their arguments.[25] The legal profession was educated in the British tradition which precluded the idea that a written Constitution could negate the decisions or actions of a parliament or government.

This made Barrington's consideration of this topic in the *Irish Monthly* in 1953 all the more interesting. Aside from Thomas Connolly, a senior counsel, and Judge George Gavan Duffy, who both pointed to the Constitution's potential and some lectures on constitutional law by the Professor of Constitutional Law at UCD, Patrick McGilligan,[26] who was the Minister for Finance during the first inter-party government, 1948–51, this was a topic that had largely been neglected by lawyers and academics. A more active judiciary was to follow the increased role which the state adopted in relation to economic and social matters from the 1950s; this, in turn, went hand in hand with greater awareness on the part of the citizenry and interest groups of their rights. Barrington also pointed to the importance of the example provided by the US Supreme Court and the fact that, in contrast to the focus on 'law and order' during its first decades, the state was 'peaceful' during the 1950s and that this facilitated a greater awareness of the importance of individual rights.[27] Though the IRA were engaged in a border campaign at the time (1956–62), the assertion that there was more space for an increased focus on issues other than the status or security of the state is accurate.

Church–state relations

Barrington's treatment of the Constitution echoed his general approach to potentially controversial matters – the need for cooperation rather than conflict and for cases to be based on rational argument not emotion. During the 1950s, it was his contention that the Constitution had struck the correct balance on important issues such as the family, education and the rights of church and state in Ireland. As with much of his writings, he provided a historical introduction to the Constitution and especially its Articles concerning religion. While he admitted that the Irish Constitution fell short of what many saw as the Catholic idea, a state-church, he questioned critics such as Marie Duce, a right-wing Catholic society active in the 1950s.[28] In response to Maria Duce's praise for regimes like those of Francis I of France and Ferdinand and Isabella of Spain in the early modern period, Barrington claimed these had 'many defects' and had been as much a 'triumph for the forces of regalism as for those of religion'.[29] He argued that the Constitution represented the best solution for Ireland and a referendum to change it would be unwise. As it was to apply to the whole island, and was therefore 'intended for a people one-quarter of whom were non-Catholics',

Barrington maintained that any effort to alter the 'special position' of the Catholic Church as expressed in Article 44 would be unwise.[30] This claim was a response to a campaign by Maria Duce which sought to amend the Constitution and replace 'special position' with the 'one true Church'.[31] Similarly, the powerful Archbishop of Dublin, John Charles McQuaid, viewed Catholicism as the 'one true Church' and thus disagreed with Barrington's view. Later, in the context of a debate on university education, McQuaid pointedly remarked that Barrington had in 1961 at a symposium in St Patrick's College, Maynooth, 'delivered a very strong attack on me personally'.[32] Barrington's claim that the position the Constitution gave to the church represented a mere 'recession from the [Catholic] ideal' was, for McQuaid and Catholic organisations such as Maria Duce, to say the least, problematic.[33] For McQuaid, Barrington was ignorant of Catholic teaching and disloyal to the Catholic Church while Marie Duce condemned him as expressing secular values and abandoning 'the ideal ... and thereby ... Christ the King'. Where Barrington had emphasised the 'paramount importance [of the] rule of law',[34] and had sought to place Catholic teaching in its historical context, the Archbishop resented such interference and Maria Duce accused him of the error of historicity. The idea that theology cannot be separated from history and therefore that the church had to respond to the needs of contemporary society, was, however, endorsed by Pope John XXIII, the Pope responsible for the Second Vatican Council (1962–65).

Whatever the truth of the assertions as to what represented best Catholic practice, it was curious that the Constitution's opponents and its supporters should choose examples from history, especially from the early modern period when the problems were very different from the modern constitutional framework and when no secular tradition or alternatives existed. Barrington recognised as much but failed to draw parallels with more recent times or experiences such as those in Italy or France or even the Commission for Vocational Organisation in Ireland. In his decision not to use examples from more recent history in Ireland or continental Europe, Barrington seemed to be inspired by the work of John Courntney Murray, a priest who defended the American Constitution.[35] More recent history when Catholicism seemed to be tied to corporatism might also have reflected Barrington's wish not to be drawn into a controversy over the implications this held for church, state and society.

Potentially, Barrington's most contentious argument was that in which he claimed that the Constitution placed the rights of the church and of religious orders in a very strong position. As it recognised the 'special position of the Catholic Church', it followed, he claimed, that church property was given greater protection than that of an ordinary citizen and that canon law had the 'same status in Ireland as the law of the foreign country'.[36] Canon law was 'recognised as binding on priests, and religious, and ordinary citizens' who may use it to, for example, make a contract and thereby they would become legally subject to it. The question as to the extent to which canon law could take precedence over civil law in a court followed from the judgment of George Gavan Duffy in the contentious Tilson case in 1950.[37] This case upheld the Catholic Church's position that children of a mixed marriage should be brought up as Catholics. The basis of this decision was that the Constitution entrusted parents with the right to choose in which religion their children would be raised and once decided, neither parent could revoke that decision. Gavan Duffy's judgment raised the possibility that the Courts could take judicial notice of Canon Law. This question as to what exactly was the position of the Catholic Church under the terms of the Constitution, how powerful this institution was or, to put it another way, was *Home Rule really Rome Rule*, remained controversial.

Most individuals who considered the 'special position' of the church seemed to be of the view that it was recognition of the factual position of the church in the state in that the vast majority of citizens were Catholic, but that it did not give the church a privileged position in the law. This was a point on which Rev. Enda McDonagh, the future Professor of Moral Theology at Maynooth College and then Professor of Sociology in Maynooth and the future bishop of Limerick, Jeremiah Newman held different positions. Whereas McDonagh argued that the Catholic Church received 'no juridical recognition from the Constitution', Newman claimed that it did in fact do just that: he stated that the Constitution obliged the state to 'take account of the official teaching of the Catholic Church' and as Catholics were in the majority they, in effect, had the power to veto any legislation 'repugnant to the Catholic conscience'.[38] In contrast to earlier positions, writing in *Hibernia* in 1962, Barrington countered that the fact that the church's teaching 'influences our lives, institutions of government and Constitution ... flow from the factual ... and not the juridical position'.[39] His position had evolved and it seems that in contrast to his earlier articles in 1953, he did not see canon law as having a significant status in Irish law. Most likely, with the death of Gavan Duffy in 1951 and perhaps influenced by McDonagh, a friend, he recognised the existence of an increasingly liberal climate within legal circles. Yet in 1954, Barrington had claimed that the rights guaranteed by the Constitution sprang from the 'relation between man and God and consequent relation between man and man'.[40] Most Judges had not yet countenanced such issues or Barrington's contention that Canon Law was in a strong position in Ireland; with the death of Gavan Duffy in 1951, the latter was an issue that remained unexamined.

The extent to which the law reflected the church's influence and Catholic teaching or a consensus on moral and social questions which was uncontested by Catholics and non-Catholics alike during the early decades of the state is a greater question. Certainly, a conservative consensus between church and state could be said to have existed on social and moral issues since independence; this began to change during the 1950s and 1960s. Increasingly, the church's traditional position was challenged by new thinking both from within the church and in society while the state responded with reforms in areas such as education and censorship. In the end, this matter was resolved when in 1972, a referendum removed the reference to the 'special position' of the Catholic Church. Barrington argued in 1998 as a Supreme Court Judge, that this step meant that under the Constitution, the state was 'obliged to respect and honour religion but was prohibited from endowing any religion or from discriminating on religious grounds'.[41] Any sense that the Constitution gave the Catholic Church additional powers was dismissed.

The extent to which the Constitution could place Protestants in a disadvantageous position had also been a divisive issue. While from an early stage Barrington maintained that 'every effort had been made to see that the law of the country should contain nothing which might offend the conscience of Catholics or of other Christians', others argued that the Constitution's ban on divorce and the special position of the Catholic Church did just that.[42] Barrington, however, seemed to believe that these constitutional provisions had been necessary to secure the support of the majority of the people for the Constitution. Given the Catholic Church's influence, this could have been the case but it is also true that Barrington might have been influenced by an admiration for Eamon de Valera, the man who was primarily responsible for the drafting of the Constitution and who ensured it was approved in a referendum. Later, Barrington held a very different position; he admitted that provisions in the Constitution 'must have been singularly offensive to Northern Protestant opinion'.[43]

The family and education

Welcoming the Constitution as giving 'to women the exact same rights as men', Barrington, nevertheless, in his articles in 1953, defended the document and its protection of the institution of marriage, the position of the woman at home as well as the rights of parents in the matter of their children's education.[44] In relation to parental rights, Barrington defended denominational education; he pointed to, without naming, 'other countries whose population consists of different religions denominations [and who having] pinned their faith on undenominational education, which has often meant the virtual elimination of religion from school life, with results which have frequently been disastrous'.[45]

While recognising the reality that mothers often needed to go out to work, Barrington, in his views on the traditional structures of marriage and the family, was a Catholic and certainly earlier in his career could be quite conservative on certain issues. Yet, with economic changes and increasingly liberal values in society in the 1960s and 1970s, Barrington's position evolved. In 1966, he acted as Counsel for the father in the Nicholaou case where the child of an unmarried father was put up for adoption by its mother and the Adoption Board without his consent.[46] Nicholaou took a constitutional case on the grounds of gender discrimination, 'in the days before equality legislation' existed.[47]

Especially interesting were Barrington's views of relations between church and state; where, for example, in 1953 he referred to divorce as 'one of the great social evils of our time', in 1978 he argued for the removal of the prohibition on divorce as well as that on contraception (a referendum removed the ban on divorce in 1995, while the first step towards making contraceptives widely available was made in 1979).[48] A later profile by Carol Coulter, the legal correspondent with the *Irish Times*, went so far as to claim that Barrington 'always had a profound concern with the nature of Irish society and the need for institutions which reflected the complexity of the origins and identities of its inhabitants'.[49] Barrington, certainly, believed that the Constitution was effective in guarding the rights of individuals and minorities while the Catholic Church and religion were treated with 'great respect'.[50] This was reflected in his defence of denominational education; this did not, for example, mean that he in 1960 shared Patrick Hillery, the Minister for Education's, interpretation that the Constitution prevented integration between University College Dublin and Trinity. Hillery's view was based on Article 42: that the 'State shall not oblige parents in violation of their conscience and lawful preference to send their children...to any particular school designated by the State'.[51] The minister argued that this prohibited any kind of arrangement between any of the four colleges in 1960 or, it seems, in the future. Barrington, on the other hand, called for UCD to remain in the city centre and not to move to Belfield and the suburbs where he believed future cooperation with Trinity would be impossible. Later, as a Supreme Court Judge, he argued that the state, in its decisions to fund primary or post-primary schools, was not to discriminate on religious grounds nor was a child who attended a school with a religious ethos different to his own to be instructed in that religion without the knowledge and consent of his parents.[52]

North and South

Social and cultural change in the South also impacted on Barrington's approach to finding a solution to divisions between nationalists and Unionists on the island. Given the new found urgency as a result of the 'troubles',[53] he now argued that Articles 2 and 3 of the Constitution, which were the basis of the southern claim to the whole island, had to be interpreted subject to Article 29 which committed Ireland to a peaceful solution of international disputes.[54] The logic of that statement, according to Barrington, was that there was 'no mandate in the Constitution'[55] for the government, or anyone else including the IRA, to use violence to attempt to end partition. Furthermore, he was, from the late 1950s, an early advocate of the principle of consent and following from the failure of the Sunningdale Agreement in 1974, he argued that in the event of an agreed settlement to the divisions on the island, not only were amendments to Articles 2 and 3 required but that a new Constitution was needed and that an agreement between the Unionist and Nationalist traditions should be put to referenda in both parts of the island.[56] It followed that, as any such agreement required the approval of the majority of people, their representatives, including Fianna Fáil, the then main opposition party, the Loyalists in Northern Ireland should also be involved in the negotiations leading to such an agreement. For Sunningdale to have succeeded, Barrington maintained that it was imperative that people be convinced that the agreement 'represented a new departure' for the South; 'nothing less than a new constitution' would have achieved that.[57] He thus laid a large part of the responsibility for the failure of the latest attempt at a resolution firmly with the southern political establishment. Perhaps most interesting was his speculation as to the effects of the Ulster Workers' Strike and the Provisional IRA campaign – the former, which effectively led to the downfall of the Sunningdale power-sharing administration, could he claimed 'break the final constitutional connection between Ireland and England' while the latter could make 'Partition permanent'.[58]

Whatever the ultimate outcome of what Barrington termed 'this strange irony of history',[59] it highlighted his concern with the deteriorating security situation during the 1970s. This was connected to his thoughts on the demise of empire and the nation state which seemed too revolutionary for contemporary political thinking. Sensitive issues included those relating to the sharing of sovereignty, policing of the border and extradition between the two jurisdictions of individuals suspected of political offences. To ensure that the police force would in the future be acceptable to both communities, it should, he argued, be made 'responsible for keeping the peace throughout the entire island' and be answerable to a Council of Ireland with representatives from both North and South.[60] This was in part inspired by the concept of a Council of Ireland which existed in the 1920 Government of Ireland Act but also the European Economic Community, which Barrington saw as the catalyst towards creating institutions of government and a basic law which would command authority and support from the vast majority of the people on the island.

In many ways, these ideas married his political and legal thinking – this was reflected in his hopes that the European Convention on Human Rights would become part of domestic law both North and South and that the European movement would make partition irrelevant. While Barrington did not suggest that nationalism would cease to exist, he was, in part, undermining a prevalent belief within Ireland; that is that membership of the EEC would lead to the unification of the island.[61] Where his faith in the European project was most clear was in his argument that issues relating to 'civil rights and state security' [should be decided by tribunals which] have the services of European Judges [rather than the] majority of Judges [being] drawn from either tradition in Ireland'.[62] It was an idea which as he admitted would 'require a revolution in our political thinking'[63] as it involved moving beyond the concept of a nation state. Moreover, the prospects in the 1970s of such an agreement securing the support of the people either north or south of the border were remote.

And yet, Barrington's views clearly found echoes in those of the political establishment and administrative elite; the thrust of government policy from the late 1950s was to create better relations with Northern Unionists rather than to persuade Britain to leave Northern Ireland. In this context, Barrington's views were, as one civil servant in the Department of Foreign Affairs put it in 1958, 'quite well known'.[64] They had not only reached a wide spectrum of opinion on both sides of the border but influenced southern attitudes and helped to change the terms of the debate. Senior politicians such as, for example, Fine Gael's Garret FitzGerald and Fianna Fáil's Jack Lynch were, by the early 1970s, committed to the principle of consent and working towards a solution of the divisions on the island. While certainly not a seamless process, the extent to which Barrington's ideas prefigured some of the thinking behind the peace process (and ultimately the Good Friday or Belfast Agreement) which emerged two decades later is striking.[65] The 1998 Good Friday Agreement included, for example, a Council of Ireland and the convention on Human Rights while an independent commission established as part of the Belfast agreement considered the future of the police in Northern Ireland.

Conclusion

In his approach to the law, church–state relations, and in seeking peace in Northern Ireland, Barrington followed an independent and, at times, paradoxical path. Where he became part of the political and legal mainstream and did not seek to represent the marginalised in society, he, as a defender of individual and minority rights was a progressive figure. Having argued since the 1950s for change and recognised the need for reform, he also admired the older generation who were responsible for the creation of the state. To summarise, Barrington, at different times, challenged and reflected dominant social and cultural attitudes in Ireland. These methods which broadly sought to persuade rather than provoke, to seek consensus not confrontation reflected his legal training, a style of advocacy. This, he believed, would be more likely to influence those in positions of power. This approach was one which he also brought to his consideration of the Irish Constitution. Over a lifetime, he was heavily involved in the debate on the Constitution's role in defending individual and minority rights and the need for it to evolve as values change in society. His wish to create institutions and a society which was tolerant and inclusive of all traditions, however, led him to question Articles of the Constitution which he previously had defended.[66] For Barrington, the questions as to the type of society that existed in southern Ireland went to the core of whether the people really wanted an end to partition. The conflict between the need for institutions which reflected societal values as against those that were appropriate to a united Ireland was one that informed much of his views. In that context, it was clear that Irish society of the 1970s was very different to that of the 1950s; the 1970s, while in many ways still conservative, was a more secular society which was more open to ideas from outside, including those from England. These in many instances would previously have been viewed as damaging to the Catholic faith and to family life. Barrington's concept of what was required for a 'better Ireland' had been transformed. His defence of Catholic values and constitutional structures was replaced with a vision for a more pluralist society that would be inclusive of all religions. Rather than the need for a balance between church and state, his thoughts were increasingly focused on the state and the need for institutions which could secure the approval of all the people on the island. This process of publicly rethinking society or seeking to reinvent the country illustrates the value of a public intellectual such as Barrington. The religious establishment seemed unwilling to engage in this rethinking but, though cautious, the political and administrative elites did participate. Barrington's role was to put forward ideas which he hoped would inform intellectual debate and persuade governmental institutions to adopt new policies. A crucial period in Ireland's development, this was a process which transformed the state's policy approach and that is central to the modernisation of Ireland.

Notes

1 *Irish Press*, 27 September 1958. Author unrecorded. 'Towards a better Ireland' was the title of Barrington's paper to the Left Review Group, Belfast.
2 C. O'Mahony, 'Societal Change and Constitutional Interpretation' [2010] I *Irish Journal of Legal Studies* 75; T. Finn, *Tuairim, Intellectual Debate and Policy Formulation: Rethinking Ireland, 1954–75* (Manchester UP, 2012) for more on Barrington's impact.
3 G. Hogan and G. Whyte, *J M Kelly: The Irish Constitution* (3rd edn, Tottel, 2007), foreword.
4 D. Barrington, 'The Constitution in the Courts' in F. Litton (ed.), *The Constitution of Ireland, 1937–1987* (IPA, 1988) p. 115.
5 O'Mahony (n. 2) 114; D. G. Morgan, *A Judgement Too Far?: Judicial Activism and the Constitution* (Cork UP, 2001).
6 For example, see Finn (n. 2); D. Keogh, F. O'Shea and C. Quinlan, *The Lost Decade: Ireland in the 1950s* (Mercier Press, 2004) pp. 105–117; T. Garvin, *Preventing the Future: Why Was Ireland So Poor for So Long?* (Gill & Macmillan, 2004); G. Murphy, *In Search of the Promised Land: The Politics of Post-war Ireland* (Mercier Press, 2009).
7 R. Foster, *Modern Ireland, 1600–1972* (Penguin, 1989); J. Whyte, *Interpreting Northern Ireland* (Clarendon, 1991) p. 120; Finn (n. 2) pp. 102–138.
8 C. de Bhaldraithe Marsh, *Text of the Introductory Address delivered by in the Royal Hospital Kilmainham on the occasion of the conferring of the Degree of Doctor of Laws honoris causa, on Donal Barrington*, Dublin, 2 December 2009, atwww.nui.ie/college/docs/citations/2009/nui/BarringtonDonal2009.pdf (accessed 14 July 2015).
9 D. H. Akenson, *Conor: A Biography of Conor Cruise O'Brien* (McGill-Queens UP, 1994); G. FitzGerald, *All in A Life: An Autobiography* (Gill & Macmillan, 1992); C. Cruise O'Brien, *Memoir: My Life and Times* (Poolbeg Press, 1998); E. Thornley, *Lone Crusader: David Thornley and the Intellectuals* (Ashfield Press, 2012); Y. Thornley (ed.), *Unquiet Spirit: Essays in Memory of David Thornley* (Liberties Press, 2008).
10 D. Ferriter, *The Transformation of Ireland, 1900–2000* (Profile Books, 2004);

R. Foster, *Luck and the Irish: A Brief History of Change, 1970–2000* (Penguin, 2008); J. J. Lee, *Ireland, 1912–1985: Politics and Society* (CUP, 1993).
11 Marsh (n. 9).
12 *Byrne v. Ireland* [1972] IR 241; *McGee v. Attorney General* [1974] IR 284; *De Burca v. Attorney General* [1976] IR 38; *McKenna v. An Taoiseach (No. 2)* [1995] 2 IR 10; *Norris v. Attorney General* [1984] IR 36; *Irish Times* (17 February 2001); D. Norris, 'Contempt of Court' *Fortnight*, 209 (December, 1990), 33; D. Ferriter, *Occasions of Sin: Sex & Society In Modern Ireland* (Profile Books, 2009) p. 500. Norris secured a favourable judgment at the European Court of Human Rights in 1988.
13 J.E. Sprang, *Abortion and Divorce Law in Ireland* (McFarland, 2004) pp. 74–80. The doctrine of unenumerated rights has allowed the Supreme Court to recognise new rights that are not specifically mentioned in the Constitution.
14 *Crotty v. An Taoiseach* [1987] IR 713; *Irish Times* (25 December 1986; 4 May 1996).
15 Finn (n. 2).
16 *Irish Times* (7 August 1989).
17 Marsh (n. 9).
18 D. Barrington, 'Christian Democracy' [April 1954], 83(968) *Irish Monthly*, 136–137.
19 *Ibid.*, 136.
20 *Ibid.*
21 *Ibid.*, 137.
22 D. Barrington, *The Purpose of the Society* (1954), Barrington papers [in author's possession].
23 M. E. Daly, *The Slow Failure: Population Decline and Independent Ireland, 1920–1973* (University of Wisconsin Press, 2006) p. 184.
24 Ferriter (n. 10) p. 463.
25 Barrington (n. 4) p. 114.
26 Hogan and Whyte (n. 3) preface to 1st edn; Barrington (n.4) p. 110; *Irish Times* (16 October 1961; 29 April 1995).
27 D. Barrington, 'Council of Ireland in the Constitutional Context' [1972] 20(4) *Administration* 40; G. Hogan, D. Barrington, P. McEntee, 'The Constitution, Law and Ideology' [1985] 9(2) *Crane Bag* 105.
28 M. Curtis, *A Challenge to Democracy: Militant Catholicism in Modern Ireland* (History Press Ireland, 2010); M. Curtis, The *Splendid Cause: The Catholic Action Movement in Ireland in the Twentieth Century* (Original Writing, 2008).
29 D. Barrington, 'The Irish Constitution X. Article Forty Four. II. Church and State' [January 1953] 81(953) *Irish Monthly* 1.
30 Barrington (n. 4) p. 4; D. Barrington, *The Church, the State and the Constitution* (Catholic Truth Society of Ireland, 1959).
31 Interview with Donal Barrington, Dublin (19 May 2005).
32 Dublin Diocesan Archives, McQuaid's papers, *Tuairim* file, McQuaid to Apostolic Nuncio, 23 January 1965.
33 Dublin Diocesan Archives, McQuaid's papers, comments by Firinne on

Barrington's pamphlet, 'The Church, the State and the Constitution', xxi/80/48/3. On the other hand, see Rev. T. Marsh, D. D., 'A Booklet on Church and State' *Christus Rex*, xiv (July 1960), 180–183 for praise for Barrington's article.
34 Dublin Diocesan Archives, Kevin McNamara, 'Maynooth Summer School' 2 November 1961, 4, Box 725, Maynooth 818.
35 V. R. Yanitelli (ed.), 'A Church–State Anthology: The Work of Father Murray' (1952) 27 *Thought* 6–42.
36 Barrington (n. 30) p. 10.
37 *Tilson* [1951] IR 1; J. Whyte, *Church and State in Modern Ireland, 1923–1979* (Gill & Macmillan, 1980) pp. 169–171.
38 *Irish Times* (1 October 1969).
39 D. Barrington, 'Morality in Politics' (November 1962) *Hibernia*.
40 Barrington (n. 18) p. 137.
41 *Campaign to Separate Church and State Ltd v. Minister for Education* [1998] 3 IR 321; *Irish Times* (26 March 1998).
42 Barrington (n. 4) p. 4; N. Gibson, *Partition Today – A Northern Viewpoint* (Tuairim, 1959) pp. 7–8.
43 Barrington (n. 27) pp. 28–49; *Irish Times* (11 August 1978).
44 D. Barrington, 'The Irish Constitution XI. The Family and Education' (February, 1953) 81(954) *Irish Monthly* 49.
45 D. Barrington, 'The Irish Constitution XII. The Family and Education II' (March 1953) 81(953) *Irish Monthly* 98.
46 *Nicholau v. An Bord Uchtála* [1996] IR 567.
47 See *Irish Times* (23 November 1977, 13 July 1978, 2 September 1985, 7 August 1989, 7 March 1997).
48 Barrington (n. 4) p. 49; *Irish Times* (11 August 1978, 7 August 1989); Ferriter (n. 12) pp. 423–426.
49 *Irish Times* (7 August 1989).
50 Barrington (n. 4) p. 3.
51 Dáil Debates, vol. 180, col. 938, Universities and colleges, 23 March 1960.
52 *Campaign to Separate Church and State Ltd v. Minister for Education* [1998] 3 IR 321.
53 T. Hennessey, *A History of Northern Ireland, 1920–1996* (Gill & Macmillan, 1997) pp. 162–168.
54 D. Barrington, 'The North and the Constitution' in Brian Farrell (ed.), *De Valera's Constitution and Ours* (Dublin, 1988) p. 67.
55 *Ibid.*
56 D. Barrington, 'After Sunningdale' [1976] 24(2) *Administration* 237–238; Barrington (n. 27) p. 49.
57 Barrington (n. 56) p. 236.
58 *Ibid.*, p. 241.
59 *Ibid.*
60 Barrington (n. 27) p. 45.
61 J. McGarry and B. O'Leary *Explaining Northern Ireland: Broken Images* (Blackwell, 1996) pp. 277–278.

62 Barrington (n. 56) p. 259.
63 *Ibid.*
64 NAI, DFA, 305/14/314, Donal Barrington's proposals for ending partition, letter, 18 July 1958.
65 Finn (n. 2).
66 Barrington (n. 44) pp. 49–54; Barrington (n. 45) pp. 88–95.

Part V

Perspectives on the Constitution and judicial power

15

Administrative action, the rule of law and unconstitutional vagueness

Oran Doyle

Introduction

The rule of law is a political ideal that legal systems can instantiate and against which they can be judged. On the one hand, those to whom the laws are addressed should be capable of following the laws. On the other hand, those in positions of power must implement the laws according to their terms. Only in such a legal system, the ideal holds, can the subjects of state power meaningfully make plans for their lives. Although it is not explicitly mentioned in the Constitution, the courts have frequently referred to the rule of law as an important constitutional value.[1] The textual prohibition on retroactive penal sanction and the judicially created rule against vague criminal offences both instantiate the ideal. In this chapter, I argue that more needs to be done to instantiate the rule-of-law ideal: administrative action potentially undermines the rule of law, since individuals may have no opportunity to tailor their activities to legally binding directives before they are issued. There are tentative indications in the case law that the courts may recognise a new constitutional doctrine constraining legislative grants of administrative power. I critically assess the emergence of this doctrine and seek to influence its development, disentangling it from a confusing association with the rule against the delegation of legislative power. Notwithstanding the absence of any clear textual basis, I argue that recognition of this doctrine would be a legitimate exercise of judicial power.

The rule of law and its place in the constitutional order

The rule of law is a contested ideal. Under one conception, the rule of law provides certain formal requirements of a legal system, such as promulgation and non-retrospectivity. The formal conception imposes, at most, very thin requirements as to the content of laws. In contrast, more substantive conceptions of the rule-of-law ideal include commitments to values such as human rights, justice and democracy.[2] These are in addition to (but often in tension with) the formal requirements. There is thus a spectrum between purely formal conceptions and conceptions that include both formal and substantive requirements. For the purposes of this paper, I adopt a formal conception,[3] drawing on Lon Fuller's eight desiderata of the rule of law: (1) there must be general rules; (2) they must be promulgated; (3) they must not be retroactive; (4) they must be clear; (5) they must not be contradictory; (6) they must not require the impossible; (7) they must not be changed too frequently; (8) there must be congruence between the law as written and the law as applied.[4] Fuller's desiderata really amount to two propositions: rules should be capable of being obeyed; officials must apply those rules.

People can therefore guide their behaviour with reference to rules, confident that those rules will be applied to them. This protects a genuine (but limited) value: no matter how restrictive the content of the rules, individuals will know that they are secure provided their behaviour is not prohibited by the rules.[5] Compliance with the rule of law does not preclude rules having a content that infringes liberty. Moreover, compliance with the rule of law may itself make it more difficult for democratic majorities to implement their projects. Nevertheless, the rule of law protects liberty in the interstices of rules; it respects the dignity of individuals as autonomous agents by allowing them to plan their lives. In a close-knit society, this predictability might be secured through convention rather than posited laws. However, once a legal system develops with officials empowered by law to inflict violence on others, there is capacity for more effective evil. The rule of law is a bulwark against the sort of evil facilitated by legal systems.[6] In some situations, of course, the content of the rules might be so evil that it would be better for the legal system to break down, notwithstanding the damage that this would cause to the rule of law.

Joseph Raz has proposed rule-of-law principles that are similar to Fuller's, but different in a number of respects.[7] Most importantly for present purposes, Raz rejects any suggestion that a legal system should consist only of general rules but holds that legally binding directives addressed to specified individuals are permissible provided they are 'guided by open, stable, clear, and general rules'.[8] General rules, provided they are not retrospective, leave a gap between creation and application, in which autonomous agents can plan their lives. Directives, in contrast, are effectively retrospective since their moment of application coincides with their moment of promulgation. They serve important purposes but must, says Raz, be made 'within a framework set by general laws which are more durable and which impose limits on the unpredictability introduced by the [directives]'.[9] This stable framework is created both by the rules that confer the powers and rules that constrain how officials can exercise those powers. This requirement is less onerous than Fuller's eight desiderata, because the penalties and privileges provided by the state through legally binding directives are less significant than criminal penalties. All that is required is that an individual be on notice that some directive, subject to guiding and constraining rules, may be issued. This allows that individual to anticipate likely directives and modify her behaviour accordingly.

The Irish constitutional order instantiates many of these rule-of-law requirements. Laws must be promulgated;[10] penal sanctions cannot be retroactive.[11] In *King v. Attorney General*, the Supreme Court held that criminal offences cannot be overly vague.[12] Justice Henchy, with whom the other judges agreed, appeared to locate this new rule in Article 38. Hogan characterises Justice Henchy's judgment as deploying the technique of 'sustained rhetoric leading to an ultimate crescendo' and as a 'legal Philippic regarding the inequities of the section'.[13] The rhetoric obscured the fact that the Supreme Court had posited a new constitutional rule without any clear textual basis.[14]

In the context of legally binding directives, the *ultra vires* doctrine protects the rule of law by ensuring that administrative agencies can only exercise the powers they have been given.[15] However, this protection would be seriously undermined if there were no limits to the sorts of powers the Oireachtas could grant to administrative agencies. If a public authority were granted the power to do *whatever* it considers right, it would be all but impossible for individuals to anticipate how that power might be exercised against them. Implicit general constraints (such as rationality and proportionality) have little purchase when the purpose and scope of the power are opaque. There is a significant gap in how the Irish constitutional order protects the rule of law, arising from the lack of any clear constraint on the extent of administrative power that the Oireachtas can grant. Over the past ten years, however, several judgments suggest the emergence of a new constitutional doctrine prohibiting the grant of overly broad administrative powers. Before analysing that doctrine, we must first disentangle a confusion that has emerged in the case law between administrative and legislative powers.

Legislative and administrative powers

Legislation involves general rules directed to general classes of persons; administrative decisions, in contrast, are directed to identified individuals. For instance, the decision as to what types of development require planning permission is a legislative decision; the decision on whether a particular development should be granted planning permission is an administrative decision.[16] The power to legislate is the power to make general rules for others without having to reason from existing validly posited norms.[17] Article 15.2 of the Constitution speaks of the Oireachtas as holding the 'sole and exclusive power of *making laws* for the State'. However, the subsequent reference to 'no other legislative authority' as well as the identification of the legislative power in Article 6 strongly implies that what is exclusively held by the Oireachtas is a legislative power. The Constitution does not grant the Oireachtas any administrative powers. Typically, the Oireachtas creates and grants administrative powers to public agencies. There is no express constitutional prohibition on the Oireachtas doing this. Importantly, when it does so, the Oireachtas does not *delegate* a power (since it does not hold an administrative power to delegate); rather it *grants* a power.

In some cases, the courts have insisted on the difference between administrative and legislative powers. In the early case of *re MacCurtain*, Justice Gavan Duffy rejected the contention that the Attorney General was exercising a legislative power in deciding whether to certify that the ordinary courts were inadequate to secure the effective administration of justice in a particular case.[18] More recently, in *Re Article 26 and the Health (Amendment) (No. 2) Bill 2004*, the Supreme Court held that the power of the chief executive officer of a health board to remit nursing home charges was not a delegated power to legislate but rather an administrative discretion.[19] In two more recent cases, however, the High Court treated grants of administrative power as if they were delegations of legislative power and thereby subject to the *Cityview* limitations on the delegation of power under Article 15.2.[20] However, this mischaracterisation prevents the rule-of-law concerns being properly addressed.

In *Sivsivadze v. Minister for Justice and Equality*, Justice Hogan granted the applicants leave to challenge the constitutionality of section 3 of the Immigration Act 1999, partly on the ground that section 3(11) breached Article 15.2 insofar as it did not specify sufficient principles and policies to guide a ministerial decision on whether to revoke a deportation order.[21] Justice Kearns heard the full application for judicial review and upheld the constitutionality of section 3(11), distinguishing between a power to make laws and policies, on the one hand, and discretionary decisions made with reference to the facts of a case on the other hand.²² In drawing this distinction, Justice Kearns seems to have accepted that section 3(11) conferred no legislative power on the minister: the power to make (and revoke) a deportation decision is administrative. On appeal, the Supreme Court was more explicit on this point.²³ Murray J. (with whom the other members of the Court agreed) held that these powers were administrative in character and that Article 15.2 therefore had no bearing on the constitutionality of section 3(11).

In *Collins v. Minister for Finance*, the Divisional High Court applied Article 15.2 to section 6 of the Credit Institutions (Financial Support) Act 2008, which allows the Minister for Finance to provide financial support in respect of the borrowings, liabilities and obligations of credit institutions.²⁴ The nub of Ms Collins's concern was that section 6 allowed too wide a latitude to the minister. The simple provision that the minister could provide financial support to credit institutions had enabled the minister to incur a liability of over €30bn for the state. Justice Hogan introduced the relevance of the non-delegation doctrine in the following way:

> While Article 15.2.1° applies generally to all legislation (and thus not just to legislation dealing with appropriations and budgetary matters), it also applies to budget measures such as the annual Appropriation Act. Article 15.2.1° vests the exclusive legislative powers in the Oireachtas and inasmuch as any appropriation for the purposes of Article 11 has to be "by law", such a law must conform to the requirements of Article 15.2.1°.

This conclusion does not follow from Article 15.2 or Article 11. The provision of financial support to particular institutions is not a legislative act; the fact that it requires an appropriation and that such appropriation must be made by law does not make the provision of financial support to particular institutions legislative in character. Section 6 did not delegate any legislative power.²⁵

The delegation of legislative power raises very different issues from the grant of administrative power. Delegation of legislative power does not infringe the rule of law because no obligations are created unless or until the delegated legislative power is actually exercised. Individuals can wait until the delegated legislator actually makes legislation; they will then be on notice of their obligations and can tailor their activities accordingly. From a rule-of-law perspective, delegated legislation is no different from primary legislation. The reasons for controlling the delegation of legislative power derive from democratic control not from the rule of law. The *Cityview* test is oriented to those democratic concerns: delegated legislators should not make decisions of principle and policy.

In contrast, the rule of law requires constraint on administrative power so that individuals can reasonably anticipate administrative decisions *before they are made*. This is important because administrative decisions – unlike delegated legislation – become applicable immediately upon being made in a way that is tantamount to retroactivity. Furthermore, the reasons for granting administrative power include allowing administrative agencies to make policy, something prohibited (at least on its face) by the *Cityview* test. The principles and policies test is therefore an inappropriate response to the rule-of-law concerns raised by the grant of administrative powers.[26]

Constraints on the grant of administrative power

In *Re Article 26 and the Health (Amendment) (No. 2) Bill 2004*, the Supreme Court upheld the power of the CEO of a Health Board to waive or reduce the charge for nursing home care. Although noting that Article 15.2 did not apply, the Court seemed to accept that the administrative power should be subject to a criterion of sufficient specificity to make judicial review a meaningful option. The Act required the CEO to exercise her discretion with reference to the criterion of undue hardship. The Court held that any arbitrary decision or other unlawful misuse of her powers could be subject to judicial review in the ordinary way; therefore, the grant of power was not constitutionally problematic.

In *Dellway Investments Ltd v. NAMA*, the Supreme Court considered a constitutional challenge to the power of the National Asset Management Agency (NAMA) to acquire eligible bank assets.[27] The appellants had credit facilities from a number of banks. NAMA had purported to acquire these credit facilities, effectively becoming the banker to the applicants. The applicants argued that the definition of 'eligible bank asset' was so broad *and* the criteria for its exercise so vague as to give to NAMA an untrammelled discretion and that this amounted to a breach of the applicants' constitutional property rights. The statutory definition of 'bank asset' is a broad one, principally relating to credit facilities for the direct or indirect purpose of purchasing, exploiting or developing development land.[28] 'Development land' included land that was intended to be developed even if planning permission would not be required for that development on account of its minor nature.[29] For instance, if a person bought her house with a mortgage and subsequently put a TV dish on the house (an act of development), the loan would be an eligible bank asset that could be acquired from the bank by NAMA. Or if a person used a bank loan to pay for a new gate on a farm, the whole farm would become development land for the purposes of the 2009 Act.

The Supreme Court held that it was, in principle, open to the Oireachtas to provide a broad definition of 'eligible bank asset'. The applicants argued that powers granted to administrative agencies must be sufficiently precise to enable individuals to know in advance whether the power could be exercised and to enable the courts to assess whether the administrative agency had remained within the scope of the power. The Court appeared to accept this requirement but held that it was satisfied by the obligation on NAMA to exercise its powers only for the purposes of the Act, as laid out in section 2, while taking account of the matters listed in section 84(4). This was a misreading of section 84(4). There is no obligation on NAMA to take account of any of the matters listed in section 84(4) – these are just matters which *may* be taken into account. The only real constraint on NAMA's jurisdiction is that section 84 allows (but does not require) NAMA to acquire a bank asset only if it considers it necessary or desirable to do so having regard to the purposes of the Act. It would appear to suffice that any one purpose would be served by acquisition. Given the breadth of some of the purposes (protect the interests of taxpayers, contribute to the social and economic development of the state), this provides little constraint.

As noted above, in *Sivsivadze v. Minister for Justice and Equality*, Justice Kearns upheld the apparently unconstrained power of the minister to revoke a deportation order.[30] He relied on case law that obliged the minister to consider any reasons put forward for revocation and consider whether any change in circumstances had occurred that would make deportation unlawful or inappropriate on humanitarian grounds. Justice Kearns also held that generally stated powers must be exercised within the boundaries of the stated objectives of the Act, fairly and in accordance with natural and constitutional justice. However, the stated objectives of the Act – to make provision in relation to the control of non-nationals – scarcely provides any real constraint. On appeal, Murray J. referred to the factors mentioned by Kearns P but did not appear to consider that these were constitutionally required in order to limit the scope of the power granted to the minister.

In *Collins v. Minister for Finance*, the Divisional High Court upheld the constitutionality of the minister's power to give credit support to financial institutions on the basis of the provisions of the Act that constrained the minister's power. The Divisional Court summarised the effect of these as follows:

> [T]he Minister can only give financial support where he is of opinion that there is (i) a serious threat to the stability of the banking sector; (ii) the giving of such support is necessary to maintain the stability of the State's

financial system and (iii) this is also necessary to restore equilibrium in the wider economy. By fixing the parameters of the Minister's discretion, the section complies with the principles and policies test. It prescribes justiciable yardsticks against which the exercise of that discretion can, if necessary, be judicially evaluated.

This depends on a highly questionable reading of sections 6 and 2 of the Act. Section 6(1) authorises the minister to provide financial support having regard to the matters set out in section 2, the extent and nature of the obligations undertaken and which might be undertaken in the future and the resources available to him or her. It is settled law that the phrase 'have regard to' does not impose any obligation to conform to or comply with the direction to which regard must be had.[31] Section 2 does not impose any requirements on the minister but instead records as a sort of legislative fact that the minister has the functions under the Act because of the factors listed by the Court at (i) (ii) and (iii). In order to exercise the power under section 6, the minister must have regard to these facts. But there is no requirement that the minister be satisfied of any of these factors as a precondition for exercising the powers under section 2.

Although stating that grants of administrative power must be subject to some constraint, the fact that the grant of power in each case was upheld makes it difficult to identify a precise standard that grants of administrative power must meet. One formulation of the standard requires that the grant of administrative power lay down principles and policies. The other formulation requires that the grant of power must be subject to a criterion that is amenable to judicial review. The courts have been willing to imply criteria into statutory grants of power, sometimes with greater plausibility than others, with the result that these tests were met. In *Collins*, the Divisional High Court read the connection between sections 2 and 6 so as to imply limitations that the legislation, on its face, sought to avoid. It seems unlikely that a court would have adopted such an adventurous reading of sections 2 and 6 if faced with a contemporaneous judicial review challenge to the minister's decision to issue the bank guarantee.

Rule-of-law constraint on the grant of administrative powers

The formal rule of law respects the dignity of individuals as autonomous agents by providing them with the freedom to make life choices, secure in the knowledge of how the state will respond to those choices. This value is undermined where people cannot know how their actions will be legally treated before they act. Administrative power is problematic since individuals have no opportunity to tailor their activities to legal directives before they are issued. Grants of administrative power may still be permissible, provided they are controlled by criteria that guide individuals as to how the power might be exercised. This imperative is partially met by an *ultra vires* doctrine but also requires limits on the scope of powers that can be conferred.

The rule of law, however, makes it more difficult to realise other values. As a constraint on state power, the rule of law impedes the sort of social projects that depend on state power for their implementation. Sypnowich, for instance, identifies equality- and democracy-based critiques of the rule of law. From this perspective, the rule of law impedes substantive justice and/or the will of the people.[32] This opposition between the rule of law and projects for social reform has been particularly acute in the context of the administrative state. Epstein bases his objection to the administrative state in terms of a defence of the rule of law, commenting that 'the administrative state gives rise to a peculiar blend of bureaucratic rule and discretion that does not comport with the historical conception of a rule of law, and its central concern with the control of arbitrary power'.[33] Brian Tamanaha traces that dynamic from the opposite perspective, showing how rule-of-law arguments have aligned in support of liberal projects over time, such as the protection of property interests and – more recently – the imposition of the 'Washington Consensus' on developing countries in return for development aid.[34]

This opposition can be perceived in the Irish case law. If the courts had required a greater level of constraint on the grants of administrative power, this would have impeded the political projects of deporting foreigners and bailing out banks. To be sure, these projects might not be first on the to-do list of those progressives sceptical of the rule of law. Nevertheless, the protection of the rule of law makes it more difficult for democratically elected majorities to achieve their projects. There is little that can be done other than recognise this tension, accept that the rule of law should be protected but also that there are other – sometimes conflicting – values, and consider how best to strike the balance between respect for the rule of law and the achievement of democratically mandated projects. In the remainder of this section, I suggest a judicial approach that meets these competing objectives. It necessarily follows from any test of this type that the Oireachtas would sometimes be unable to grant the sort of administrative power that it wishes to grant. This is the price we pay for conformity to the rule of law.

The Oireachtas should be empowered to give an administrative agency as much power as is necessary to achieve the purposes that the Oireachtas holds for that agency. This leaves to the Oireachtas the democratic choice of which projects should be pursued, but constrains the Oireachtas to empower administrative agencies no more than is necessary to implement those projects. No matter how broad the power, if it is genuinely necessary to meet the purposes set by the Oireachtas, it is permissible. However, it may not be possible to design a grant of administrative power that perfectly allows the administrative agency meet only the purposes that the Oireachtas holds for it. If the Oireachtas chooses to grant an over-inclusive power, then the Oireachtas must impose duties on the decision-maker that provide meaningful constraint, and hence guidance to individuals as to whether the power may be exercised.

Obliging a decision-maker to take certain matters into account constrains that decision-maker (to some extent) and increases (to some extent) the predictability of the decision-maker's actions. The more matters that the decision-maker *must* take into account, the greater the constraint and the greater the predictability. In contrast, merely *allowing* the decision-maker to take certain matters into account provides considerably less constraint. Moreover, the more matters that may be taken into account, the less the constraint on the decision-maker. At this point, the damage to the rule of law simply becomes too great to be justifiable by reference to the desirability of effective administration. Reflecting these concerns, the courts should hold unconstitutional powers that are wider than necessary to achieve their purpose, unless the decision-maker is obliged (as distinct from merely authorised) to take specific matters into account when making its decision.

Three clarifications are necessary. First, if this test is to be meaningful, one cannot infer the purpose of the power from the scope of the power. If one took that approach, the scope of the power would always be deemed coextensive with the purpose for which it was conferred.[35] The courts should instead infer the purpose of the power from the statute as a whole (including its long title), evidence as to the sorts of cases in which the administrative agency has in fact exercised the power, and common-sense observations about what the purpose of the power is likely to have been. This avoids any difficulty that might be caused by recourse to parliamentary debates or other parol evidence.[36]

Second, the courts should show some judicial deference to any assessment by the Oireachtas of what powers are necessary to achieve the purposes that the Oireachtas has set for the administrative agency. The courts should ask whether the scope of the power is reasonably necessary to meet the purpose for which it is being conferred. However, this deference must be checked as otherwise the doctrine would become meaningless.

Third, the constraining factors referred to above should be present in the statute itself that confers the power. The rule of law gives us reason to constrain administrative powers not for the sake of constraint but in order to make the exercise of those powers more predictable for individuals. This does not occur if individuals do not know of the constraints. The courts have consistently held that apparently absolute administrative powers are subject to implied constraints, such as fairness[37] and rationality.[38] Requirements of rationality and fairness, however, bring little predictability to the exercise of a broad administrative power. A power to make any 'rational and fair' decision would not provide much guidance to those potentially affected, if they even knew who they were. Moreover, it is no answer to a charge of vagueness to read constraints into a statutory provision through the double construction rule. It is not appropriate for the Oireachtas to seek to 'hide the ball' and require individuals to engage in constitutional litigation so as to discover what constraints applied to the decision-maker. Since this guidance comes after the fact, it does not increase predictability. Long-standing and well-known common law restraints (including those based on previous interpretations of the statute) have some force, but not as much as constraints stipulated in the statute itself.[39]

This doctrine for the control of administrative powers is fundamentally different from the principles and policies test set out in *Cityview*. It starts from the assumption that the Oireachtas can grant administrative powers. It recognises that the Oireachtas and administrative agencies have very different functions: they are not rival legislators competing to exercise the same role. It does not exclude administrative agencies from a policy-making role. It allows for the grant of very broad administrative powers without any constraining guidance, provided those powers are necessary to achieve the objective that the Oireachtas has set for the administrative agency. Finally, where the power is broader than might be necessary, the test requires constraint but does not preclude the administrative agency from developing principles and policies consistent with that constraint.

Bearing these points in mind, we can reconsider the cases above. The decision in *Re Article 26 and the Health (Amendment) (No. 2) Bill 2004* to uphold the CEO's power to waive or reduce charges is unproblematic. The scope of this power was no broader than necessary. Moreover, this limiting criterion was laid down in the statute itself. In the context of *Sivsivadze*, it is problematic that the criteria that guided the revocation power were not laid down in the statute but were instead the result of judicial interpretation. That said, the fact that these interpretations predated the case did reduce the force of the applicants' claim. The obligation on the minister to revoke a deportation where there is a material change in circumstances is a genuinely constraining factor.

The power conferred in *Dellway* was far wider than conceivably necessary to meet its objective. It is difficult to avoid the conclusion that the Oireachtas was assigning to NAMA the hugely important decision about what types of bank assets should be acquired. Moreover, the constraining factors – as illustrated above – provided little or no constraint. The powers conferred on NAMA would not survive the test suggested in this chapter. *Collins* raises fewer concerns than *Dellway*. The scope of the power here – although wide – was probably no broader than was necessary to meet its objective. It is troubling that the Court read in constraining factors that probably do not exist on a fair reading of the statute. However, it is significant that the Act was – in substance but not in the precise constitutional sense – emergency legislation. The state was immediately faced with a crisis situation, the possibility of a run on the banks. It is of course questionable whether the bank guarantee was the correct response to that situation, but this is not a rule-of-law concern. Bearing in mind that there must be a balance between rule-of-law concerns and the need to facilitate the achievement of democratically endorsed programmes, *Collins* seems an appropriate case in which to favour the latter over the former.

Implications for judicial power

The argument in this chapter has implications for judicial power at two levels. First, some might be troubled at the absence of any clear textual justification for the power of the courts to strike down grants of administrative power. This should not be a concern. The formal rule of law is the quintessential value of legality: a legal system that evinces no commitment to the rule of law is little more than a regime for control of the masses. Judges have a role to play, irrespective of any explicit constitutional authorisation, in ensuring compliance with the rule of law. The Irish courts have accepted this role, on several occasions emphasising the commitment of the constitutional order to the rule of law.[40] It provides the best explanation of the prohibition on vague criminal offences, a doctrine likewise lacking any clear textual basis. Rather than unconvincingly cobble together several vaguely related constitutional provisions, it is better to assess the doctrine as a judicial elaboration of the constitutional order's fundamental commitment to the rule of law. The doctrine's justification turns on whether it is a reasonable response to that commitment, consistent with the other objectives of the constitutional order. The doctrine is minimally restrictive of legislative choice while providing a baseline of rule-of-law compliance for the grant of administrative powers. It would be a justified elaboration of Ireland's commitment to the rule of law.

Apart from the constitutional basis for its existence, the doctrine also has implications for the judicial power in its operation. In policing the boundaries between legitimate and illegitimate grants of administrative power, the courts obtain power for themselves, arguably at the expense of administrative agencies.[41] This concern, however, is offset by a number of factors. The doctrine only controls the means through which the Oireachtas can pursue its objectives. It allows for broad grants of administrative power and requires the courts to be deferential to the assessment by the Oireachtas as to what powers are necessary to meet the objectives of an administrative agency. Moreover, in a legal system where the government is guaranteed a majority in the legislature, the implications of a declaration of unconstitutionality are less significant. The government can always secure the passage of new legislation that allows the administrative agency to achieve the same objective, but in a manner that complies with the rule of law. This should assuage concerns about the power that such a doctrine would grant to judges.

Notes

I presented earlier drafts of this chapter to the annual meeting of the Irish Association of Law Teachers in Belfast on 24 November 2013 and to the Judges, Politics and the Constitution conference held at Dublin City University on 4 September 2014. I am grateful to all who commented in both forums and especially to Paul Daly who read and commented on a previous draft.

1. *Re Article 26 and the Illegal Immigrants (Trafficking) Bill* 1999 [2000] 2 IR 360, 385; *Maguire v. Ardagh* [2002] 1 IR 385; *Mallak v. Minister for Justice, Equality and Law Reform* [2012] IESC 59.
2. See for instance R. Dworkin, 'Political Judges and the Rule of Law' in *A Matter of Principle* (Harvard UP, 1985).
3. It is more analytically useful than the substantive conceptions, since it focuses on a discrete value of legality rather than merging that value with other values. If one sympathises with more substantive conceptions of the rule of law, one can read this chapter as an inquiry into how Irish constitutional law instantiates the formal aspects of the rule of law.
4. L. Fuller, *The Morality of Law* (Yale UP, 1967) pp. 46–91.
5. N. E. Simmonds, 'Straightforwardly False: The Collapse of Kramer's Positivism' (2004) 63 *Cambridge Law Journal* 98.
6. L. Green, 'Positivism and the Inseparability of Law and Morals' (2008) 83 *NYU Law Review* 1035, 1054–1058.

7 J. Raz, 'The Rule of Law and its Virtue' in *The Authority of Law* (OUP, 1979) pp. 214–219.
8 Raz refers to 'particular legal orders' to connote a legal order directed to an individual; I use 'directives' to avoid confusion with the other sense of 'legal order'.
9 Raz (n. 7) p. 216.
10 Article 25.
11 Article 15.5.
12 *King v. Attorney General* [1981] IR 233.
13 G. Hogan, 'The Judicial Thought and Prose of Mr Justice Seamus Henchy' (2011) 46(1) *Irish Jurist* 96.
14 This principle has been subsequently applied in *Dokie v. Director of Public Prosecutions* [2010] IEHC 110, *Douglas v. DPP* [2013] IEHC 343, and *McInerney v. DPP* [2014] IEHC181. For discussion, see D. Prendergast, '*Douglas v. DPP* and the Constitutional Requirement for Certainty in Criminal Law' (2013) 50(2) *Irish Jurist* 235.
15 In *Kennedy v. Law Society of Ireland (No. 3)* [2002] 2 IR 458, 486, Justice Fennelly explicitly related this doctrine to the rule of law.
16 The existence of Private Acts does not fit easily within this account. If they are correctly called legislation, they are a peripheral instance of legislation.
17 For Gardner, this distinguishes legislative lawmaking from judicial lawmaking (J. Gardner, 'Legal Positivism: 5½ Myths' in *Law as a Leap of Faith* (OUP, 2012) p. 40).
18 [1941] IR 83.
19 [2005] IESC 7.
20 The Oireachtas may delegate its lawmaking power provided that the delegating instrument deals with all matters of principle and policy, leaving only matters of detail to the delegated legislator. *Cityview Press v. An Comhairle Oiliúna* [1980] IR 381. This is the articulation of the test but it has never been applied by the courts in this way. See O. Doyle, *Constitutional Law: Text, Cases and Materials* (Clarus Press, 2008), [11–19]–[11–28].
21 [2012] IEHC 137.
22 [2012] IEHC 244.
23 [2015] IESC 53.
24 [2013] IEHC 530.
25 In *McGowan v. The Labour Court* [2013] IESC 2, Justice O'Donnell held that measures that do not breach the principles and policies test are for that reason not legislative in character. This cannot be correct: the character of a power as legislative is in no way affected by the breadth of that power.
26 As a foundation for the doctrine, Article 15.2 would be highly insecure, given the Supreme Court's clear recognition in *re Health (Amendment) (No. 2) Bill 2004* and in *Dellway Investments Ltd* (see below) that grants of administrative power are not subject to Article 15.2. Indeed, the Supreme Court in *Sivsivadze* largely exhausted its consideration of whether section 3(11) granted too much power with its conclusion that Article 15.2 did not apply to the grant of an administrative power.

27 [2012] IESC 13.
28 National Asset Management Agency Act 1999, s. 69 and SI 568/2009 National Asset Management Agency (Designation of Eligible Bank Assets) Regulations 2009, reg. 2.
29 *Ibid.*, s. 4.
30 [2012] IEHC 244. It might be thought that any rule-of-law concern is diminished by the fact that section 3(11) can only be exercised in favour of a person. However, rule-of-law concerns arise just as much in respect of possibly favourable decisions: individuals should know what they are legally entitled to and not have to tailor their activities to anticipate the whim of unfettered bureaucrats. Moreover, the existence of section 3(11) was part of the state's defence of the constitutionality of section 3(1) which provided only for indefinite deportations. In the absence of section 3(11), deportation orders would be permanent and most likely unconstitutional.
31 *McEvoy v. Meath County Council* [2003] 1 IR 208.
32 C. Sypnowich, 'Utopia and the Rule of Law' in D. Dyzenhaus (ed.), *Recrafting the Rule of Law* (Hart, 1999).
33 R. A. Epstein, 'Why the Modern Administrative State is Inconsistent with the Rule of Law' (2008) 3 *NYU Journal of Law and Liberty* 491, 495.
34 B. Z Tamanaha, 'The Dark Side of the Relationship between the Rule of Law and Liberalism' (2008) 3 *NYU Journal of Law and Liberty* 516.
35 A similar problem arises in respect of the constitutional review of legislative action. See O. Doyle, *Constitutional Equality Law* (Round Hall, 2004) pp. 117–122.
36 *Molyneux v. Ireland* [1997] ILRM 241; *Crilly v. Farrington* [2001] 3 IR 267; *Controller of Patents v. Ireland* [2001] 4 IR 229.
37 *East Donegal Co-operative Ltd v. Attorney General* [1970] IR 317, 344.
38 *State (Keegan) v. Stardust Compensation Tribunal* [1986] IR 658.
39 From a rule-of-law perspective, there would be no difficulty with an administrative agency fettering its own jurisdiction in advance. However, this does raise democratic concerns and is generally prohibited in administrative law. See G. Hogan and D. G. Morgan, *Administrative Law in Ireland* (4th ed, Round Hall, 2010) pp. 793–799.
40 (n. 1).
41 For this type of argument, see E. Carolan, 'Democratic Control or High-Sounding Hocus-Pocus? A Public Choice of Analysis of the Non-Delegation Doctrine' (2007) 29 *Dublin University Law Journal* 111.

16

Article 16 of the Irish Constitution and judicial review of electoral processes

David Prendergast

Introduction

Constitutional referendums tend to dominate discussion of the Irish courts' interaction with political processes. The *McKenna* judgment of 1995,[1] ruling out one-sided public spending on constitutional amendment advocacy, has had contentious and enduring effect.[2] This chapter looks past the referendum cases to examine judicial development of Article 16. This Article provides for the composition of, and election to, Dáil Éireann, Ireland's lower house of parliament. The chapter first introduces a way of thinking about democracy to ground the evaluation of Article 16 case law that follows. I give an overview of Article 16, rejecting the view that it is a 'total code' for Dáil elections. Finally, I defend the restrained yet occasionally creative path the courts have taken under Article 16; the courts' work can be overall characterised as seeking to protect the electoral process, but not perfect it.

The concept of democracy

Democracy is a system of political government orientated around the principle that the people rule themselves. Evaluation of legal practice by reference to democratic principle must articulate and defend its conception of democracy. This chapter's assessment of Irish constitutional practice relies on a broad notion of democracy with minimal assumptions about its nature. Democracy is a contested concept.[3] This contestation is evidence (though not proof) of its non-essentialist nature. Democracy is a humanly constructed complex good that is not immutable. Details of democratic government are to be worked out and are always up for debate in light of experience and reasoned argument. So far as these claims about democracy are sound, the following three principles are plausible: first, the contours of democracy should themselves be worked out primarily by democratic processes; second, there is a danger of decay in democracy in part because it is an ongoing experiment; and third, notwithstanding the first principle above, we should be sceptical about *a priori* arguments completely ruling out judicial review of democratically enacted legislation. The next section elaborates on these principles.

A role for the courts in protecting, not perfecting democracy

The impulse that suggests democratic processes settle substantive political questions also suggests democratic processes settle their own content. Democratic processes are self-defining because democracy needs laws to constitute itself and yet democracy produces laws. The understanding of democracy as non-essentialist and always answerable to the reality of people's lives carries a danger of decay. That is, democracy, in working out its own shape, might change itself with the eventual result that it is no longer recognisably democratic (because it is no longer reasonably orientated around the idea that the people rule themselves). The vulnerability of democracy points to value in having constraints on democratic decision-making that mitigate the danger of decay. This is where judges as guardians or protectors of democracy may have a role in enforcing ground rules about how much the democratic processes can be altered and what political practices and arrangements are compatible with those processes. Hence, there is scope, within the argumentative space of democratic values, for a judicial power to strike down or invalidate democratically enacted measures. This is a power above and beyond the inescapable power that judges have as interpreters of law to decide whether legal requirements relating to democratic processes have been complied with. Clearly, for an unelected and not popularly accountable judge to invalidate a law with democratic provenance troubles a democrat;[4] but the idea is that in the long run democracy can be strengthened by this practice. The judges should understand their role as restrained and bounded. In reviewing the processes of democracy, they should intervene only to catch or prevent democratic processes going awry or malfunctioning.[5] Judges ought to protect democracy but not take on the task of perfecting it. They should not lose sight of their lack of democratic representativeness and accountability; their role is subsidiary and reactive, the lead role is for democratically elected organs of government.[6] That courts write reasoned judgments explaining decisions is a valuable practice. The need to give a reasoned judgment restrains the extent to which the conclusion can be arbitrary or motivated by improper reasons. Decisions must be an application of the law

– properly identified and using legal reasoning where appropriate to fill gaps – to the true facts of a case. Of course, with skill, a judge can make a decision appear legally constrained when in reality factors not listed in the judgment have influence. But not every conclusion can be rationalised in a written judgment. That lawyers, judges themselves, law professors, and other observers and commentators on the workings of the legal system are reading court judgments, and to varying degrees, scrutinising, criticising and commending them may help reinforce the felt duty to give soundly reasoned judgments.[7] Hence it is valuable to analyse closely the reasons for decisions; the content as well as the net result of a judgment is apt for scrutiny. What follows reports the main conclusions of a critical analysis of the case law on Article 16.

Article 16: not a 'total code'

Article 16 stipulates certain limits on who can be an elected representative and who can vote; prescribes assembly composition through an electoral constituency system with proportional representation by single transferable vote; and gives guidance on the duration and changeover of parliament, polling, and a Dáil Chairman. It is key to note that Article 16 resides in a system with a textually mandated and firmly established practice of superior court constitutional review of legislation and executive functions. This section seeks to correct a misleading view of Article 16 adopted in *Re Article 26 and the Electoral (Amendment) Bill 1983*.[8] In that case the Bill under review purport to entitle British citizens ordinarily resident in Dáil Éireann constituencies to register to vote in Dáil elections. At the time, Article 16.1.2° stated simply that 'every citizen' – subject to the age requirement and without distinction on the basis of sex – had the right to vote in Dáil elections. The Supreme Court held that Article 16.1.2°, as it then was, could not be construed as permitting the extension of the franchise by legislation to certain non-citizens and accordingly the 1983 Bill was held to be repugnant to the Constitution. This conclusion was based in part on the Court's observation that Article 16 provided a 'constitutional code for the holding of an election to Dáil Éireann'.[9] The 'essential features' of this framework for election to Dáil Éireann cannot be altered by ordinary legislation, the Court said. This meant that if Article 16, given the way it is structured overall, says citizens have the right to vote, it means *only* citizens have the right to vote.[10] The Supreme Court judgment in *Re Article 26 and the Electoral (Amendment) Bill 1983* has a tendency to mislead as to the way Article 16 sets up a framework for elections to Dáil Éireann. The judgment's description of Article 16 as a 'total code' for Dáil elections, with only 'minor regulatory'[11] aspects left to be legislated for, can make sense in the context of the particular focus of the Court's inquiry into the permissibility of extending the franchise.[12] However, it is an inapposite description of Article 16 as a whole that led the High Court into unpersuasive reasoning in *Redmond v. Minister for the Environment*[13] and which was largely corrected by the Supreme Court in *King v. Minister for the Environment (No. 2)*.[14]

In *Redmond* Justice Herbert struck down a statutory requirement for monetary deposits to stand for election; it had been argued that would-be electoral candidates of little financial means were discriminated against in running for office. The judgment had a constitutional equality basis under Article 40.1 but as regards Article 16, the judge said that the Oireachtas did not have the power to put in place the impediment, as he considered it, of a deposit to stand for election to the Dáil. Justice Herbert reasoned that the deposit requirement falls somewhere between, on the one hand, the very substantial power (based on 'weighty and objective reasons' such as preserving the separation of powers) to disqualify or render persons (such as judges) ineligible from the Dáil under Article 16.1.1° and, on the other hand, the power to put in place the necessary regulations (the 'rules and procedures') for elections under Article 16.7.[15]

The *Redmond* judgment did not appreciate that the deposit requirement, if aimed at stopping a multiplicity of candidates crowding out the ballot, contributes to a workable ballot, which is an aspect of the regulation of elections. This was subsequently recognised by the Supreme Court in *King v. Minister for the Environment (No. 2)*.[16] In *King*, the impugned legislation discriminated against electoral candidates who did not have affiliation with a registered political party. In order to get on the ballot non-party (or independent) candidates had to provide signatures of thirty supporters or assentors, as well as have these assentors present themselves at the local authority offices to have their identity verified. Political party candidates had no such task to perform. The High Court upheld this arrangement, but the Supreme Court said it was incompatible with the Constitution. While the Supreme Court recognised a legitimate purpose in ensuring electoral candidates sought election in good faith and that there was a rational basis for distinguishing between party and non-party candidates, the Court concluded that the measures adopted were disproportionate. The Supreme Court in *King* overruled *Redmond's* identification of Article 16.7 as an inapt base for grounding the power to impose restrictions on candidates getting on the ballot paper. The electoral process that was concerned and accordingly Article 16.7, calling for the Oireachtas to regulate the electoral process for the Dáil, founds the power that the Oireachtas had exercised in this context. Thus, for the Supreme Court, Justice Herbert's approach, whereby deposit requirements or indeed other conditions for getting on the ballot are said to be *ultra vires*, was incorrect.[17] *King* obliquely rejects the *dicta* in *Re Article 26 and the Electoral (Amendment) Bill 1983* describing Article 16 as a total code for Dáil elections.

The provisions of Article 16, along with other provisions of the Constitution, provide a plan for a democratic system of government. It is a '*basic* blueprint',[18] indicating the general electoral architecture and being quite detailed in places, but also conspicuously lacking detail in other places. A number of vital matters are left for the Oireachtas to prescribe the details; for example, the machinery of balloting and procedures for guarding against electoral fraud. Article 16 plays a key part in setting up an electoral democracy that has room to evolve and vary within certain parameters without the need for constitutional amendment. Sometimes the incompleteness of the constitutional text is clearly by design, other times it is not so clear that the constitutional text was knowingly crafted to be indeterminate on a point of democratic structure. Either way there is work to be done, as Article 16.7 envisages, to maintain a functioning democracy and the remainder of this chapter continues to survey the contribution of the superior courts to this task.

The courts' interaction with Article 16

As in *Redmond* and *King (No. 2)* above, statutory arrangements for elections have been constitutionally challenged with varying success by reference to the provisions of Article 16. The following tour of the most notable cases shows judicial choice to intervene and not to intervene, and the pattern more or less overall conforms to a model of protecting, not perfecting democratic processes. The main evaluative claims are that *O'Donovan v. Attorney General* in 1961[19] and *Murphy v. Minister for the Environment* in 2007,[20] both concerning equally proportioned electoral constituencies, are exemplars of a court protecting – but not seeking to perfect – democracy. *McMahon v. Attorney General* in 1972, on the secrecy of the ballot, and *Doherty v. Ireland* in 2009,[21] on the filling of Dáil vacancies through by-election, come in for critical comment but are nevertheless defensible interventions. A qualified defence is provided in respect of the decisions not to strike down statutes in *O'Reilly v. Minister for the Environment* in 1986 (alphabetic listing of candidates on ballot), *Draper v. Attorney General*[22] in 1984 (disabled voters' exercise of the franchise) and *Breathnach v. Ireland*[23] in 2000 (prisoner voting), though these three cases contain weak judicial reasoning.

Balloting and the exercise of the franchise

The mechanisms of balloting and the exercise of the franchise are vital matters in elections genuinely reflecting popular choice. *McMahon v. Attorney General*[24] is notable in showing an exacting standard of constitutional review in upholding Article 16.1's requirement of a secret ballot. In *McMahon* both the High Court and a three-two majority of the Supreme Court held that the Constitution required a level of strict ballot secrecy that the impugned arrangement violated. The impugned statutory scheme left it possible to ascertain how a person voted on foot of a Dáil or court order where there was a question of personation. Voter identity could also be discovered pursuant to an election petition for the purpose of enquiring into the validity of votes cast.[25] At the time of the case, this procedure had not yet been utilised. Chief Justice Ó'Dálaigh, for the majority, recognised the importance of a secret ballot in enabling people to vote independently, free from threats and intimidation.[26] Implicit is an understanding that the secret ballot guards against bribery. The judgment did not explain precisely why the strict secrecy approach was needed over the qualified secrecy approach of the impugned scheme.[27] Only if the scope for revelation of the ballot could be abused would the rationale push beyond qualified secrecy to demand strict secrecy. An unspoken premise to the argument in favour of strict secrecy that bolsters the finding in *McMahon* is that the potential avenue for abuse ought to be closed off even if it is unlikely to happen.

Among the cases showing a much more lax standard of review, is *O'Reilly v. Minister for the Environment*.[28] Justice Murphy in the High Court refused to declare unconstitutional the practice of listing electoral candidates' names in alphabetical order on ballot papers. The Court accepted evidence that the alphabetic listing did indeed tend to favour candidates whose surnames were closer to A in the alphabet. But the 'defect', according to Justice Murphy, was 'a defect or a want of care or a want of interest by the electorate'[29] rather than a defect in the system. The result of *O'Reilly* – refraining from striking down the alphabetical ballot – is defensible from the point of view that sees judicial review of electoral law not as an avenue for perfecting the system but rather as a safeguard on the system. However, the cited reason for upholding the legislation – blaming voter laziness and not the ballot arrangements for the problem – reflects a principle unsuitable for generalisation. It would, for instance, be an unsatisfactory rationale for upholding a scheme that in effect allowed minor bribery of voters on the basis that voter weakness of will is to blame rather than the system. In terms of protecting and not perfecting democracy, *O'Reilly* gets the result right but its lax review should not be repeated because if there is to be constitutional review of electoral processes, it must be rigorous; it must not lend itself to being a potential whitewash.

Like *O'Reilly*, *Draper v. Attorney General*[30] and *Breathnach v. Ireland*[31] show highly deferential review of statutory rules on voting. The applicants in both *Draper* and *Breathnach* could not in practice exercise their Dáil votes because they could not travel to a polling station. Physical disability prevented voting in *Draper*, lawful imprisonment in *Breathnach*. In both cases the applicants sought a method such as postal voting to be put in place for them for Dáil elections. The *Draper* and *Breathnach* judgments frequently note that the legislation enjoys the presumption of constitutionality; it seems all that was needed to uphold the unavailability of postal voting was any sort of rationalisation why it was unavailable. In the *Draper* judgments, there is the idea that if provision was made for postal voting for voters with disabilities, then it would have to be made for those who are temporarily away from their residence and so on. This was added to assumptions that postal voting is more vulnerable to abuse than voting in person to rationalise the prudential restriction of postal voting. *Breathnach* followed *Draper* and said that if the state was not obliged to extend postal voting to voters with disabilities, then it was not obliged to extend it to prisoners.[32] In a concurring judgment in *Breathnach*, Justice Denham treats the case as only about the right to equality in Article 40.1, thus implying that the right to vote in Dáil elections in Article 16.1 was not in issue; the imprisoned applicant still having, according to the electoral register, the right to vote. This understanding has the curious implication where, suppose, the state arbitrarily detained or otherwise impeded certain persons for the duration of electoral polling days, there would be no Article 16.1 issue. Absent from the *Breathnach* judgment are references to political equality that featured prominently a few years previously in *McKenna (No. 2)*[33] where Article 16 and Article 40.1 were said to be in play together, being expressions of 'the concept and spirit of equality'.

While the *Draper* and *Breathnach* applicants were unsuccessful, subsequent statutory law provided what the applicants had sought. Persons with disability or illness,[34] as well as prisoners,[35] are now facilitated under Irish law for postal voting. No doubt the relevant reforms should have occurred earlier but the pattern of court rejection followed by statutory reform is somewhat reassuring in terms of democratic health. That the Oireachtas subsequently addressed the problem that the courts declined to rectify tends to vindicate the courts' decisions not to intervene since the political process proved to be able to improve itself without court intervention. The reforms have come via legislation from the elected assembly, not directed or constrained by unelected judges. The lesson of *Draper* and *Breathnach* – it might be said – is that very facility of judicial review, even when exercised with restraint, may help encourage reform.

Electoral constituencies

O'Donovan v. Attorney General[36] is the earliest superior court case reviewing a political process under the Irish Constitution, predating the US Supreme Court's reapportionment cases,[37] and with no attempt on the court's part to avoid reviewing the matter via the political question doctrine or a standing requirement. The High Court struck down an electoral scheme[38] for failing to comply with Articles 16.2.3° and 16.2.4°, which require, respectively, the constituencies to be equally proportioned throughout the country and revised in light of population changes. Under the impugned scheme, certain Dublin constituencies had as many as 24,000 citizens to one Dáil deputy while some rural constituencies in Galway, Kerry and Donegal had as few as 16,000 per deputy. Justice Budd rejected the Attorney General's argument that the disparity in ratio of population to elected representatives was needed to equalise the difficulties in representation faced by deputies in rural areas, stating there is:

> [N]o direction whatsoever contained in the Constitution that these matters of difficulties of communications, differing economic interests, differing modes of life or the convenience of constituents or the difficulties of deputies or any of the other matters relied on by the defendant, should be taken into consideration when the Legislature is performing its functions in enacting the electoral laws. All of these are, in their own sphere, important matters, and if those who enacted the Constitution had intended them to be taken into consideration when the Legislature was enacting the electoral laws, pursuant to subclause 2 of Article 16, it is scarcely credible that they would not have said so.[39]

Justice Budd saw the purpose of Article 16.2.3° as adding a further constraint on the construction of constituencies, that of achieving 'equality of ratio and representation'.[40] So while *O'Donovan* was a straightforward application of Article 16.2.3° and 16.2.4°, Justice Budd nevertheless constructed a theory of what is required in a democracy in rebutting the Attorney General's argument. Justice Budd went beyond Article 16 in defending his reading of Article 16.2.3°. He concluded that the equality in question 'is not maintained if the vote of a person in one part of the country has a greater effect in securing parliamentary representation than the vote of a person in another part of the country'. He said that the three constitutional Articles (Articles 5, 16 and 40) 'harmonise'[41] and their 'spirit' 'demands equality of voting power and representation'.[42] Though rebutting evidence was heard,[43] Justice Budd's rejection of the Attorney's argument does not deny the difficulties of representation for the West. The Attorney's argument was an argument from equality. Justice Budd's rejection is based on there being no express textual invitation in the Constitution to assess the electoral process in these terms.[44] Justice Budd's judgment rejects an argument for lacking express textual support and then proceeds to 'support' this rejection with a non-express principle of equality of voting power and representation that is, at best, consistent with the text apart from that of Article 16.2.3°. In this regard, *O'Donovan* foreshadowed the more recent interventionist approach to democratic processes of the Supreme Court in *McKenna v. An Taoiseach (No. 2)* and the High Court in *Doherty v. Ireland* in its implication that even absent the concrete requirements of Articles 16.2.3° and 16.2.4° the Court could still have found the impugned electoral constituency scheme to be invalid. Part of the *O'Donovan* judgment reasons from broad democratic structures to concrete requirements. Though *obiter dictum*, this part of *O'Donovan* crossed a threshold in opening up space for creative judicial review of political processes.

Since *O'Donovan* the courts have not identified a precise measure by which departure from parity of ratio is tolerable as a matter of course. There is no 'magic formula' such as a 5% tolerance level readily available that can identify a permissible departure from exact parity.[45] Deviations in the ratio of Dáil seats to population in the order of 25% from a national average have been considered impermissible.[46] Deviations are defensible by reference to a variety of factors including the desirability of adhering to 'well-known boundaries such as those of counties, townlands and electoral divisions' as well as allowing for the 'existence of divisions created by such physical features as rivers, lakes and mountains'.[47] The obligation on the Oireachtas in Article 16.2.4° to 'revise the constituencies at least once in every twelve years, with due regard to changes in distribution of the population' is not necessarily discharged by revision of constituencies once every 12 years.[48] Population for the purposes of the ratio in Article 16.2.3° is that 'as ascertained at the last preceding census'. This has been held to mean that the ratio is calculated by reference to the population figures in the most recently published final official census report rather than what may be the true population figures at any point in time, as might be revealed in various estimates or preliminary census results.[49] When final census figures become available, revealing population changes such that the ratio of Dáil members to population is no longer the same throughout the country, the existing constituency scheme does not automatically become invalid. Rather, there arises an obligation on the Oireachtas to have the constituency scheme altered accordingly within a reasonable time. This is because Article 16.2.3° requires the ratio to be the same throughout the country 'so far as it is practicable'.[50] The Oireachtas has taken up the High Court's suggestion[51] to minimise the time during which existing constituencies are disproportioned by having the redistricting process commence using preliminary census data rather than wait for final census data to trigger the process.[52]

Settling uncertainty in the constitutional framework for electoral law

The Irish superior courts' interaction with the provisions of Article 16.2 shows a judicial role in helping stabilise an electoral system in the face of uncertainty. As noted in Part I, Article 16 provides an incomplete plan for the electoral part of the Ireland's democracy but it is a framework nonetheless for a large body of legislation to make the electoral system a functioning reality within constitutional limits. Uncertainty will arise as to those limits and the task for the courts is to settle these uncertainties without unsettling what is certain. Justice Budd recognised in O'Donovan that '[t]he object of the Constitution was to provide in the form of a fundamental law a code of rules within which the organs of government and the people might function in an orderly way of life befitting a modern state'.[53] He continued, '[w]hile it necessarily contains certain philosophical principles, its purpose was to set up institutions which would be workable'.[54] This appreciation of the Constitution as an essential source of stability in political structures and not, for instance, a vehicle for judges to refashion structures such as electoral law as it ideally ought to be, motivated a forensic judgment in O'Donovan. So far as indeterminacy arises with the proviso 'so far as it is practicable' appended to the requirement to have equally proportioned constituencies, Justice Budd settled the matter in O'Donovan, steering between two pitfalls. One pitfall was the temptation to reinvent the constitutional rule, as the Attorney General's arguments encouraged. The danger of this path is that the court's background understanding of the functions and qualities of an electoral system tend to oust what the Constitution purported to settle originally. The Court becomes the redesigner of the electoral framework. The other pitfall was to require strict mathematical parity between the constituencies. As the experience in the United States with one person, one vote for federal congressional districts shows, this requirement can provide cover for gerrymandering.[55]

The Supreme Court judgment in *Re Article 26 and the Electoral Amendment Bill 1961*[56] cohered with Justice Budd's judgment in *O'Donovan* and thus has the merit of not undermining the degree of certainty brought in the previous case. It repeats the message that the requirement for equally proportioned constituencies must be respected but that the requirement is not for exact parity. It also adds an important gloss that in revising constituencies, geographical boundaries and traditional political boundaries can be legitimately preserved. This conveys the message that the process of revising the constituencies should be done in a restrained way, not redrawing from a blank canvas, but adjusting what is already in place to recognise population changes in accordance with the constitutional requirement. Justice Clarke's judgment *Murphy v. Minister for the Environment*[57] continued the tradition of not looking behind what Article 16.2.3° specifically prescribes even if greater equality of voting power could arguably be achieved otherwise.[58] While the previous case law from the 1960s had settled the question of what degree of parity is needed between constituencies, there remained space to chip at the certainty of the requirement regarding the timeframe for revising the constituencies and furthermore to rekindle doubts arising from Article 16.2.3°'s referring to ratio of Dáil members to *population* rather than to voters. Justice Clarke pointed out how true proportionality is a function of many factors: Constituencies may have especially low voter turnout, large numbers of non-citizens not entitled to vote, or high proportions of children.[59] Justice Clarke noted:

> [F]reed from any specific constitutional requirement as to how proportionality between population/electorate on the one hand and numbers of elected representatives on the other was to be determined … there are a whole variety of ways in which one might seek to achieve an appropriate level of proportionality … Bunreacht na hÉireann selects one model and one model only by reference to which proportionality is to be determined. It is the population as ascertained by the last census. Whatever may be the merits or otherwise of that benchmark, it is the benchmark that has been adopted for this State.[60]

It is clear from this passage and elsewhere in Justice Clarke's judgment that it respects the settlement function of the constitutional provisions on electoral processes and bolsters that function in precluding potential uncertainty about the timeframe for the constituencies to be revised following a census.

Filling Dáil vacancies: *Doherty v. Ireland*

In *Doherty v. Ireland*[61] Justice Kearns in the High Court granted a declaration that there had been 'unreasonable delay in moving the writ for the by-election in Donegal South West'. The vacated Dáil seat had been left unfilled for near eighteen months. In identifying the applicant's case as justiciable, Justice Kearns cited the description in Article 5 of the state as democratic as well as the provisions in Article 16. He emphasised that Article 16.7 envisaged 'the *filling* of casual vacancies'.[62] Justice Kearns read s. 39(2), Electoral Act 1992 Act to include a requirement that the process for holding a by-election to fill a Dáil vacancy must take place within a reasonable time of a vacancy arising. The words of this subsection did not include reference to an overall temporal requirement, distinct from the Chairman of the Dáil having to act 'as soon as he is directed by the Dáil', and the respondents argued the correct interpretation was that the provision left it entirely at the discretion of the Dáil when to hold a by-election. For Justice Kearns, however, the subsection, on the respondents' reading, would be unconstitutional and the presumption of constitutionality required him to prefer constitutional to unconstitutional readings. The judge also stated that ordinary statutory interpretation principles lead to this reading of the subsection since it would otherwise produce an absurd result (that is, the filling of a vacancy being at the discretion of the Dáil). It would also, for Justice Kearns, be 'absurd to apply a requirement of reasonable time to the holding of a general election' – under the European Convention on Human Rights requirement for free elections by secret ballot at 'reasonable intervals'[63] – 'and then to flout or altogether ignore the same principle at the micro level of a by-election'. Thus, for Justice Kearns, any one of three routes – the constitutional double construction rule, ordinary principles of statutory interpretation, and the obligation to read statutory rules in a Convention compliant manner[64] – led to reading s. 39(2) of the 1992 Act as imposing an expedition requirement on the Dáil in moving to have its vacancies filled.

What Justice Kearns castigated as an absurd arrangement – that the filling of casual vacancies would remain at the discretion of the Dáil – was in fact the understanding expressly identified and successfully defended in Oireachtas debates on the 1992 Act.[65] The *Doherty* judgment reversed an Oireachtas enactment on an electoral matter by reference to the judge's notion of what ought to be in a democracy, loosely supported by vague constitutional terms, and masked by the rhetorical use of 'absurd'. After *McKenna (No. 2)*, *Doherty* is a stand out case involving reasoning from a judge's vision of democracy to constitutionalising a specific requirement. In *Doherty*, it was said that the delay in holding the by-election 'offends the terms and spirit of the Constitution and its framework for democratic representation'. This echoed Justice Denham's statement in *McKenna (No. 2)* that partisan state spending in a referendum campaign offended the 'spirit of equality', which in turn repeated *dicta* from *O'Donovan*. In *McKenna (No. 2)* the impugned conduct of the government's spending on partisan advertising was something that neither constitutional nor statutory law had provided a rule either way. Nor was it clear that a background closure rule – such as what is not prohibited is permitted – ought to apply. The *Doherty v. Ireland* case, in contrast, involved a question on which the law had already spoken. A legislative determination had already been made on the question of the timeframe for the filling of casual Dáil vacancies. The Constitution in Article 16.7 said it was for the Oireachtas to regulate the matter and the Oireachtas had legislated to give the Dáil discretion as to when to cause a by-election to be held. The *Doherty* judgment refuses to countenance this law as it was enacted. On this view, *Doherty* is an example of what a court should not do in the realm of judicial review of electoral processes: It should not try to perfect the process or reinvent the arrangements in place, where such arrangements cannot be said to be defeating real democracy, though they may be clearly suboptimal. The court is simply not appropriately qualified, both in terms of expertise and being empowered by democratic process, to take a proactive role in shaping democratic processes. The court's role should be reactive, receptive, and subsidiary; performed only when needed. On another view, however, the readiness in *Doherty* to intervene ought to be valued. If a significant number of vacancies arose in the Dáil and were left unfilled as the Oireachtas continued to enact legislation, the proper functioning of democracy would tend to be undermined and an obligation to have the vacancies filled within a reasonable time is a worthy rule to consitutionalise to guard against that event. Although the facts in *Doherty* did not disclose the above scenario, they still provided an opportunity to constitutionalise a protection against a possible degradation. A democracy may suffer death by a thousand cuts and the threshold for intervention may be the point where democracy is on the way to degradation rather than actually degrading. *Doherty* looks like *McMahon v. Attorney General* where strict ballot secrecy was insisted upon even though there was no evidence that the qualified secrecy arrangement had been, or was likely to be, abused. Importantly, in *Doherty* Justice Kearns laid down a flexible constitutional standard of a reasonable time for casual Dáil vacancies to be filled. This left open a number of legislative options;

as it turned out the Oireachtas put in place a six-month time limit for the triggering of a by-election to fill a vacancy.[66] In this light, the High Court's intervention ultimately managed to respect the idea that the exact contours of the democratic system should be worked via that democratic system.

Conclusion

Writing extra-judicially in 2001, Mr Justice Declan Budd characterised the courts' interaction with electoral law and referendums as 'treading delicately'.[67] This description is apt to describe the bulk of the case law on elections so far as it means proceeding carefully and being reluctant to intervene just because an impugned arrangement seems democratically imperfect. Nevertheless, the superior courts, starting with *dicta* in *O'Donovan v. Attorney General*, have been ready and willing to constitutionalise aspects of the conduct of elections in the absence of a firm textual basis in the Constitution. The courts have embraced a role guarding Ireland's democracy that somewhat illustrates in practice the idea identified early in this chapter that judicial review of electoral processes can be acceptable in democratic terms. That is a subsidiary role of protecting democratic processes.

Notes

This contribution was presented at the Judges, Politics and the Irish Constitution conference, DCU School of Law and Government, 4 September 2014 – I am grateful to the organisers and participants for a stimulating day. This chapter is drawn from a doctoral thesis completed at Trinity Law School under Oran Doyle's supervision. I thank Dr Doyle for brilliant guidance. I also thank my Ph.D. examiners, Conor O'Mahony and Dimitrios Kyritsis, for probing and very helpful assessment. Finally, I thank the editors whose comments improved this chapter. Defects are mine.

1 *McKenna v. An Taoiseach (No. 2)* [1995] 2 IR 10 (SC).
2 See G. Barrett, 'Building a Swiss Chalet in an Irish Legal Landscape? Referendums on European Union Treaties in Ireland and the Impact of Supreme Court Jurisprudence' (2009) 5 *European Constitutional Law Review* 32.
3 Democracy was an example of an essentially contested concept in W. B. Gallie, 'Essentially Contested Concepts' (1956) 56 *Proceedings of the Aristotelian Society* 167. An essentially contested concept, in Gallie's account, is marked by endless dispute of a philosophical, reasoned kind that goes to the essential features of the concept, not just the margins.
4 Recent scholarship on the Irish constitutional system shows renewed appreciation of the democratic problems with constitutional review: T. Hickey, 'Revisiting *Ryan v. Lennon* to Make the Case against Judicial Supremacy (And

for a New Model of Constitutionalism in Ireland)' (2015) 53 *Irish Jurist* 125; Daly, Chapter 2, this volume.
5 The most eloquent account of the courts protecting the processes of democracy remains J. Hart Ely, *Democracy and Distrust: A Theory of Judicial Review* (Harvard UP, 1980).
6 D. Kyritsis, 'Constitutional Review in Representative Democracy' (2012) 32 *OJLS* 1, 3, 22–24.
7 M. Dorf and S. Issacharoff, 'Can Process Theory Constrain the Courts?' (2001) 72 *U Colo L Rev* 923 p. 925 suggest 'informed and balanced criticism of judicial overreaching' as a subtle mechanism for deterring judges from straying from independence.
8 [1984] IR 268 (SC).
9 [1984] IR 268, 275.
10 Following the Supreme Court's ruling in the *1983 Bill case* a referendum was held and Article 16.1.2° was amended with 'such other persons in the State as may be determined by law' added to 'citizens' as being entitled to vote.
11 [1984] IR 268, 274.
12 See *King v. Minister for the Environment (No. 2)* [2007] 1 IR 296, 320–321.
13 [2001] 4 IR 61.
14 [2007] 1 IR 296.
15 [2001] 4 IR 61, 78.
16 [2007] 1 IR 296 (SC).
17 [2007] 1 IR 296, 320.
18 S. Issacharoff, 'Constitutional Courts and Democratic Hedging' (2011) 99 *Georgetown Law Journal* 961, at 971 (emphasis added).
19 [1961] IR 114 (HC).
20 [2008] 3 IR 438 (HC).
21 [2010] IEHC 369.
22 [1984] IR 277 (HC) (SC).
23 [2000] 3 I R 467 (HC); [2001] 3 IR 230 (SC).
24 [1972] IR 69 (HC) (SC).
25 Rules 38 and 39 in Part I of the Fifth Schedule of the 1923 Act as inserted by s. 26, Electoral Act 1963.
26 [1972] IR 69, 102–103.
27 This is the basic point made in Justice McLoughlin's dissent in *McMahon v. Attorney General* [1972] IR 69, 119–120.
28 [1986] 1 IR 143 (HC).
29 [1986] 1 IR 143, 153.
30 [1984] IR 277 (HC) (SC).
31 [2000] 3 I R 467 (HC); [2001] 3 IR 230 (SC).
32 [2001] 3 IR 230, 238–239.
33 [1995] 2 IR 10, 53–54, *per* Denham J.
34 The Electoral (Amendment) (No. 2) Act 1986 facilitated postal voting for disabled persons for all relevant elections. The main provision regulating the matter now is s. 17, Electoral Act 1992, as amended.

35 Electoral (Amendment) Act 2006. This statute was enacted after the European Court of Human Rights indicated that prisoners not facilitated to vote was incompatible with the ECHR: *Hirst v. United Kingdom* [2005] ECHR 681.
36 *O'Donovan v. Attorney General* [1961] IR 114 (HC).
37 *Colgrove v. Green* (1946) 328 US 549 said the disproportioned electoral districts question was nonjusticiable. *Baker v. Carr* (1962) 369 US 186 marked the turning point on justiciability and *Wesberry v. Sanders* (1964) 376 US 1 and *Reynolds v. Sims* (1964) 377 US 533 started the redistricting.
38 The Electoral (Amendment) Act 1959 set out the invalidated electoral scheme.
39 [1961] IR 114, 135–136.
40 *Ibid.*, 137.
41 *Ibid.*, 138.
42 *Ibid.*, 137.
43 *Ibid.*, 134.
44 *Ibid.*, 138.
45 *Murphy v. Minister for the Environment* [2008] 3 IR 438, 446–447.
46 *O'Donovan v. Attorney General* [1961] IR 114, *O'Malley v. An Taoiseach* [1990] ILRM 461, *Murphy v. Minister for the Environment* [2008] 3 IR 438.
47 *In re Article 26 of the Constitution and the Electoral (Amendment) Bill 1961* [1961] IR 169, 183.
48 *O'Malley v. An Taoiseach* [1990] ILRM 461.
49 In *re Article 26 of the Constitution and the Electoral (Amendment) Bill, 1961* [1961] IR 169, 181, *Murphy v. Minister for the Environment* [2008] 3 IR 438, 466–467.
50 *Murphy v. Minister for the Environment* [2008] 3 IR 438, 457.
51 *Ibid.*, 469–470.
52 s. 5, Electoral Act 1997, as amended by s. 9, Electoral (Amendment) Act 2009; 2011 saw the new approach come in to practice.
53 [1961] IR 114, 126.
54 *Ibid.*
55 M. McConnell, 'The Redistricting Cases: Original Mistakes and Current Consequences' (2000) 24 *Harvard Journal of Law and Public Policy* 103, 112. Note that Ireland's multi-member constituencies are less vulnerable to gerrymandering than the US's single member districts.
56 [1961] IR 169 (SC).
57 [2008] 3 IR 438 (HC).
58 *Ibid.*, 464.
59 *Ibid.*, 463.
60 *Ibid.*, 464.
61 [2010] IEHC 369.
62 Kearns P.'s emphasis in quoting Article 16.7 of the Constitution.
63 Article 3 of Protocol 1, ECHR.
64 s. 2, European Convention on Human Rights Act 2003.
65 See D. Prendergast, 'By-elections and the Filling of Dáil Vacancies within a

Reasonable Time – A Note on *Doherty v. Ireland*' (2011) 34 *Dublin University Law Journal* 242.

66 s. 2, Electoral (Amendment) Act 2011 substituted a new ss 2A into s. 39, Electoral Act 1992. The criticism in Prendergast (*ibid.*) was overstated in saying that the High Court had precluded the Oireachtas from choosing a rule on the timeframe; clearly a specific rule (six months, or another period) can be enacted on top of the flexible constitutional standard of a reasonable time.

67 D. Budd, 'Electoral Law, Referenda, and the Courts: "Treading Delicately"' in J. Sarkin and W. Binchy (eds), *Human Rights, the Citizen and the State – South African and Irish Perspectives* (Round Hall, 2001) 117–139.

17

Social and economic rights in the Irish courts and the potential for constitutionalisation

Claire-Michelle Smyth

Introduction

In recent years, the momentum to judicially protect social and economic rights has grown in national, regional and international spheres. Debates evident during the transposition of the Universal Declaration of Human Rights centred on the status of social and economic rights, resulting in a division of the rights, has largely been concluded.[1] Contemporary considerations focus on how these rights should be protected, or, more appropriately, what role, if any, the judiciary should play.[2]

The theory that the most appropriate and effect manner in which to protect these rights is through constitutionalisation, elevating them to a status comparable to their civil and political counterparts is gaining dominance.[3] This is evidenced through the emergence of a trend towards constitutionalising social and economic rights internationally, regionally and domestically. In international terms, the Optional Protocol to the International Covenant on Economic Social and Cultural Rights bridges a significant gap by creating the first international forum where violations of social and economic rights may be heard.[4] While there are criticisms of this system, particularly in terms of its enforcement mechanisms, the same can equally be applied to the system of protection afforded to civil and political rights.[5] This elevates the protection of social and economic rights to a level comparable with that of their civil and political counterparts. Within regional systems, the European Court of Human Rights has indirectly given life to social and economic rights by expansively interpreting the textual rights of the European Convention.[6] The Inter-American Court has taken a similar approach by interpreting the Inter-American Convention in a harmonious manner with the American Declaration of Human and Peoples Rights,[7] and the African Commission has interpreted certain textual social and economic rights to include other non-specified rights.[8]

Within national systems India, South Africa and Canada have garnered significant attention for constitutionalising social and economic rights. While these are the three foremost jurisdictions, there is evidence of a growing trend in national systems. More recent constitutions such as that of South Africa are beginning to incorporate specific protection for social and economic rights. The Croatian Constitution,[9] the Charter of Fundamental Rights and Freedoms of the Czech Republic, which is justiciable under article 4 of Constitution of the Czech Republic,[10] the Constitution of Finland,[11] the Constitution of Moldova,[12] the Constitution of Hungary[13] the Constitution of Poland[14] the Constitution of Serbia[15] and the Swiss Constitution[16] provide express protection for various social and economic rights and for their enforcement through the court. Others have begun to expansively interpret existing rights to protect social and economic rights in line with the reasoning of the Indian and Canadian courts. In Latin America, several states have made significant moves to protect these rights, including making orders with significant cost effects. In Argentina, the court in the *Viceconte* case[17] interpreted existing constitutional provisions in light of obligations under the ICESCR to indirectly constitutionalise the right to health.[18] Brazil has recognised the justiciability of social and economic rights, in particular the rights to education and health,[19] with more HIV / AIDS sufferers receiving treatment due to court orders than government treatment programs.[20] Similar approaches have been taken in Colombia[21] Costa Rica[22] and Venezuela among others.[23]

The status of social and economic rights in Ireland was solidified by the Supreme Court judgment in *TD v. Minister for Education*,[24] which confirms them as non-justiciable rights. Continued support for this positing is declining with the Constitutional Convention recently voting, with an overwhelming majority, in favour of an explicit insertion of specific social and economic rights into the text of the Constitution.[25]

With this emerging trend towards judicial intervention, coupled with the clear desire to see such in Ireland, this chapter seeks to identify the avenues for constitutionalisation without the need for express incorporation by way of referendum. Beginning with an overview of the case which cements the status of social and economic rights in the Irish Constitutional order, this chapter examines the potential of reinvigorating the doctrine of unspecified rights, utilising the power of Article 45 and analysing the legitimacy of the Supreme Court's reasoning to refuse judicial intervention.

TD v. Minister for Education: a brief overview

The position of social and economic rights in Ireland is governed by the Supreme Court judgment in *TD v. Minister for Education*.[26] This judgment relates to an appeal brought by the state against a mandatory order made in the High Court.[27] TD was the first named applicant seeking a mandatory injunction compelling the state to provide the urgent treatment that he, and others, required in a secure residential unit.[28] In granting the order, the High Court had particular regard to the ongoing nature of the violations, which had previously been identified.[29] Further, it observed that the mandatory order of a similar nature previously granted had not been appealed and had in fact been complied with.[30] The order was appealed to the Supreme Court, where it effectively had the choice of two High Court decisions to endorse.[31]

In the High Court case of TD detailed plans were presented to the court outlining additional facilities and detailing access to these services.[32] Lengthy adjournments had previously been granted on the basis of these plans however, they were not implemented, resulting in a 'scandalous situation that has now obtained for years'.[33] Kelly J. set down four considerations in determining whether or not a mandatory injunction should issue in such cases:

> Whether a declaratory order has already been granted in a case of this type affording the government an opportunity to put matters right;
> (a) The need to act quickly in order to secure rights to applicants before they attain the age of majority and lose their entitlement to those rights;
> (b) The effect of a failure to provide the appropriate facilities on the lives of those who are entitled to them (including risk of harm);
> (c) Due regard is to be had to the efforts of the government to address the difficulties to date, if all reasonable efforts have been made then normally no order of this type should be made.[34]

The conditions established are quite restrictive and clearly only apply in the most extreme cases where other remedies had been tried, leaving the primary responsibility with the executive. Referring to the separation of powers, Justice Kelly suggested that the doctrine was not absolute and where the choice before the court is observing the separation of powers or vindicating a constitutional right it should always choose the latter.

Rather than endorsing this test, the majority of the Supreme Court relied on the reasoning espoused by Justice Costello in the earlier case of *O'Reilly v. Limerick Corporation*.[35] This case was brought by members of the Travelling community who resided in unofficial halting sites in a situation of extreme poverty and deprivation. Their claim was that the state had an obligation to provide them with a minimum standard of living, including access to sanitation. Justice Costello found that this matter was a non-justiciable political one, which involved distributive justice and not commutative justice. Justice Costello relied heavily on the distinction between the two in concluding the case:

> What could be involved in the exercise of the suggested jurisdiction would be the imposition by the Court of its view that there had been an unfair distribution of national resources. To arrive at such a conclusion it would have to make an assessment of the validity of the many competing claims on those resources ... in exercising those functions the Court would not be administering justice as it does when determining an issue relating to commutative justice, but it would be involved in an entirely different exercise, namely an adjudication of fairness or otherwise of the manner in which other organs of the State had administered public resources.[36]

While, somewhat paradoxically affirming that the Constitution exhibits concepts of distributive justice,[37] Justice Costello refused the adjudicate the claim determining that the court was not in a position to make determinations on competing state resources and, in the absence of legislation conferring such power, it remained entirely within the remit of the Oireachtas.[38] The Supreme Court in relying on this determination conveniently overlooked the fact that Justice Costello had subsequently publicly[39] and judicially resiled from this position.[40]

In determining the case of *TD* and in establishing the precedent that the court could not vindicate cases of social and economic rights former Chief Justice Keane doubted as to whether the courts should declare 'what are frequently described as socio-economic rights' as unspecified rights under Article 40.[41] Justice Murray also confirmed that there is no obligation on the state to provide, or on a citizen to receive medical and social services as a constitutional obligation. He went further to state that the failure to include social and economic rights in the various referenda showed a conscious decision to exclude them from constitutional protection.[42]

Justice Hardiman was of the opinion that relief for cases such as this ought to be sought in Leinster House and not the Four Courts.[43] He reiterates reasons already espoused in his judgment in *Sinnott v. Minister for Education* as to why the courts should not engage with issues of a social and economic nature:

> Firstly, to do so would offend the constitutional separation of powers. Secondly, it would lead the courts into the taking of decisions in areas in which they have no special qualifications or experience. Thirdly, it would

permit the courts to take such decisions even though they are not, and cannot be, democratically responsible for them as the legislature and the executive are. Fourthly, the evidence based adversarial procedures of the court, which are excellently adapted for the administrative of commutative justice, are too technical, too expensive, too focused on the individual issue to be an appropriate method for deciding on issues of policy.[44]

In addition, Hardiman fears that judicial involvement would downgrade the power of the political arms of the state and involve the court in politics.[45]

As such the majority of the Supreme Court agreed that these rights should remain firmly non-justiciable, however they do not appear able to advance a cohesive reason as to why that is. This decision was not unanimous and in her dissenting judgment, the now Chief Justice Denham took the position that policy considerations which would require expenditure is not adequate reason to abdicate judicial responsibility in deciding an issue, reasoning more in line with the High Court judgment.[46] The Supreme Court decision in *TD* is overwhelmingly harmful to the protection of rights as it does not limit the right on grounds of practicality or proportionality as had been done in the past, but rather fetters the power of the judiciary in granting a remedy for the violation of rights.[47] The developing line of jurisprudence in the High Court relating to these types of cases was abruptly halted by this decision. It was accepted that there may be certain exceptional circumstances[48] in which it would intervene, however its failure to clarify precisely the contours of this exception further hampers the development of this area.[49] Subsequent cases seeking mandatory orders must fall within the narrow exception accepted by the Supreme Court to succeed.[50] The elusive 'exceptional circumstances' sets an excessively high barrier.[51]

The doctrine of unenumerated rights

One way in which social and economic rights could be constitutionalised is through a reinvigoration of the doctrine of unenumerated rights. This doctrine in the Irish context arose from an expansive interpretation of Article 40.3, where the court determined that it ultimately had jurisdiction to determine what rights were protected.[52] Yet, the fact that there is no reference to unenumerated rights within the text of the document itself makes their development one of judicial activism.[53] The inception of this doctrine is credited to the dictum of Justice Kenny in the landmark case of *Ryan v. AG*, which challenged the constitutionality of compulsory fluoridation of water, upheld in the Supreme Court, in which he stated: 'I think that the personal rights which may be involved to invalidate legislation are not confined to those specified in Article 40 but include all those rights which result from the Christian and democratic nature of the State.'[54]

This hitherto dormant power of the court was the catalyst for the most innovative feature of our Constitutional law,[55] the importance of which is significant.[56] However it has been argued that there is no logical reasoning to Ryan, that the decision is fundamentally flawed and that at no time did the drafters envisage Art 40.3 protecting a cache of unspecified rights,[57] a 'supertextual' development in excess of the jurisdiction of the court.[58]

While ultimately unsuccessful in her claim, the declaration of the unspecified right to bodily integrity spurred a period of judicial activism with the court discerning the existence of new fundamental rights. Among these rights the right to privacy,[59] the right to earn a livelihood,[60] the right to travel,[61] the rights to marry, and, found a family,[62] the right to fair procedures were declared.[63]

Despite the clear link with many of the unenumerated rights, social and economic rights have not been classified as such. Cases such as *Ryan v. Attorney General*[64] and *McGee v. Attorney General*[65] which created the unenumerated rights to bodily integrity and privacy respectively, had strong links with the right to health, although not framed them in those terms.[66] What appeared to be a declaration of unspecified rights to health and adequate housing where Justice O'Flaherty opined that it was 'beyond debate that there is a hierarchy of constitutional rights and at the top of that list is the right to life, followed by the right to health and with that the right to the integrity of one's dwelling house' has remained relatively undeveloped with unclear parameters.[67]

An explanation for this may lie in the fact that support for the judicial activism which followed the Ryan case was decidedly waning within the judiciary by the time cases involving social and economic rights fell to be decided.[68] Not only was the court loath to declare new unspecified rights, but it was also extremely reluctant to expand existing express or implied rights. The declaration of new unspecified rights was cautioned against in *TD v. Minister for Education* where it was opined that: 'Save where such an unenumerated right has been unequivocally established by precedent, as, for example, in the case of the right to travel or the right to privacy, some degree of judicial restraint is called for in identifying new rights of this nature.'[69] Further, he contends that even those who are in agreement with the decision of Ryan would agree that judicial restraint is required in order to preserve the 'delicate balance' of the separation of powers.[70]

Despite the criticisms directed towards the doctrine for its lack of clarity, placing social and economic rights within the broader concepts of justice and dignity, there appears to be an inherent argument for their inclusion as unspecified rights. Justice Kenny in *Ryan* explicitly referred to natural law in coming to his conclusion and stated that rights which flowed from the 'Christian and democratic nature of the state' should fall to be protected.[71] The concept of natural law became a recurring theme in constitutional cases, these concepts, vague as they were, have been seen as part of Ireland's rebellion against the positivist approach of the UK system.[72] Interpreted as having religious, specifically Catholic, meaning initially, the decline in influence of the church coincided with a decline in the use of natural law.[73] However natural law, morals or ethics do not necessarily require a religious connotation.[74] It recognises that there are certain rights antecedent to positive law, which could equally be interpreted as deriving from 'the nature of man and society',[75] or through concepts of justice, prudence and charity values which may 'be conditioned by the passage of time in light of prevailing ideas and concepts'.[76]

Given the strong influence of Christian democracy on the Constitution which recognises social and economic rights as 'indispensable to the common good',[77] the argument to include them as unspecified rights is strong,[78] should the will exist.[79]

The potential of Article 45

The placement of social and economic rights specifically within the non-justiciable clause of the Constitution is viewed as another stumbling block to justiciability.[80] However, despite the lack of explicit protection, Article 45 does present an opportunity for indirect constitutionalisation.[81] The potential of using this article to indirectly give effect to other rights is evidenced in *Murtagh Properties Ltd v. Cleary*.[82] Here, Justice Kenny held that the preamble to Article 45 does not 'involve the conclusion that the courts may not take [this article] into consideration when deciding whether a claimed constitutional right exists'.[83]

Thus this provision is not legally irrelevant and can be used to interpret the content and existence of other rights, and further can assist in the interpretation of legislation.[84]

Former Chief Justice Keane has referred to Article 45 as a 'particular problem' in relation to the judicial determination of social and economic rights in Ireland.[85] In agreement with this sentiment, Justice Niall Fennelly distinguishes between legal rights and desirable policy. Legal rights, he states, infer a corresponding obligation cognisable in law, declared in objective legal terms by the text of law, while policy is for the politicians and is not justiciable, save where such conflict with legally justiciable rights.[86] Thus these vague concepts seeking to guide the politicians in their policy making[87] serve no more than pious aspirations[88] remain beyond the purview of the courts.[89]

The potential of Article 45 to indirectly constitutionalise social and economic rights can be demonstrated by considering the Indian Supreme Court's interpretation of an identical provision. Article 37[90] of the Indian Constitution was inspired by the Irish Constitution's Article 45.[91] However, the 'particular problem' which perplexes Keane does not seem to have the same effect on the Indian judiciary, who has utilised them to interpret and expand existing textual fundamental rights.[92] The Supreme Court has continually expanded the right to life to include social and economic rights, holding that it entails a 'right to live with human dignity and all that goes along with it'.[93] In *Olga Tellis v. Bombay* Chief Justice Chandrachud observed that it would be 'sheer pedantry to exclude the right to livelihood from the content of the right to life'.[94]

It is briefly worth noting that the court has used this interpretation to uphold compulsory purchase orders of private land to provide housing for poverty stricken classes,[95] the right to health,[96] emergency health care,[97] adequate emergency healthcare,[98] and the right to food.[99] Not only has the Supreme Court identified the rights that are protected by an expansive interpretation of the right to life, but it has placed positive obligations on the state to ensure that such rights are vindicated and protected. This is a position which however has not found favour within the Irish judiciary to date. While retaining the option, and the ability, to use Article 45 to interpret existing provisions in a manner conducive to the constitutionalisation of social and economic rights, it remains unlikely given the current composition of the Supreme Court[100] who appear to follow the view that 'poverty is a misfortune for which the law cannot take any responsibility at all'.[101]

Distributive justice and the separation of powers

The Irish Supreme Court has primarily justified its refusal to adjudicate on social and economic rights on the basis of the separation of powers doctrine; in that, to engage with matters of distributive justice is to go beyond its sanctioned function.

The Constitution itself does not mention the phrase 'separation of powers', rather Article 6 acknowledges three separate and distinct limbs of the state: the executive, the legislature and the judiciary. The court has explained that the: 'Separation of Powers involves for each of the three constitutional organs not only rights but duties also, not only areas of activities and functions but boundaries to them as well with regard to the legislature the right and duty of the Court to intervene is clear and express.'[102] Despite the court acknowledging that it has not only a role, but a duty to intervene to protect the constitutional rights of individuals,[103] the position is that they should not revisit the current doctrine of separation of powers in order to address violations of social and economic rights.[104] The separation of powers has been interpreted in a rigid manner – one, which is inflexible and precisely delineated.[105]

In essence, the central contention then becomes that cases which involve distributive justice breach the separation of powers doctrine. [106] They are, as such beyond the scope of the judicial review and enforcement. The reason for this, according to Gerard Hogan, is that social and economic rights are resource dependent whereas civil and political rights are not.[107] This evidences the continuing and fundamental misconception by the Irish judiciary as to the cost implications surrounding the protection of rights, effective conservation of all fundamental rights necessarily requires both positive and negative obligations.[108]

On a more extensive examination of the separation of powers doctrine, it is apparent that the rigid interpretation as determined by the Irish courts is not the sole method of interpretation. Alternative understanding of this doctrine could be based on the Catholic ethos of the Constitution[109] or more generally, on accountability and justification.[110] This is supported by doctrine's purpose as one based on protecting the citizen from state tyranny, where all power is vested in one organ of the state.[111] Unlike the austere position taken in Ireland, it has been argued that a central feature of the doctrine is that its boundaries are flexible and undetermined,[112] with any stringent features mostly ameliorated by the 'checks and balances' system introduced.[113] The most common form of such checks and balances in action is the judicial review of executive and legislative decisions.[114]

As the courts are the sole body with the power to administer justice[115] they have determined that the supremacy of the Constitution trumps the separation of powers.[116] Thus where the executive or legislature has exceeded its power the court retains the ability to nullify the action. The issue with certain social and economic rights is the inaction of the state and whether the court has the power to compel action, rather than merely prohibit. To this end it has been categorically determined that issues involving distributive justice cannot be adjudicated upon as such would breach the separation of powers. Arguably, by remitting an entire cache of rights from judicial review it is giving sole power to one branch of state, creating a situation that the doctrine of separation of powers was designed to prohibit. Such an uncompromising application of the doctrine weakens judicial review to the 'point of futility'.[117]

The argument that the court cannot engage in distributive justice shows a flawed understanding of the difference between distributive and commutative or corrective justice and it has in several cases blurred the lines between the two, undermining the cogency of its reasoning.[118]

The case of *Magee v. Farrell* considered the provisions of civil legal aid,[119] for representation at an inquest into a death in custody.[120] In the High Court Justice Gilligan found fair procedures guaranteed under the Constitution required the state to provide legal aid in these circumstances.[121] The Supreme Court unanimously overturned the decision of the High Court, ending speculation over the precise advancement of legal aid for civil matters, and held that civil legal aid will only be available within the parameters of the Civil Legal Aid Act 1995.[122]

Some three months later, a case relating to criminal legal aid came before the Supreme Court. The Appellant in *Carmody v. Minister for Justice, Equality and Law Reform* argued that the right to legal aid extended to him an entitlement to be represented by a barrister in addition to a solicitor in a District Court case.[123] Under the Act,[124] a District Court Judge has no power to appoint a barrister save in the exceptional circumstances where the accused is charged with murder.[125] The accused had been charged with 42 offences in what was a relatively complex case, wherein the state was using a specialist barrister to prosecute the matter. The Applicant was unsuccessful in the High Court and appealed the decision to the Supreme Court. Therein it was noted that the right to legal aid in criminal cases was a constitutional right, and the Act was merely a means of vindicating that right. Ultimately it held that criminal law had changed drastically since the enactment of the legislation and that the complexity of the case was something that the Judge should be able to consider. It also noted that where the prosecution was represented by a barrister, this could be a relevant factor in determining the type of representation that was appropriate for the defendant.[126]

The *Carmody* case illustrates that the courts have no issue in ordering what amounts to distributive justice where they feel that the right in question is significant enough, and what the Supreme Court did in this case was, in essence, to engage in distributive justice. Arguments that resource implications are secondary in cases involving civil and political rights are misnomers.[127] This ruling ensures that accused persons have the right to apply,[128] for the assistance of counsel in addition to a solicitor in District Court matters. Where this is granted, it will involve significant costs to the state. Even where it is not granted, the application process and potential appeal to its refusal will cost, and this is something clearly not considered apposite to the discussion of fundamental rights.

Equally, the very recent Supreme Court decision in *DPP v. Gormley* determined that an accused has the right of access to a solicitor prior to questioning by Gardai.[129] Prior to this ruling, the access rights of an accused to a solicitor in Garda custody was defined as 'reasonable access'[130] and this was interpreted restrictively.[131] This extension of the right to access a solicitor prior to questioning is clearly engaging in distributive justice, particularly in circumstances where the legal advice is being provided through the system of legal aid. It remains to be seen the exact parameters of this extension, however its implications are apparent.

Hogan's argument that resource implications are secondary in vindications of civil and political rights when viewed through the prism of the above cases shows the arbitrary and nonsensical nature of the distinction.[132] In vindicating the right to a fair trial in criminal procedures it was declared in Carmody that the complete exclusion of the ability to appoint a barrister was unconstitutional, while in Magee the complete exclusion of legal aid for inquests into death was not. Hogan's argument would be that the court in Carmody was not ordering the state to provide for a barrister in all cases in the District Court but merely that the judge would have the ability to appoint one should the case require it. Resource implications would be secondary as one would only be appointed where the seriousness of the case warranted it, and where existing criteria for the grant of legal aid had been met. This could equally be applied to Magee. The resource implications would only arise in circumstances where existing criteria for the grant of legal aid had been met, and is not a blanket guarantee that all cases of this nature would be provided with state funded legal aid.

The strict interpretation of distributive justice as a bar to justiciability appears to be losing some traction, in the High Court at least. In disagreeing with the state's contention that that the court could not entertain claims of distributive justice it determined that where: 'State action results in a breach of human rights and where the only remedy is the expenditure of additional money, the Court, in my opinion, must be entitled to make an appropriate order, even if the consequence is that the State must spend money to meet the terms of that order.'[133]

The stark inconsistency with which the court has interpreted obligations on the state involving distributive justice undermines their position in relation to social and economic rights. If it is to apply this argument, it should do so in a consistent manner. The reality, as outlined above, is that it does engage in distributive justice in order to vindicate constitutionally protected rights. Should it then directly or indirectly recognise social and economic rights as fundamental rights, this distributive justice argument becomes impertinent. Further should a given case seek to assert negative obligations on the state, the argument becomes fruitless.

Conclusion

The law must develop with societal changes. It is clear from national and international movements that judicial protection is the most effective way to protect and vindicate social and economic rights. As such the Irish courts need to re-evaluate their stance and embrace the value of social and economic rights and to actively engage with their obligation to protect and vindicate the personal rights of the citizen. In the absence of a referendum specifically incorporating social and economic rights there are a number of ways in which the court could bring these rights within their remit. Through reinvigorating the doctrine of unspecified rights, utilising Article 45 to read these rights into existing provisions akin to the Indian courts, or simply an acknowledgment that they do engage in distributive justice could all result in meaningful judicial engagement.

Notes

1 P. Alston and R. Goodman, *International Human Rights, The Successor to International Human Rights in Context* (OUP, 2013) pp. 277–284; E. Wiles, 'Aspirational Principles or Enforceable Rights? The Future for Socio Economic Rights in National Law' (2006) 22(1) *American University International Law Review* 35.
2 See P. O'Connell, *Vindicating Social Rights* (Routledge 2012); C. Gearty and V. Mantouvalou, *Debating Social Rights* (Hart, 2011); K. Young, *Constituting Economic and Social Rights* (OUP, 2012); J. King, *Judging Social Rights* (CUP, 2012).
3 P. O'Connell, *Vindicating Social Rights* (Routledge 2012); C. O'Cinneide 'The Constitutionalization of Social and Economic Rights' in H. A. Garcia, K. Klare and L. Williams (eds), *Social and Economic Rights in Theory and in Practice: Critical Enquiries* (Routledge, 2014).
4 Resolution of the Human Rights Council 8/2 of 18 June 2008 adopted by the General Assembly under resolution A/RES/63/117 10 December 2008, entered into force 5 May 2013. For a detailed analysis of the background to the drafting of the Optional Protocol, see C. Mahon, 'Progress at the Front: The Draft Optional Protocol to the International Covenant on Economic Social and Cultural Rights' (2008) 8(4) *Human Rights Law Review* 617; T. Melish, 'Introductory Note to the Optional Protocol to the International Covenant on

Economic Social and Cultural Right' (2009) 48 *International Legal Materials* 256; S. Leckie, 'Another Step Towards Indivisibility: Identifying Key Features of Violations of Economic, Social and Cultural Rights' (1998) 20 *Human Rights Quarterly* 81.

5 See A. Vandenbogaerde and W. Vandenhole, 'The Optional Protocol to the International Covenant on Economic Social and Cultural Rights: An Ex Ante Assessment of Its Effectiveness in Light of the Drafting Process' (2010) 10(2) *Human Rights Law Review* 207; L. Chenwi, 'Correcting the Historical Asymmetry between Rights: The Optional Protocol to the International Covenant on Economic Social and Cultural Rights' (2009) 9(1) *African Human Rights Law Journal* 23; B. Simmons, 'Should States Ratify? – Process and Consequences of the Optional Protocol to the ICESCR (2009) 27(1) *Nordic Journal of Human Rights* 66.

6 See E. Koch, *Human Rights as Indivisible Rights: The Protection of Socio-Economic Demands under the European Convention on Human Rights* (Martinus Nijhoff 2009); C. O'Cinneide, 'A Modest Proposal: Destitution, State Responsibility and the European Convention on Human Rights' (2008) 5 *European Human Rights Law Review* 583; E. Palmer, 'Protecting Socio-Economic Rights through the European Convention on Human Rights: Trends and Developments in the European Court of Human Rights' (2009) 2(4) *Erasmus Law Review* 397.

7 T. Melish, *Protecting Economic Social and Cultural Rights in the Inter American Human Rights System* (Yale Law School, 2002).

8 *Social and Economic Rights Action Centre (SERAC) and the Center for Economic and Social Rights (CESR) v. Nigeria* Communication No. 155/96; Justice C. Nwobike, 'The African Commission on Human and People's Rights and the Demystification of second and Third Generation Rights under the African Charter: *Social and Economic Rights Action Centre (SERAC) and the Center for Economic and Social Rights (CESR) v. Nigeria*' (2005) 2 *African Journal of Legal Studies* 129; C. Heyns 'The African Regional Human Rights System: The African Charter' (2004) 108(3) *Pennsylvania State Law Review* 681.

9 Entered into force on 22 December 1990 and protects the Right to Social Assistance (Article 58), the Right to Healthcare (Articles 59 and 70) and the Right to Education (Article 66).

10 Entered into force 1 January 1993 and protects the Right to Social Assistance (Article 30), the Right to Health (Article 31) and the Right to Education (Article 33).

11 Entered into force 1 March 2000 and protects the Right to Social Security and Housing Assistance (Section 19) and the Right to Education (Section 16).

12 Entered into force 29 July 1994 and protects the Right to Education (Article 35), The Right of Health Security (Article 36), The Right to Life in a Healthy Environment (Article 37) and the Right to Social Assistance to include food, clothing, shelter and medical care (Article 47).

13 Entered into force 25 April 2011 and protects the Right to Education (Article

XI), Social Security (Article XIX) The Right to Health (Article XX), the Right to Decent Housing Conditions (Article XXII).
14 Entered into force 2 April 1997 and protects the Right to Health (Article 68).
15 Entered into force 8 November 2006 and protects the Right to Health (Article 68), the Right to Education (Article 71) and Social Protection (Article 69).
16 Entered into force 18 April 1999 and protects the Right to Social Assistance (Article 12) and the Right to Basic Education (Article 19).
17 *Viceconte, Mariela Cecelia v. Argentinian Ministry of Health and Social Welfare* Case No. 31.777/96, 2 June 1998.
18 The Supreme Court has expanded this to require states make access to medical care available in a timely fashion; *Asociacion Benghalensis v. Ministry of Health and Social Welfare* Case No. 16.986, 13 August 2000.
19 These rights are textually recognised in Articles 6 and 196 of the Brazilian Constitution. Article 6 provides 'Education, health, nutrition, labour, housing, leisure, social security, protection of motherhood and childhood and assistance to the destitute are social rights as set forth in this constitution.' Article 196 states 'health is the right of all and the duty of the State and shall be guaranteed by social and economic policies aimed at reducing the risk of illness and other maladies by universal and equal access to all activities and services for its promotion, protection and recovery'.
20 O. Motta Ferraz, 'Harming the Poor Through Social Rights Litigation: Lessons from Brazil' (2011) 89 *Texas Law Review* 1643, 1651.
21 M. Cepeda-Espinoza, 'Transcript: Social and Economic Rights and the Colombian Constitutional Court' (2011) 89 *Texas Law Review* 1699.
22 B. Wilson, 'Rights Revolutions in Unlikely Places: Colombia and Costa Rica' (2009) 1 *Journal of Politics in Latin America* 59.
23 M. Langford, *Social Rights Jurisprudence: Emerging Trends in International and Comparative Law* (CUP, 2009) pt 1.
24 [2001] 4 IR 259.
25 Of the Convention, 85% voted for specific inclusion of social and economic rights. Full breakdown of the votes is available at www.constitution.ie/AttachmentDownload.ashx?mid=adc4c56a-a09c-e311–a7ce-005056a32ee4 (accessed 18 August 2015).
26 [2001] 4 IR 259.
27 [2000] 2 ILRM 321.
28 Also joined in the case were DB, MB, GD, PH, BJ, TL and ST.
29 *FN v. Minister for Education* [1995] 1 IR 419, *DG v. Eastern Health Board* [1997] 3 IR 511.
30 *DB v. Minister for Justice* [1999] 1 ILRM 93.
31 [2001] 4 IR 259.
32 In *DB v. Minister for Education* [1999] 1 IR 29 mandatory injunctions had been granted compelling the introduction of specialised facilities which was being complied with, but was confined to a certain geographical area. *TD* sought an order compelling an extension of these facilities geographically and numerically.

33 [2000] 2 ILRM 321, 334.
34 *Ibid.*, 84.
35 [1989] ILRM 181.
36 *Ibid.*, 195.
37 'I am sure that the concept of justice which is to be found in the Constitution embraces the concept that the nation's wealth should be justly distributed' (*ibid.*, 195).
38 C. McHugh, 'Socio Economic Rights in Ireland: Lessons to be Learned from South Africa and India' (2003) 4 *Hibernian Law Journal* 109, 113.
39 *Irish Times* (14 November 1998).
40 *O'Brien v. Wicklow UDC* unreported High Court 10 June 1994.
41 [2001] ILRM 259.
42 *Ibid.*, 316–317.
43 [2002] 4 IR 259, 357.
44 [2001] 2 IR 545, 710 reiterated in [2002] 4 IR 259, 361. The *Sinnott* case concerned considerations of the extent to which the right to primary education provided for in Article 42 could apply. Jamie Sinnott, an autistic man, argued through his mother that the right should extend as long as an individual can benefit from such education; a contention rejected by the Supreme Court who determined that any obligations on the state to provide for free primary education was termination when the individual attained the age of eighteen. See S. Quinlivan and M. Keyes, 'Official Indifference and Persistent Procrastination: An Analysis of Sinnott' (2002) 2(2) *Judicial Studies Institute Journal* 163; O. Doyle, 'The Duration of Primary Education; Judicial Constraint in Constitutional Interpretation' (2002) 10 *Irish Student Law Review* 222; G. Whyte, *Social Inclusion and the Legal System* (IPA, 2002).
45 [2002] 4 IR 259, 361.
46 [2002] 4 IR 259.
47 F. Kiernan 'TD Reconsidered; Constructing a New Approach to the Enforcement of Rights' (2004) 7 *Trinity College Law Review* 62.
48 A position reiterated in *Re Article 26 and the Health (Amendment) (No. 2) Bill 2004* [2005] IESC 7.
49 P. O'Connell, *Vindicating Socio-Economic Rights* (Routledge, 2012) 160.
50 *Ibid.*, 159.
51 Whyte (n. 44) p. 359.
52 Article 40.3.1 'The State guarantees in its laws to respect, and as far as practicable to vindicate the personal rights of the citizen.'
53 Unlike the American Constitution which expressly acknowledges the existence of unspecified rights. Amendment IX 'The enumeration in the Constitution of certain rights shall not be construed to deny or disparage others retained by the people.'
54 *Ryan v. AG* [1965] IR 294, 312.
55 B. Doolan, *Constitutional Law and Constitutional Rights in Ireland* (3rd edn, Gill & Macmillan, 1994) p. 156.

56 J. Casey, *Constitution Law in Ireland* (3rd edn, Thompson Round Hall, 2000) p. 386.
57 D. Clarke, 'Unenumerated Rights in Constitution Law' (2011) 34 *Dublin University Law Journal* 101, 116.
58 G. Carey, 'Police Targeting and Equality Rights' (2001) 19 *Irish Law Times* 8, 14; O. Molloy, 'Unenumerated Constitutional Rights: The Current Problematic Position' (2007) 3 *Galway Student Law Review* 209; D. Morgan, 'Judicial Activism – Too Much of a Good Thing?' in T. Murphy and P. Twomey (eds) *Ireland's Evolving Constitution 1937–1997* (Hart, 1998); G. Hogan, 'Unenumerated Personal Rights: Ryan's Case Re-evaluated' (1992) 25 *Irish Jurist* 95.
59 *McGee v. AG* [1974] IR 284; *Norris v. Ireland* [1984] IR 36.
60 First recognised by Kenny J. in *Murtagh Properties v. Cleary* [1972] IR 330.
61 In *Ryan v. AG* [1965] IR 294 a right to travel within the state was declared by Kenny J. and broadened by Finlay P in *State (M) v. AG* [1979] IR 73 to a right to travel outside the state and to obtain a passport for this purpose.
62 Recognised in *Ryan v. AG* [1965] IR 294; see also *Murray v. AG* [1985] IR 532.
63 *Garvey v. Ireland* [1981] IR 75 elevated the common law position of procedural fairness in decision making to an unenumerated right. Casey (n. 56) ch. 12; G. Hogan and G. Whyte, *JM Kelly; The Irish Constitution* (4th edn, Butterworths, 2003) 1389–1494; M. Forde and D. Leonard, *Constitutional Law of Ireland* (3rd edn, Bloomsbury Professional, 2013) ch. 12.
64 [1965] IR 294.
65 [1974] IR 284.
66 In *Ryan* the case dealt with a claim that fluoridation of drinking water would adversely affect her health. In while accepting and creating the unenumerated right to bodily integrity the plaintiff ultimately failed as she did not show sufficient evidence that the fluoridation would cause adverse effects to her health. Mrs McGee's challenge to a criminal prosecution for importing contraception was grounded on medical advice that a further pregnancy could endanger her health the Court accepted that the decision whether or not to reproduce would fall within the unenumerated right to marital privacy.
67 See *Re Art 26 and the Health (Amendment) (No. 2) Bill 2004* [2005] IESC 7 where the Supreme Court accepted that there may be particular circumstances where the state may have to maintain patients free of charge, however they rejected the argument of an entitlement to free healthcare.
68 See *O'T v. B* [1998] 2 IR 321 where Keane CJ opined that the absence of legislation did not justify the court intervening as they lacked the democratic mandate to do so.
69 [2001] 4 IR 259, 281.
70 R. Keane, 'Judges as Lawmakers: The Irish Experience' (2004) 4(2) *Judicial Studies Institute Journal* 1, 6.
71 [1965] IR 294, 312.

72 A. Kavanagh, 'The Irish Constitution at 75 Years: Natural Law, Christian Values and the Ideals of Justice' (2012) 2 *Irish Jurist* 71, 99.
73 For analysis of Natural Law in the Irish Constitution, see A. Greene, 'Natural Law and the Basic Norm of the Irish Constitution' (2012) 30 *Irish Law Times* 298; A. Keating, 'Natural Law and Natural Rights' (2013) 31(4) *Irish Law Times* 61; C. O'Connor, L. Kelly and E. McSwiney, 'Natural Law: A Bible for Judicial Reasoning?' (2012) 1 *Trinity College Law Review* 75; O. Doyle, 'Legal Positivism, Natural Law and the Constitution' (2009) 31 *Dublin University Law Journal* 206; R. J. O'Hanlon, 'Natural Rights and the Irish Constitution (1993) 11 *Irish Law Times* 8; T. Murphy, 'Democracy, Natural Law and the Irish Constitution' (1993) 11 *Irish Law Times* 81.
74 O. Molloy, 'Unenumerated Constitutional Rights: Current Problematic Position' (2007) 3 *Galway Student Law Review* 209, 222.
75 *Finn v. AG* [1983] IR 154.
76 *McGee v. AG* [1974] IR 284, 319.
77 G. Whyte, *Social Inclusion and the Legal System* (IPA, 2002) p. 361.
78 D. McGrattan, 'The Constitutional Vindication of Socio-Economic Rights: A Catholic Perspective' (2007) 7 *University College Dublin Law Review* 29, 42.
79 P. O'Connell, 'The Death of Socio-Economic Rights' (2011) 74 *Modern Law Review* 532, 540.
80 Referred to as a 'particular problem' by former Chief Justice Ronan Keane, 'Judges as Lawmakers: The Irish Experience' (2004) 4 *Judicial Studies Institute Journal* 1, 6.
81 J. O'Dowd, 'ESC Rights as Legal Rights' Conference on Economic, Social and Cultural Rights: Models of Enforcement (Irish Human Rights and Equality Commission, 9 December 2005). Full text available at www.ihrec.ie/publications/list/john-odowdesc-rights-as-legal-rights-9–december-20 (last accessed 4 April 2015).
82 [1972] IR 330.
83 *Ibid.*, 337.
84 M. Tushnet, 'Social Welfare Rights and the Forms of Judicial Review' (2004) 82 *Texas Law Review* 1895, 1989.
85 R. Keane, 'Judges as Lawmakers: The Irish Experience' (2004) 4 *Judicial Studies Institute Journal* 1, 6.
86 N. Fennelly, 'Judicial Decisions and Allocations of Resources' (2010) 23 *Advocate* 48, 48.
87 S. Yildirim, 'Expanding Secularism's Scope: In Indian Case Study' (2004) 52 *American Journal of Comparative Law* 901, 910.
88 G. Jacobsohn, 'The Permeability of Constitutional Borders' (2004) 82 *Texas Law Review* 1763, 1772.
89 As G. Hogan 'Directive Principles, Socio-Economic Rights and The Irish Constitution' (2001) 1 *Irish Jurist* 174, 196 points out that the Supreme Court have not given a definitive ruling on this issue. The cases of *Sinnott v. Minister for Education* [2001] 2 IR 545 and *TD v. Minister for Education* [2001] 4 IR 259 did not raise Article 45 in their claims.

90 Article 37 states: 'The Provisions contained in this part shall not be enforced by any Court, but the principles therein laid down are nevertheless fundamental in the governance of the country and shall be the duty of the State to apply these principles in making laws.'
91 J. Usman, 'Non-Justiciable Directive Principles: A Constitutional Design Defect' (2007) 15 *Michigan State Journal of International Law* 643, 647.
92 E. Keane, 'Socio-Economic Rights and National Law' (2008) 36(4) *Irish Law Times* 62.
93 *Francis Coralie v. Union of India* AIR 1981 AC 746.
94 AIR 1986 SC 180, 194.
95 *Chameli Singh v. State of Uttar Pradesh* (1996) 2 SCC 549.
96 *Consumer Education and Research Centre v. Union of India* AIR 1995 SC.
97 *Parmanand Katara v. Union of India* AIR 1989 SC 2039.
98 *Pascham Banga Khet Mazdoor Samity v. State of West Bengal* 1996 3 SCJ 25.
99 *Peoples Union for Civil Liberties v. Union of India* Writ No. 196/2001.
100 A. Nolan, 'Holding Non State Actors to Account for Constitutional Economic and Social Rights Violations: Experiences and Lessons from South Africa and Ireland' (2014) 12(1) *International Journal of Constitutional Law* 61, 72; A. Nolan, 'Ireland: The Separation of Powers Doctrine vs Socio-Economic Rights' in M. Langford (ed.), *Social Rights Jurisprudence: Emerging Trends in International and Comparative Law* (CUP, 2008) p. 319.
101 J. Cooper, 'Poverty and Constitutional Justice: The Indian Experience' (1993) 44(1) *Mercer Law Review* 611.
102 *Crotty v. An Taoiseach* [1987] ILRM 400 *per* Finlay CJ, 449.
103 *Ibid*.
104 S. Quinliven and M. Keyes 'Official Indifference and Persistent Procrastination: An Analysis of Sinnott' (2002) 2 *Judicial Studies Institute Journal* 163; N. Daly, 'Unenumerated Rights Reconsidered' (2007) 3 *Galway Student Law Review* 226, 230.
105 J. Wakely, 'Social and Economic Rights – A Retreat by the South African Constitutional Court' (2010) 28 *Irish Law Times* 153.
106 E. Keane, 'Socio-Economic Rights and National Law' (2008) 36 *Irish Law Times* 62.
107 G. Hogan, 'Directive Principles, Socio-Economic Rights and the Constitution' (2001) 179 *Irish Jurist* 1, 4.
108 C. Gearty and V. Mantouvalou, *Debating Social Rights* (Hart, 2011), p. 110; E. Wiles, 'Aspirational Principles or Enforceable Rights? The Future for Social and Economic Rights in National Law' (2006) 22 *American University International Law Review* 35, 47; S. Liebenberg, 'The International Covenant on Economic Social and Cultural Rights and Its Implication for South Africa' (1995) 11 *South African Journal of Human Rights* 359, 362.
109 G. Whyte, 'The Role of the Supreme Court in our Democracy: A Response to Mr Justice Hardiman' (2006) 28 *Dublin University Law Journal* 1, 4.
110 N. Haysom, 'Giving Effect to Socio-Economic Rights: The Role of the Judiciary' (1999) 1 *Economic and Social Rights Review* 11.

111 For analysis of this point, see D. Gwynn Morgan, *The Separation of Powers in the Irish Constitution* (Round Hall 1997); M. de Blacam, 'Children, Constitutional Rights and the Separation of Powers' (2002) 37 *Irish Jurist* 115; P. B. Kurland, 'The Rise and Fall of the "Doctrine" of Separation of Powers' (1986) 85 *Michigan Law Review* 592; B. Ackerman, 'The New Separation of Powers' (2000) 113 *Harvard Law Review* 634; M. Pieterse, 'Coming to Terms with Judicial Enforcement of Socio-Economic Rights' (2004) 20 *South African Journal on Human Rights* 383.
112 J. Cassels, 'Judicial Activism and Public Interest Litigation in India: Attempting the Impossible?' (1989) 37 *American Journal of Comparative Law* 495, 513.
113 As initially introduced in American Constitution Law, M. Pieterse, 'Coming to Terms with Judicial Enforcement of Socio-Economic Rights' (2004) 20 *South African Journal on Human Rights* 383, 386. See also E. Carolan, *The New Separation of Powers: A Theory for the Modern* State (OUP, 2009).
114 The Constitution provides for a tripartite split of executive, legislature and judiciary however the practicality of this is that the executive and the legislature have now merged and such division no longer exists. See D. Gwynn Morgan, 'Judicial-o-centric: Separation of Powers on the Wane?' (2004) 1 *Irish Jurist* 142 who argues that technically there are two: the judiciary and the 'political organs'.
115 Article 34.1 'Justice shall be administered in courts established by law by judges appointed in the manner prescribed by this Constitution, and, save in such special and limited circumstances as may be prescribed by law, shall be administered in public.'
116 *Crotty v. An Taoiseach* [1987] IR 713; *McKenna v. An Taoiseach (No. 2)* [2003] 2 IR 10; *McCrystal v. Minister for Children and Youth Affairs* [2013] ILRM 217.
117 T. R. S. Allan, 'Human Rights and Judicial Review: A Critique of Due Deference' (2006) 65 *Cambridge Law Journal* 671, 677.
118 G. Whyte, 'A Tale of Two Cases – Divergent Approaches of the Irish Supreme Court to Distributive Justice' (2010) 1 *Dublin University Law Journal* 365.
119 [2009] ILRM 453.
120 This particular area was not covered in the Civil Legal Aid Act 1995 and therefore her claim was based on a constitutional right to legal aid.
121 [2005] IEHC 388.
122 Relying on the case of *O'Donoghue v. Legal Aid Board* [1976] IR 325 the Court held that the constitutional right was to have the Act administered in a fair way and not to infer a right to legal aid based on the unspecified right of access to the Courts contained within Art 40.
123 [2010] 1 ILRM 157.
124 s. 2(1)(b), Criminal Justice (Legal Aid) Act 1962 provides: 'If it appears to the District Court ... (b) that by reason of the gravity of the charge or of exceptional circumstances it is essential in the interest of justice that [a person charged before it] should have legal aid in the preparation and conduct of his defence before it, the Court shall, on application being made to it in that behalf,

grant in respect of him a certificate for free legal aid (in this Act referred to as a legal aid (District Court) certificate) and thereupon he shall be entitled to such aid and to have a solicitor and (where he is charged with murder and the Court thinks fit) Counsel assigned to him for that purpose in such manner as may be prescribed by regulations under S 10 of this Act.'

125 This exception was made redundant by the Criminal Justice Act 1999 which abolishes the preliminary examination procedure in the District Court for murder charges. This was pointed out by Murray J. in *Carmody v. Minister for Justice, Equality and Law Reform* [2010] 1 ILRM 157, 161.
126 [2010] 1 ILRM 157 at 181–182.
127 G. Hogan, 'Directive Principles, Socio-economic Rights and the Constitution' (2001) 179 *Irish Jurist* 1, 5.
128 Not an automatic entitlement.
129 [2014] IESC 17.
130 *DPP v. Healy* [1990] 2 IR 73.
131 See *DPP v. Buck* [2002] 2 IR 268.
132 G. Hogan 'Judicial Review and Socio-Economic Rights' Jeremy Sarkin and William Binchy (eds), *Human Rights, The Citizen and the State: South African and Irish Perspectives* (Clarus Press, 2001) 1,8.
133 *CA and TA v. Minister for Justice* [2014] IEHC 532 Judgment of MacEochaidh J. [12.6].

Index

A v. The United Kingdom, case of 98
A, B and C v. Ireland, case of 114–115
abortion 15–16, 21–23, 51, 66, 114, 213
academics, legal 31
   appointed to the judiciary 131–132, 141
administrative powers, granting of 239–249
   constraints on 242–248
African Commission on Human and People's Rights 269–270
Akdivar v. Turkey, case of 88, 101, 113
Anglo-Irish Agreement (1985) 207
'anticipatory obedience' 13
Argentina 270
Article 16 of the Irish Constitution 4, 252–264
Article 26 of the Irish Constitution 44
Article 44 of the Irish Constitution 200–201
Article 45 of the Irish Constitution 275–276
Association of Judges of Ireland 153–159
Atkin LJ 102
Attorney General, Irish 40, 162, 240

balloting 257
   see also secret ballot
Bangalore Principles of Judicial Conduct 157–158
Barrington, Donal 207, 217–230

interest in the Irish Constitution 220–229
Beatson J 131
Belgium 189
Bellamy, Richard 36, 70–71
Bingham LJ 103
'black letter' legal rules 68–69
Boland, Kevin 204–205
Bowers v. Hardwick, case of 50
Boyle, Hilary 177
Brady, Patrick 176
Brazil 270
Breathnach case 256, 258–259
Brown, Bernard 175
Budd, Declan 56, 259–262, 265
Bunreacht na hÉireann 169, 183–184
de Búrca, Máirín 177, 219
'bureaucratic' mindset 193
Butler J 174–175
by-elections, timing of 263–265
Byrne, Isolda 176
Byrne, Kathleen 219

Cahillane, Laura x, 3; *author of Chapter 8, co-author of Introduction and co-editor*
Canada 3, 131, 155–163, 188, 270
Canadian Bar Association (CBA) 160–162
canon law 224–225
Carmody case 278–279
Carrigan Report (1931) 117
Carroll, J. 143
Casey, Gerard 49, 52

Casey, James 182, 189–190
Catholicism and the Catholic Church 41, 183, 200–201, 217–226
Chandrachud CJ 276
Charleton J 89, 101 112, 117
Chester case 103–104
Chief Justice, Irish 153–156, 159–163
child sexual abuse 3, 85–92, 99, 101, 109–110
Chubb, Basil 171
church–state relations 220–226, 229
Cityview test 241–242, 247
Clarke, Joseph 176
Clarke J 262
Coffey, Donal x, 4; *author of Chapter 12*
Collins case 241, 243–244, 248
Colombia 270
Congress of Irish Unions (CIU) 182, 186
Connolly, Thomas 222
consent, principle of 218, 227–228
consequentialist theories 34–35, 38
constituencies 259–262
Constitution, Irish 4, 18, 21, 65, 199–213
  of 1922 32, 171
  of 1937 29, 32, 46, 169–171, 175, 178–179, 183, 204, 217–219
  amendments to 154–156, 161, 192, 200–207, 210
  excision of Article 44 from 200–201
  judges' role in relation to 217–218
  legal profession's attitude to 219, 221–222
  seen 'from below' 169, 179
  see also Article 16; Article 26; Article 44; Article 45
constitutional adjudication 67, 71, 144
Constitutional Convention, Irish 270
constitutional evolution 9–10, 16–21
constitutional interpretation 10–18, 22–24, 42, 45, 66, 145, 218
  common elements across systems 23
  courts' role in 18
  indirect 16–17
  knowledge ecosystem of 11–16, 74–75
constitutionalisation 269–270
  of political discourse 39–46

constitutionalism 29–34, 171–172
  Irish version of 36–45
  'new commonwealth' model of 75, 77
  see also legal constitutionalism; political constitutionalism
constitutional jurisprudence 2, 59
constitutional law as an expert practice 43–44, 77
constitutional review 44–45
  academic literature on 31
contraception 18, 69, 219, 226
Cooper v. Millea, case of 184
corporatism 183, 185, 188–189, 193, 223
Cosgrave, Liam 201, 204
Costa Rica 270
Costello, John A. 141, 189, 271–272
Coulter, Carol 226
Council of Europe 95, 98, 105
Council of Ireland 204–205, 228–229
Credit Institutions (Financial Support) Act (2008) 241
Criminal Jurisdiction Act (1975) 208
Croatia 270
Cross, Kevin 138, 140–144
Czech Republic 270

D v. Ireland, case of 114–115
Dáil Éireann 252
Daly, Eoin x, 2, 64, 76; *author of Chapter 2*
Davis, E.E. 204
delegated legislation 15, 241–242
Dellway Investments case 242, 248
de Londras, Fiona x, 2–3, 74–75; *author of Chapter 1*
democracy
  concept of 252–253
  danger of decay in 253
  protection of 253–257
democratic processes 30, 33–36, 39–40, 67, 69, 73, 264
Denham J 71, 155–156, 258, 264, 273
Dennehy, Dennis 174–176
Department of External Affairs 201–202
Department of Industry and Commerce 184–185
Department of Justice 123, 133
deportation 243, 248

de Valera, Éamon 51–53, 184–186, 190–191, 225
directives on law 238–239
disciplinary procedures for judges 160–161
discretionary powers granted by legislation 4
distributive justice 276–280
divorce 202–203, 219–220, 225–226
Doherty case 68–71, 74, 76, 256, 260, 263–264
domination, social and economic 35–36
Dorr, Noel 209–210
Douglas, Lori 160
Doyle, Oran x–xi, 4; *author of Chapter 15*
Draper case 56–57, 256, 258–259
Dublin City University (DCU) xiv–xv, 1, 94
Dublin Housing Action Committee (DHAC) 4, 169, 172–178
Dublin Trades Union Council 185–186
Duffy, Gavan 182, 184, 188–189, 222, 224–225, 240
Dworkin, Ronald (and Dworkinian thought) 31, 67–70, 75

economic rights 270
  see also social and economic rights
Electoral Act (1992) 263
England and Wales 128–132
Enright, Máiréad 76
Epstein, R.A. 245
equality legislation 40–41, 66
'essential grievance', concept of 108, 111–112, 115, 118
European Convention on Human Rights 3, 18, 54, 85–92, 95–98, 102–106, 114, 117, 219, 228, 263, 269
European Court of Human Rights 3, 85–92, 95–106, 108–118, 269
European integration 228
European Union (EU) 18–19
executive's role in constitutional interpretation 12–13
extradition 207–212
Extradition Act (1987) 211

Farrell, Brian 171–172
Faulkner, Brian 204–205
Fennelly, Niall 86, 99, 275–276

Ferdinand and Isabella, King and Queen of Spain 222
Ferriter, Diarmaid 218–219
Finland 270
Finn, Tomás xi, 4; *author of Chapter 14*
Fish, Stanley 137–140
FitzGerald, Garret 200, 203, 205–206, 228
Fleming, Eric 176
Fleming case 37
fluoridation 273
Foster, Roy 218–219
France 34, 44, 126, 189
Francis I, King of France 222
Franck, Louis 188–189
Fuller, Lon 238

Gallen, James xi, 3; *author of Chapter 5, co-author of Introduction and co-editor*
Gardaí, the 176
Gardbaum, S. 13
Geraghty, Patrick 176
Germany 18, 54–55, 57–58
Gilligan J 278
Good Friday Agreement (1998) 96, 219, 228–229
Gormley case 279
Gramsci, Antonio 171
Grant v. Roche Products, case of 52
Griffin J 56

Hale, Lady 131
Hamilton J 57
Handyside case 101
Hanna J 190
Hardiman, Adrian xi, xiv–xv, 3, 55, 66, 85–92, 99, 108–112, 115–118, 154, 272–273; *author of Chapter 6*
Harlan J 51
Harte, Paddy 199, 203
Heaney case 37
Hearne, John 51–53
Henchy J 56, 239
Herbert J 255–256
Hickey, Tom xi, 2–3; *author of Chapter 4, co-author of Introduction and co-editor*
High Court, Irish 12, 108–110, 113, 115, 174–175, 188, 204–205, 210, 240, 255–265 *passim*, 271, 273, 278–279

Hillery, Patrick 226
Hirst case 103–104
Hobbes, Thomas 65, 67
Hogan, Gerard xi, 2–4, 66, 71, 96, 171, 191, 204, 209, 239–240, 277, 279; *author of Chapter 3*
Holloway, John 171
homosexuality 219
hospital practices 15–16
Hourican, Liam 206
housing
   Irish state policy for 176
   poor condition of 173, 176
   seen as a *commodity* or as a *social need* 170, 178
human rights, domestic thinking on 105–106
Human Rights Commission, Irish 219
human rights law 91, 97, 104
   Irish 22, 95–96, 103–106
   in the UK 96
human rights violations 212
Hungary 270
Hyde, Douglas 185–186

Immigration Act (1999) 240
implicit principles in constitutional text 69
implied rights 50–56, 274
inalienable rights 65–66
India 270, 276
Industrial Relations Act (1946) 193
Inter-American Human Rights Court and Convention 269
International Commission of Jurists (ICJ) 155, 157, 163–164
International Covenant on Economic, Social and Cultural Rights (ICESCR) 269–270
international law 208–211
'interpretative community' of judging 139–143, 146–147
'Irish dimension' debate 205–206
Irish Independent 189
Irish jurisprudence, distinctive features of 29, 32
Irish Press 183–184
Irish Republican Army (IRA) 173, 208, 211, 218, 222, 227
   see also Provisional Irish Republican Army

Irish unity 201–206, 212–213
Italy 188–189

JC case xv
John XXIII, Pope 223
Judges' Report (2014) 138, 143, 145–146
judicial appointments 3, 123–133
   comment on 153
   current system for 123–124, 137
   diversity needed in 125–126, 132–133, 136–137, 143, 146–148
   eligibility criteria for 129–132
   future prospects for 145–148
   and the *merit* principle 136–138, 145, 148, 164
   politics of 137–148, 154
   possible reforms of 126–133, 154, 159, 163–164
   problems with the present system 124–126
   profile of 125–126
Judicial Appointments Advisory Board (JAAB) 123–129
   membership of 128–129
Judicial Appointments Review Committee 159, 163–164
   Preliminary Submission *see* Judges' Report
judicial comment on matters of public interest 158
judicial communication with the executive 153–158, 162–164
   three models for 153, 155–158
Judicial Council proposals 153–159, 162–164
judicial independence 17, 20, 124, 129, 154, 157–159
judicial innovation 9–11, 16–24, 74, 182
   definition of 9
   legitimacy of 19–24
   need for 16–19
judicial misconduct or incapacity 155–156
   investigations into 159–163
judicial power 248–249
judicial remuneration 154–159
judicial review 3–4, 22, 69, 71–77, 172,

Index

182, 190, 242, 244, 253, 257, 260, 265, 277
rights-based 69
'strong-form' 29–46, 77
judicial supremacy 2, 29–39, 42–45, 64, 71, 74–77
descriptive and *normative* uses of term 30
in the Irish constitutional tradition 30–33
objections to 33–36

Keane J 272, 275–276
Kearns J 37–38, 68–69, 71, 74, 240–241, 243, 263–264
Kelly, J. 50–53, 171–172, 182, 189–190, 271
Kelly, Peter 125, 154
Kennedy, Eamon 212
Kennedy case 57–59
Kennedy J 19, 71
Kenny, David xi–xii, 3; *author of Chapter 9*
Kenny J 49–50, 52, 273–275
Kenny Report on land prices 40
Keogh, D. 183
King v. Attorney General, case of 239
King v. Minister for the Environment (No. 2), case of 255–256
Kissane, Bill 171–172

Larkin, James 185–187
Laskin, Bora 131
Latin America 270
Lavery SC 188–189
law, role of 65
law officers 12, 52
Laws LJ 97, 103
lay participation in the handling of complaints against and disciplining of judges 160–161, 163
Lazarus, E. 51, 58
Lee, J.J. 193, 218–219
legal aid 278–279
legal constitutionalism 14, 64–77
legal research in Ireland, deficiencies of 172
legislative powers 240–241
legislative supremacy 29, 33, 35
legislature's role in constitutional interpretation 13–14

Lehane, Con 175–176
Lemass, Seán 187, 193, 200
Leo XIII, Pope 184
'LGBT' rights 19
LH case 85–86
liberalisation, legal 219, 224
libertarianism 201
Limbach, J. 13
Liversidge v. Anderson, case of 102
Locke, John 65
Lucey, Cornelius 193
Lynch, Jack 201, 228

MacBride, Seán 185, 192
McCarthy, A. 183
McCarthy, Charles 186
McCartney, Robert 200–201, 207
Mac Cormaic, Ruadhán xiv
MacCurtain case 240
McCusker, Harold 206, 212
McDonagh, Enda 224
McDunphy, Michael 185
MacEntee, Sean 185, 187
McGee case 38, 56, 65, 69–71, 76, 274
McGilligan, Patrick 190, 222
McGimpsey, Christopher and Michael 207
McGlinchey, Dominic 209, 212
McKenna case 258, 260, 264
Mackey, Rex 175
McLachlin CJ 155
McLoughlin, Richard 191–192
McMahon case 95, 256–257, 254
McMahon J 57
McQuaid, John Charles 223
Magdalene laundries case 92
Magee v. Farrell, case of 278–279
Maguire v. Ardagh, case of 95
Mansergh, Martin 201, 210–211
Marbury v. Madison, case of 23
Marie Duce society 222–223
Milhench Rory xii, 4; *author of Chapter 13*
'minimal state' thesis 66–67
minorities, protection of 33
Moldova 270
moral principles 68–69
Morgan, David Gwynn 1, 9, 21, 127, 157
Murnaghan J 189, 191
Murphy case 256–257, 262

Murray, John Courtney 223
Murray, Thomas xii, 4; *author of Chapter 11*
Murray J 109, 115, 241, 243, 272
Murtagh Properties v. Cleary, case of 275

Nadon controversy 155–156, 162
National Asset Management Agency (NAMA) 242–243, 248
National Union of Railwaymen v. Sullivan, case of 4, 182, 184, 191–194
natural law 51, 275
natural rights 65–66
Neuberger LJ 103
Neumann, Franz 171
Newe, Gerard Benedict 199–200
Newman, Jeremiah 224
New Zealand 30
Nicholaou case 226
norms, commonly avowable 72, 75, 77
Norris case 69, 219
Northern Ireland 199–207, 213, 218, 227–229
   territorial claim to 203–207, 227

O'Brien, William 186–187
O'Brien case 55
O'Byrne J 189
Ó Dálaigh, Cearbhall 218
Ó Dálaigh CJ 257
Ó Domhnaill v. Merrick, case of 96
O'Donovan case 256, 259–265
O'Dowd, John xii, 3; *author of Chapter 10*
O'Flaherty J 274
O'Higgins J 57, 69
Oireachtas, the 32, 37–38, 41–42, 53, 57, 144, 183–185, 190–191, 239–240, 243–249, 255–264 *passim*, 272
   Committee on the Constitution 123
   committee hearings on judicial appointments 146
   Education Committee 41
O'Keeffe, Louise 3, 85–86, 90, 109–117
O'Keeffe v. Hickey, case of 3, 99–103
O'Keeffe v. Ireland 85–92, 99, 108–118
O'Leary, Don 187

O'Leary, Michael 207
O'Mahony, Conor xii, xiv, 18, 85, 88–91; *author of Chapter 7*
O'Neill, Terence 200
Ontario 129
O'Reilly v. Limerick Corporation, case of 271–272
O'Reilly v. Minister for the Environment, case of 256–258
'original position' (Rawls) 67
Osborough, Nial 172
O'Sullivan, Jan 90
Ovey, C. 97–98, 104

Pacem in terris (Papal encyclical) 50
Paine, Thomas 53
Paisley, Ian 205–206, 210
Papal encyclicals 50, 97, 183–184
parliamentary sovereignty 31–32
party political systems 14
Patwell, Michael 124–125
Pettit, Philip 71–73
Pigs Marketing Board v. Donnelly, case of 190
Pius XI, Pope 184
Poland 270
political appointments to the judiciary 124–125, 127, 136
political constitutionalism 29, 70–71
popular sovereignty 32–33
populism 76
Portmarnock Golf Club case xv
positivism, legal 275
Posner, Richard 137, 139, 141
postal voting 57, 258
Prendergast, David xii, 4; *author of Chapter 16*
Presbyterian Church 201
presidents of Irish courts 155–156, 161–163
Preuss, Hugo 53
principle in constitutional adjudication, role of 64
   see also moral principles
Prior, James 211
proceduralist political theories 34, 38
Prohibition of Forcible Entry and Occupation Act (1971) 177
property rights 4, 170–172, 175–178, 191
Protection of Life during Pregnancy Act (2013) 16

Provisional Irish Republican Army (PIRA) 205, 207, 227
public authorities' role in constitutional interpretation 12–16
public intellectuals 230

Quadragesimo Anno (Papal encyclical) 183
Quinn v. Wren, case of 210

Rajagopal, Balakrishnan 170
Rawls, John (and Rawlsian thought) 67, 72–73
Raz, Joseph 238–239
Re Article 26 and the Electoral (Amendment) Bill (1983), case of 254, 256, 262
Re Article 26 and the Health (Amendment) (No. 2) Bill (2004), case of 240, 242, 247
Redmond case 255–256
referendums 12, 15, 21–22, 45, 53, 155, 200, 204, 222, 225, 227, 252, 265
representation of the interests of judges 157–158, 162–163
restraint on the part of judges 142–143, 253, 274
Riggs v. Palmer, case of 67–68
rights
  positive and *negative* 66–67
  protection of 65, 178, 269, 273
rights-based adjudication 30, 33–34, 43–45, 69
Roche, Stephen 52
Roche v. Roche, case of 38
Roe v. Wade, case of 23, 58
Roosevelt, F.D. 189
rule of law 67, 104, 237–249
  as a political ideal 237
  Fuller's eight disederata of 238–239
  place in the constitutional order 237–239
  Raz's principles of 238
rule-of-law constraints on the grant of administrative powers 244–248
Russell v. Fanning, case of 210
Russia 95
Ryan, James 187
Ryan case 2, 37, 43, 49–59, 273–275
Ryan Report (2009) 89, 117

same-sex marriage 12
Scalia, Antonin 104
Scappola case 103–104
School Attendance Bill case 190–191
Scotland 129–130, 132
secret ballot 257, 264
Selmouni case 113–117
separation of powers 94–95, 144, 171–172, 271, 274–278
Serbia 270
Shatter, Alan 154
Single European Act 219
Sinn Féin Funds case 95, 182
Sinnott, R. 204
Sinnott case xv, 94–95, 273
Sivsivadze case 240, 243, 247
Smyth, Claire-Michelle xii, 4; author of Chapter 17
Smyth, Martin 206
social and economic rights 171–172, 269–280
social inclusion 2
social justice 190
social movements 169, 172, 177–179
socio-legal analysis 170–171
Solum, L. 10
de Sousa Santos, Boaventura 170
South Africa 128, 270
squatting campaigns 169–179
Stalin, Joseph 95
state, the, role and power of xv, 220–222
'state of nature' thinking 65
State (Ryan) v Lennon, case of 71, 182
strike action 193
subsidiarity 85, 87, 97, 183
suicide 37
Sullivan CJ 191
Sumption LJ 95
Sunningdale Agreement (1974) 204–205, 227
Sunstein, C. 74
Supreme Court, Irish 22, 32, 37–38, 42–46, 52, 56–57, 86–88, 94, 99, 108–110, 115–116, 131–132, 186–191, 209–211, 217, 221, 239–243, 254–257, 262, 270–273, 276–279
Switzerland 270
Sypnowich, C. 245

Tamanaha, Brian 245
TD case xv, 71, 94–95, 270–274
Teitgen, M. 54
Terrorism Convention (1977) 208–209
terrorist offences 207–209
Thatcher, Margaret 206, 210
Tilson case 224
de Tocqueville, Alexis 94
Trade Union Act (1941) 182–192
Tuairim sociey 218–220
Tuohy v. Courtney, case of 37
Tushnet, M. 13

Ulster Defence Association (UDA) 207
Ulster Unionists 4, 199–207, 210–213, 228
Ulster Workers' Strike 227
ultra vires doctrine 239, 245, 256
Underwood, Ivor 174–175
unenumerated rights 49, 54, 56, 59, 73–75
United Kingdom (UK) 30, 74, 91, 208
  Human Rights Act (1998) 96
  Supreme Court 95, 103–104
United Nations (UN) 212

United States (US) 13, 22–23, 31
  Constitution 18
  Supreme Court 23, 35, 58, 222
Universal Declaration of Human Rights 269
University College Dublin 226

Venezuela 270
vicarious liability 85–88, 91, 99–102, 108–112, 115–118
vocationalism 182–188, 192–193
vote-based processes 69

Waldron, Jeremy 33, 35–36, 45, 70–71
Walker, C. 209
Walsh, Brian 218
Walsh J 38, 56, 65–66, 71, 145
Ward, Alan 171
Whelan, Anthony 193
White, R. 97–98
White J 50
Whyte, Gerry 2, 182
Whyte, J.H. 188, 192–193, 218

Z v. New Zealand, case of 110
Ziemele J 89

EU authorised representative for GPSR:
Easy Access System Europe, Mustamäe tee 50,
10621 Tallinn, Estonia
gpsr.requests@easproject.com

www.ingramcontent.com/pod-product-compliance
Ingram Content Group UK Ltd.
Pitfield, Milton Keynes, MK11 3LW, UK
UKHW021847140426
5217IPUK00022B/1637